# The Lion and the Lamb

# The Lion and the Lamb

*Evangelicals and Catholics in America*

WILLIAM M. SHEA

2004

# OXFORD
UNIVERSITY PRESS

Oxford    New York
Auckland    Bangkok    Buenos Aires    Cape Town    Chennai
Dar es Salaam    Delhi    Hong Kong    Istanbul    Karachi    Kolkata
Kuala Lumpur    Madrid    Melbourne    Mexico City    Mumbai    Nairobi
São Paulo    Shanghai    Taipei    Tokyo    Toronto

Copyright © 2004 by Oxford University Press, Inc.

Published by Oxford University Press, Inc.
198 Madison Avenue, New York, New York 10016

www.oup.com

Oxford is a registered trademark of Oxford University Press

Library of Congress Cataloging-in-Publication Data

Shea, William M., 1935—
The lion and the lamb : evangelicals and Catholics in America /
William M. Shea.
p.    cm.
Includes bibliographical references and index.
ISBN 0-19-513986-0
1. Catholic Church—Relations—Evangelicalism.    2. Evangelicalism—
Relations—Catholic Church.    3. United States—Church
history.    I.    Title.
BR1641.C37 S53 2003
280'.042'0973—dc21        2003005368

9 8 7 6 5 4 3 2 1

Printed in the United States of America
on acid-free paper

*With every breath I draw I am grateful*
*To the woman who gave me life, Sarah Margaret Shea,*
*And to the woman who saved my life, Helene Anne Lutz*

The wolf shall dwell with the lamb,
and the leopard shall lie down with the kid,
and the calf and the lion and the fatling together,
and a little child shall lead them.
The cow and the bear shall feed;
their young shall lie down together;
and the lion shall eat straw like the ox.
The suckling child shall play over the hole of the asp,
and the weaned child shall put his hand on the adder's den.
They shall not hurt or destroy
in all my holy mountain;
for earth shall be full of the knowledge
of the Lord
as the waters cover the sea.

Isaiah 11: 6–9

# Acknowledgments

This project began in 1980 when I met evangelical Christians for the first time at the University of South Florida. I wrote my first essays on fundamentalism there. I wrote the early versions of some of the chapters of this book at Saint Louis University between 1991 and 1997, and the full manuscript between 1997 and 2002. I have a lot of people to acknowledge.

Michael J. Lacey is Director Emeritus of the American Program and a Senior Scholar at the Woodrow Wilson International Center for Scholars. It is difficult for me to imagine what the last fifteen years would have been without his encouragement to scholarship and his friendship. Of the same order of importance in my small life has been the friendship and inspiration of Jacob Neusner, the great scholar of Talmud, now Research Professor at Bard College and Senior Fellow at Bard's Institute for Advanced Theology. As a professor I sat in his classroom at the University of South Florida and found out anew what it means to be a student, a teacher, and a scholar. Mark Noll, McManis Professor of Christian Thought at Wheaton College, has written historical reflections on the subject of this book that every Catholic historian should envy and supported my interest in the subject since we first met at the Wilson Center in 1986. These three are human beings and relentless hunters of knowledge for the sake of humanity. No one has taught me as much as they, with the exception of Bernard Lonergan, S. J., who knew "only a few things" but knew them very well indeed.

Saint Louis University gave me time and support in the form of a sabbatical and a research leave with pay, and several Mellon travel grants. The librarians at Pius XII Library were unstinting in their efforts to show me how to find what I needed. Ronald Crown, the theology librarian, and S. J. Waide, the archivist, not only helped me but came to be my companions in the quest for an honest intellectual life.

The Institute for Ecumenical and Cultural Research, with Patrick Henry at its head, and the Library at St. John's University and St. Benedict's College in Collegeville, MN, welcomed me and my family and warmed us through a winter. Westminster Theological Seminary and D. G. Hart, who was librarian there, and the Billy Graham Center and Buswell Memorial libraries at Wheaton College all provided me with research material in evangelical theology and the Catholic Church, as did Covenant Seminary Library in St. Louis. I also received a generous summer research grant from the Louisville Institute for the Study of American Religion.

My colleagues and friends at Saint Louis University, James Fisher, Belden Lane, Michael McClymond, Francis Nichols, Kenneth Parker, John Pauly, John Renard, Jose Sanchez, and Joseph Tetlow all shared expertise, criticism, encouragement, and laughter. Clarence Miller, an Erasmian beyond compare, paid the ultimate price and read the entire manuscript. The work would have been dreary indeed had they not been there. Every one of them is a model of academic life. So, too, my old friends and colleagues at the University of South Florida, Ap Zylstra, Darrell Fasching, and Mozella Mitchell, all of whom showed me the strength of evangelical faith and shared with me their hard won knowledge. Another group of scholars and friends from the University of Dayton showed constant interest and provided just as constant inspiration: William Portier, Terrence Tilley, Dennis Doyle, and James Heft. Now I have been welcomed to a new academic home among the faculty of the College of the Holy Cross by such outstanding scholars of American Catholicism as David O'Brien, Thomas Landy, and John Schmalzbauer. As one looks back the hand of God is evident.

The authors who loaned me their knowledge would fill pages but I cannot fail to mention Joel Carpenter, Jose Casanova, Bishop Thomas Curry, Jenny Franchot (may she rest in peace), Anthony Kemp and George Marsden. I must also mention that Mark Massa, Philip Jenkins, and John McGreevy each recently published a book on anti-Catholicism in America that I have read with deep appreciation but not in time to include in this book. I must address them in other circumstances.

I am grateful for the help of Saint Louis University graduate student research assistants over the past dozen years, among them Mindi Cromwell, Dan Dunavan, Zaida Perez, and Kyle Rose. Mark Reynolds and Guido Stucco wrote dissertations on evangelical theology and became my companions in the process. The participants in the American doctoral seminar (especially the evangelicals among them) at that university read several chapters and criticized them liberally, thereby helping me to produce a better book.

Rev. Margaret Pride, pastor of the Memorial Boulevard Christian Church in St. Louis, was for a dozen years our neighbor and friend who shared with us a back yard and a common journey in faith. Joel Delpha, who walks the walk, taught me more about faith and hope than he will ever admit. Father Kenneth Brown's gentle and sure hand guides the Christians of St. Margaret of Scotland Parish in St. Louis and without fail, Sunday after Sunday, spoke wisely to us. He is the best pastor I have known in my sixty-eight years and too many parishes. Old friends kept asking me "When will it be finished?"—Joe Komonchak, Nancy Malone, and Alice Gallin the most beloved among them. Thank you all.

I am grateful to Nathanael and Christopher, my sons, who must have wondered why so much time and thought would go into a profitless project, and gave me support nonetheless and reason for pride beyond reason. And to Isis, my old friend, who kept me company, talked to me everyday, and cheered me to the finish line.

Catherine Read, Theo Calderara, and Bob Milks of Oxford University Press graciously and expertly helped me through rewriting the manuscript, and Melanie Piper made up a far better index than I could have done.

Finally, I am grateful to the editor of *Theological Studies* for allowing me to use an essay published in that journal in the composition of the 12th and 13th chapters of this work.

# Contents

# PART I

# The Landscape of a Quarrel

# I

# Terminology, Myth, and Tribes

To begin at the end of my story, one of the more intriguing questions in contemporary American Christianity is whether the current warming of relations between Catholics and conservative evangelicals promises a thaw in the ice age in place since the sixteenth century. Following their northern Irish cousins in the peace accord of Good Friday, 1988, evangelicals and Catholics in America may have the like of a Good Friday treaty staring them in the face. Like their Irish cousins, they may reach an agreement that will catch hold, slowly and perhaps painfully. Like the treaty of their Irish cousins, the prospective truce is controversial, provoking both suspicion and opposition, and the outcome is uncertain. The notion of American conservative Presbyterians conversing with American Catholics is no more unlikely than that of northern Irish Presbyterians conversing with Irish Catholics, for the historic bitterness between the communities, although less bloody, has been as corrosive and pervasive here as there. The current occasions and justifications for a contemplated *rapprochement* offered in both cases are political and cultural, to be sure, but in neither case, across the Atlantic or here, can they remain solely political and cultural if the relationship is to improve. These are religions, after all, and for them religious meanings are decisive. And, finally, I think it safe to say that if improvements catch hold, in both nations the societal results will be formidable.

American evangelical Protestants and Roman Catholics have hated one another since the colonial period. In the mid-twentieth century, an event took place in each community, namely, the founding of the National Association of Evangelicals (NAE; 1942) and the second Vatican Council (1962–65), that brought notable change to each community, forming one and reforming the other. If only gradually and perhaps initially unintended, the change within each led to a change in the relationship between the two. This is not a book pumping for change, although I favor and hope for it. Nor does it lay out a path that makes change more likely, though at the end I make a suggestion or two which seem to me to condition the possibility of improvement. The conditions favoring stasis have long been in place and remain operative today, and it is these that need attention.

This is a book about change and continuity, then, about an ice age and a warming trend, about meanness and its grip on souls, but also about the blessed weight of the past and the meaning of old words in the present, and about how communities may learn to use them anew. The book dips into the past, rummaging in the detritus, in order to find how the two communities explained their war, and it traces some of the signs of warming since the founding of the NAE and the decisions of Vatican II. In the sense that it interprets texts from the past, the book is historical and literary; in the sense that it deals primarily with religious meanings embedded in those texts it is theological; in the sense that it is about hatred and fear communicated in tales and symbols, it is psychological. And because it is about two American religious behemoths, it is part of a story of profound importance for the politics and culture of the United States and beyond.

The title is both symbolic and ambiguous, deliberately so. It is adapted from Isaiah 11 (it might be a leopard and a kid). Isaiah knew that lions don't lie with lambs except to eat them, and that the lamb's fear of the lion is as permanent and proper as is the lion's hunger for the lamb. But Isaiah uses the incongruity of a series of such images to suggest that God's power will undo instinct and that history will surprise us with happiness if we wait and watch the signs. I choose the image as a title because each one of these two communities has for four centuries regarded itself as the lamb and looked on the other as the lion as a matter of historical, if not eschatological, fact. Neither community has "seen through" Isaiah's symbol nor heard his call for a transformation of nature and history though hope and love. This book seeks to display the historical enmity and at the end to suggest that, as a healing balm, the eschatological promise to lions and lambs is worth prayerful meditation in the present.

## American Evangelical-Catholic Relations

In 1993, a group of American evangelical Protestants and Roman Catholics signed a declaration entitled *Evangelicals and Catholics Together: The Christian Mission in the Third Millennium* (*ECT*).[1] It surprised many, and it prompted vigorous debate on the evangelical side. Although it was written with other more formal discussions between Catholics and evangelicals in its back-ground,[2] the evangelical signers of *ECT* were not representatives of anyone or any official body; the Catholic signers included bishops who always represent the church, but who were not assigned to the dialogue by Catholic headquarters in Rome. *ECT* was not sent to any ecclesiastical bodies for formal approval—a fact unusual in ecumenical dialogue. The document did not commit anyone other than the signers to any course of action. As a theological document, *ECT* is underdeveloped, unimpressive, and unimportant.[3] It simply declared that old enemies ought to start collaborating for the common social and cultural good on the basis of a common Christian faith.

The document, its significance, and its critics will be discussed in the course of this book. Here it must be noted that its mere existence served as a signal to nonsigning observers that a turn had been taken, or was threatening to be taken, that had high theological and religious significance to evangelicals. By this time, thirty years after Vatican II, alert Catholics were used to ecumenical dialogues and documents, and to them the only surprising thing would have been that the other parties in this discussion were the heirs and associates of the most anti-ecumenical and separatist of Protestants (fundamentalists, that is) whose ecclesial communities and organizations were explicitly opposed to the ecumenical and "modernist" Protestantism of the twentieth century and whose uncritical biblicism supplied the arsenal of anti-Catholicism. To many it must have seemed a document *de novo*. How, given their history of mutual animosity, could members of these two communities cooperate on the basis of *a common Christian faith* when one of them has consistently denied that the other is Christian at all? This simple question has, and deserves to have, both historically and systematically, a very complex answer.

The state of this relationship is important. If *ECT* is in fact more than another "event" put on by religiopolitical operatives left over from the culture wars of the Nixon and Reagan era, if it is a signal of change already occurring with more to come, then its historical context must be explored, for present discussion invariably includes the past, and the past, if it is ignored, will exact its price in the future. These quite self-conscious heirs of the sixteenth century Reformation and the Council of Trent need to face, understand, accept, and resolve their past if they are to be free to deal with the deep issues separating them and with the projects of common action for the common good. Each knows that there once was a man who tried to build a castle on sand (Mt. 7: 24–27). What shall these parties build on? Is there a theological or even a religious foundation? What precisely are the limits to a structure erected on it?

Historical theology plays a pivotal role in the overall theological task by determining "what was going forward" in the past, and so enabling intellectual and institutional leaders to decide exactly what in the past contributes to a desirable future and what in the past must be repudiated or corrected. To do so theologians have to put aside their apologetic and polemical armor, and historians must cease their search for supporting evidence for the status quo. And risks must be taken, for this conversation will involve obvious candidates for clarification and even correction, perhaps even Roman Catholic doctrines of the church and evangelical understandings of the Pauline *sola gratia* and *sola fide*. Facing these together was not within the scope of *ETC*. In fact, the signers skirted them for the purposes of the moment, but surely not, even the authors might agree, for long.[4]

The signers, as Christians, know it is vital for Christian communities to deal reflectively with their relationship for religious reasons (*caritas Christi urget nos*) and also for theological reasons (*fides quaerens intellectum*). In the case of the evangelical and Roman Catholic communities, historical static in the relationship is especially great, and the religious ethos, practices, and doctrines of the two are so different and at odds that they raise the question whether they are the same religion or in fact two different religions, or at least two permanently opposed Christianities, although this would be curious indeed. Until *ECT*, one might well have supposed that the only recourse was for each to call for the conversion of the other. The one has been an apostate church and the other a conventicle of heretics. But ambiguity, "crisis," double-mindedness has remained, however muted. A logic of ecclesiological and soteriological beliefs and practices led each side to conclude that the other is not a legitimate form of Christianity, while, by contrast, a commonsense interpretation of common symbols and traditions would lead each to conclude of the other that it, too, is a legitimate form of the one religion. In either resolution it has now become imperative that theologians and church leaders not rest content with judgments of each other formed in quite different historical and cultural circumstances.

The conversation and cooperation suggested in *ECT* are important not only for the churches but also for American culture at large. The combined membership of the two communities is close to one half of the American population. While the dissolution of the religious underpinnings of the public culture has proceeded steadily, the religious communities have remained strong and increasingly vigorous in their intent to have their say in it. Distinguishing culture from politics, it seems inevitable that the religious communities (of all sorts) establish collegial relations for the sake of their common values. In a society in which religion and politics are an explosive mix and religions themselves seem often to go to the mat with one another, immense discipline is required on their part, for old prejudices gnaw at intellectual, spiritual, and political freedom and energy. The just shaping of cultural and political discourse will rest to a significant degree on whether evangelicals and Catholics can learn to talk civilly to and about one another, and to establish a common voice. For the health of the Christian churches only the relationship of Christians and Jews surpasses in cultural and religious import the relationship between Catholics and evangelical Protestants.[5]

It will serve the good of both communities to retell the story of the relations between the two communities, to clarify barriers to discussion and action, to deal with the ugly past for the sake of a better future, and to sketch the response of both parties to the "modern world" and to its ideologies as a key to any attempt at mutual understanding and acceptance.[6] On a superficial level, one might agree with the godfather, "the enemy of my enemy is my friend," but let us take the fact as a clue: both American communities struggled against the "modern world" and its effects on them, one for at least two centuries and one for a century. Why? And what does that repudiation, and its subsequent modifications, tell us about the two, not to say about the modernity to which they have objected?

Although the slant I take here on this relationship is primarily concerned with the history and theology of the relationship between two American Christian communities and only secondarily with modernity, my own long-range academic interest is in four discernible approaches to the understanding of Christianity developed in the twentieth-century United States, the paradigmatic modern culture: philosophical naturalism, religious modernism, fundamentalism, and orthodoxy (evangelicalism and Catholicism I would list under the last in spite of their differences).[7] Although my intent in this book is to understand a history and literature of antagonism between two putatively orthodox Christian communities, the study is spurred on by a personal fascination with walls and boundaries, hatreds and incomprehensions so deeply planted in a religion that, according to its great apostle, was meant to eliminate them, and in a nation whose quest for liberty and justice would seem to include an imperative for mutual comprehension. A puzzle indeed! But only a piece of the puzzle need be dealt with at this point: What have American evangelicals and Roman Catholics been saying about one another, what are they saying now, and how might they learn to speak differently in the future?

I begin, in the second chapter, with a stage-setting sketch of the separate paths of evangelical Protestants and Roman Catholics in coping with modernism in the twentieth century, and with an initial look at the differences between them.

Weeding out the powerful strand of the American nativist movement against the Catholic immigrants and their church will occupy us in the third chapter. We will visit Samuel Morse, Lyman Beecher, Josiah Strong, and Paul Blanshard. Although they are inextricably intertwined in many texts, nativist and evangelical apprehensions must be distinguished if we are to concentrate on the theological aspects of the "Great Struggle" between Protestantism and popery in our nation's history. The point is to discover why evangelical Americans thought that Catholics were not Christians and could not be good Americans. The answer to the first question is religious, and to the second political, a crucial distinction as it turned out, for when popular nativism wore out in the face of political experience and Hot and Cold War expediency, the theological concern remained prominent and continues to be so. For that brief period after World War II and before the Cold War began in earnest, even secularized white Anglo-Saxon Protestants (Paul Blanshard will be taken as a representative) retained the nativist worry that Catholic authoritarianism and American democracy were incompatible.[8] While religious and theological judgments often seem mixed with nativist anxieties over the century, the link weakened in the aftermath of the Kennedy campaign of 1959 and was largely resolved by the second Vatican Council (1962–65) and the Kennedy presidency (1961–63).

Theology proper we meet in the fourth chapter when I examine the roots of the nineteenth-century evangelical critique of Catholicism in Britain and the Massachusetts Bay colony. The literature of these two communities is vast and unconquerable. What shall one attend to? My choice has been to study historically influential and representative evangelical assessments of Catholicism (chapters 5 through 8) and Catholic assessments of American evangelical Protestantism (chapters 9 through 13) over the past century and a half. My initial focus on representatives of nineteenth-century denominations that, in a simpler usage than is possible now, were collectively called evangelical, will narrow to conservative neo-evangelicalism in the second half of the twentieth century, especially to representatives of the Calvinist or Reformed wing of that movement. Beginning, then, with the colonial commentary of John Cotton on the Book of Revelation in 1642 and the Dudlean lecture of Jonathan Mayhew in 1765 ("Papal Idolatry") as a convenient link between the American anti-Catholic diatribe and its British roots, I pass on to William Nevins, pastor and columnist for one of the earliest antipopery sheets, to the Restorationist Alexander Campbell's debate with Bishop Purcell, to prominent Presbyterian and Congregationalist pastors and theologians in the mid-nineteenth century, and then to a short list of mid-nineteenth-century evangelical leaders, Presbyterian and Congregationalist. The twentieth century provides us with two outstanding Reformed theological critics of the Catholic church, Loraine Boettner and Cornelius Van Til. Almost all of these men regarded the Catholic Church as a body that had long ago abandoned the Christian gospel in a massive compromise with paganism.

The eighth chapter ("The Heretical Church") takes on an ambiguity in the evangelical argument by dealing with an unlikely pair: William Ellery Channing's essays on Catholicism and Charles Hodge's disagreement with his own Presbyterian General Assembly over the Christian credentials of the Catholic Church, as well as with Hodge's letter to Pius IX in the matter of an invitation to the first Vatican Council. In the twentieth century, J. G. Machen and Samuel Craig continue a clear and consistent Reformed theology, and give us a more considered yet still ambiguous weighing of Catholicism from the vantage point of that influential tradition. In this chapter, I find another side to the evangelical argument in addition to the continuing antagonism. The evangelical (especially the Reformed) critique develops in two incompatible directions: Catholics are not Christians at all or Catholics are Christians who have made serious mistakes, an apostate church or a heretical church. The distinction is active in current evangelical discussions about a dialogue and cooperation with the Roman Catholic Church.[9] In addition, the change, even among the strongest opponents of dialogue with Catholics, involves a purge of apocalyptic, nativist (political), and erotic themes, and a sharpening focus on Reformation theological principles. It would seem now that the post–Vatican II Catholic Church must meet the sixteenth-century reformers again, but now dealing head on with their theological arguments without the accompanying apocalyptic and erotic fanfare!

I turn, in the ninth through the thirteenth chapters, to the Catholic responses. Some of the classic texts of responses of the nineteenth-century Catholic bishops to the evangelical critique will be examined to determine the structure of Catholic apologetic self-understanding. In the twelfth chapter, I find that the late twentieth century yielded up renewed Catholic pastoral polemics against "biblical Christianity" in the years immediately preceding ECT (1993). There were theological and historical, personal and official, defensive and offensive responses and expressions of self-understanding throughout a two-century period, but the twelfth and thirteenth chapters attempt to catch Catholics as they come to terms with the Reformation from the vantage point of the second Vatican Council. Although it has been deeply modified in the last third of the twentieth century, there was an American Catholic apologetic answering Protestant criticisms, laced with charges undercutting both the religious legitimacy and political hegemony of evangelicalism. Catholics had found evangelical Protestantism to be an illegitimate and incomplete form of Christianity (i.e., heretical), a force for religious and cultural oppression (convent and church burning), a root cause of modernity's loss of Christian faith, and a symbolically inadequate support for a healthy American democracy (the Reformers' repudiation of church authority becomes modernity's anarchy). The older Catholic apologetic has lately been replaced by an ambiguous reaction especially evident in recent theological, curial, and episcopal documents on "biblical Christianity" as the latter makes deep inroads into previously impenetrable American Catholic territory. The fascinating and unexpected turn to ecumenism at the Council presents Reformed Protestants with a two-headed contemporary Catholic Church: one willing to listen and talk, and at the same time refusing to budge on the still nettlesome anathemas of the Council of Trent and the peculiar beliefs and practices of traditional Catholicism. The "crux," as it confronts Catholic leaders and theologians, is forced by three decades of dialogue with a variety of evangelical communities and by recent restatements of reformation criticisms by hard evangelicals: Is there only one true church, and what exactly is it that makes it or any other church true?

As the twentieth century ran down, demonization was no longer the first weapon grasped. Catholic authors tired of looking for psychological and moral reasons for the "revolt" of Luther and Calvin, and evangelical historians took another look at the "Whore of Babylon" as a proper image for the interpretation of the history of Christianity from the fourth through the sixteenth centuries. The evangelical commitment to a transformation of American culture in addition to evangelization of individuals made at the founding of the NAE in 1942 resulted in evangelical conversation about alliances to combat what Pope John Paul II later named "the culture of death," and a widening recognition of the need to reinsert Christian moral values into what had become a "naked public square."[10] The overall response of evangelicals to Catholic ecumenism, although short of the mainline Protestant enthusiasm, was less negative and suspicious than one would expect from the heirs of Calvin and Luther.[11]

In retrospect, it appears that the path was being cleared for initiatives such as *ETC*, but *ETC*, once signed and published, brought a flood of old light reaction to dalliance with Roman Catholics. The critics echoed the rock-bottom Reformation criticisms of Catholic doctrine, polity, and practice, and pointedly denied that the Roman lion had lost its teeth. But they did so in the face of increased and perhaps unavoidable nonsacramental religious, political, and cultural intercommunion between evangelicals and Catholics. As a result, evangelical and Catholic theologians are now required to clarify the principles on which such conversation can be based. The older (and lower!) themes still dominate some popular polemics, but the discussions among evangelical intellectuals about relations with the Catholic Church have already undergone a sea change. Nativism has disappeared, the most strongly worded and deeply felt critiques are now civil in tone, and conspiratorial and erotic fantasies are largely restricted to Jack Chick's comic books and the trick photography of Tony Alamo.[12] The argument is far from over and may well threaten ecclesial relations between the evangelical disputants themselves (the Protestant curse!), but it would seem that the evangelical relations with Roman Catholicism will not be what they were. Ironically, but perhaps predictably, it is the most conservative of the evangelicals and the most liberal of the Catholics who worry about the improvement.

The final chapter will confront the remaining and imposing religious and theological differences between the two communities, especially as these are reiterated by current bearers of the old relationship. The most succinct way to summarize the basic differences is to say that they reflect deeply held convictions regarding the mediation of religious meaning, the relation between religious myth and history, whether evangelicalism and Catholicism can be considered distinct forms of one religion, and the relation between Christian faith and its cultures. To reach and cope with that difference requires a commonly recognized theological aim and method, something of the sort suggested by John Warwick Montgomery's proposal to deal with "deep structural differences" among Christian communities and on Bernard Lonergan's "horizon analysis" as a method for dealing with basic differences in theology.[13] They constitute a methodological step toward clarification, contrast, and, above all, self-criticism. Differences will not evaporate, however.

Surely the religious foundations for dialogue are being laid down in both communities: deepened religious and affectional conversion, clarification of the nature of Christian faith, worship with a lessened tribalism, and a common plumbing of the scriptures with a commitment to their truth. In addition, conditions for cooperation are evident: an increase in understanding the/a church and its ethos, and coming to grips with decisive and seemingly everlasting issues such as "pure gospel" and "holy church" (or learning how to handle doctrines in conversation). If religious motivation and intent replace cultural and political, perhaps authentic Christian faith can counter the inherent pull of Christian tribalism, participants will recognize that, in the relations between the two communities, and between them and the environing society, what is at stake is a responsible and common religious witness rather than sociological conversion or cultural and political hegemony. We also may recognize a religious and theological witness of each community to the other on principles that should not be abandoned. In the end, it is only the forbearance of friendship and the grace of intellectual and spiritual conversion that can create and sustain such a relationship in the face of ineradicable structural and doctrinal difference and continuing exchange of members. Perhaps, in the end, the old antagonists, even though they judge each other wrong, will find each other's contra-diction necessary to their own authentic Christianity. A pipe dream, perhaps, but one worth chasing down.

## Terminology

Participating regularly in a doctoral seminar on American Christianity populated with students of various ecclesial backgrounds is an enlightening experience, especially for a bookworm. There is a bit of irony to begin with in the fact that young evangelical theologians now frequently receive doctoral education in Catholic universities, but more in the fact that Catholic professors are receiving their education in the lively tangle of contemporary evangelicalism from evangelical students who, in several Catholic doctoral programs, make up 50 percent or more of the student body.[14] *Evangelical* has not proved an easy term to define in the books, and it borders on the prickly in seminar interchanges. Although at first sight there is little to distinguish the anti-Catholicism of Calvin from that of Wesley, so different are the theological and religious interests of Wesleyan evangelical churches from those of students in the Reformed tradition, that, listening to them, one wonders how the term evangelical can cover both comfortably. Those in the Wesleyan (and typically Arminian) stream of conservative Protestantism stare unsympathetically as their Calvinist counterparts tie themselves tightly in the silken loops of the *sola Scriptura* and *sola fide* of the continental Reformation, while the Reformed student might express her disapproval of the current usage of *evangelical* because it now evokes a form of piety intellectually vapid, doctrinally soft, and culturally uncritical. Catholic students and professors are reminded of the mutual incomprehensions and antagonisms in the many hues of the contemporary Catholic theological spectrum.

The experience of the seminar reflects the ambiguities found in the literature on twentieth-century American Protestantism. *Evangelicalism* is as slippery as *fundamentalism,* a term that once applied solely to a movement of theologically conservative and separatist Protestant Christians in the United States and now is stretched to cover violence prone Muslims and "ultra-orthodox" Jews.[15] *Fundamentalism,* if we follow the lead of the editors of the massive academic study of that worldwide phenomenon, can no longer be defined; we must settle for sixteen traits in a family resemblance, adapting our usage in each case. We have two valuable studies that attempt to save evangelicals from such a fate: Mark Ellingsen's *The Evangelical Movement,* a comprehensive study of European and American evangelicals, and the British historian David Bebbington's "Evangelicalism in its Settings." The latter, for example, suggests a four-point definition. *Evangelicals* have in common (1) a stress on conversion; (2) an activism focused especially, but not exclusively, in evangelization; (3) an unequivocal affirmation of the authority of the Bible; and (4) a soteriological focus on the suffering and death of Jesus normatively understood as atonement for sin.[16] Whereas one can work with such a definition at the outset, there are tortures of terminology: *evangelicalism* varies from church to church, continent to continent, and age to age.

Historically, the term meant the churches of the European Reformation and their linear descendants, and simply referred to the fact that Protestant Christians lived by "the gospel" in distinction from Roman Catholics who added tradition(s) that compromised "the gospel." This gospel was rediscovered by Martin Luther in his liberating reading of the letters of Paul to Rome and Galatia. The banner terms for these communities of Pauline Christians were *sola scriptura, sola gratia,* and *sola fides.* While the communities differed among themselves in significant ways, they were united in their suspicion and rejection of the Catholic Church, which condemned their doctrines as heretical at the sixteenth-century Council of Trent (1545–63). The Lutheran and Reformed (Calvinist) churches were the *evangelical* churches. The Church of England, although it harbored evangelicals, retained many of the elements of medieval English Catholic church, and so remained torn between what were regarded as ancient and proper forms of worship and church polity on the one hand, and the recovery of an even more ancient and purer gospel, worship and polity on the other.

The stories of the Puritans and Pilgrims tell us of their devotion to the pure gospel and pure church, and of their hatred of Rome and suspicion of Canterbury. They, too, were *evangelical,* continuing in the tradition of the continental Reformation. But the pietist revivals of the eighteenth century took a particular hold of the American churches. The second birth canonized in these revivals became a central feature of American evangelicalism, as did sanctification in the holiness movement of the nineteenth century and faith *versus* culture dualism of the American fundamentalist revolt against Christian modernism and secular culture in the twentieth century. All of these movements, along with the frequent establishment of new Protestant denominations and the doctrinal liberalism of the mainline Protestant communities, complicate the use of the term enormously. In one historically profound sense they are all *evangelical,* for they regard themselves as children of the Great Reform, born again and governed by the scripture. Yet, by the end of the nineteenth century, the mainline churches (even in the Reformed tradition!) appeared no longer to be Calvinist but Arminian, no longer Augustinian but Pelagian; they no longer lived by faith and grace alone, but by "faith working through love" in people who prized their freedom of will and their cooperation with the grace of God in constructing the "evangelical empire" of redeemed Christian souls in America and throughout the world. Can one, then, any longer speak of the pure gospel recovered by Luther and Calvin? Luther and Calvin, not to say Jonathan Edwards and perhaps even Charles Finney, would be surprised and even repelled by elements of the current American evangelical subculture.[17]

A further terminological complication arose in the middle of the twentieth century, when many fundamentalists reversed their parents' ecclesiastical separatism and cultural isolation, and, while clinging to the Bible and to revival, reestablished the older American evangelical tradition of ecclesial cooperation and culture construction. The National Association of Evangelicals was founded in St. Louis in 1942 and another remarkable chapter in American Protestant history opened. The *neo-evangelicals,* as they came to be called, set out to revive American Christianity and America itself in the name of Jesus Christ and under the inspired and inerrant scriptures, yet the historical and demographic base on which they stood mixed Calvinist and Arminian theologies drawn from churches of quite different experiential and doctrinal leanings. We are now left with a highly fluid use of *evangelical,* embracing people in varied communities such as Free Methodist, Presbyterian, Southern Baptist, Assemblies of God, Pentecostals, and even some who are *evangelical Catholics.* Joel Carpenter has written this history in *Revive Us Again,* and I shall rely on his work at several points.[18]

How, then, do I dare use the term here and what can we hope for from it? This book is immediately concerned with one aspect of this historical and terminological jungle: anti-Catholicism. While not as virulent in every decade and in every segment of American evangelical history, it seems to cut across all. Sidney Ahlstrom once wrote in an attempt to answer the question, "Who are the Evangelicals?" that anti-Catholicism is an essential ingredient in the evangelical recipe: evangelicals are ". . . those Protestants who . . . repudiate Roman Catholic polity, liturgics, piety, and doctrine, and at least used to regard the Roman Catholic Church as the Anti-Christ."[19] At the outset, in our dealings with the evangelical critique of Catholicism between 1830 and the present, I draw materials from the American churches of the Reformation, including churches that later are recognized as mainline and even modernist, and then, especially in the twentieth century, churches of a more conservative bent in the newly formed communities of fundamentalism and neo-evangelicalism. Because my interest is in the current dialogue between Catholics and conservative evangelicals, I find myself narrowing the focus to those theologically conservative evangelicals who regard themselves as the legitimate heirs of the Reformation, for they are embroiled in a battle over the implications of Reformation doctrine for any conversation and cooperation with Catholics. The most highly strung among them tend to be Calvinist in doctrine and theology, and they remain vigorously critical of the Catholic Church.

"Evangelicalism" and "evangelicals," then, have three referents, and the referent in each use will be garnered, I hope, from the context of the discussion: the Reformation churches and theologies (*evangelische*), the American churches and figures who stood in that Reformation tradition in the nineteenth century and that were by then much shaped by the experience of the revivals and the influence of pietism, and finally, those figures and churches associated with the mid-twentieth-century neo-evangelical revival. In contexts in which the twentieth century is the field of discussion, evangelical and evangelicalism will not refer to the mainline Protestant churches, although good argument can be mounted that they are at least as fully "reformed" churches as are those now commonly called evangelical. *Fundamentalism* used in the discussions of twentieth-century evangelicalism and neo-evangelicalism requires special care, for American religious historians use it of the militant and separatist evangelicalism in conflict with Christian modernism, while Catholics late in the century use the term to cover evangelistic anti-ecumenical Christians who try to convert Catholics to what the bishops call "biblical Christianity," and even use the term "fundamentalist" of Catholics whom they judge to be overly devoted to the papacy and doctrinal orthodoxy.[20]

*Catholicism* has its own terminological morass. A student of mine who specialized in Hinduism once told me that the Catholic Church is the Hinduism of the West—a collection of religions that are covered for the sake of convenience by a single term. The term refers to an attempted unification of cultures as much as a religion. There are many evangelicals who would agree

with him. When one uses the term *Catholicism,* is one speaking of an ecclesiastical structure, an ancient religious culture, a worldview, a sacramental/
ritual way of life, or a Christian orthodoxy? Is Catholicism the gospel of Paul
or of Peter or perhaps a social and political gospel of this-worldly liberation, or
even a gospel of mysticism? Some evangelicals, as we shall see, find in Catholicism a form of Christianity in tune with cultures into which it has injected
itself, and an inauthentic form of Christianity in any of them.

Until Vatican II, when the Catholic Counter Reformation ended and Catholic anti-modernism collapsed, at least evangelicals (and Catholics!) had little
problem identifying what Catholicism was and who was a Catholic, and, when
the evangelical commentators were in doubt, they could rely on Roman authorities to settle the question in short order. Since then, the public strife
among Catholics, widespread theological and religious dissent from official
teaching, the appearance of competing interpretations of the Council and of
doctrine, the emergence of Tridentine separatist movements, the new papal
attitude toward Judaism and other world religions, an intensified theological
syncretism, and explicit doctrines of inclusivism and inculturation, one is
forced to wonder how much of Tridentine Catholicism is left.[21] This polymor-
phous character of contemporary Catholicism makes it as difficult to define as
evangelicalism. What were named "models of the Church" just two decades
ago by a distinguished Catholic theologian have now become conflicting ways
of practicing the Catholic religion: the institutional church, the mystical communion, the sacramental church, the prophetic church, the servant church,
and the Council's "people of God."[22] Equally distinguished Catholic historians
have found four types of American Catholicism distinguishable by eras: enlightenment, romantic, immigrant and now evangelical Catholicism.[23] Add to
these categories radical orthodox, neoconservative, conservative, liberal, neo-
liberal, modernist and postmodernist, cafeteria and cultural Catholicism, and
we get some sense of how complex the current Catholic scene is. Some even
suggest that there is an American Catholicism that must be distinguished from
the Roman variety, and others that there is no Catholic Church at all but only
the local churches tenuously united in artificial historical bonds to the Roman
See (nominalism is still among us!). Evangelicals, for their own purposes, have
taken to using their own category, "committed Catholics," to distinguish the
sort of Catholics with whom an evangelical may converse without evangelizing.[24]

To cut the knot in this case is nowhere as complicated a task as in the case
of evangelicalism. My purpose is to lay out a Catholic assessment of evangelical
Protestantism in the United States from the middle of the nineteenth to the
end of the twentieth centuries. I have chosen texts written by self-described
Catholics, lay and clerical, theologians and other intellectuals, whose communion with the church in Rome and in the United States stands as a matter
of unchallenged public record. Even after the second Vatican Council, with

attendant and subsequent confusions, determining this is not difficult. Some of these texts are official—letters of the American Catholic bishops and a document or two from the Roman congregations—but most, especially in the last two decades, were penned by Catholics to defend their religion against challenges posed by fundamentalists and evangelicals and were published in Roman Catholic media. Whereas the views of conservative spokespersons Karl Keating, James Hitchcock, Scott Hahn, and Peter Kreeft are vital to understanding contemporary Catholic reaction to evangelicalism, the views of schismatic Traditionalist Catholics repeat the assessments of pre–Vatican II, post–Tridentine Catholic apologetics in the middle of the nineteenth century. I will, therefore, report on the spokespersons of conservative Catholicism as well as on dozens of Catholics who cannot easily be classified in any particular wing of American Catholicism.

## The Scholarly Literature

Although there is a small and respectable scholarly literature on the subject of evangelical-Catholic relations in general, it barely begins to address the mountain of polemic literature piled up since the colonial period. There are two outstanding books on nineteenth-century Protestant anti-Catholicism, Ray Allen Billington's *The Protestant Crusade* (1938) and Jenny Franchot's *Roads to Rome* (1994),[25] and there is no parallel study of the Catholic responses. Billington's and Franchot's are sharply different tellings of the same story, valuable for their extensive bibliographies as well as their narratives. Originally a Harvard dissertation, Billington's work is an academic historian's account of the Protestant polemic against Catholicism that supported and surrounded the nativist movement in the 1840s and 1850s. The material dealt with by him is primarily popular and political, and the narrative is a decade-by-decade account of the rise and waning of antebellum nativism. Franchot's is a splendid example of postmodernist culture study, embracing history, biography, art and architecture, and high culture, as well as popular literature. Where Billington covers the debate between Campbell and Purcell, the hysteria of the Beechers, and the nativist arguments in Congress and the Massachusetts legislature, Franchot plucks the more subtle anti-Catholic (and in some cases philo-Catholic) meanings from the historical works of W. H. Prescott and Francis Parkman, the literary works of Poe and Hawthorne, travel journals of American tourists, and the pictographs of *Harper's New Monthly Magazine*—while not neglecting the escapades of Maria Monk and Rebecca Reed, and the fanaticism of the dean of nineteenth-century antipopery, Samuel F. B. Morse. While Billington's prose is spare and linear, Franchot's is lush and suggestive. One overall conclusion I draw from them is that anti-Catholicism, and the Catholic response to it, was a trope of American political, literary, religious, and psychological life up to the Civil War, and was displaced (all too briefly, alas!) by that tragedy.

John Higham's study, *Strangers in the Land,* covers the period from the Civil War to the passage of restrictive legislation on immigration after World War I. He follows the thread of nativist sentiment, organization and political activity from the immediate post–Civil War hiatus to its revival in the 1880s, its ebb in the 1890s, its revivals again before and after World War I, tying it to the fortunes of capital and labor, the criss-crossings of politics and religion, and its rural and urban flowerings. Anti-Catholicism is only one of nativism's many forms, steady though it is throughout the period. In fact, the tale of its gradual transformation from ethnic to racial forms seems the most pernicious and dangerous historical tendency. Hatred of Catholics is only part of the story. There is a protean "paranoid style" to American politics and intellectual life, as Richard Hofstadter maintained, rooted in an instinctive hatred of the stranger.[26] Our interest here is in the relations between evangelical Protestants and Roman Catholics, not in nativism itself, but we cannot tell our own story without alluding at least to Higham's broader study of American postbellum culture.

This book will suppose these work and rely on them wherever possible. I can only envy Billington's and Higham's achievements in historical investigation and Franchot's extraordinary command of American literature and practice of literary hermeneutics. Although I discuss at length some of the literature of the period, my special interest runs from the close of theirs into and through the twentieth century, and my question is different from theirs. Billington and Higham want to tell us what happened, Franchot wants to explore the dreams and nightmares of American identity, and I want to know, from a philosophical and theological standpoint, what evangelicals and Catholics meant about one another and what that means in the present and the future. I shall adapt from Billington his narrative of the nineteenth-century debates and from Franchot her bent-back question, "While they seemed to talk to and about each other, were Protestants and Catholics in fact talking to and about themselves?" In addition, there is a significant, albeit not yet daunting, literature on anti-Catholicism by historians, Protestant and Catholic; this will prove helpful. There is precious little scholarly work on Catholic anti-evangelicalism, and my hope is that this book will serve as a modest first step in analysis of it.[27]

## Three Myths

What will soon oppress the persistent reader is a theological gauntlet. Before that begins, it might help to lay out the point of view taken in approaching it. According to Jacob Neusner, there are three components to the definition of a religion: a worldview; a way of life; a people.[28] This is a useful, and common, way to approach a religion, or, indeed, several of them in an academic setting. This section addresses two of those terms: a worldview expressed in symbol and narrative (a myth) and the importance of a myth to a people. I assume for present purposes that Protestants and Catholics are two distinct and often opposed peoples. American historians such as Sydney Ahlstrom and Mark Noll now tell their stories in one interconnected narrative, but each people retains its own view and its own story (its myth) that the historians are dedicated to refinishing.

But we have here a triangle: the third people can be called naturalists or humanists or atheists who have yet another story that they like to think is the "real" story. Each of the three peoples, or what I want to call tribes, must explain to itself what it is and why it is this. But it must also explain why it is not that, accounting for "the others" in relationship to the tribe. Such an account may be in part historical but it is not fully or simply historical. One might even call the three stories "folk history," because they are concerned to tell their story as it truly happened. But it palpably is not the academic sort of history no matter how much it may intend to resemble it. Even footnotes do not help its classification. It remains the sort of history written by the authors of Exodus and the New Testament gospels, "sacred history," the story of God and the community. And so I prefer to call these stories myths. A myth is perhaps typically about the beginning and/or the end of things, but it may be also about the middle, about "the way things really happened."

In my view, for a variety of reasons, sacred history or myth is different from, and perhaps more important than, secular history. Academic history informs ordinary life only indirectly, but sacred history or myth does so directly. These myths are the "history" we tell our children, the ones that are permeated by the love God has had for our foremothers and fathers. As the son of an Irish immigrant I know full well how my family survived the famine, British tyranny, and the great journey across the sea—and I knew it before I read a single academic account. My memory of a discussion in 1986–87 at the Smithsonian's Woodrow Wilson Center between C. Vann Woodward and John Hope Franklin is tenuous no doubt, but, as I recall it, these two giants of the history of the American South fell out over the relation between myth and history, with Vann Woodward coming down hard on the side of the incompatibility of the two and the value of history in breaking myth, and Franklin insisting on the necessity of both, with myth carrying the meanings and values of a people. The options were: history corrects myth, which yet remains the story (Franklin), or history demythologizes and so becomes the "true" story itself (Vann Woodward). My option is the first one, the one supported, if my memory serves me, by John Hope Franklin.[29]

All three of the myths I retell here are utterly true, in the sense in which the four canonical gospels about Jesus are true. These myths are etiological, explaining the origins and progress of a people. But they are distinct even from folk history, for two of them pull God into the narrative and the third is cradled in the myth that God is not necessary for its story. Yes, all three are capable of distorting or ignoring history on one side, but they carry the meaning of two modern movements of Christianity on the one side and of Enlightenment naturalism on the other. Can we read them as history? No, although there may be history in the secular sense in them. Must we read them as myths control-ling historical meaning and expressing basic religious meaning on the other? Yes, although they are not thereby untrue or useless. In fact, they are the data for an academic history of the tribes' self-understanding.

Two of the myths tell the stories of different Christianities. The Roman Catholic myth is wrong, to judge by the Protestant Bible. The Protestant myth is wrong, to judge by the ongoing life of a spirit-led church hierarchy. Both claim to be history, they often look like history, they often are intended to be history, but neither myth acts like a history. They cement adherence, explain origins, warn, justify practice, direct decisions, draw boundaries, and place and judge "the others." The Catholic myth is clerical, hierarchical, organizational, sacramental, analogical, communitarian, and culture-absorbing. The Protes-tant myth is anticlerical, liberational, dialectical, antimediational, individualist, and culture-suspecting. "What actually happened" is understood differently in the two, and so are authentic Christian doctrine and practice. Getting at the roots of the myth, political, religious, and psychological, is important, as is relating them to their cultural conditions of origin and transmission. The ac-ademic study of the myths, as important as that is, is not as important as the fact that peoples live in them, for to understand a people one must understand its myths. To understand Catholicism, one must understand the story of God's establishment of the one true church and the Protestant revolt against it. To understand Protestantism, one must understand God's call of the reformers to Christian liberty and the Roman attempts to crush any and every sign of that liberty given by God in Christ to those who believe.[30] To understand the Enlightenment one must understand how it brought down the power of Chris-tian churchmen to enslave the human spirit.

## *The Protestant Myth:* Ex tenebris lux

The churches the Apostles left behind were true Christian churches adhering in belief and practice to the Apostolic witness. The New Testament replaced that witness as the *norma normans non normata,* the only inspired container of the apostolic preaching and of the inerrant revelation, and the symbol of the definitive break with Judaism. Christianity was to be a religion of spirit and truth. The preaching of the gospel and the life of apostolic Christianity was gradually perverted by the reestablishment of Jewish institutions and the im-portation of pagan practices. The unscriptural and illegitimate invention of the priesthood, and the extension of the authority of the monarchical bishops over the churches and of bishop of Rome over other bishops, weakened the New Testament rule of the churches and of church leaders, subjecting the churches to non-Christian and finally to anti-Christian institutional governance, doctrine, and custom. These officeholders responded to the flood of new members into the established churches by restoring the old paganism in the form of monastic communities and convents that in fact have been cesspools of iniquity and fonts of works-righteousness. Religious asceticism replaced faith. The Christian people were taught that they were saved by undergoing clerically controlled ceremonies rather than by faith, and that the scriptures were joined by, in fact dominated by, an infallible and "apostolic" tradition, which meant in practice whatever the bishop of Rome and his supporters taught. Thus, both belief and practice were so thoroughly corrupted, and the churches so controlled, that those who lived by the scriptures were subject to persecution by the papal anti-Christ. The faith was kept alive by these so-called heretics and by pious and trusting souls who lived by the scriptures. God preserved them and the Bible.

By the sixth (or fifth or fourth or third) century, the pope grew so powerful that he not only supported idolatrous pagan and Jewish forms of worship but also blasphemously demanded and accepted worship of himself as the presence of God in the world, styling himself "universal bishop" and "vicar of Christ." At one point (perhaps 606 CE) the papacy itself became the anti-Christ. The Christian world was corrupted in its teaching, its worship, its art, its intellectual and spiritual life, its governance to the point that many, including the leaders, rejected the simple Christian gospel of salvation by faith through grace when they were reintroduced to it by the Reformers in the sixteenth century. Those who heard it worked to spread the true gospel and, as a result, true Christian churches were founded in northern Europe and the American colonies.

That true gospel was formally condemned by the Roman church at Trent, as a vigorous and Satanic opposition to the preaching of the gospel was launched by the popes and controlled from Rome. In anticipation of the final, eschatological battle of Satan against the Kingdom of God, papal forces struggled against every true Christian church and sought to reestablish control over every Christian nation. They plotted and carried out the murder of believers and the suppression of the gospel. The most prominent servants of this Romish hatred of the gospel were the Jesuits who led, among other enormities, the plot to slaughter the king of England, the royal family, and the entire Parliament in the Gunpowder Plot of 1605.

The pope and his Jesuits planned to control the entire Christian world, including an imminent takeover of the United States, utilizing the sacramental system, especially the sacrament of penance, and the naiveté of American Protestants. Only a clearheaded and constant reaffirmation of the pure gospel in a pure church can save the Christian people from enslavement once again to

Roman error. Only in the last days will the efforts of the Antichrist of Rome be definitively defeated and he and his servants be chained in the lake of fire.[31]

## The Roman Catholic Myth: Extra ecclesiam nulla salus

The Roman Catholic Church is the church commissioned by Christ when he appointed his twelve Apostles who were its first priests and bishops, commanding them to govern the church, to baptize all nations, and to be the instruments of grace through the administration of the sacraments to all who believe. The legitimacy of the papacy, the monarchical episcopate, and the sacramental system are all established by the words of Christ and the words of the authors of the New Testament. Christ taught much that was not contained in the scriptures that has been passed down in unbroken written and oral tradition of the church, teachings whose truth is guaranteed by the ubiquity of its acceptance by the bishops of the churches under the leadership of the chief of the bishops and successor of St. Peter, the bishop of Rome and vicar of Christ on earth. The life of the Christian people is instituted and fed by the mediation of priesthood in the sacrifice of the Mass whereby Christ's saving death on Calvary for the remission of sins and the continuing offering at the heavenly throne of His Father are renewed for each generation of Catholic Christians.

Since the very beginning this saving truth, sacramental life, church governance, and unity have been threatened time and again by the errors and deliberate distortions of heretics, including the Arians of the fourth century, the Albigensians of the thirteenth, and the Protestants of the sixteenth. Although the true church has gone on to preach and practice the true religion commanded by Christ, these Satanic movements, as tares among the wheat, have spread confusion in the flock of Christ. The heretics have been exposed and contained by the vigorous action of church leaders, including lawful condemnation of heresy and punishment of heretics by the leaders of Christian nations. The heretics deserved no better, for error has no rights. The errors of the Protestant movement were catalogued and refuted, and the true gospel reasserted, at the Council of Trent. Those Protestant errors had severely strained communion in belief and sacrament, and threatened the very existence of the true church, yet the church was reinvigorated and has prospered under the leadership of the Roman pontiffs. Protestant subjectivism and antinomianism have led to the decline of Christendom in spite of the efforts of the church of Rome, spawned the series of revolutions that have wracked Europe, and revealed its Satanic origin in the Enlightenment, which completed the denial of Christian truth and the rights of the church, and stripped society of its divinely established political and social order.

The true church alone has the right to preach and teach the gospel of Christ and shape the worship practice of the Christian people. The bishops alone have the right to commission missionaries, ordain ministers, order worship, and teach definitively in the name of Christ. Through all its historical sufferings, the church's teaching and its basic religious life have not changed and will never change, echoing the revelation of the eternal and unchanging God whose Son died once for all and whose Holy Spirit ever reminds the lawful rulers of the church of the truth revealed. The papal universal jurisdiction over the church is a theological deduction from Matthew 16:18ff and John 21:15ff, was recognized in the practice of the apostolic and patristic churches, and implies papal infallibility, which has been explicitly affirmed by the bishops in communion with the pope at the Councils of Trent, Vatican I, and Vatican II. The central message of this long history of God's true church is apostolic succession and communion.[32]

The Catholic myth is reiterated in the documents of Vatican II, embodied in a benign form to suit the times, corrected and reshaped by the historical theologians and the bishops, maximizing inclusiveness and minimizing exclusiveness.[33] The boundaries are shifting, yet the myth is being rewritten.

### The Enlightenment Myth: Sola scientia!

The progress of humankind has been slow and difficult, its way blocked by ignorance and superstition, by adherence to traditions, and by wiles of the religious specialists who controlled both salvation and knowledge. There were moments of light in the work of the Greek naturalist-philosophers who sought to break through the old stories, from *mythos* to *logos,* but religious controls on inquiry and communication were reimposed, first in the Hellenistic and then in the Christian eras.[34] Myth rather than reason once again dominated humanity. Significant and irreversible steps toward the liberation of Reason were taken in the eighteenth century, first with the philosophical criticism of the churches' reactionary hold on the masses and literary criticism of the sacred documents, then by political revolution against tyranny, by the establishment of inalienable human rights and of democratic governments committed to maintain them, and finally by the rise and institutionalization in the universities of *Naturwissenschaften* and *Geisteswissenschaften* as the only way to know the truth about the world and humankind. Immanuel Kant defined the heart of the Enlightenment as a moment in which human beings take responsibility for their own knowing and their own moral activity rather than resting in the soporific arms of superstition, tradition, and the priesthood. The spirit of the Age of Enlightenment is captured in the atheism of Feuerbach, discovery of the goals, the flow and mechanisms of historical progress by Hegel and Marx, and the mapping of the interior bonds of humanity's psyche by Freud in the twentieth century. The hope of humanity lies not in religious dogma or political despotism but in the courageous affirmation of science and the critique of religious superstition and doctrine; the affirmation of democratic polity against tyranny; and the proclamation of the moral gospel in its ideal of reason, responsibility, and freedom against traditions and obscurantist institutions. Religions, including all forms of Christianity, are the implacable enemies of human progress and liberation with their emphasis on divinely established order, truth by revelation, and salvation by faith alone. The triumph of science and the elimination of religion is assured by the progress of humanity through self-knowledge and knowledge of the cosmos.[35]

In its latest phase, post-Enlightenment or postmodernism, the Enlightenment reaches another stage in its development wherein all claims to truth, even its own, are affirmed to be relative to context. All knowing, including science, and moral evaluation are seen to be shaped in traditions and so are subjective, historical and contextual, and permeated by ideology. The contribution of postmodernism in correcting the Enlightenment-modernist myth is cognitive and moral relativism. Surpassing the vigor of the modernist forms of criticism, postmodernism is doubly opposed to uncritical and obscurantist traditional religions with their claims to unconditioned truth and their service to power.[36]

## The Tribes

Tribes live by myths.[37] By this term, I mean not only an important element of religion and culture but also an important element in the horizon of the interpreter of religion. The term in this context is not a metaphor of opprobrium. We can ill afford to look down on tribes, for we belong to them; without them we are nothing. By tribe, I mean the community established by bonds of common experience, understanding, and intersubjectivity that set a people apart in the sea of humanity: the tribe has its common past and its hopes for the future, and has the symbols by which these meanings find expression.[38] The family, the extended family, the clan, the ethnic group, the people, the nation, and even the political party would more or less fall under my usage, but so prominently do the Roman Catholic Church, the Protestant churches, and Enlightenment movements such as Marxism and secular humanism. Even the modern academic class, one of the many offspring of the Enlightenment, is a tribe, although not an especially cohesive or attractive one. The academic class is a guild of professional knowers, the ones who know the signs of our culture and other cultures, how to interpret them, and how to impart knowledge and proper usage to the young and to apprentices.

In the modern world of differentiation and specialization, we may belong to several tribes and find our loyalties divided among them. I, for example, am a Roman Catholic, an American citizen, an ethnic Irishman, an academic, a student of religions, a Democrat. I confess that I do not find my multiple tribal membership at all easy. In addition, we may be at odds with other members of our tribes—witness the liberal-conservative split that runs across the Christian churches in the United States.[39] The ample number of tribal memberships possible for us characterizes the modern world—the phenomenon is called pluralism and multiculturalism by academics and politicians. There were always many tribes, but I doubt that there ever was an equal possibility of multiple memberships—perhaps Hellenistic culture with regard to religion would run a distant second.

Moreover, the tribe today often recognizes itself as a tribe among many, not as the norm of the human as was reportedly the case in tribal, archaic, and classical cultures, in early modern Western nations. Today they are tribes in relation to others, a situation that counters claims to normativity. Nazism and the Communist movements were examples of extreme ideological tribalism, but they remain, one hopes, the horrific aberration rather than the rule in the twentieth century. But even the history of advanced first-world societies in Western and central Europe in the twentieth century can be told in good part in terms of the struggle for ethnic and cultural purity and dominance.[40] Xenophobia is the ghost in modern cultures.

There is a certain irony to this pluralism. The Enlightenment, which is at least in part responsible for it, is so by indirection, for the Enlightenment set out to liberate us from the old tribes in favor of a new tribe, a universal tribe of the Enlightened that would embrace all, if only the Enlightened could get the rest of us into state controlled public schools and keep us there until we are civilized.[41] This is typical, for tribes suspect one another. A tribe excludes as well as includes; it not only distinguishes but in doing so it draws lines; beyond the line fall those about whom the tribe cares not or stands against. The term "tribe" brings out that moral ambiguity more sharply for our purposes than the more morally neutral, indeed flaccid, term "community." One of the characteristics is suspicion of the stranger and unease in the presence of the strange. The tribe lives by its inherited commonsense wisdom and aesthetics, and by its unquestioned and unquestioning group loyalty, by its own myth of origins, and by conviction of its own normativity. The stranger threatens all this. When the tribe meets the stranger or a tribe of strangers, there is swift recognition ["They are not us"], a conclusion ["They are perverse insofar as they are not like us"] an alternative imperative ["Draw the wagons round" or "Make them like us."].[42]

In contemporary intellectual culture, subtribes abound: naturalists, pragmatists, existentialists, Marxists, Freudians, and so on, a list as endless as the subtribes of Christians. The modern world, the modern mind, the left wing of modern culture has been suspicious of the old religious tribes, their traditions, and their authorities, and are deeply hostile to them, as well they might be. For the religions wisdom has been given once for all; for the Enlightenment tribes it is just over the next hill if only we can cling to science.

The irony is twofold: the Enlightenment meant to transcend tribalism, yet became another tribe in its very efforts to destroy tribalism; and, second, the Enlightenment thereby set conditions in place that assured the resurgence of tribalism, for, in its destruction of the "old ways," myths, and traditions, it left a vacuum that its own spare myths of reason, progress, and equality could not possibly fill, a vacuum to be filled at times with new and far more brutish versions of the ancient myths.[43] Some of the worst of that resurgence we see in the ethnic wars in the Balkans and crimes of racism in Germany, Britain, and the United States. Some of the best we see in the remarkable persistence and renewal of ethnic communities in parts of central Europe and in the United States, and, above all, in the survival and health of the Jewish and Christian tribes and in the renewed vigor of Islam. Ah, if only we could have many tribes and no strangers! If only Enlightenment without disdain for the past!

But these are high and great matters. I have in mind a narrower and more lowly focus: tribalism and the study of two bodies of Christians. The bonds of affection and loyalty over time and the sharing of meaning that constitute religious communities are ambiguous. The religious tribe not only gives life and spirit and provides the beginning of any understanding we possess but also breeds bias, blocks understanding, and demands a loyalty that cuts into freedom. Religious tribes, like others, outlaw the very questions of meaning and value that constituted them in the first place. The United States is founded on a revolution, the like of which it now thoroughly excludes by means of the largest military, economy, and bureaucracy in history. Christianity, that foundation of which involves a Man who was regarded as a Stranger and even, by his murderers, an enemy, and a Christianity that itself has claims to universality, can only contradict itself when it outlaws the stranger and oppresses the strange in its midst. Dostoevski caught the irony beautifully.[44] It would appear that this particular tribe's very existence and meaning is bound up with welcoming the stranger as the bearer of God.[45] A tribe that presents itself as the "one true tribe" and separates itself from its many less true and even untrue neighboring tribes has only a surface logic in its favor, for it acts on the logic of survival, the ordinary logic of the tribe; it has lost the logic of its Master who, according to its own central tradition, did not choose survival over other values. The historical tribal warfare among Christians has become an irony indeed if the tribe claiming eternal affinity with the Stranger-in-our-midst should become, in the attitudes and action of his earthly body the Church, the systematic enemy of all that is different and strange.

Enlightenment liberalism clearly does not escape this ambiguity. It set out to teach us all tolerance, yet has not gotten beyond patronizing and scornful tolerance toward the old religious and ethnic tribes. The "mere tolerance" of the Enlightenment carries in its bosom a secret wish for the death of those who refuse enlightenment. At bottom, the Enlightenment tribe doesn't think the others should exist. No wonder then, that the others, the religious tribes of Christians such as the Catholics and the conservative evangelicals, retain their suspicious, often hostile, attitude toward Western tribes descendent from the Enlightenment—political tribes such as liberals and socialists, cultural elites such as the academic tribe, and task-based tribes such as the bureaucrats. The old religious tribes exist outside the knowledge and care of the modern tribe.

The instinct of the modern tribe for survival and for dominance of the environment (whether literal or metaphorical), and so on, has little changed, though its specific forms differ markedly in many instances from older examples. The modern and postmodern tribes, too, confront the stranger in ways continuous with the ancient ways of rejection and elimination. In a valuable essay Bernhard Asen lays out the biblical understandings of the stranger and of the stranger's basically ambiguous self-presentation, an ambiguity that puts the tribe in moral crisis.[46] Thus, not only the sojourner in Israel is the stranger but also Yahweh and Jesus may be the Stranger; and the despised stranger (the Samaritan) may turn out to be the neighbor to one in need. Thus, the response of the Christian and Jew to the stranger is complicated well beyond politics, economics, intertribal rules of hospitality, and even the memory of a former state of oppression. The stranger can be a bearer of God.

In our common history, evangelicals have been taken by Catholics as strangers and sometimes enemies, and conservative evangelicals have so regarded Catholics.[47] The Catholic and Protestant myths are crucial carriers of the enmity. The myths enable the tribe to hold on to its past, and so promote its intellectual, spiritual, and moral cohesion. The rise of critical history does not entail a decline of myth in my view, but it may mean a purification and rewriting of myths. The myth, being the story of how God has brought things to be as they are and why they are that, must be sifted if the old hatreds are to be left behind and if our present and future together is to be seen as the will and gift of God. The critical history of Christian enmity is well on its way, and, partly as a consequence, the myth can be retold.

At present, I would tell the story this way: Protestantism and Catholicism are modern versions of medieval Christendom, which in turn grew, by the grace of God, from "the early church." The two are seemingly incompatible postmedieval developments of Christianity. Neither is simply medieval, and neither continues or breaks with the parent religion cleanly and definitively, but the different paths taken in the sixteenth century imply such a profound transformation of medieval Christendom that they are close to being two distinct religions, not subspecies of one religion as are Eastern and Western Catholicism. In spite of their own stories, Protestantism is as much an heir of medieval Christianity as Roman Catholicism claims to be, and Catholicism is as new or modern and "apostolic" a Christianity as Protestantism claims to be. Neither is or could be purely or surely apostolic Christianity outside their respective myths. They are both *nova et vetera,* the new and the old, they are equally legitimate forms of Christian community life that differ in their understandings of what a Christian life and community should or may be. Their myths are true insofar as they accurately claim the inspiration of the Spirit of Jesus of Nazareth and insofar as they point to sin as the source of their division; and they are both authentic and inauthentic expressions of that same Spirit in so far as they have been faithful or unfaithful to its leading. They both now show signs of a critical-historical remythologization of their pasts; that is, they are beginning to imagine their pasts freshly in terms of sin and grace. The older account on either side will not hold. The Enlightenment myth has also undergone revision in the same period. Its two claims, that human beings are best understood as autonomous individuals free of restraints of traditional religious and social organization, and that religion will fade as science advances, have been discovered to be inadequate even by its spiritual heirs. The story of the Enlightenment, too, may be retold. The latter may turn out to be a chapter in the story of Western Christianity.[48]

The three stories are, by the grace of God, breaking down and God is acting once again to anticipate the kingdom of justice and peace, and catching us all once again asleep, comfortable in our dreams of ourselves, while His Son suffers over our sins. In my version, there is a confluence of myths and a newly imagined future. If the traditions are to rewrite their myths, can we imagine an historical, premillennial future for the relationships between them? Will the lion and the lamb rest together?

# 2

# The Perils of Modernity

When the Christian church entered the Gentile world it ceased to be a messianic sect of Judaism. Luke told the story in *The Acts of the Apostles,* and Paul provided the theological argumentation in his letters to Galatia and Rome: there would be no more Jew and Greek. Among other problems facing the new religion, the church was fated over the centuries to come to terms with the intellectual and religious life of Hellenistic culture, and it did so, one halting step at a time. In the century after the Christians came out of the catacombs they took on the responsibilities of the religious life of the empire. Christianity became a church, a catholic church, preserving not only its gospel but also the inherited culture of Greece and Rome, and it helped to create a new culture out of the ruins of the old. There can be no question that the church began to change Hellenistic culture and the culture began to change the church.

When Tertullian asked in the third century, "What has Athens to do with Jerusalem?" he meant by that, "What has pagan learning to do with the Christian gospel?" That question has been put to the church throughout its history, and, in most cases, the answer has been, "More than you think, yet less than you fear." Tertullian's negative answer to his own question,[1] his condemnation of pagan learning, was rejected by the Fathers of the church in the third and fourth centuries, by Aquinas in the thirteenth, by Erasmus and the learned men and women of the Renaissance, by the Protestant theologians of the nineteenth century, by both Protestant and Catholic theologians in the twentieth, and by every sustained Christian tradition, whether Orthodox, Roman, or Protestant. Christianity has been

a constructor of cultures, not separatist or sectarian within cultures; its problems have stemmed from its construction of culture rather than from avoiding
it. True, under certain conditions, Christians have been tempted to sectarianism,[2] but its leaders have consistently attempted to dominate and direct cultures or have fallen under the direction and dominance of other forces in
cultures. Before entering the dark tunnel of evangelical–Roman Catholic relations, we should take account, at least in broad strokes, of the immense
struggle of Protestants and Catholics with the rapid and profound changes in
western culture that alienated some of them and smothered others, challenged
them all, and now may even have turned them toward one another. The point
of this chapter, then, is to set a general context for the chapters to follow.

From their different starting points, modern evangelical Christians and
Catholics have undergone social and cultural displacement and now, it seems,
have adjusted and emerged from that process without some of their worst fears
being realized. In the course of their journey some in the evangelical movement and the Catholic Church assumed a sectarian posture (Protestant fundamentalism and Catholic integralism) and formed their own inclusive sub-
cultures and societies, to become countercultural in the very cultures they felt
they had created in the first place. As we make our way through an admittedly
selective narrative, we will be laying stress on those aspects of the conservative
Christian reaction to modernity that seemed most evident and important to
them at the time. Perhaps in the long run modern democratic politics, economies, and technologies will have the greater impact on them and their institutions, but for my purpose, to sharpen the differences between the two communities in their common experience in modernity, I shall concentrate on the
cultural changes that had the most immediate and direct effect on them and
called forth their vigorous negative responses. "Modernity," I hope, will stand
here for antireligious ideological factors in the changes in the West since the
Enlightenment.

The publication of Darwin's *Origin of Species* (1858) and *The Descent of Man*
(1871) and their reception, and the irresistible spread of historical and literary
study of the Bible in European and American universities and seminaries are
the outstanding instances of modernity's impingement on the life of the
churches. The implications of the new biology and the new methods of biblical
study were at first obscure, and then gradually clearer: Darwinism claimed that
the present could be explained as an evolution from the past and explained
without appeal to supernatural causes. This claim implied that the account of
human origins given in the book of Genesis (1–3) is historically inaccurate;
indeed, the account, as it was determined by academic experts, is not historical
at all. For the six days of creation, the new science substituted almost unima-
ginable eons of development. For a special creation of two individuals in a
garden, it substituted hundreds of thousands, and then several millions of

years of development of our species from humanoid and nonhuman ancestors. For the fall from primitive innocence, it substituted a rise from primeval slime.[3]

These implications touch on the doctrines of Christian anthropology, removing humanity even further from the center of the cosmic stage than had Copernicus, Kepler, and Newton, confining human beings to the last split second on the march of cosmic forces, and simultaneously outlawing any notion of humanity as the "end" or "culmination" of a divine creation. This would prove more than enough to turn Christians, both Protestant and Catholic, against "Darwinism." In two widely read essays by American naturalist philosophers the broader intellectual and cultural significance of Darwinism was made clear:

- Change is the fundamental reality, not some timeless "essence" or "substance" behind the processes of nature.
- Human thought is concerned with the specific and the particular, with concrete problems rather than with the general and transcendental, with how things interact rather than the fact that they do.
- Human striving is for concrete, historical goods and values, "direct increments of justice and happiness."
- Humanity's concern now moves from discovering the "purposes of the Creator" and the Creator's design to how creation's natural processes can be used for human purposes.

Darwin was directly a cause of worry to those conservative Christians, Protestant and Catholic, who read the scriptures as if they reveal scientific data. But in the long run Darwin was as much worry to those who, by drawing accommodating intellectual categories such as literary forms in the scriptures, think they have escaped Darwin's science. Then even liberal theologies could not escape the naturalist net. Reflecting on the hundred years after publication of *Origin of Species,* John Herman Randall Jr., a twentieth-century naturalist philosopher, wrote:

> These changes which Dewey signaled fifty years ago (1909) are all in what he called our "mode of thinking." . . . the employment of this new, genetic, pluralistic, experimental, and functional, mode of thinking led to a great change in substantive views. Man's relation to nature was basically altered. He was no longer a fallen angel, but a great ape trying to make good, the last and best-born of nature's children. This alternation effected two great transformations: it transformed man, and it also transformed nature.[4]

During that same century, in the university departments of ancient culture and humanities, and in theology departments and seminaries, the sacred books of Judaism and Christianity were subjected to the methods and criteria of historical and literary study. The Bible was examined in the same way one would study any ancient document, with much the same kind of startling conclusions: Moses did not write the Pentateuch; the book of Isaiah was not the product of one prophet but of three over a period of as much as 250 years; the psalms were not written by King David but by a succession and variety of Hebrew poets over some six hundred years whose work was attributed to the Israelite bandit-king; St. Matthew did not write the Gospel of Matthew; St. John did not write John; Jesus did not say what the four evangelists say he said, and so forth.[5] It seemed that every assumption and teaching of the Bible and the Christian churches with regard to the origins of the earth and human life, the history of the Jews, the origins of Christianity, and the development of the Bible was under serious question in universities, in the books read by intellectuals, in journals, in newspapers, and even in seminaries and their Bible classes.[6]

## Evangelical Protestants and Modernism

At the very time that the questions were being raised, America was undergoing the third of its vaunted "great awakenings." The first of these periods of religious revival among American Protestants occurred in all the colonies in the 1740s. The second broke out in the states of Kentucky and Tennessee in 1800 and spread through the other states to the north and south, reaching its high point between 1820 and 1830. Even New York City got a bit of religion in that one. And the third revival began after the Civil War and ran over into the first decade of the twentieth century. The revivalists in this third, Dwight Moody the most prominent among them, went from town to town, city to city, in the United States and even in England, preaching the evangelical gospel of sin, second-birth, salvation, and the imminent second coming of Christ.[7]

As the new biology and biblical studies intruded themselves into the lives of ordinary citizens, the revivalists came to feel that the foundations of Christian faith were being attacked by godless professors of a pseudoscience and by compromising Christian theologians. Some were convinced that to accept the new science and biblical studies was to deny Christian faith. As one of the later fundamentalists put it in 1920:

> Every honest man knows that accepting evolution means giving up
> the inspiration of Genesis; and if the inspiration of Genesis is given
> up, the testimony of Jesus to the inspiration of the scriptures, goes
> with it; and if his testimony to the scriptures is given up, his deity
> goes with it, and with that goes his being a real Redeemer and we
> are left without a savior and in the darkness of our sins.[8]

The concern of Christian revivalists became the concern of thousands and later millions of American evangelical Christians. Not all Protestants, not even all evangelical Protestants, thought that the new science was inimical to Christian faith, although some of the hawkers of its methods were, Thomas Huxley, Darwin's booster, most notable among them. Many Protestants accepted the methods of the sciences and biblical study, and adjusted to the findings of both without altering the beliefs they cherished. But others thought that, by the use of scientific methods, the church could be rescued from some of its age-old misconceptions and set free of dogmas that no longer served to illuminate human life and to guide it, enabling theologians to engage in wholesale and open-ended reinterpreting of Christian belief. These Christians were called modernists, and they became the primary enemy of the revivalists, even more so than the "godless" scientists and philosophers themselves.

The reactions to Darwinism, then, varied widely among evangelical Protestant theologians and pastors. "Modernists" were the more radical wing, apprehending the basic issue to be methodological, that is, the procedures by which knowledge is established. They accepted unequivocally the recognized methods of the sciences including history and literary criticism. Many moderate evangelicals, doctrinally conservative, saw no contradiction between science and faith, and worked out solutions to specific problems as they arose; witness theistic evolution, the variety of "symbolic" interpretations of the Genesis narratives, and the rapid absorption of literary and historical criticism in the study of the entire Bible. The fundamentalists saw every bit as clearly as did the modernists that the issue was methodological or, as they might put it, a matter of authority. In their case, the authority for knowledge, historical as well as religious, remained Scripture.[9]

Between 1910 and 1915 a group of revival leaders and conservative evangelical scholars published twelve short volumes of essays entitled *The Fundamentals*.[10] The volumes were a ringing defense of traditional Christian orthodoxy, and a sharp criticism of the new science and the methods of biblical study and of the Christian theologians who would adopt them. The authors were not separatists, however, although at this point the acceptance of Darwinism and especially the practice of biblical criticism were branded infidelity to the church and apostasy from the orthodox Christian faith. A minister in the Canadian church objected to the acceptance of German higher criticism as follows:

It is not possible, then, to accept the . . . [Higher Critics'] . . . theory
of the structure of the Old Testament and the . . . theory of its inspiration without undermining faith in the Bible as the Word of God.
For the Bible is either the Word of God, or it is not. The children of
Israel were the children of the Only Living and True God, or they
were not. If their Jehovah was a mere tribal deity, and their religion
a human evolution; if their sacred literature was natural with mythi-

cal and pseudonymous admixtures; then the Bible is dethroned from its throne as the exclusive, authoritative, Divinely inspired Word of God. It simply ranks as one of the sacred books of the ancients with similar claims of inspiration and revelation.[11]

Darwinism receives similar treatment at the hands of "an Occupant of the Pew":

> But when we consider that the evolutionary theory was conceived in agnosticism, and born and nurtured in infidelity; that it is the backbone of the destructive higher criticism which has so viciously assailed the integrity and authority of the Scriptures; that it utterly fails in explaining—what Genesis makes so clear—those tremendous facts in human history and human nature, the presence of evil and its attendant suffering; that it offers nothing but a negative reply to that supreme question of the ages, "If a man die, shall he live again?" that it, in fact, substitutes for a personal God "an infinite and eternal Energy" which is without moral qualities or positive attributes, is not wise, or good, or merciful or just; cannot love or hate, reward or punish; that it denies the personality of God and man, and presents them, together with nature, as under a process of evolution which has neither beginning or end; and regard man as being simply a passing form of this universal Energy, and thus without free will, moral responsibility, or immortality, it becomes evident to every intelligent layman that such a system can have no possible points of contact with Christianity. He may well be pardoned if he views with astonishment ministers of the Gospel still clinging to it, and harbors a doubt of their sincerity or sanity.[12]

If these are the alternatives, as our authors find them, no Christian could hesitate to declare for Christian orthodoxy against unbelieving scientists. Nor can one say that these essays are at all inaccurate portraits of the threat facing the evangelical churches at the end of the nineteenth and the beginning of the twentieth centuries. Nor can one fail to appreciate the energy and commitment of fundamentalist Christians in opposing what they were convinced meant the end of Christianity.

The volumes were mailed free of charge to hundreds of thousands of ministers and Bible teachers throughout the country—-production and mailing costs borne by two oil tycoons, Lyman and Milton Stewart. In the end, over three million copies of *The Fundamentals* were distributed.[13] American ministers then had in their hands, if they chose to accept it, a rationale for rejection of Darwinism and biblical criticism.

In 1919 a group of conservative pastors, revivalists, and theologians formed the World's Christian Fundamentals Association in direct opposition to what was then known as the Federal Council of Churches (later the World Council of Churches), an organizational outcome of the interdenominational and missionary spirit of nineteenth-century evangelicals.[14] The fundamentalists, as they were soon called, were ready to do battle with their liberal and modernist counterparts in the decade from 1920 to 1930.[15] They moved to gain control of the northern Presbyterian General Assembly and the Northern Baptist Convention, denominations in which liberals were prominent but far from a majority.

The liberals rose to the occasion.[16] In 1922, a leading liberal, Harry Emerson Fosdick, a Baptist preacher and pastor of the First Presbyterian Church in New York (and so subject to Presbyterian polity), read and then published a sermon entitled "Shall the Fundamentalists Win?" in which he pinpointed the issues from a liberal perspective.[17] He was joined in 1924 by Shailer Mathews, a professor in the University of Chicago divinity school, in *The Faith of Modernism,* which identified the cause of science and modernist Christianity.[18]

Before Mathews's volume appeared, Professor J. Gresham Machen of Princeton Seminary, in *Christianity and Liberalism,* the finest theological essay by a leader of the antimodernist wing of evangelical Protestants, responded with a charge he had been honing for a decade, that Protestant modernist theology was not Christian at all but a new religion. Indeed, as far as Machen was concerned, Modernism is more objectionable than Catholicism.[19] The fundamentalists moved to have the modernists, Fosdick among them, censured by their denominations and excluded from pulpits and teaching posts.[20] The crucial stage of the intradenominational war came in 1926 and 1927 when, finally, the Presbyterian General Assembly and the Northern Baptist Convention refused to expel or censure the modernists. The fundamentalists had lost the battle for the large denominations in the north. Princeton Seminary, a prize of the Presbyterian conflict, quickly changed to a more liberal stance and, as a result, Machen and several of the traditionalist professors, including the young Cornelius Van Til, withdrew to found Westminster Theological Seminary near Philadelphia.[21] A few years later, after a trial by his own presbytery (Brunswick, NJ) for the act of establishing an independent missionary society in violation of the accepted procedures of the Presbyterian Church in the United States of America, Machen and others left the Presbyterian General Assembly and founded the Orthodox Presbyterian Church (1936).[22] The outcome in the Northern Baptist Convention was similar: the seminaries remained in the hands of liberals and moderates, and the fundamentalists withdrew to found new seminaries.[23]

While the war over seminaries and denominational leadership was under way, fundamentalists also led a national political campaign to exclude Darwinian evolution theory from the public schools, denominational colleges, and state-supported colleges and universities. Several states passed statutes banning Darwin from the public schools. In 1925 a biology teacher named John

Scopes, agreeing to a court test of the law, admitted teaching evolution in his high-school class in Dayton, Tennessee, and the "Monkey Trial" was under way. Two of the most famous men in America fought one another in the courtroom over science, religion, and the law. William Jennings Bryan, several-times candidate for the presidency, recently secretary of state under Woodrow Wilson and the year before candidate for moderator of the Presbyterian General Assembly, prosecuted the case for the state of Tennessee and the fundamentalists; and Clarence Darrow, fresh from his highly publicized defense of Leopold and Loeb, two young men who had murdered a child in Chicago for the thrill of it, stood at the bar for John Scopes supported by *The Baltimore Sun* and the American Civil Liberties Union.

The Dayton trial received national attention. Bryan and the fundamentalists won a court victory—Scopes was fined a small sum and the verdict was later reversed—but lost the case in the national press when Darrow got Bryan himself on the stand to defend the Bible and made a fool of him. Fundamentalists were subjected to nationwide mockery. By the end of the decade they had lost a bid to save their churches from modernism and to save the nation's schools from evolution, or, as they called it, "devilution" and "evilution." Modernist polemical writings and caricatures by newspaper men such as H. L. Mencken convinced the intellectual reading public that fundamentalism was the death spasm of an outmoded worldview and was now retreating to the ill-educated, rural haunts from whence it came.[24]

But being quiet and being dead are not quite the same thing, and the fundamentalists were far from dead. They simply receded, reorganized, and rebuilt. They formed their own churches, their own associations, their own seminaries, Bible schools, and colleges such as Bob Jones University, recalling the vigor and the success of American Catholics who built a school system from kindergarten to graduate schools over the century from 1850 to 1950 for some of the same reasons. Many of the fundamentalists retained membership in the associations, conventions, and assemblies of the more conservative evangelical denominations such as Southern Baptists. They taught, they wrote, they preached on radio. They watched with dismay the effect of liberal ideas and policies on the public morality and political ethos of the nation, fought with one another over doctrines and worried over one another's ideological purity.

George Marsden defined fundamentalism as "militantly anti-modernist Protestant Christianity."[25] Some would add the implied term *separatist*. It took its rise at the end of a century of political and intellectual revolution, of a terrible civil war in America, of innovations in science and learning, of a flood of unwelcome Jewish and Catholic immigrants into the United States and its attendant threat to the cultural and political hegemony of American evangelical Christianity, and at the beginning of a century that would see a world war and its slaughter, a Marxist revolution in Russia, and the increasing strength of a liberal theology and its step-child neo-orthodoxy. For the fundamentalists, the whole mess, from flappers to a Roman Catholic running for the White House in 1928, signaled the decline of Christian civilization and an increase of the power of Satan in the world, a sign of the End. The first editor of *The Funda-mentals*, A. C. Dixon, wrote: "If Darwin was right and the evolutionists . . . are right, Germany was right and Lenine [*sic*] and Trotsky are right."[26] Tie modern science and Bolshevism into a knot, throw in higher criticism of the Bible, and what good American Christian would not rise up against them?

Many did. Revivalists such as Billy Sunday, millennialists who expected the return of Jesus momentarily, orthodox Presbyterian theologians at Prince-ton, and people from the Pentecostal and Holiness traditions, and even older religiously conservative yet socially and politically liberal evangelicals, joined in the battle for the Bible against the Beast. They came together to fight for supernaturalism against naturalism, to support the truth of the ancient doc-trines of the virgin birth and the divinity of Jesus, the historical accuracy of the biblical narratives, the bodily resurrection of Jesus, and his second coming. To defend the ancient orthodoxy they erected an impregnable line of defense drawn from the Princeton theologians of the nineteenth century: the doctrine of plenary verbal inspiration and the inerrancy of the Scripture. Furthermore, they insisted that the Bible can judge, but cannot be judged by, any modern science, and that the Bible has a commonsensical saving meaning that can be apprehended by the ordinary believer without the learned machinations of infidel professors. Perspicuity became crucial when academics asserted control over interpretation.[27]

The fundamentalists were soteriological exclusivists and ecclesiastical sep-aratists. For them, the Protestant ecumenical movement and the other religions of the world were Satanic in inspiration. They denounced the National Council of Churches as a haven for apostate Christians. Some of them later criticized Billy Graham for talking and praying with mainline Protestants and with Cath-olics. The mainline churches were condemned because they had refused to purge their leadership and their seminaries of moderates and liberals. The traditional Protestant anti-Catholic rhetoric was retained: Roman Catholicism was still the Whore of Babylon and the pope the apocalyptic beast from the sea.[28]

Fundamentalism was not the usual disagreement among American Prot-estants over a doctrine or two; it was a religious worldview distinct in decisive respects from its parent, nineteenth-century American evangelicalism, based often on a revivalist experience of salvation, and associated with attitudes and theological convictions at times different from anything evangelical Protes-tantism had seen before, and, interestingly enough, the same holds true for modernist Christianity.

Basic to fundamentalism was (and is!) the supernaturalist cosmology and history no longer taken for granted as it had been for two millennia but now explicitly reaffirmed as factual in the face of its denial by secularists and modernist Christians. The debating rule, "Never deny your opponent's major premise," was abandoned when the supernaturalist myth was attacked, and the debate turned ugly. The fundamentalists and their neo-evangelical offspring understood themselves to be the true Christians, steering between the rationalist subjectivism of their moderate and liberal Protestant brethren, on one hand, and the Satanic, antibiblical authoritarianism of the Catholic Church, on the other.[29] They claimed that they had inherited the mantle of the sixteenth-century Protestant reformers and that they were carrying forward the faith and practice of the old American evangelical movement.[30]

There were, however, some notable differences. Protestantism, in its origins, was biblical, appealing to the Bible against the authority of the Roman ecclesiastical establishment; it was not biblicist, restricting all expression and practice to biblical language and form. In several respects the reformers carried forth the ancient and medieval faith and forms of piety.[31] The reformed communions rather quickly developed traditions of their own, which functioned as interpretative stances and were recognized as such; one need only recall the importance of the Pauline distinction between law and gospel for the entire Lutheran theological tradition, and of Calvin's emphasis on the sovereign power of God to this day in Reformed churches. Although their proponents claim biblical status for them, as doctrines they remain hermeneutical tools more than doctrinal shibboleths—as verbal plenary inspiration and perspicuity seem to have become in the American neo-evangelical movement.

Second, the reformed churches were not anticultural. They were broad enough in their self-understanding to embrace both liberal and traditionalist emphases, and in this way they resembled more the Catholic tradition than they did the fundamentalist; they were churches rather than sects, to use the sociological terms, and were not religious or cultural separatists (sects). To the contrary, mainline Protestant theologians led the effort to mediate between Christianity and the new scientific culture, and absorbed most of the shocks of the rise of historical consciousness over the past two hundred years—while the Catholic leadership stonewalled the issues. For this attempt, mainline Protestantism earned the same scorn from the fundamentalists as Catholic liberals in the nineteenth century and modernists in the twentieth earned from Rome and its theological integralists. Moderate and liberal Protestant theology and leadership inherited from Luther and Calvin the sense of responsibility for culture, while the fundamentalists exhibited a consistent drive to cultural separation in order to preserve purity of doctrine.[32]

Third, fundamentalism is distinct from its parent, nineteenth-century American evangelicalism—the evangelical alliance that Martin Marty called the "righteous empire"—made up of Congregationalists, Presbyterians, Methodists, and Baptists. Emphasis on verbal inerrancy was not a formulated theological doctrine of evangelicals before the end of the nineteenth century. The plenary verbal inerrancy of Princeton Seminary lasted only half a century within Presbyterianism itself and was rejected by that community in the late 1920s.[33] Even Machen himself, otherwise the carrier of the consistent Calvinism of Alexander, Hodge, and Warfield, did not promote it.[34] For the most part the older evangelical churches were not exclusivist (of one another, at any rate), separatist, or dogmatic. American evangelicalism is a rich and complex tradition in church order, in practice, and in theology that, at bottom, insisted on conversion of heart against Protestant rationalist tendencies in the eighteenth century and against the reemergence of ritualism in the nineteenth. Through its intellectual meanderings evangelicalism remained, and still remains, true to Jonathan Edwards's classic definition, "True religion, in great part, consists in holy affections."[35] The return to prominence of this theme in neo-evangelicalism in fact shows fundamentalism and its abandonment of culture to be a theological as well as religious dead end.

Fundamentalism is dogmatic rather than theological, conceptualist, or rationalist rather than affectional, and followed a deductive and polemical theological method that Jonathan Edwards, the founder of the evangelical revivalist theological tradition in America, or Horace Bushnell, the nineteenth-century evangelical theologian and the father of American liberalism, or even Charles Hodge who articulated the theory of biblical inerrancy, which has proved so useful to fundamentalists, would have found intellectually emaciated.[36] After all, the fundamentalist would say, what can one add to the Bible except a defense couched in its own terms? The evangelical theological tradition is quite broad-ranging and inclusive, from Jonathan Edwards's and Charles Hodge's neo-Calvinism to Charles Finney's and Horace Bushnell's disregard of much of the Calvinism. Most of the exemplars of the American evangelical theological tradition from 1740 to the present would be regarded by fundamentalists as infidels of varying degrees.[37] Billy Graham and his neo-evangelical allies stand in this older evangelical stream, recognizing as he does the role of the gospel and the Christian in the culture. Without profound distortion Protestantism cannot be sealed up against culture, although it often must be pitted against it.

The evangelical tradition in America has also shown a deep concern with social structure, political inequalities, issues of community, and public responsibility for the deprived and the poor, and so it remains with many evangelicals today.[38] For fundamentalists, the range of cultural, social, and political concerns remains narrow, limited largely to issues of individual morality and need. It may well be that the neo-evangelical repudiation of dispensational premillennialism is intimately linked to the evangelicals' sense of public responsibility. A return to social ethics found expression in the second generation of fundamentalist leaders, the founders of the National Association of Evangelicals, who were neither ecclesial nor cultural separatists. Freeing orthodox Protestants from the cultural pessimism and isolation of the fundamentalist movement in the twentieth century was an important aim of those founders, and their intent bore fruit on the public stage three decades after the initial meeting in St. Louis in 1942.

The smashing defeat of Barry Goldwater in 1964 was reversed finally in the equally smashing victory of Ronald Reagan in 1980. In the same years (1976–80) that the public saw the resurgence of the political right, it saw as well the growing power of the religious right, conservative in public policy and fundamentalist in theology. Jerry Falwell became a TV personality and a conservative political power to be reckoned with for a decade, but he remained primarily pastor of a large independent, fundamentalist Baptist church and the founder and chancellor of Liberty Baptist College, an educational institution training young missionaries to a pagan America (and elsewhere). The very year (1976) when some of us first became aware of the political muscle of fundamentalism, a fundamentalist bestseller penned by Harold Lindsell bemoaned the lapse of Fuller Theological Seminary from its inerrantist heritage and called for a renewal of *The Battle for the Bible* in American evangelical denominations nationwide.[39] School boards in several parts of the nation began to hear of an alternative to Darwinism, "Scientific Creationism"[40] and Jimmy Swaggart continued his attacks on the "works-righteousness" teachings of the Catholic Church and the liberal Protestant denominations.[41] Dispensationalism made its return to the American vocabulary in Hal Lindsey's *Late, Great Planet Earth*, the first of his series of bestsellers offering to tell Americans when and how their history would end. Now dispensationalism constitutes the dramatic spine of a bestselling series of novels by Tim LeHaye.[42]

The century-long struggle of American Protestants with the function of gospel and faith in a world no longer Christian continues. Left, center, and right Protestantism took shape in this struggle, as did reform, conservative, and orthodox Judaism. The contest has been as much between the various responses of Protestants to the modern world and its variety of secular and naturalist ideologies as it has been with the ideologies themselves. The effort to reconcile the twentieth-century versions of the Protestant spirit and faith to one another has been as expensive and expansive as the Protestant efforts to understand the world slipping out from under its intellectual and spiritual tutelage after the American Civil War. The fundamentalist and evangelical movements are, by many standards, the most vital and successful Protestant revival and resistance to modernity in the last century. It is not slighting the important intellectual and social achievements of that other offspring of nineteenth-century American evangelical Protestantism, namely, mainline Protestantism, to note that the fundamentalists and neo-evangelicals have carried on the orthodox temper and the revivalist piety so much a prominent feature of their ancestors, and have proved instinctively suspicious of the glories of the Enlightenment and modernity. For this reason they invite comparison with that most dedicated enemy of modernity and its ideologies, Roman Catholicism.

## Roman Catholics and Modernism

There is a second story.[43] The Catholics, too, had to respond to the new biological and human sciences, and to the new methods of study of the Bible and
their conclusions, and they had an added problem: a century of struggle with
secular, anticlerical governments in France, Italy, and Spain, and nativist attacks in the United States. At the turn of the century, despite some gains in
the British Isles and increasing numbers in the United States, the church faced
a deteriorating political situation on the continent and danger of assimilation
in modern cultures generally. Gregory XVI and Pius IX both condemned "liberalism," including Catholics who seemed in sympathy with modern political
and cultural forms.[44] The doctrine of the freedom of Mary from original sin
was formally defined by Pius IX in 1854 and papal infallibility ratified in 1869
by the first Vatican Council. Each of the dogmas was meant to draw boundaries
between Catholicism and the rising secular culture. In 1899 Leo XIII and his
theologians warned the American bishops in *Testem benevolentiae* against
"Americanism,"[45] that is, the adjustment of Catholicism to American cultural
norms and values. Several American bishops and archbishops had been expounding on the compatibility of Catholicism and American political practice
and ideals, seemingly contradicting the Roman teaching on the dangers of
modern culture and the countercultural task of the church in the modern
world.[46] Catholic integralism, a Roman theology, aimed at rolling the Catholic
inheritance up in a ball impervious to intellectual accommodation and cultural
assimilation, forbad any such mixture of ideals. The church's life and doctrine
were understood by integralists to be a logical whole, inalienable in any of its
parts. The distinction between it and the "modern world" was drawn in near-
Manichean terms.

The bishops and Rome were confronted by a problem in Europe similar
to that facing conservative evangelicals in the United States. The handful of
European Catholic modernist scholars were busy adopting and adapting to the
new intellectual methods and publishing their conclusions in books and theological journals in France, England, Germany, Italy, and even in the theologically unadventurous American church.[47] The confrontation began in France,
where the diocesan priest Alfred Loisy taught the languages and cultures of
the ancient biblical lands at the Sorbonne and the Institute Catholique in Paris.
In England the Jesuit priest and author George Tyrrell taught, lectured, and
wrote on how the Catholic Church might enter the life of the new culture of
Europe. They and their colleagues were convinced that the historic commitment of Catholicism to culture and intelligence demanded that the church
abandon the methods and expressions of a dying culture, especially scholastic
philosophy and theology, and use modern intellectual methods.

The papal response to the crop of modernizers was cautious under Leo

XIII (1878–1903) who, succeeding two popes who were vigorous critics of modernity, was careful to cultivate a progressive image of the papacy. In 1893 Leo published an encyclical on Sacred Scripture, *Providentissimus Deus,* in which he reiterated the traditional Catholic doctrine of the divine authorship and inspiration of the Scriptures. He wrote:

> God so moved the inspired writers by his supernatural operation
> that he incited them to write, and assisted them in their writing so
> that they correctly conceived, accurately wrote down, and truthfully
> expressed all that he intended and only what he intended; and only
> thus can God be the author of the Bible.[48]

The divine inspiration of scripture was an ancient Catholic doctrine, and Pope Leo did little else than repeat what was already believed. Simply put, it means that the Bible is wholly God's book as well as the human authors' book. Thus had the scriptures been treated throughout the history of Christianity. The pope expressed a doctrine much like the Protestant one, minus the Princeton additions of perspicuity and verbal plenary inspiration. But the Catholic modernists, like their Protestant counterparts, treated the scriptures far more like a human document than the Roman theologians and the Roman pontiff could abide. The Catholic modernists undercut the inerrancy of the Bible as well as the traditional Catholic theological method for expounding its meanings. For a modernist like Fr. Loisy to dismantle the liberal Protestant historical reconstruction of the New Testament era, which concluded that the Catholic Church abandoned the gospel, one had to dismiss subtly the a-historical Roman theology that made no distinction between the New Testament church and the Catholic Church. The irony ran through Loisy's *The Gospel and the Church.*[49] The new pope was not willing to swallow the dismissal of scholastic theology's control of history, although the dismantling of von Harnack's view must have been tasty indeed.[50] The Roman theologians knew that a theological notion of "development of doctrine" would lead to the priority of historical investigation over the traditional scholastic dogmatic theology. They were not willing to accept a theory that had led John Henry Newman into the Catholic Church. Loisy's book was placed on the Index on Forbidden Books in 1903. Leo died in that year. He had communicated privately with bishops, with the superiors of the modernist priests, and with the modernists themselves, attempting to dam the stream of explosive modernist literature on the Bible, on church history, and on scholastic theology. He failed, but his successor would not.

Pius X was elected to succeed Leo in 1903. Less reticent than his predecessor, he gave orders that Fr. Loisy and Fr. Tyrrell and other modernists were to be silenced. A cat-and-mouse game, including their formal submissions to papal authority and much pseudonymous publication by them and other modernists, was conducted until Pius X's patience wore out. In 1907 he issued an encyclical letter to all the Catholic bishops (*Pascendi dominici gregis*), and signed a document (*Lamentabili*) that listed the errors of the modernists and condemned their teaching, their disobedience, and their pride in opposing the authority of the church's leaders.[51] Pius X's harsh judgment of the collusion of Catholics in the modernist ethos equaled that of his predecessors, Gregory XVI and Pius IX. These priests, Pius X wrote, are "the most pernicious of all the adversaries of the Church":

> It may seem to some, Venerable Brethren [he writes to the bishops] that We have dealt at too great length on this exposition of the doctrines of the Modernists. But it was necessary that We should do so, both in order to meet their customary charge that We do not understand their ideas, and to show that their system does not consist in scattered and unconnected theories, but, as it were, a closely connected whole, so that it is not possible to admit one without admitting all. For this reason, too, we have had to give this exposition a somewhat didactic form, and not to shrink from employing certain unwonted terms which the Modernists have brought into use. And now with Our eyes fixed upon the whole system, no one will be surprised that we should define it to be the synthesis of all heresies. Undoubtedly, were anyone to attempt the task of collecting together all the errors that have been broached against the faith and to concentrate into one the sap and substance of them, he could not succeed in doing so better than the Modernists have done. Nay, they have gone farther than this, for, as We have already intimated, their system means the destruction not of the Catholic religion alone, but of all religion.[52]

Pius's logic uncovered the final implication of the Modernist position, namely agnosticism and atheism. As he calls it, the first step in the logical progression is Protestantism, then Modernism, then atheism, each step a rebellion against legitimate authority. How does one explain this radical departure from the Christian spirit? In the first place, the modernists' unregulated curiosity "accounts for all error." There is also ignorance, for the Modernists know nothing of scholastic philosophy and theology, and so cannot think straight. But basic to it all is their intellectual pride, a disease to which he knows the cure:

> It is pride which exercises an incomparably greater sway over the soul to blind it and lead it into error, and pride sits in Modernism as in its own house, finding sustenance everywhere in its doctrines and lurking in its every aspect. It is pride which fills Modernists with that self-assurance by which they consider themselves as the sole possessors of knowledge, and makes them say, elated and inflated with presumption, "We are not like the rest of men," and

which, lest they should seem as other men, leads them to embrace
and to devise novelties even of the most absurd kind. It is pride
which rouses in them the spirit of disobedience and causes them to
demand a compromise between authority and liberty. . . . For this
reason, Venerable Brethren, it will be your first duty to resist such
victims of pride, to employ them only in the lowest and obscurest
offices. The higher they rise, the lower let them be placed . . . and
when you find the spirit of pride among them [i.e., young clerics]
reject them without compunction from the priesthood.[53]

There is, no doubt, a foundation in Christian spiritual teaching, Protestant and
Catholic, for his analysis, if not for his judgment of the particular men involved
in the Modernist movement he detects. There is a great deal of anger in the
encyclical and a disdain for the modernist priests, which rivals the disdain for
authority he attributes, not without cause, to them. But it is easy for the reader
to find in his letter the deep sense of betrayal and alarm he and his court
theologians experienced as the "modern world," so clearly condemned by his
predecessors, insinuates itself into the priestly sanctuary. The nineteenth-
century popes had drawn the line between the church and the world, and it
was crossed by the Catholic modernists. The laity, such as Baron von Hugel,
might have to live in two worlds but the clergy dare not.[54]

In 1908, Fr. Loisy and Fr. Tyrrell were suspended from their practice of
the priesthood and then excommunicated from the church. The *excommuni-
catio vitandus ("he must be avoided")* pronounced on Loisy is the exact equivalent
of Mennonite shunning.[55] In 1909, Tyrrell was refused burial in a Catholic
cemetery and Fr. Henri Bremond was suspended from the priesthood for blessing his friend Tyrrell's Anglican grave.[56] Their associates in France, England,
Germany, and Italy were disciplined and forbidden to publish. The Pontifical
Biblical Commission, set up by Pope Leo to deal with the proper interpretation
of the scriptures in the universal church, proceeded under Pius X to issue over
the next few years a series of decrees commanding a historical interpretation
of the creation account in Genesis and forbidding departure from traditional
interpretation of biblical texts and traditional attributions of scriptural authorship.[57] Pius X ordered every diocese in the church to establish a society (*So-
dalitium Pianum*) that would inform the Vatican of the slightest departure of
any priest (and even any bishop) from the teaching set down by himself and
his theologians.[58] There ensued, over the next four decades, a reign of terror
in theology whose parallel in the United Sates might be the McCarthy era.
While it had long since been impossible to burn heretics, the campaign had
profound effects on the Catholic intellectual ethos, especially in clerical education. The papal success in shutting down the movement could well have
been the envy of American Protestant fundamentalists.

In 1943, the fiftieth anniversary of Leo XIII's *Providentissimus Deus,* Pius

XII issued a letter on Sacred Scripture, *Divino Afflante Spiritu*. In it he called for an end to the persecution of Catholic scholars in these words:

> Let all the sons of the church bear in mind that the efforts of these resolute laborers [i.e., the scripture scholars] in the vineyard of the Lord should be judged not only with equity and justice, but also with the greatest charity; all, moreover, should abhor that intemperate zeal which imagines that whatever is new should for that very reason be opposed or suspected.[59]

With Pius XII, the persecution of Catholic biblical scholars came to an official end, but the struggle within clerical ranks did not cease. It had become a partisan affair. Prior to the Second Vatican Council many were determined to retain the integralist position sponsored by Pius X. Theologians of the stature of John Courtney Murray, Henri deLubac, Karl Rahner, and the priest-scientist Teilhard de Chardin were silenced by Roman authorities in the 1940s and 1950s for taking positions in theology that could not be easily reconciled with the reigning theological integralism. As late as 1958, Bernard Lonergan, a Canadian Jesuit professor of theology at the Gregorian University in Rome and now recognized on the highest rank of twentieth-century Christian thinkers, was accused of Christological heresy in a Roman theological journal.[60] Immediately prior to the Vatican Council in 1962 two New York biblical scholars were denounced, one priest was delated to the Vatican, and another, his student, was threatened with a denial of priestly orders for articles they published on the literary form of the infancy narrative in Matthew and Luke.[61] They would have been done injury had not Francis Cardinal Spellman, their own archbishop, intervened to protect them. Paulist Press, publisher of a series of pamphlet commentaries on the Bible written from the point of view of a modified high criticism, was the subject of complaint to Rome by the Apostolic Delegate, Archbishop Egidio Vagnozzi. Once again Spellman intervened. To his last days, Father Raymond Brown, the noted scripture scholar, was recorded on tape in his public lectures by traditionalist Catholics and denounced for heresy.[62]

The second Vatican Council (1962–65) was called by Pope John XXIII precisely because the church needed to dispel the dank atmosphere of its antimodern war and become a contributor to rather than an enemy of the culture of the West. In a stunning and entirely unexpected series of documents the Catholic bishops, turned loose all too briefly from Roman Curial control to do their own thinking and deciding, reversed two centuries of antimodern rhetoric and church policy and four centuries of enmity toward other Christian churches. A reformulated Catholic position on scripture emerged out of this political and theological struggle:

> Sacred Scripture is the utterance of God put down as it is in writing under the inspiration of the holy Spirit. . . . Since, therefore, all that

the inspired authors, or sacred writers, affirm should be regarded as affirmed by the holy Spirit, we must acknowledge that the books of Scripture firmly, faithfully, and without error teach that truth which God, for the sake of our salvation, wished to see confided to the sacred scriptures. . . . Seeing that in sacred scripture, God speaks through human beings in human fashion, it follows that the interpreters of sacred Scripture, if they are to ascertain what God has wished to communicate to us, should carefully search out the meaning the sacred writers had in mind, that meaning which God had thought well to manifest through the medium of their words. In determining the intention of the sacred writers, attention must be paid, among other things, to *literary genres*. The fact is that truth is differently presented and expressed in the various types of historical writings, in prophetic and poetical texts, and in other forms of literary expression. Hence the exegete must look for that meaning which the sacred writers, in given situations and granted the circumstances of their time and culture, intended to express and did in fact express through the medium of contemporary literary forms.[63]

While the Council affirmed inspiration of the Bible, it did not affirm inerrancy, although by an older logic one might infer inerrancy from an affirmation of inspiration (God cannot inspire an error nor lie). A subtle but theologically crucial distinction is adopted, one that has until recently been rejected by some American evangelicals and would have been rejected in all likelihood by Pius X. While the whole of scripture is inspired, inerrancy applies to the essential *religious* affirmations of scripture, those (including historical affirmations), which are made for "our salvation," and does not mean that the authors were protected from the limits of their existence in the first century and miraculously turned into authors who could speak over and outside of human history and their own human condition. The author's religious message, not his commonsense historical knowledge, was saved from error.[64] To be specific, the gospels inerrantly proclaim the resurrection of Jesus but may not be inerrant when they place the Transfiguration on Mount Tabor or place it before the resurrection in their narrative when it may have occurred after it.

And how do Catholics know that the Bible is free from error in these religious matters, and how shall the faithful know what is inerrant and what is not? The Council fathers take a stand that would not make American fundamentalists and evangelicals happy:

Thus it is that the Church does not draw its certainty about all revealed truths from the holy Scripture alone. Hence both scripture and tradition must be accepted and honored with equal devotion and reverence. . . . It is clear, therefore, that in the supremely wise arrangement of God, the sacred tradition, sacred scripture, and the

magisterium [teaching authority] of the Church are so connected
and associated that one of them cannot stand without the others.[65]

And so we have the reiteration of an old difference between the evangelical
and Roman Catholic positions on scripture: the Catholic Church has a tradition
and a teaching authority that are linked with scripture as interrelated principles
of Christian religious life and faith. We catch here the echo of the Reformation
and Counter Reformation argument.

The tension between the church and culture is omnipresent in Catholic
history. One form of it in the medieval period was the question, "May theologians use a pagan philosophical language in the interpreting Christian teaching?" namely, the language of Aristotle. St. Albert, St. Thomas Aquinas, and,
finally, the Catholic Church as a whole, said yes, if it serves the Gospel. Biblical
language is not the *only* Christian language, then; it is *not* unambiguous; it
needs clarification and interpretation. It may be perspicuous for some purposes
and not for others, in some respects but not in others. The same answer was
given by the first Vatican Council in 1869 when it rejected fideism and reaffirmed the link between faith and reason; and by the second Vatican Council
in 1965 when it affirmed the church *in* rather than *against* the modern world;
and by Pope John Paul II when he insisted that *fides et ratio* (1998) are permanently coupled.[66] The church lives in and with and through a culture—and
with the culture's problems, its questions, its methods and inquiry, and its
various technical languages. To go back on this historic commitment would be
for Catholicism to give up being a church and to become a sect, an elect set
apart from the life of the culture, in effect creating its own culture. Catholicism
is committed to the life of mind, not to its death; it is not antitheological or
antiphilosophical.[67] The continuing struggle by Catholics against integralism
in the Roman Catholic Church is fought to keep the church catholic and public,
to keep it from becoming a sect existing in self-imposed exile awaiting a res-
urrected Christendom. The struggle closely resembles the neo-evangelical
search for a relationship with American culture of which fundamentalist separatism despaired.

If this is the case, if Catholicism is essentially constructive in its attitude
toward culture and theology, why was there a repression of theological inquiry
in the first half of the century? Why did the Roman Catholic Church for forty
years take the same position on the new methods of biblical study as did the
American fundamentalists, and for two hundred years denounce the formation, indeed the existence, of modern Western culture? For several very good
reasons.

First of all, the Reformation of the sixteenth century was a terrible, a shat-
tering, blow to the Catholic Church. The Europe to which Catholicism had
given birth was no longer to be Catholic; there was now a Protestant Christian
culture in large parts of Europe, and by the nineteenth century that culture

was clearly becoming secular. *Post hoc, ergo propter hoc.* The Roman bitterness toward the Protestant reformers and the defensiveness of Roman leaders in the face of a disenfranchising secularism rather easily became suspicion of the "modern" culture that Protestant Christianity had spawned. Most of the practitioners of the new biblical criticism were Protestants, some were unbelievers, and the Catholic modernists were interested in history.

Second, modern culture turned out badly for the church. The nineteenth was a century of revolution, from the American and French revolutions, through the unification of Italy under the king and the loss of the papal states to the king's armies, to the enforced collapse of the church's role in French education. This kind of disorder made order, unity, and authority even more desirable to Rome. The answer? The declaration of papal infallibility demanded by Pius IX at the first Vatican Council, and the crushing of a nascent modernism by Pius X. The loss of external political prestige and stability was compensated for by insisting on internal conformity.[68]

Third, the intellectuals of Europe, from Deists through Rationalists to the Romantic philosophers (and the American nativists and evangelicals!) constantly attacked the Roman church as obscurantist and authoritarian. Rome was resolved that there would be no infidelity within the Catholic intellectual world, and no compromise with the modernity that despised her.[69]

Fourth, the Catholic modernists themselves did not successfully distinguish methods of study and conclusions, ran too rapidly and happily to embrace the conclusions of the young disciplines, and were sometimes as intransigent as their ecclesiastical critics. In addition, the archmodernist Alfred Loisy admitted himself that by the time he published *The Church and the Gospel* several years before he was excommunicated, he believed nothing of orthodox Christianity. Seeing this as a process of dissolution, it was not hard for the ecclesiastical leaders to connect loss of faith with modernist intellectual and cultural suppositions in every case, however slow the decline in any given case. Pius X saw modernism as a disease where Loisy saw it as a progression in authenticity with a high cost.[70]

Fifth, the nineteenth century had seen a startling centralization of church authority in Rome; one of the consequences of this was that Roman theology became the *only* Catholic theology—something that would have mystified Thomas Aquinas in thirteenth-century Paris and Duns Scotus at Oxford in the fourteenth as it did John Henry Newman in the nineteenth. This standardization of theology may fit a *Roman* church, but surely not a *catholic* church. The Council, although immensely influential in broadening the possibilities for Catholic theology, has not solved this tension once and for all. Perhaps it is not solvable in a church committed to clerical autocracy and Roman centralism in its form of government. No church leader charged with maintenance of orthodoxy can allow ten thousand flowers to bloom.

One might have hoped that the leaders of the Catholic Church would have handled the crisis better than they did in the early years, and perhaps the waning years, of the twentieth century; but given the painful history of the church since the Reformation, there is little wonder that it took the leaders of the church some fifty years to adopt the inclusive and catholic attitude displayed at the second Vatican Council. Roman Catholicism, by the nineteenth century, had opted for a vigorous form of authoritarianism and centralism in ecclesiastical politics and theology as it continued to support monarchy and the union of church and state. Its leaders, with few exceptions, were unable to imagine alternatives.[71] In the first half of the twentieth century, Catholic theologians and the entire church paid the price of that choice. Michael Gannon described the effect of that option in his essay "Before and After Modernism":

> As 1908 progressed on its course a gradually enveloping dread of heresy settled over episcopal residences, chanceries, seminaries, and Catholic institutions of higher learning. Security, safety, conservatism became national imperatives. Free intellectual inquiry in ecclesiastical circles came to a virtual standstill. The nascent intellectual movement went underground or died. Contacts with Protestant and secular thinkers, never very many in the first place, were broken off. It was as though someone had pulled a switch and the lights had failed across the American Catholic landscape.[72]

So also Jesuit historian James Hennessy in *American Catholics*:

> The post-Pascendi years in American Catholicism were marked by intellectual retreat and theological sterility. Cultivation of the life of the mind became suspect. A thoroughgoing and immensely effective educational police action isolated the theological reaches of the Catholic community from the contemporary world. . . . the powerful integrist reaction which set in after 1907 effectively put an end for the next fifty years to further development of Catholic thought in authentic American dress.[73]

It must be said that Catholics pay the price still. To put the matter in terms that are alien to the antimodernist Catholic theological tradition but that nonetheless have some bearing on the fundamentalist deformation of American evangelicalism, one might say that when the virtues needed in a society with egalitarian ideals and democratic processes are neither prized nor cultivated in the church, the vices endemic to authoritarian societies are cultivated, prized, and named virtues. Questioning, conversation, contradiction, inquiry, the joy of discovery, independence, and daring of mind, all these prizes of the Enlightenment are despised, and we are left with respect turned to wariness, intellectual and spiritual trust soured by the power of corrupted symbols, servants acting as masters, and shepherds become sheepdogs snapping at their own flock and at one another. Catholic and Protestant antimodernists removed themselves from the drama of Western intellectual life and left the stage to their modernist antagonists.


## Differences on Modernism

We have seen some of the responses of fundamentalists and integralists to modernity and Christian modernism. On the surface they appear remarkably the same: they show the same concern for biblical teaching and inerrancy, for the supernatural worldview of the Bible, and for ancient doctrines of Christianity, and they exhibit much of the same antagonism toward a culture gone secular. But there are several notable and crucial differences.

First, American evangelical antimodernism remained fiercely egalitarian while the Roman Catholic response was just as fiercely authoritarian. Where the Protestant critics of modernism lost control of denominational assemblies and bureaucracies, the Catholic Church became even more Roman than it had been in terms of subjection of the local churches to the papal offices and commissions. "Subsidiary" as a principle of Catholic life became, and continues to be, an ideologized "communion" with centralized authority.[74]

Second, the Protestants have usually affirmed the Bible as the single, sufficient, and binding authority for knowledge of God and salvation, and as the rule for Christian practice. The fundamentalists and evangelicals among them wanted subordination of theological scholarship to the biblical text. For them, the key issue has been the availability of the biblical text for personal religious interpretation. The Catholics integralists reaffirmed the precritical *ecclesiastical* interpretations of the Bible, insisting that it be available for scholastic doctrinal use. Pope Pius X and the integralists affirmed as much the authority of church pastors to interpret the Bible as they did the historical character of the biblical narrative and the inerrancy of the Bible itself. What Rome wanted was total subordination of biblical and historical scholarship to ecclesiastical authorities. As fundamentalism objected to control of biblical meaning by scholars, so it objected to its control by any ecclesiastical authorities. For the fundamentalists, the Bible judges the church as well as the scholars; for the integralist Catholics the Bible is the book of the church to be read authoritatively by the *Magisterium*, the primary teachers of the church, the bishops under papal oversight.

Fundamentalists and many of their evangelical descendents transformed the ancient Christian teaching of the inspiration of scripture into the dogma of absolute inerrancy.[75] The popes, while upholding inerrancy, asserted the right and authority of the church's leadership to interpret the scriptures, and so placed considerably increased weight on the infallibility of the pope and bishops acting as teachers of the church. Ironically, this allowed a certain measure of flexibility with regard to biblical interpretation later taken advantage of by Pius X's successors, Pius XII and Paul VI, in elevating the position of scholars of the Bible. These latter popes had far less fear than their predecessor that biblical and historical scholarship would undermine the church's life and teaching.

Fundamentalists, then, answered Protestant liberalism and modernism by intensifying concern for the inerrancy and perspicuity of scripture, rendering its interpretation a matter of common sense rather than academic expertise: where there is any question about the meaning of a passage of scripture, one settles it by appeal to another passage, even from another book or another testament.[76] The Bible, for the Princetonians, for example, is made up of a "system" of logically interrelated propositions, much as for the integralist Catholicism is a system of interrelated doctrinal meanings and practices. For Rome, the answer to Catholic liberalism and modernism, and the encroachments of secularism in general, is found in loyalty to the teaching and the teaching authority of the officers of the ecclesial body, its traditional interpretation of scripture and its direction of theological research and teaching.

Moreover, the fundamentalists insisted on the supernatural character of the biblical events, most especially as stated in the key doctrines about Christ: the virgin birth, miracles, the resurrection, and the second coming. Rome, for its part, reaffirmed not only biblical supernaturalism but also Catholic sacramentalism, tying supernaturalism to the life of the church as well to the Bible.[77] Both answers to modernism are deeply dogmatic (insistence on the unquestionable truth of an assertion), but the dogmas at issue are quite different. One is a dogmatism of the written word, the other a dogmatism of official teacher, the first an aberration of religion formed in a culture of literacy and the second an aberration of a religion still grounded in a culture of orality.[78] In order to protect the foundations of the Christian faith against the threat of modern science, history, and literary criticism, the fundamentalists highlighted the infallibility of the bible; Rome reasserted the infallibility of the leaders of the church.

Protestant fundamentalism was and is a mistake insofar as it rejects in toto modern hermeneutics and relies on separation as the method of dealing with Christian heterodoxy and modern culture, and insofar as it departs from some of the intellectual and spiritual resources of the American evangelical tradition and from its three-centuries-old investment in American culture. The mistakes were corrected later by a broader and new evangelical alliance of former fundamentalists (NAE).

The Roman reaction was also a mistake, a forgetfulness of its own history by a church that prides itself on its sense of history, and a flight from constructive discernment of cultural values. Roman separatism was corrected later, significantly if not entirely, at the second Vatican Council. The best instinct of Catholicism and American evangelical Protantism has been to embrace, support, expand on, challenge, correct, and bless human culture—with all the possibilities of confusion and sin attendant on this. Many in both communities lost their moorings under pressure; both began to act as sectarians, even if in different ways and to different degrees, and both have had to modify judgments and redirect commitments.

The immense capacity for recovery displayed in the reflection and hard work that led to and followed on the founding of the NAE in 1943 and in the second Vatican Council in 1962, and its aftermath gives one hope for a recovery of both sides from the lacerations of the Reformation era. Their different problems with modernity have converged and now push the two together. Each has accepted disestablishment, though with much pain, and has assumed the role of mediating rather than dominating institutions in a state and a secular culture. Each still wants a normative status in the culture for Christian virtues. Both fear that the culture, whose politics disestablished the church, could suffocate believers, for both still wonder how Christians can breathe in a world that excludes God and ignores the gospel. Both insist on the freedom to be faithful to the gospel and the freedom to preach faith and have it respected in the public forum. This perception of the problem is a more promising than the older formulation of separatists and integralists, "Who owns this culture anyway?" At the highpoint of his own review of Christianity in modern culture, J. Gresham Machen recognized something in common between evangelical Protestants and Catholics over against religious liberalism and secularism, namely, clarity and consistency in upholding the truth of the orthodox faith, in "battle," if necessary. The difficulty faced by the two was practical: displacement and how to survive and overcome it.

But also great historical ideals were and perhaps still are at issue: each community was possessed by a dream. American evangelicals thought that this land was their land, destined to be a Righteous Empire whose legitimacy stood foursquare on the Protestant gospel. Catholics, in their long wrestling with modernity, dreamt of a restored Christendom in which the church's rights and mission would be upheld by the state and accepted by the society. What happens when the dream of each community dies, the Righteous Empire and the medieval Christendom? There must be release of imagination for a new dream and a new struggle under different circumstances. This began a half century ago in each community, but recent events show that the two communities' hopes involve each other, willy-nilly. They have accepted emersion in a culture no longer their own, accepted political and religious rights of dissent, and the legitimate existence of religious difference, imagining a world in which the church is free but not culturally dominant. They have emerged from a culture in which they were free to resent and suspect one another, into a world in which they need one another, where disagreement makes sense but recrimination does not, and where mutual respect may replace resentment. From this point of view disestablishment and cultural alienation have proved to be a gift of God. This possibility suggests another: perhaps the evangelical-Catholic rift also may be a gift God has given to each through the other.

Catholics do not carry the Bible to church on Sunday morning; evangelical Protestants still do. Catholics start off their Sunday Mass with a procession in which the Bible is held high by a lay reader, but the last place in the procession, the place of highest honor, is still taken by the priest, the *alter Christus*. There is biblical Christianity and there is liturgical Christianity, and we should have no illusions about the difference between them. Harold Bloom recently claimed that most American religion is gnostic, including American evangelicalism.[79] Although he confesses that he himself is a gnostic and so we should not take the term as an epithet when he uses it, in this respect Bloom sounds like an old-time Catholic apologist writing about Luther. And he trips over the old-time and some contemporary evangelical apologists who claim with surpassing conviction that Catholicism is a syncretic paganism rather than a form of Christianity. Those Protestant and Catholic apologists were and are not fools—the differences are sometimes stunning in their depth and intensity. Our tour of evangelical anti-Catholicism and Catholic anti-evangelicalism should dispel any naivete about the readiness of the mass of evangelicals to join hands with Roman Catholics or of Roman Catholics to develop any interest in and understanding of evangelicalism—except when a beloved relative joins a Pentecostal church. Most will not be moved until an intervening experience invites it. Religious tribalism is like racism—talk is cheap, and racism is extensive and deep among white liberals, no matter how liberal! Perhaps a seed permitting conversation between evangelicals and Catholics was planted long ago when Calvin himself admitted that there may be Christian churches in communion with Rome although there shouldn't be, and Catholics admitted that, although formal heretics like Luther and Calvin are destined to the eternal flames if they do not repent, those material heretics (the heresiarch's religious offspring) are invincibly ignorant and so may yet be saved without foreswearing their heresy. Through such small holes in the dyke do creative floods pour.

# 3

# Nativism and Politics

The peculiar virulence of American anti-Catholicism can be traced to British origins. Colonists, or at least their leaders, knew the sixteenth-century reformers' histories of the papacy and were acquainted with the acts of the Roman leaders and English Catholics against the British crown.[1] England had been at war with Catholic France and Catholic Spain and would be again. The colonists' grandparents and parents had lived under the reign of Queen Mary (1553–58) with its vigorous persecution of Protestants, through the Catholic intrigues against Queen Elizabeth, her successor (1558–1603), and the attack of the Spanish armada (1588). The colonists had probably been weaned on Foxe's "Book of Martyrs,"[2] (1563) a primary tool of British Protestant education about the unspeakable cruelty, treachery, and apostasy of the Catholic Church.

John Cotton was a student of divinity at Trinity College, Cambridge, when the Gunpowder Plot was uncovered in 1605. The unfortunate plotters were tried and executed as Cotton read theology and Oliver Ormerod wrote his dialogues with a papist and the aptly titled companion piece, *Pagano-Papismus*.[3] Only fifty years lay between the Gunpowder Plot and the publication of Cotton's commentary on Revelation.[4] A century later Jonathan Edwards, the greatest of the American Calvinist theologians, feared that Catholics from Canada would overwhelm New England. Two decades later the decidedly anti-Calvinist Jonathan Mayhew lectured at Harvard College that the pope was not only an idolater and an idol, and the prime historical corruptor of Christian faith, but that he also plotted the destruction of British and American liberty and the restoration of the hated medieval Christendom.⁵ The conviction was intensified among Puritans by their dread of any church leadership, Anglican or Roman, which threatened the autonomy of the local Christian congregation.⁶ Anti-Catholicism was never purely a religious matter for American Protestants; it was from the outset a political fear as well, for the Catholic Church was never a purely or merely objectionable *religious* system.⁷

We must break up into currents what is in fact a single historical stream: American nativism, political fear of Rome, and evangelicalism. Evangelical Protestantism is not nativist; in fact, its theology runs counter to nativism. The gospel is good news for all human beings, and transcends ethnic barriers and political and economic group bias. Evangelical theory and historical practice are normatively inclusive while nativism in its raw form is ethnic and political xenophobia. Yet through most of American history, evangelicalism and nativism are nearly inextricably joined, and what joined their unlikely seams was a rabid political fear of popery. I must discuss nativism in this chapter in order to extricate evangelicalism from its historical link to nativism, for what I am interested in here is not American nativism but American evangelicalism, that is, theology rather than politics.⁸ I shall discuss in the fourth and fifth chapters some of the chief carriers of the theological banner. Here I engage four influential American Protestants who set aside theological arguments to make the case for the political and cultural incompatibility of the Catholic Church and American ideals and political practice.

As a historical phenomenon, nativism took public form in the 1830s, was shaped into a political party over the 1840s, arrived at national prominence in the early 1850s, and perished in the rush to war at the end of that decade. But as a mood it has never been long absent from American politics and social life, and has been presented as an ideology against each new wave of immigrants. Forms of nativism resisted Irish, Italian, central European (Polish and Russian), as well as current Hispanic immigration, over the last two centuries. In order to distinguish what in many instances cannot be separated, evangelical Christianity and nativist ethnic prejudices and politics, I will discuss the beginnings of the link in the 1830s and what, one may be permitted to hope, is anti-Catholic nativism's last gasp in the 1940s and 1950s.

The American Catholic bishops met in Baltimore in 1829 for the first time. There had been one bishop in 1807, and by 1829 there were ten. Ray Allen Billington, the chronicler of the antebellum nativist movement, commented:

> Although the council's purpose was to quiet nativistic fears its effect
> was exactly the opposite, for the assembling of the American hierar-
> chy in all its glory was a sight which caused grave concern among
> the simplicity-loving Americans. Still more alarming were the thirty-
> eight decrees issued by the council, warning Catholics against "cor-
> rupt translations of the Bible," urging parishes to build parochial

schools to save children from "perversion" and approving the baptism of non-Catholic children when there was a prospect of their being brought up in the Catholic faith. This open flaunting not only of
the power but also of the ideals of Catholicism, turned many Americans against the Church. The Baltimore Council for the first time
taught them something of the strength of the dreadful enemy and
definitely placed them on guard.[9]

In addition, the American Catholic bishops' condemnation of the trustee movement among Catholic laity with the support of some priests called the attention
of Protestants to the hierarchical character of Catholic polity, so much at odds
with American Protestant practice and theory. Fr. William Hogan was excommunicated by Bishop Conwell of Philadelphia in 1821 for supporting independent lay ownership of the cathedral church.[10] The next bishop, Francis Kenrick,
facing the continued "rebellion" of lay trustees in 1830, placed his own cathedral church under canonical interdict forbidding the celebration of Mass and
the sacraments there. Twenty years later, the archbishop of New York, John
Hughes, who had supported the two Philadelphia bishops in their struggle
with Hogan and the trustees, found himself dealing with a similar situation
in a parish at the western edge of his own archdiocese. The battle over church
ownership was intense and public, was fought in several courts and state leg-
islatures, and was accompanied by a flood of controversial literature. The trustees won sympathy from American Protestants by pointing out that the bishops' position was out of line with the country's tradition and ideals. The
trustees steadfastly held that the issue was one between the democracy of the
congregation and the autocracy of the clergy. The inference might easily have
been made that Catholicism was a sworn enemy to democratic institutions and
thus a dangerous influence in the United States.[11]

But there is more. The first three decades of the nineteenth century saw
the improvement of the political position of the papacy after the defeat of
Napoleon and the restoration of the papal states in 1815. Again, 1814 saw the
rebirth of the hated Society of Jesus (the Jesuits) under Pius VII after its ban
by Clement XIII in 1773. To boot, the British Parliament passed the Catholic
Emancipation Bill in 1829, restoring some civil rights to Catholics. The print
controversy that accompanied the bill made its way to the United States.[12]

Gregory XVI (1831–46), once abbot of the Camaldolese monastery in Rome
and professor of theology, was known for his intense interest in missions in
his work for the Sacred Congregation of the Propagation of the Faith. He was
widely viewed as the "Austrian candidate" for the papacy and had the support
of Metternich, the mastermind of Austrian foreign policy, at his election. Gregory's opposition to the French revolution and Enlightenment rationalism was
matched by his personal asceticism, displayed by his choice to live as a monk
when he was pope. In 1832 Gregory issued *Mirari vos,* an encyclical letter to

the Catholic bishops that added considerable heat to the American fire even though the encyclical was directed toward a specific problem in France and contained no reference to the United States.[13] *Mirari vos* contained a condemnation of liberal democracy, specifically its French anticlerical form, that reinforced evangelical and rationalist convictions about the incompatibility of the Catholic Church and the new "liberal" world.

Gregory's encyclical figured large in expressing and shaping the attitude of the Catholic Church toward and relationship with modern European politics and culture. It registered high on the Richter scale of American anti-Catholic sentiment, from its issuance to the mid-twentieth century. For American Catholic-watchers from Samuel Morse to Paul Blanshard, *Mirari vos* revealed the dangers posed by the church to democratic cultures. Chiefly concerned with French Catholic liberalism and Italian revolution in the papal states, Gregory identified the religious independence of the papacy with its continued hold on the papal states. But Gregory spoke not only for papal monarchy but monarchy as an organizing principle of politics, as well as for the "union of church and state" as the preferable, indeed the normative, relation of church and society. He also managed to condemn most of the civil liberties achieved in Europe and the United States. Gregory failed to distinguish anticlerical ideological liberalism and those civil liberties.[14]

Finally, in the first decades of the nineteenth century, an extensive revival was going forward among evangelical Protestants called the second Great Awakening. That, and the considerably expanded number of Irish and German Catholic immigrants after the Napoleonic wars, favored a rebirth of traditional anti-Catholicism. Some of the men who, from the young republic to the 1950s, helped create the waves of antipopery now concern us.[15]

## Samuel F. B. Morse

Samuel Finley Breese Morse (1791–1872) developed the electric telegraph (1835) and the Morse code (1838). His father was a Congregational minister.[16] Samuel graduated from Yale University in 1810. He began painting portraits in 1815 to make a living, painting some of the best ever done in America, and later turned to grand vistas and historical subjects. As a young man he traveled widely in Europe, including the papal states, and did some of his best artistic work there. When he returned he founded and was first president (1826–45) of the National Academy of Design, and taught art at the University of the City of New York (later New York University). Politically and culturally conservative, he was a Jacksonian Democrat by affiliation but a Federalist/Whig by inclination and a staunchly orthodox Presbyterian. Founder, trustee, and benefactor of Vassar, he donated generously in his later life to Yale and to seminaries, to mission and temperance societies, and to poor artists. His large personality and vigorous intellectual powers made him an outstanding artist, then a great inventor and, through the second half of his life, an outstanding anti-Catholic in a crowded field. He wrote one of the most influential books in the no-popery crusade of the nineteenth century, *Foreign Conspiracy against the Liberties of the United States* (1835).[17]

Morse interpreted the St. Leopold Foundation (*Leopoldinen Stiftung*, 1828–1921), set up in support of American Catholic missions by the Austrian emperor with the blessing of Pope Gregory, as a political shoehorn to get Catholic missionaries into the United States, there to tamper with the American political system. He linked it to the post-Napoleonic conservative arrangements in Europe under Metternich, as well as to the pope's restorationist agenda. He was convinced that American liberty caused so much heartburn and envy among the aristocrats of European nations that the vigorously restored despotism, to protect itself, must crush it.

Morse did not focus on a religious critique of Roman Catholicism, although he might well have done so in other circumstances.[18] Some of his close friends, sponsors of Maria Monk among other things, took good care of that. Morse's appeal was across denominational lines in the United States, which he took to be a Christian (i.e., Protestant) nation. While strongly anti-Roman, he is not easily classified as a nativist. He lacks entirely the racism and ethnicism of the ideal nativists—say, the Ku Klux Klan or the Aryan Nation. So there is a bit of a peculiarity here: *Foreign Conspiracy* is not religious or theological, and it is not nativist in the abstract sense. It is a political assault on what he regarded as a political threat—not immigration but the political and civil ramifications of the immigrants' religion. If immigrants had been pouring in from Protestant Norway, Sweden, and Scotland, Morse would hardly have objected. Perhaps his assault is best understood as an expression of the tribalism of American politics and culture, with its habitual suspicion of the stranger and fear of betrayal, as Senator Joseph R. McCarthy's 1950s anticommunism should be. The book is not easily placed in relation to Anglo-Saxon convictions of cultural and even biological superiority, which I identify as the heart of nativism. Thus the danger of working with the abstraction "nativism." In the concrete, what exists are the books of Morse and Lyman Beecher—a mixture of religious, political, and cultural concerns perhaps driven by the demons of ethnicism and xenophobia, and perhaps by the drive to make a little money for a good cause.

Morse made out that the foreign conspiracy was a political endeavor under a religious cover—why else would the emperor of Austria rather than the pope run it? He wrote: ". . . I have nothing to do in these remarks with the *purely religious* character of the tenets of the Roman Catholic sect. . . . If any wish to resolve their doubts in the religious controversy, the acute pens of the polemic writers of the day will furnish them abundant means of deciding for themselves."[19] The distinction without a difference was repeated by most of the political critics over the next century, for all of them announced that it is the Roman "system" they are concerned with, a system in which religion and politics are inextricably mingled. Morse intended to compare political principles and regimes, contrasting absolutism and democracy, Austria and the United States, and Catholic and Protestant political theories.

Morse quoted *Mirari vos,* Gregory's encyclical outlawing liberty of opinion, of conscience, and of the press, and stressing the need for censorship. He contrasted "Popery, from its very nature, favoring despotism, and Protestantism, from its very nature, favoring liberty." The Leopold Foundation, in the first few years after its origin in 1828, siphoned $100,000 and missionaries from Europe into the United States, and Morse took this as a signal of Austrian intentions:[20]

> And who are these agents? *They are,* for the most part *Jesuits,* an ecclesiastical order, proverbial through the world for cunning, duplicity, and total want of moral principle; an order so skilled in all the arts of deception that even in Catholic countries, in Italy itself, it became intolerable, and the people required its suppression. . . . they are *foreigners* under vows of *perpetual celibacy,* and having, therefore, no deep and permanent interest in this country . . . bound by strong ties of *pecuniary interest* and *ambition,* to the service of a foreign despot.[21]

Catholics ". . . are already the most powerful and dangerous sect in the country, for they are not confined in their schemes and means like other sects to our borders, but they work with the minds and the funds of all despotic Europe." The international character of Catholicism and the Jesuits were sources of great bother to Morse. Protestant communities answer to no foreigner, and are weak and disunited in political action.[22] The Catholic immigrants, poor and ignorant, were guided by priests

> . . . imported from abroad, bound to the country by none of the usual ties, owing allegiance and service to a foreign government, depending on that government for promotion and reward, and this reward depends too on the manner in which they discharge the duties prescribed to them by a foreign master; which is, doubtless for the present, to confine themselves simply and wholly to increasing the number of their sect and the influence of the Pope in this country. . . . The Roman church is the body of *priests and prelates;* the *laity* have only to *obey* and to *pay,* not to exercise authority.[23]

The view that the Catholic laity and lower clergy are passive and "slavish" is nearly universal in anti-Catholic literature, from Morse to Blanshard and Boettner. Most often the Catholic laity is an object of pity, sometimes of contempt. Among Catholics, so wrote Morse, antirepublican sentiment is widespread; witness their fascination with titles and people who bear them. In addition, Catholics use American freedom of religion as a shield for their activities and to protect themselves from public scrutiny. Let them believe what they want in religion, said Morse, but not in political doctrine such as expressed by Pope Gregory.[24] For Catholic doctrines and American doctrines in politics are contradictory. Protestants will see that

> . . . Popery is now, what it has ever been, a system of the darkest *political intrigue and despotism,* cloaking itself to avoid attack under the sacred name of religion. . . . Popery is a political as well as a religious system; that in this respect it differs totally from all other sects, from all other forms of religion in the country. *Popery embodies in itself* THE CLOSEST UNION OF CHURCH AND STATE. Observe it at the fountain head. In the Roman States the civil and ecclesiastical offices are blended together in the same individual. The *Pope* is the *King.*[25]

Americans must demand that the prelates and priests in their midst declare their allegiance to our civil government and renounce all "allegiance to a FOREIGN SOVEREIGN. . . . Open your financial records. . . . *Come out and declare your opinion on the* LIBERTY OF THE PRESS, *on* LIBERTY OF CONSCIENCE, *and* LIBERTY OF OPINION." Morse challenged the Catholic clergy: Let us see if American Catholic opinion accords with the encyclical of the pope. The bishops themselves, he wagered, dare not disagree with the pope.[26]

He estimated that loss of American religious liberty was already "probable," given the progress of popery in the country. What was to be done? Engaging in double-speak, on the one hand, he forswore a Protestant Party in American politics and, on the other, gave advice on the principles on which it should be founded. After all, if the foreigners can organize the Irish especially are "clannish"—why not "American Christians"? And if they decided to do so he provided them grounds in what he called its manifesto:

> Popery is a *political system, despotic* in its organization, *anti-democratic* and *anti-republican,* and cannot therefore coexist with American republicanism.
> The ratio of *increase of Popery* is the exact ratio of the *decrease of civil liberty.*
> The *dominance of Popery* in the United States is the *certain destruction of our free institutions.*
> Popery, by its organization, is wholly under the control of a FOREIGN DESPOTIC SOVEREIGN.
> Austria, *one of the Holy Alliance of Sovereigns* leagued against the liberties of the world, HAS THE SUPERINTENDENCE OF THE OPERATIONS OF POPERY IN THIS COUNTRY.

The agents of Austria in the United States are Jesuits and priests in the pay of that foreign power, in active correspondence with their employers abroad, not bound by ties of any kind to our government or country. . . .

Popery is a UNION OF CHURCH AND STATE . . . and so destructive to our *religious* as well as civil liberty.

Popery is more dangerous and more formidable than any power in the United States.[27]

He piously added "But whilst deprecating *a union of religious sects* to act politically against Popery, I must not be misunderstood as recommending no political opposition to Popery by the American community," and he warns that the Romanists should not "whine" about religious persecution when their fellow citizens are aroused to defend their liberties.[28] In 1836 Morse ran for mayor of New York on a nativist ticket, and lost.[29]

Was Morse a nativist? No, if, as I define it, nativism involves a fear and hatred of immigrants. Yes, if fear and hatred of immigrants *who are Catholic* is essential to nativism in the period. Morse was a xenophobe when the stranger was a papist. He apparently got on quite well with strangers, witness the pleasure he took in his European journeys. His time in Italy, including the papal states, England and France, were highly productive. But he didn't cotton to English hierarchical society any more than to papal gendarmes, and returned appreciating his country, its freedoms, and its Protestantism above all. He inherited the Congregationalist orthodoxy of his minister father as well as his father's apocalyptic view of the Catholic Church. The "foreign potentates" and their plots against American liberty aroused him, but the potentates turned out to be European *Catholic* rulers, and so his Presbyterian prejudices provided the strong flow of negative feeling that pervades his writings on the Catholics. Perhaps he didn't need his religious convictions in order to see a threat in Catholic Austria and the Jesuits, but they certainly turned up the passion of his writing. In its turn, the writing sold very well and the money helped in his laboratory. He had the happiness, all too rare, of making a great deal of money by exercising his favorite prejudices and apocalyptic vision at precisely the time when to do both solidified his social standing as a patriot and a religious man. We shall have to wait for Paul Blanshard to see the like.

## Lyman Beecher

Lyman Beecher (1775–1863) graduated from Yale College in 1797. He studied theology with Timothy Dwight, the president of Yale, in 1798. He held pastorates in East Hampton, NY; Litchfield, CT; Boston; and Cincinnati. He took on the presidency of Lane Seminary in Cincinnati in 1832 in part in order to meet the threat posed by immigration of Catholics and the growth of the Catholic Church in the East and Midwest. His "fiery sermons" on a money-raising return trip to Boston in 1834 "apparently helped incite mob action and the burning of an Ursuline convent and school in August of that year."[30] He was thought in the West to be theologically liberal and too attached to the Arminian camp of Nathanael Taylor, was tried for heresy after criticism by Calvinists, and acquitted. Catholicism was not his only fear. He also vigorously opposed rationalism and the liquor trade.

Beecher collected Eastern funds to support his seminary in Cincinnati and the erection of other educational institutions in the West. The lands of the Louisiana Purchase needed intellectual and religious culture and education: schools, colleges, seminaries, pastors, and churches. "We must educate! We must educate! Or we must perish by our own prosperity."[31] The plea for educational support is primary, at least in the printed text of A Plea for the West. There, immigration and Roman Catholicism are brought in as an afterthought, but his sermons may have reversed this. Perhaps the verbal "Plea" was "Save us from Catholic tyranny!" while the printed version banked the fire of the Boston pulpit. Prudence would have dictated such a course in view of the uproar over the convent burning.

Echoing Morse, Beecher was worried that uneducated immigrants would dilute the strength and clarity of the community's intelligence on voting day—they were a "terrific inundation." The flood is connected to "continental powers alarmed at the march of liberal opinions, and associated to put them down . . . waiting for our downfall." Three quarters of the immigrants, he maintained, were controlled by potentates of Europe through Catholic priests. The papacy was in his view a creature of Austria and the priests did Austria's bidding. The outcome would be a nation within a nation, and before long a union of church and state.[32] Like Morse, Beecher saw an erosion of American liberties, the result of a foreign conspiracy of aristocrats working through Catholic immigrants. He wrote, we must remember, before the Irish immigration to the eastern cities has hit its peak in the 1840s. The only "potentate" involved there would have been the queen of England, and she surely wanted and could achieve no control of uneducated Irish minds through priests. A decade after his book, the priests would be on their own with no one but the pope behind them, and the Irish could only have been charged a threat to the East.

> The ministers of no Protestant sect could or would dare to attempt
> to regulate the votes of their people as the Catholic priests can do,
> who at their confessional learn all the private concerns of their peo-
> ple, and have almost unlimited power over the conscience as it re-
> spects the performance of every civil or social duty.

Catholic Europe would soon control 10 percent of the suffrage of the nation, deciding elections, perplexing policy, dividing the nation, breaking the bonds of unity, and throwing down free institutions. He had no fear of the Catholics simply as a religious denomination unconnected to European governments hostile to republican institutions. Surely the song would have had different words a decade later.

> Let the Catholics mingle with us as Americans and come with their children under the full action of our common schools and republican institutions, and the various powers of assimilation, and we are prepared cheerfully to abide the consequences. If in these circumstances the Protestant religion cannot stand before the Catholic, let it go down, and we will sound no alarm, and ask no aid, and make no complaint. It is no ecclesiastical quarrel to which we would call attention of the American nation.[33]

"We" welcome "them," he said, they and their property are safe; "we" abhor violence against "them." "We" want "them" to become Americans. To do that as Beecher would define it, of course, is to become Protestant. No, it is not their religion but the church's political claims and character of it, its alliance with the states hostile to liberty, he claims. If only they were just another American denomination, with equal rights and privileges, no one would be upset. But they:

> are taught to believe that their church is the only church of Christ, out of whose inclosure none can be saved. . . . if such, I say, are the maxims *avowed by her pontiff, sanctioned by her councils, stereotyped on her ancient records, advocated by her most approved authors, illustrated in all ages by her history, and still* UNREPEALED and still *acted upon* in the armed prohibition of free inquiry and religious liberty, and the punishment of heresy wherever her power remains unbroken: if these things are so, is it invidious and is it superfluous to call the attention of the nation to the bearing of such a denomination upon our civil and religious institutions and equal rights? It is *the right of* SELF-PRESERVATION, and the denial of it is TREASON or the INFATUATION OF FOLLY.[34]

Catholics in his view were a threat to the political *status quo*; they operate by different rules and will not keep "ours." They insist they are right on moral issues and will not put issues to a vote in their church. Their clergy are in charge of their life, civil as well as religious, he said, and their institutions are formally opposed to republicanism. He traced the Catholic problem to Constantine and "the kings of the earth who gave their protection to a despotic form of corrupted Christianity. . . ."[35] Again, in its alliance with despotic powers over the centuries the papacy "by a death of violence is estimated to have swept from the earth about sixty-eight millions of its inhabitants, and holds now in darkness and bondage nearly half the civilized world."[36] And again, "It is the most skillful, powerful, dreadful system of corruption to those who wield it and of debasement and slavery to those who live under it, which ever spread darkness and desolation over the earth." The papacy, he admitted, had not for ages had the military power to compel the assent of its neighbors. Instead it used "the terrors of [its] spiritual power over the consciences of their dark-minded subjects. . . ." Protestantism had benefited the civilization of Europe, but Austria, Bohemia, and Ireland were still under the papal spell—and under civil despotism.[37] The immigrants were a class of people least enlightened and most subject to the priesthood.

> And is there no danger from a population of nearly a million, aug-
> menting at the rate of two or three hundred thousand a year by im-
> migration; whose physical power, and property, and vote, are as en-
> tirely as in Europe, within the reach of clerical influence? If the
> Catholic religion were simply an insulated system of religious error,
> it might be expected to fade away without a struggle before the aug-
> menting, overpowering light of truth; but it has always been, and
> still is, a political religion—a religion of state . . .[38]

His solution to what he painted as a desperate problem was uncommonly mild, given the magnitude of the threat: he called for a book collecting "the authentic documents of the Catholic church, accessible to ministers and intelligent laymen of all denominations . . . *without note or comment* . . . ," part of "rearing up" literary and religious institutions necessary to the intellectual and moral culture of the nation. He urged schools for cheap and effectual education to compete with Roman Catholic schools; he wanted to extend to the Catholic population "intellectual culture and evangelical light."[39] Finally, straining once again to distinguish good Catholic laity from their evil clerical masters, he requested that Protestants were be nice to ordinary Catholics for they may be unconscious of "designs and higher movements" of their system against republican government.

However, it seems obvious that Beecher hated both Catholics and the Catholic Church. In addition, he feared the resurgent monarchy in Europe and the restored papal states, and he was aware of the support of Austria in conclave for the election of Gregory, all of this fuel for a fire already burning in his evangelical breast. Beecher does not mention the Leopold Society, although this organization is Morse's clue to the papal plot to annex the American West. Nor does he allude to the highly touted controversies of John Hughes with John Breckinridge in Philadelphia.[40] There is no mention of the conversions to Rome that had been taking place,[41] and no mention of Maria Monk or the convent scandals that were breaking about this time. There are only oblique references to celibacy, with a quick run through the distinctive Catholic doctrines and practices. He stayed focused on civil disruption and the threat to Protestant political hegemony (church and state). Throughout he assumed that the nation is Protestant, that Protestants are tolerant, that assimilation to that norm is desirable, and that Catholicism and democracy are fundamentally incompatible.

The structure of the book is peculiar. He was half way through before he got to the flaming issue, popery. He argued for strong literary and intellectual institutions without mentioning the "threat" he saw. And he got through the immigrant problem before he tells us that it is the *Catholic* immigrants who pose the threat. And more before he tells us why it is a threat in a brief mention of Morse's "plot between Metternich and the pope." Harding, his biographer, comments: "In his plea he now became no longer a Christian seer, but an American with strong tendencies toward nativism and incipient Know-Nothingism—perhaps the inevitable fate of any person who identified the salvation of the world with his own nation, culture, and religious community." Beecher wanted two things in order to check Roman influence: choke off immigration and build more schools. Is he a nativist? The answer is the same as in Morse's case. He would, I suspect, have been happy to receive the immigrants who were not under clerical and autocratic domination.[42]

## Josiah Strong

Born Naperville Illinois in 1847, Josiah Strong descended from a 1630 immigrant ancestor who was an elder in the Boston Congregational church in which John Cotton taught.[43] No wonder Strong thought of himself as a native American. He was a Congregationalist, graduated from Lane Seminary (1871), was several times a pastor in Wyoming and Ohio and then in New York City, where he resided as a pastor and General Secretary of the Evangelical Alliance (1886–98). *Our Country* illustrates amply that he was Arminian Calvinist and a firm believer in American manifest destiny.[44] He was as well an ecumenist among Protestant churches and a founder of the Federal Council of Christian Churches (1908). A dedicated Social Gospeler (he has a good deal to say about capitalism, its dangers and limits), he worried most about the urbanization of American culture and liquor consumption. The next to the last chapter in *Our Country*, on "The Anglo-Saxon and World Future," is racist (with some qualifications). In fact, the prominence of its racism or ethnicism is even more distressing than its antipopery. Read over a century after its publication, the book is astounding on this score. There is no mention of slavery except that abolition was the result of Christian principle of individual liberty, nor any mention of the American freedmen, nor of the violence committed by whites against Native Americans in the name of national expansion. One would think that all that Anglo-Saxons were doing in the American West and South was leading the natives on to higher forms of life and religion. The destruction of Native American civilization and culture seems just one more step in the westward flow of "higher culture" and its torchbearers, the Anglo-Saxons. This is a book by a man who can think, who can write, who is obviously high-minded and utterly dedicated to the good and who is blinded by group bias. He was attempting to raise money for the Home Missionary Society in the footsteps of Beecher and Horace Bushnell, both of whom also had put on their antipopery epaulets for the Society's good. Strong shared Bushnell's conviction of destiny of Anglo-Saxons. Strong was as well a worthy successor to Morse and Beecher in his hopes for and fears about the nation and the West. Worry about the survival of a Protestant America is common to them all.

There were 175,000 copies of *Our Country* sold by 1916 and, while not matching Maria Monk's sales, it was considerable for the time. According to the editor, Jurgen Herbst, Strong "had gauged correctly the mind and mood of Protestant America" and his book "mirrors the thought and aspirations of this dominant segment of American society towards the close of the nineteenth century . . ."[45] Who is the "Our" in *Our Country*? Well, it certainly is not me and mine. The "Our" were people who assumed that Protestant America was God's special instrument in His Great Work of spreading the Gospel to the ends of the earth, and so to be a Protestant Christian and an American patriot was one and the same.[46] To be a Catholic, a Mormon, a Campbellite, a "foulmouthed rationalist" was to be an obstacle to the national and Gospel progress. Herbst wrote: "*Our Country* is a mirror of Protestant America in the 1880's, reflecting its image of the past, its sense of present realities, and its dreams of the future."[47] Strong himself believed in the timeliness of his work:

> There are certain great focal points of history toward which the lines
> of past progress have converged, and from which have radiated the
> molding influences of the future. Such was the Incarnation, such
> was the German Reformation of the sixteenth century, and *such are
> the closing years of the nineteenth century,* second in importance to
> that only which must always remain first; viz, the birth of Christ. . . .
> Many are not aware that we are living in extraordinary times. . . .
> (N)o generation appreciates its own place in history. Several years
> ago Professor Austin Phelps [who wrote the preface] said: "Five hun-
> dred years of time in the process of the world's salvation may de-
> pend on the next twenty years of United States history." It is pro-
> posed in the following pages to show that such dependence of the
> world's future on this generation in America is not only credible,
> but in the highest degree probable. Like the star in the East which
> guided the three kings with their treasures westward until at length
> it stood still over the cradle of the young Christ, so the star of em-
> pire, rising in the East, has ever beckoned the wealth and power of
> the nations westward until today it stands still over the cradle of the
> young empire of the West, to which nations are bringing their offer-

ings. The West today is an infant, but shall one day be a giant, in each of whose limbs shall unite the strength of many nations.[48]

God has determined all this, but still there were perils to this divinely willed expansion. The first was immigration. It threatened the precious morals of the Anglo-Saxon society: "The typical immigrant is a European peasant, whose horizon has been narrow, whose moral and religious training has been meager or false, and whose ideas of life are low. Not a few belong to the pauper and criminal classes." The low life is linked to the liquor traffic, "debauching popular morals . . ." In addition, immigration influenced American politics: there was a liquor vote; Mormons get these low people and then there is a Morman vote; there is a Catholic vote; immigration is the "mother and nurse of socialism"; and immigration especially floods the cities. Nothing is more of a threat than cities. Intelligence and virtue are needed for the republic and the immigrants are in short supply of both. The struggle is joined: are "we" to "Americanize them" and go on to the glory of God or are they to "foreignize" us and see our divine mission cancelled?[49]

The second multifaceted peril was Romanism. It was a challenge to our "free institutions." "We" believe in popular sovereignty while Catholics hold to Papal supreme sovereignty.[50] The Catholic code of canon law trumps the law of the land, the church trumps the nation. Boniface VIII in *Unam Sanctam* (1302) wrote: "it . . . [is] . . . altogether necessary to salvation that every human creature should be subject to the Roman Pontiff." No commonplace denial of unconflicted loyalty will do. The protestations of John England and other American bishops cannot outweigh this high doctrine of church authority. For American Catholics, too, political conscience must be subordinate to the Pope. Unlike the Protestant who stands with his Bible in adjudicating possible conflicts between the spiritual and the state,

> . . . the Roman Catholic is not at liberty to weigh the Pope's judgment, to try his commands by his own conscience and the Word of God—to do this would be to become a Protestant. There can be no appeal to his reason or conscience, the decision is final and his duty absolute. And, moreover, he stands not alone, but with many millions more, who are bound by the most dreadful penalties to act as one man in obedience to the will of a foreign potentate and in disregard of the laws of the land. *This, I claim, is a very possible menace to the peace of society.*[51]

"The two greatest living statesmen, Gladstone and Bismarck, hold that the allegiance demanded by the Pope is inconsistent with good citizenship."[52] The problem posed by Strong, repeated in the presidential campaigns of 1928 and 1960, is transatlantic in its dimension, and is another instance of the struggle between the church and modernity (in this case, the modern nation state). This gives us the second of the three strands of anti-Catholicism: American nativist, modern political, and Protestant theological.

To this, Strong adds the Catholic objection to religious liberty: "heresy has no right." Strong quotes *Brownson's Quarterly Review* as follows: "Heresy and infidelity have not, and never had, and never can have, any rights, being, as they undeniably are, contrary to the law of God."[53] Other modern liberties such as speech and press fall before papal teaching, as does the separation of church and state and the public school.[54] Strong remarked that Catholics said and wrote such shocking things as if no one but Catholics were in the audience, or perhaps because they wished to provoke the non-Catholics in the audience. Admittedly there was a certain bravado in the Catholic language, a kind of stick-it-to 'em attitude characteristic of the mythical Catholic beast of Britain, the Chesterbelloc.[55] This may be the rhetoric of wartime, but Strong was correct that the positions were espoused as he quotes them. Strong summarizes in a comparison of fundamental principles:

1. We have seen the supreme sovereignty of the Pope opposed to the sovereignty of the people.

2. We have seen that the commands of the Pope, instead of the constitution and the laws of the land, demand the highest allegiance of Roman Catholic in the United States.

3. We have seen that the alien Romanist who seeks citizenship swears true obedience to the Pope instead of "renouncing forever all allegiance to any foreign prince, potentate, state or sovereignty," as required by our laws.

4. We have seen that Romanism teaches religious intolerance instead of religious liberty.

5. We have seen that Rome demands the censorship of ideas and the press, instead of freedom of the press and speech.

6. We have seen that she approves the union of church and state instead of their entire separation.

7. We have seen that she is opposed to our public school system.

Manifestly, there is an irreconcilable difference between papal principles and the fundamental principles of our free institutions. . . . Our fundamental ideas of society, therefore, are as radically opposed to Vaticanism as to imperialism, and it is as inconsistent with our liberties for Americans to yield allegiance to the Pope as to the Czar.[56]

The institutional conflict was as inevitable as it was profound. In addition, it was clearly and publicly part of the purpose of Roman Catholics to convert all Americans to the Roman Catholic Church. Thus, the conflict of principles will thus inevitably become a conflict in practice. Nor did Strong, some fifty

years down the line, share in Beecher's optimism about the American Protestant ability to assimilate Catholics. Catholic enthusiasm for the pope appeared universal, and unqualified. The outlook for a change in the Roman
Catholic mind was not good.[57] Their reliance on authority and rejection of
independence in believing and thinking has taken its toll on the character of
Catholics:

> Everyone born a Roman Catholic is suckled on authority. His train-
> ing affects every fiber of his mental constitution. He has been
> taught that he must not judge for himself, nor trust to his own con-
> victions. If he finds his sympathies, his judgment and convictions in
> conflict with a papal decree, it is the perfectly natural result of his
> training to distrust himself. His will, accustomed all his life to yield
> to authority without question, is not equal to the conflict that would
> follow disobedience. How can he withstand a power able to inflict
> most serious punishment in this life, and infinite penalties in the
> next?[58]

The foreign threat was an immediate challenge from within, for the Catholics
were citizens and still Romanists. The West was in particular danger. The
Jesuits brought their talent for intrigue; they were there "with empires in their
brains . . . proposing to Romanize and control our western empire." He ended
the chapter with a much-used quote from Lafayette, "If the liberties of the
American people are ever destroyed, they will fall by the hand of the Romish
clergy."[59]

The third peril, religion and the public schools, was in good part presented
by Catholics and their schools. The public schools aim at making good citizens,
the Catholic schools aim at making good Catholics; the American independence of character is replaced by Roman submission, American self-control by
control by superiors, and American intelligent obedience to rightful authority
by unquestioning obedience to arbitrary authority. "When, therefore, the Catholic hierarchy and press assert that the only way to make a good Catholic out
of a child is to keep him out of the public school and separate him from
American children, it is an acknowledgment that Romanism is un-American
and represents an alien civilization."[60]

In his final chapter, "The Anglo-Saxon and the World's Future," we read
that the superiority of the Anglo-Saxon rests on two ideas: civil liberty and pure
spiritual Christianity.[61] Protestantism has failed in Europe, is even fleeing from
Britain, and has taken up residence among American Anglos. The English and
Americans, he hoped, will convert the world. The Anglos are "divinely commissioned" to stamp other peoples with these ideas, in fact to "Anglo-Saxonize
mankind."?[62] The American Anglos are even superior to the English in height,
chest measurement, and weight. Ironically, superiority is due in part to the fact
that Anglo-Saxons are a mixed race—but then all the great races have been

mixed. But, with the flood of immigrants, the blood type had to be maintained. Anglos also have a genius for moneymaking and an instinct for colonizing. Because of their superiority—intellectual, moral, economic, and political—we were heading for a new stage of world history, namely:

> . . . the final competition of the races, for which the Anglo-Saxon is being schooled. Long before the thousand millions are here, the mighty centrifugal tendency, inherent in this stock and strengthened in the United States, will assert itself. Then this race of unequaled energy, with all the majesty of numbers and the might of wealth behind it—the representative, let us hope, of the largest liberty, the purest Christianity, the highest civilization—having developed peculiarly aggressive traits calculated to impress its institutions upon mankind, will spread itself over the earth. . . . And can anyone doubt that the result of this competition will be the "survival of the fittest"? . . . Notwithstanding the great perils which threaten it, I cannot think our civilization will perish; but I believe it is fully in the hands of Christians of the United States, during the next ten or fifteen years, to hasten or retard the coming of Christ's kingdom in the world by hundreds, and perhaps thousands of years. We of this generation and nation occupy the Gibraltar of the ages which command the world's future.[63]

The satisfaction of possessing the key to human history, and finding out that one's age is the pivot of it all, must be huge. Marx, I suppose, had something of that sort. Surely Catholic apologists had it: after all, they clung to the Rock on whom Jesus built a church, which would withstand the powers of Hell. The Reformers, too, knew that God was acting in them to save his people from popery. It is all of a piece with the apocalyptic convictions of Jesus and Paul. Strong added his bit to a history of a satisfying Protestant and Catholic illusion, a touch of racial/ethnic/national superiority. In this way only did he depart from his predecessors in the evangelical and the national tradition, and in doing so, violated its basic anthropological assumption, that "All men are created equal . . ." But his political and moral arguments against Catholicism remain essentially the same, long hallowed in evangelical tradition.

## Paul Blanshard

Paul Blanshard (1892–1980) was the most important American political critic of the Catholic Church in the twentieth century, certainly the most widely read and influential.[64] In 1947 he revived the old no-popery crusade in a new context. In post–World War II America, Catholics were rapidly climbing the social and economic scale.[65] Membership had continued to increase rapidly.[66] The church's bishops were assumed to be more influential than they had ever been, from pursuing public funds for parochial education to exercising the function of censorship over the film industry.[67] To the great bother of American liberals, the church continued to support Francisco Franco, the dictator of Spain. Democracy had nearly been defeated in Europe by fascism, and tensions with totalitarian communism were growing. And Paul Blanshard had just retired from public service and needed to make money.

Blanshard himself was an example of the secularized American Protestantism of the period. He remarked about his first ministerial work in a Boston Congregational church while a student at Harvard Divinity School, "I preached more socialism than Christianity in my first year in the pulpit, relying more on Bernard Shaw and H. G. Wells than on St. Paul."[68] In 1916, with the tension of unbelief below the surface, he was ordained pastor of a small Congregationalist church in Tampa, Florida.[69] In 1917, although his congregation voted unanimously to continue his contract, he "finally decided to leave for a very odd reason: I read the New Testament through carefully for the first time in my life . . ."[70] He worked in the government of the city of New York and in the State Department, and retired to Vermont in his mid-fifties to "write books," among which was to be a book attacking Christianity.[71] He found an even readier target.

While wandering among the shelves in the Dartmouth College Library, Blanshard came across a textbook in moral theology by an English Jesuit, Henry Davis, and was so shocked by its treatment of medical ethics, abortion, sex, and marriage that he determined to make a study of "the Catholic underworld and do a deliberate muckraking job. . . . Why not? This was apparently one field not yet preempted by the muckrakers."[72] The result of a couple of years' reading, three articles in *The Nation* and the book *American Freedom and Catholic Power*, was a sensation among American intellectuals as well as the general reading public.[73] Ten New York publishers refused to publish the book manuscript before the Unitarian-owned Beacon Press picked it up and became Blanshard's chief publisher. Three hundred thousand copies of the first edition were sold, the book made the bestseller list for seven months, and was a Book of the Month Club pick.[74]

In the same period liberal Protestants were voicing complaints identical to his. They were deeply apprehensive about the effect of the muscular Catholic Church on the civil and political order for which they felt a proprietary responsibility. But they no longer traded in Reformation doctrinal or theological worries. The complaints they made were expressions of Enlightenment-assimilated Christianity in America, dominated by the democratic values common to the left-wing Christians and secularists. Blanshard had a youthful fling with the former and spent most of his adult life with the latter. He expressed the concern shared by leading American secular and religious intellectuals such as Walter Lippmann, Reinhold Niebuhr, William Sloan Coffin, Talcott Parsons, Robert K. Merton, Justices Hugo Black and Robert Jackson, Harvard president James Bryant Conant, Perry Miller, John Dewey, Corliss Lamont, and others.[75] Morse and Beecher found heirs, no longer Christians but just as viscerally and instinctively anti-Catholic as their more pious ancestors had been.

In fact, the political and social no-popery had concentrated its focus on the contradictions between democracy and hierarchy, surrendering the religious and theological language of traditional evangelical criticism of the Catholic Church. Blanshard's issues are different from those catalogued in the traditional table of contents of the evangelical religious and theological attack still evident in Loraine Boettner's 1962 summary of evangelical problems with the Catholic Church in his *Roman Catholicism* and in the lurid *A Woman Rides the Beast: The Roman Catholic Church and the Last Days* by Dave Hunt in 1994.[76] Blanshard's list approximates the stream of political no-popery concerns: foreign control of American Catholics; anti-democratic Catholic ecclesiastical structure; Catholic religious propaganda and the attempt to control education; public education and the public treasury; Catholic use of censorship and boycott; and the Church's attempt to make America Catholic. Blanshard adds to the list: medical practice in Catholic hospitals and by Catholic doctors; Catholic opposition to current liberalized sexual practice, birth control, and eugenics; enforcement of the Church's own code of marriage and divorce on the public; manipulation of science and Catholic superstition; Catholic association with fascism and an exercise of authority similar to Soviet communism, the other anti-individualist system in the twentieth century. This is a book that, like Boettner's, took more than faith; it took work and a lot of it on the Catholic bibliography.[77]

In the first two chapters he repeated an old Anglo-American argument. American Catholics are subjects of two conflicting social, political, intellectual, and spiritual centers. They suffer alien imposition from abroad. Their religious community, unlike any other, is antidemocratic, clannish, and intolerant. Blanshard intended a book "not about the Catholic faith but about the cultural, political, and economic policies of the Catholic Church," and about a "relatively unexplored underworld of medieval policy and practice which has been prettified and camouflaged by clerical window dressing, . . . an autocratic moral monarchy in a liberal democracy . . ." Of course, his distinction between religious faith and national politics does not hold, at least from a Catholic viewpoint. What he is objecting to is crucial to the Catholic religion. He is objecting to "The Church," that entity of which Lenny Bruce said "Everyone knows which church you mean when you say The Church." It is the church of "big shows and displays," "a militant and exclusive faith." Its "[p]riests are the victims of the medievalism of their own Church, imprisoned by ancient beliefs and forced into the role of a 'good' magician . . . a salesman for magic."[78]

The framework of the power of the Catholic church *is* medieval. The clerical caste, on the whole, corresponds to the nobility, and the Pope corresponds to the king. In the total authoritarian scheme the people are subjects, as they were in the Middle Ages, not partici- pants in the government.[79]

In his third chapter he gets to the heart of the issue. The Catholic doctrine of union of church and state contradicts the United States constitutional sep- aration of church and state. The church wants special consideration from gov- ernment, to control the free practice of other religions, and to charge its edu- cational expenses to the public treasury. American Catholic leaders avoid this kind of talk in public, and they "disguise . . . [the doctrine] by semantic arti- fice . . ." The basic terms state, church, and democracy are used differently by Americans and Catholic leaders in this country and elsewhere. What are clearly economic and social goals are spoken of as religious, and so their meaning is not evident. The church doesn't get "into politics" on one occasion or another; it *is* political!

In particular areas, the authority of the church is superior to that of the United States government and of all governments, and no gov- ernment is conceded the moral right to deny this. The Pope is a kind of special world monarch who rules a synthetic moral empire that overlaps and penetrates the sovereignty of all earthly govern- ments.[80]

Nowhere does a pope endorse "democracy as a superior form of govern- ment."[81] One might ask Blanshard: But wouldn't that be a political act itself? Yes, it would. Would Blanshard have preferred that the pope do that? Did he want the church to become a supporter of a specific form of government? Yes, he did. Yet, how were the popes to abstract themselves from the history of anti- Catholicism practiced by modern democracies, most especially socialist? It took a church council (1962–65) to begin a change of direction in that relationship, and it took a lot of learning on the side of secularist, anticlerical democracies as well. Although church leaders had to learn that democracies were not nec- essarily tied to antireligious policies, democratic leaders had to learn that tra- ditional religions, especially Catholicism, were not in the last stages of decrep- itude and were ready to support democracy if they could see its benefits. Blanshard wanted the popes to "support the American conception of the sep- aration of church and state as set forth by the Supreme Court." And he wanted the bishops to stop trying to get public support for the Catholic schools.[82] Nowhere does he note that a plural school system is not only constitutional but may be a signal benefit to democracy. He wanted the church to be assim- ilated to American law, mores, and procedures. He demanded that it become an American Catholic Church, another American denomination like the Methodists, Presbyterians, and Baptists.[83] The notion that a church might have a notion of itself as transcending the modern democratic political order was deeply abhorrent. That Catholics who experienced American democracy should support a Falangist Spain, even after the violent persecution of the church by Spanish republicans, was unintelligible.

Blanshard went on to maintain that, although Catholics have the right to disagree, they have no right to disobey the law: "Unquestionably Catholics have a moral right to oppose any law in a democracy so long as they believe in submission to law. . . . [But] In some cases the alien-controlled hierarchy demands defiance of existing American law," including laws mandating sterilization and proposed laws compelling children to attend public schools, offer only conditioned acceptance of a law (e.g., freedom of religion), and impose ecclesiastical penalties against Catholics who exercise the rights of a citizen (e.g., canon law blocks Catholics from suing a priest or the church). He quotes Hilaire Belloc: "On the one side you have a plain affirmation that the law is the law and must be obeyed, and indignant surprise on the rejection of what seems so obvious and universal a rule. On the other, you will have, as you have had throughout history, resistance to and denial of that rule."[84]

Blanshard turned to education, a thorn in Protestant-Catholic relations since the 1830s. The "tremendous revival of anti-Catholic feeling" that Blanshard discerned was because of the hierarchy's "educational aggressiveness." In the post–World War II generation it was not the old Ku Klux Klan nativist bigotry shown to Al Smith, or the religious onslaughts of the nineteenth century, but the "tolerant liberals" who were upset by public transportation of private school children and the fight for universal school aid, tied into church opposition to any federal aid to education that doesn't include the parochial schools. In addition, Blanshard cites the poor quality and separatist nature of parochial education. In the Catholic schools, children are not taught democracy, freedom, tolerance, and national solidarity, and they are taught in conditions markedly inferior to public education.[85] The bishops divide the American community emotionally and culturally by separating immigrants from the public schools. The church claims primacy over education. Although it says that the parents have primacy, it never grants that in fact; and it insists the government has no *primary* right to educate Catholics at all. Education is the crucial issue—all depends on it in this struggle with the hierarchy. The possibility of the hierarchy winning this battle is "remote" because non-Catholics are "aroused as never before . . ." In fact, the Catholic schools are on the verge of collapse since the number of nuns will decline, for "Catholic young women, reared in the free and hearty atmosphere of modern America, are beginning to regard the whole segregated system of nuns, wimples, and convents as medieval posturing and useless mortification."[86]

But none of the states questions the spirit and outlook of the segregated Catholic system. No one asks whether the system is producing
Catholics first and Americans second, or whether the closed system
develops real community spirit, or whether the nuns who are shut
off from the outside world are competent to teach children about
that world.[87]

The Catholic Church provides second-rate education, segregates its members,
undermines their participation in American culture, attempts to obtain tax
money for its private system, and undercuts and infiltrates the public school
system. He sums up his case by quoting John Dewey in *The Nation's Schools*
on the hierarchy's blocking aid to colleges when it doesn't include Catholic
colleges: "It is essential that this basic issue be seen for what it is—namely, as
the encouragement of a powerful reactionary world organization in the most
vital realm of democratic life with the resulting promulgation of principles
inimical to democracy."[88]

The national problem of education and the church is matched by the international problem of the church and antidemocratic forces at mid-century.
The pope did not oppose Mussolini in 1922. Quite the contrary. The church
has more affinity in social ideas with fascism than with democracy. Christopher
Dawson, the noted Catholic historian at Columbia University, wrote that "Catholicism is by no means hostile to the authoritarian ideal of the state."[89] The
pope signed the Lateran Treaty, "one of the most important and one of the
most tragic events in modern history. . . ." It blessed the war on Ethiopia, helping to destroy the League of Nations. It proposed corporate state models in
social teaching. It supported Franco and helped him, along with Hitler and
Mussolini, to destroy Spanish democracy. It protested Hitler only when its own
interests were infringed on and signed a concordat with him. It supported
General Petain in Vichy France. It favored the murderous Joseph Tiso in Slo-
vakia. So long as clerical hegemony is guaranteed, it will support fascist regimes. Spain and Portugal are its model Catholic states. There and elsewhere
"Catholicism conditions its people to accept censorship, thought control, and,
ultimately dictatorship." All the ideals of democracy and liberalism are opposed
by the church, while authoritarianism in politics is approved if it can be ma-
nipulated to support the church's status. In the course of this indictment, he
takes no notice of a tension between his demand that the church stay out of
politics, his desire for papal backing for democracies, and his denunciation of
the church's desire to protect itself as far as possible from fascist regimes.[90]

Once again, nativism is a misleading term for Blanshard's approach. Like
most high-culture American critics, Blanshard confesses that it is difficult to
criticize the Catholic "system" as distinct from the Catholic faith, for "the system" is as much a part of Catholic faith as beliefs about God, Jesus Christ, and
the sacraments. "The Catholic problem as I see it is not primarily a religious

problem: it is an institutional and political problem," and he will deal with it as such. He objects not to a church, but to "a state within a state, a state above a state, and a foreign-controlled society within American society."[91] Why does he worry about it? Although he revives the old nativist and Protestant fears, both here and in England, he displays an extraordinary lack of historical awareness of this. In English-speaking Christianity, the "problem" presented by the Catholic Church has never been far from the public mind since Henry VIII. It has only been "settled" (so far as it can be) in the past fifty years, and even now the Catholic Church is as resolutely transnational as ever, the pope still the center of "the system." Blanshard is the latest in a centuries-old string of messengers. He is not a nativist in the ethnic sense, nor is he interested in putting a stop to immigration—he's a nationalist, perhaps even a statist whose own religion is the democratic national community and its ideals, a Deweyan sanctified and capitalized "Democracy." He fears dual loyalties and anything transcending the actually existing democratic community. In this way, he's a Deweyite, sharing with Dewey a Congregational background and a conversion to democratic idealism, to a new "church." He wants all Americans safely and soundly within American culture and living by its democratic rules, suppositions, and ideals.

Blanshard provided a culmination of the Puritan distaste, indeed fear of a Catholicism that invades and threatens the democratic (read: Protestant) ethos of American culture and politics. He shared this with predecessors such as John Cotton, Jonathan Edwards, and Jonathan Mayhew, Morse, and Beecher. His protests, made by Morse and Beecher as well, that his attack is not on Catholicism as a faith or on Catholic fellow citizens rings hollow, however, for he seems to realize that what he does attack as basic to "the system" is also basic to the "faith." To mention only two issues central to the system and the faith, the Catholic Church was and is unlikely, to put it mildly, to agree to being just another denomination, and unlikely to agree that democratic procedure and political structure are part of the "one true faith" by which it lives. But it seems that the Roman Church cannot commit itself to any form or government or social order except its own, and its own as given to it. The ecclesiological dogma is immensely important to its self-understanding as well as to a scholar's understanding of it.

## James T. O'Neill's Response to Blanshard

James O'Neill was chairman of department of speech in Brooklyn College and the author of a study of education and the U.S. Constitution.[92] In the preface to *Catholicism and American Freedom*, O'Neill says of himself that he is not a philosopher or a theologian but a teacher of rhetoric, of argument and debate. He had never taught in or been a student in a Catholic educational institution, but his six children attended both public and Catholic schools. He taught for forty-five years in eight different states, from first grade in public grammar schools to graduate schools in universities. He was a member and then chair of the Committee on Academic Freedom of the American Civil Liberties Union for twelve years, a card-carrying member of a constituent organization in Paul Blanshard's America.[93]

When O'Neill read Blanshard's articles in *The Nation,* they bored him. He read the book when it was reviewed and recommended by "men who had reputations for responsible scholarship." He found in it all the "worst faults of argument" that had stopped his reading of *The Nation* articles. In the preface he sums up his charge:

> Mr. Blanshard's basic thesis is that the Catholic Church is an enemy of American freedom. . . . My position is that Mr. Blanshard's basic thesis is false, and that the discussion of the belief and practice of American Catholics which he presents in support of his thesis is so biased and inaccurate as to be substantially worthless. Anyone, of any religion or of none, with some knowledge of the Church's doctrines, and of the history and practices of American Catholics, should have known that the book's central thesis is false; and anyone with elementary knowledge of the principles of argument and proof should have known that Mr. Blanshard does not prove his case.
>
> If the Blanshard book is so bad, why take it so seriously? The answer is, because it has been *praised and promoted* by men who, on account of the positions they occupy and the ideals they advocate, should have been expected to expose its antireligious, anti-Catholic bias, its basic freedom-smothering philosophy of the omnipotent state, and its erroneous scholarship. The betrayal of American scholarship by the encomiums heaped on Mr. Blanshard's book has done more to produce what has been called the "tension" between Catholic and non-Catholic Americans than all of Mr. Blanshard's inaccuracies and insults put together.[94]

O'Neill sketches in three chapters the history of the church in the United States, focusing primarily on its support of the Constitution and of American freedoms. He then deals in order with the church and the separation clause of the Constitution, democracy, religious freedom, Catholic education, censorship, social policy, medicine, and papal infallibility, all of which Blanshard had especially fixed on to prove his thesis. Then he answers Blanshard's attack on American Catholics by reviewing the flaws in Blanshard's use of documents, Blanshard's correction of Catholic propaganda, and his presentation of the "Catholic Plan for America." O'Neill reviews Blanshard's reviewers, favorable and unfavorable, and then projects what he calls Blanshard's own "Plan for America." He does this with careful attention to the presuppositions and implications of Blanshard's claims, to the logic of his arguments and his use of language, to his distortions of documentary evidence and his failure to produce evidence of any sort of most of his charges, and to Blanshard's own worldview. This is a smart, well-written, and tough piece of polemic that cannot but have bothered Blanshard and his secularist confreres had they read it.

O'Neill argued that Blanshard wrote a sloppy and biased book on an important topic, and that the genuine point of conflict and tension is not between the church and the national ideal, but between the church and Blanshard's secularist and statist version of that ideal. Blanshard added a dimension to Morse, Beecher, and Strong: he supposes a world in which nothing transcends the decisions and interests of the citizens and their state as these are defined from an entirely secularist point of view.

Blanshard was mistaken, O'Neill claims, in three of his most important criticisms. O'Neill was an established expert in the history of the constitutional separation of church and state. Blanshard's first mistake was to assume that "separation" is total, and that the famous Jeffersonian metaphor of the "wall" is in fact the meaning of the amendment. But for one hundred and fifty years the "establishment" eschewed by the First Amendment meant an exclusive arrangement created by government giving preferential treatment to one religion over others, that is, it forbade only discrimination in government policy. Liberal intellectuals carried some evangelicals along with them in a long campaign to change the amendment's meaning from anti-establishment to a "wall" forbidding even nondiscriminatory support or cooperation.[95] This effort brought to its term the secularization of the schools, which had been the objective of many educators over the previous half-century. The traditional understanding of cooperation between the government and religion expressed by the majority of the Supreme Court in the Everson bus case (1947) and then set aside the following year in the McCollum decision, codified what in effect was an informal amendment of the Constitution.[96]

In other words, what Blanshard blamed the Catholics for holding is in fact the traditional legal interpretation of the amendment, while he himself pushed the recent secularist version announced by Justices Black and Rutledge. Catholic leaders support separation when it does not involve discrimination against religion and consequent secularization of the public order, and in doing so they thought they were in line with the thinking of the framers. What forced the secularization of the public schools, which were in fact Protestant at the outset, was the danger of the application of the amendment as originally conceived and so the danger of nondiscriminatory aid to Catholic and other religious schools.

Second, Blanshard maintained the incompatibility of Catholicism and democracy, and proclaimed the Church's preference for authoritarian forms of government. O'Neill counters that the Catholic Church doesn't "approve" *forms* of government; it either approves or disapproves of the *actions* of governments.

The church does not "favor" governmental and political systems. However, Catholic citizens may favor political systems. The historical record of the American Catholics, both clergy and lay, gives close to unanimous support to the American form of democracy. But Blanshard was not appeased by the record in this matter. He was not able to get past the fact that the church is a "foreign power with international jurisdiction" in which a hierarchy exercises "totalitarian" control over the lower clergy and laity. What Blanshard wanted, wrote O'Neill, was a democratically organized church, which is simply "one agency of the state . . . a private organization trying to do some good which is agreeable to 'the will of the people' as a whole," much like the American Civil Liberties Union or the League of Women Voters.[97] This cannot be done, said O'Neill, without the Catholic Church ceasing to be Catholic. But then neither Protestantism nor Judaism could meet his demand for conformity to the will of the majority. Neither of them can offer unconditional acceptance of the state and its laws. Rather than Catholic authoritarianism, we should be concerned about Blanshard's "totalitarian philosophy of the omnipotent state."[98] In fact, O'Neill's criticism amounts to a charge that Blanshard has switched religions, from Christianity to Statism.

Third, Blanshard's designation of Spain as the ideal Catholic state and his use of it to indicate the Catholic threat to American freedom of religion revealed a great deal about Blanshard's methods. According to O'Neill, who was far from defending the Spanish constitution and government action in these matters, Blanshard ignored the recent comparative research on seventy-two national constitutions published by a Protestant scholar.[99] The research showed that "the record of Catholic and Protestant civic units in the matter of granting religious liberty is about equal. . . ."[100] Sweden balanced Spain, so to speak.[101] Why did not this substantial study and its conclusions have impact on Blanshard's considerations? Once again, his abhorrence of the Catholic notions of "two perfect societies" and the "two powers" that forbid church submission to the state and to democratic majoritarianism, made it impossible for Blanshard to see research evidence that might have countered his thesis, and renders him unable to read and absorb the American Catholic historical record on religious liberty. Like many of the Protestant critics of Catholicism who assume an identity of American Christianity and Protestantism, Blanshard assumes that the real America is his secularist America, a surprising piece of naivete for a democratic pluralist.

Blanshard's book is in the long American Protestant tradition from Cotton, Mayhew, Morse, Beecher, and Strong but also a part of the broader modernist worry about the Roman Catholic Church. Blanshard's concerns echo those of Gladstone, Friedrich Nippold, H. G. Wells, Avro Manhattan, and James Hastings Nichols in their political distrust of the "Catholic system," namely, the conflict between an authoritarian religious institution and a populist democracy, whether the latter be in an ecclesiastical or a civic community.[102] From this perspective, the Catholic Church is inverted, upside down, incompatible with any political or religious organization that accepts the basic laicism of the Reformation, the Enlightenment, and modernity. O'Neill, for his part, also stood in a long tradition, namely, that of American Catholic Church leaders who have practiced and believed that a religious community that recognizes and accepts apostolic authority in its present embodiment is no threat to political democracy. Indeed, the case is quite the contrary. As de Tocqueville wrote:

> I think it is wrong to look on the Catholic religion as by its very na-
> ture hostile to democracy. Of all the various interpretations of Chris-
> tianity, Catholicism strikes me as by far the one most favorable to
> the equality of [social and political] conditions. In Catholicism, the
> religious community is made up of two elements only: priest and
> people. Only the priest is raised above the rest of the faithful. All
> below him are equal. In Catholicism, so far as dogma is concerned,
> men of every degree of intelligence are placed on the same level.
> The wise man and the ignoramus, the man of genius and the man
> in the street, all are subject to the same creed in all its details.
>       . . . It strikes no bargain with any child of the earth, and, weigh-
> ing each man by the same standard, it brings every class of society
> without distinction to the foot of the same altar, just as such distinc-
> tions are confounded in the sight of God.[103]

My task has not been to refute but to recount the challenge posed to American Protestants and liberals by the Catholic Church, namely, its authoritarian and hierarchic structure, its supranational character, its forthrightness (not to say aggression) in pursuing its social, political, and moral agenda, the tightness of its discipline and its consistent rejection of individual liberties, its conviction of unique divine foundation, its independence and aloofness, its particular and peculiar moral code. The church's record of acceptance of American political arrangements for two centuries was not enough to offset the fears of fellow citizens. Only in the last forty years have we seen a significant lessening of those fears.

I also have attempted to distinguish three aspects of the challenge that the presence of a large and active Catholic Church has posed in the nation's history. First, it was, and remains, the church of millions of immigrants, and those who objected to uncontrolled immigration found it bothersome. Some of this opposition is connected with ethnicism and racism. Second, there were serious tensions to be resolved between American political ideals and Roman Catholic Church structure and practice. The men discussed in this chapter we found to be not nativists in the sense that they opposed all immigration, or even the immigration of ethnic groups from Southern and central Europe because they were not up to the standards of Anglo-Saxons (Josiah Strong's is the exception here). These men were opposed to Catholicism on political grounds primarily, whatever their ethnic sensibilities might have been. Finally, we saw the deeper and wider stream of Protestant hostility to the Roman Catholic Church as a religion. We turn now to that companion stream, the religious and theological objections. The Roman Church has been the object of suspicion and rejection as a Christian communion since colonial days by American evangelical Protestants.

# PART II

# Paul Speaks of Peter

# 4

# Roots

The Reformers and the Antichrist

Between 1512 and 1515, Martin Luther identified the enemy of the true gospel he had discovered in his meditations on Paul's letters to Rome and Galatia, and he pinned down the supernatural character of that enemy.[1] His construction of a reformed Christian faith had begun with the "tower experience" in those years. While the experience itself may have been religious, it had immediate political as well as ecclesiological implications. The Donation of Constantine had for several centuries played a key role in the papacy's justification of its claims of primacy over the patriarchs of the Eastern churches, its dominance of the Western church, and its political and territorial rights in the West.[2] In 1440 Lorenzo Valla (1406–57), a humanist scholar and severe critic of the papacy, had exposed the Donation as an impious rather than pious fraud. Luther, when still a monk, became an admirer and avid reader of Valla's works. In 1520, the same year in which Luther authored *De captivitate babylonica ecclesiae,* his indictment of Roman corruption of the Christian gospel, he wrote to Georg Spalatin, his fellow monk and close friend, that the exposure of the Donation of Constantine led him to conclude that the pope was the Antichrist. Not only was the Roman exegesis of Matthew 16:18 a tortured bit of ideological posturing, but the entire historical foundation of the papal claim to leadership of the church and to political headship in Europe had been proved a lie.

The Donation was in fact a political forgery, backing the popes' struggle against imperial iconoclasm. Luther's deduction from the lie to its supernatural source ought not to be particularly startling—no forgery of this sort could be other than satanic to a mind and soul like Luther's and in a time like his. Judgments of a similar nature were made of him by his Roman opponents.[3] The judgment shaped Luther's attitude toward Rome from the earliest days of his efforts at reform. Especially in his last years, when it was evident that the reform was being successfully resisted by Rome and internal tensions in the reformation movement mounted, the Augustinian clash of the forces of evil and good, the false church and the true church, dominated his religious imagination. Luther's growing expectations of the End, the pressure of politics (Rome, the Holy Roman Empire, the princes, the Turks, and even his fellow reformers), and the routinization of the reform itself provided the context for his later teaching on the Roman church. He had good reason to be morose and fearful, for it looked to him as if the enemies of the gospel were gaining strength.

The Council of Trent met for the first time in 1545. In that same year, the year before he died, Luther published *Against the Papacy at Rome, Founded by the Devil*, a scathing renewal of his thirty-year denunciation of the doctrinal and ethical condition of the Roman church, accompanied by apocalyptic and scatological woodcuts on the papacy.[4] Displaying his lack of hope that the convening Council of Trent would heal the break between the reformers and Rome, Luther set out in *Against the Papacy* to explain theologically Christendom's ghastly state of affairs:

> Rather [the pope] is the head of the accursed church of the very worst rascals on earth; vicar of the devil; an enemy of God; an opponent of Christ; and a destroyer of the church of Christ; a teacher of all lies, blasphemy, and idolatries; an arch-church-thief and church-robber of the keys [and] all the goods of both the church and the secular lords; a murderer of kings and inciter of all sorts of bloodshed; a brothel-keeper above all brothel-keepers and all lewdness, including that which is not to be named; an Antichrist; a man of sin and child of perdition; a true werewolf.[5]

The pope was not only an enemy of reform; he was Antichrist, while the Turk was merely the Devil incarnate, GOG, and "the little horn" of Daniel, and Luther's Protestant critics were false prophets, all of them signs of the end time.[6] Luther's fear of "the Turk" as a threat to Europe ceded to his fear of the papacy though it was the chief organizer of opposition to the advance of the Ottoman empire. But, although the Turks were straightforward in their wish to destroy the church of Christ, the Arch Liar in the Vatican ruled and perverted the church. The Antichrist in Rome had produced a Roman antichurch:

> But for us the pope is the true Antichrist who has the high, subtle, beautiful, glittering devil, who sits inside Christendom, allows the

holy Scripture, baptism, Sacrament, keys, catechism, [and] marriage
to remain. As St. Paul says, he sits (that is, rules) in God's temple,
that is, in the Church or Christendom, namely among such people
that have baptism, the Sacrament, the keys, the holy Scripture and
God's word. And nevertheless he rules so masterfully that he at the
same time elevates his "decraptals," his Koran, his human teaching
above God's word. . . . Christ and Paul prophesied that the pope
should sit in God's temple, pass himself off as God, and do many
false signs and wonders. If you wish to know what these wonders
are, then read the legends of the saints, the monks, the pilgrimages,
the masses, and the like—then you will indeed see what false signs
are and what sorts of wonders the poltergeists and pilgrimage-devils,
saint worship or prayers have accomplished in all the corners of
Christendom.[7]

Yes, one fears being conquered in battle and enslaved by the Muslim enemy of God. But one even more fears the millennium-old web of deception,
of dissimulation and simulation, wherein many of the forms of true Christianity are retained and only its reverse and perverse meanings are contained.
What is proclaimed as freedom produces slavery, what appears to be Christ is
not, what appears to be the true gospel and holy sacrament are not, what
appears to be a shepherd of Christ's flock is a minion of Hell. Behind these
masks of Christian life there lurks only eternal death. For Luther, Rome is
something much more terrible than an apostate church, which is led from
Christian faith by Satan. The Roman church is a sacrament of Satan under
whose appearances or "accidents" there lurks the substance of evil.

John Calvin (1509–64) agreed fully. He had published several editions of
*The Institutes of the Christian Religion* before the Council of Trent met in 1545.
There he echoed the tale of the Roman Antichrist told by Luther:[8]

Daniel and Paul had predicted that Antichrist would sit in the temple of God (Dan ix.27; 2 Thess. ii.3, 4). The head of that cursed and
abominable kingdom, in the Western Church, we affirm to be the
Pope. When his seat is placed in the temple of God, it suggests, that
his kingdom will be such, that he will not abolish the name of
Christ, or the Church. Hence it appears, that we by no means deny
that Churches may exist, even under his tyranny; but he has pro-
faned them by sacrilegious impiety, afflicted them by cruel despotism, corrupted and almost terminated their existence by false and
pernicious doctrines, like poisonous potions; in such churches,
Christ lies half buried, the gospel is suppressed, piety exterminated,
and the worship of God almost abolished; in a word they are altogether in such a state of confusion, that they exhibit a picture of
Babylon, rather than that of the holy city of God.[9]

. . . Now, when he (Paul, in 2 Thess ii.4) designates Antichrist by this character,—that he would rob God of his honour in order to assume it himself,—this is the principal indication which we ought to follow in our inquiries after Antichrist, especially where such pride proceeds to a public desolation of the Church. As it is evident therefore that the Roman pontiff has impudently transferred to himself some of the peculiar and exclusive prerogatives of God and Christ, it cannot be doubted that he is the captain and leader of this impious and abominable kingdom.[10]

Although we do find some reserve in his judgment of all Roman Catholic churches (there are some believers in it, and there may even be "true churches" among them), the condemnation is unremitting and the final statement clear: it is an apostate church, the Antichrist, and the enemy of all believers and all true churches.[11] The Roman church in the view of the great reformers was the legion of the Antichrist, a false church, a heretical and an apostate church. So evil its "system," so corrupt in doctrine and practice, that it can only be adequately dealt with in the language of apocalyptic invented to pierce through an opaque history to its roots in the infernal mind. The Reformation was thus inextricably tied to Manichean [and Johannine!] rhetoric.

## A Seventeenth-Century British Dialogue and Comparative Apologetics

The evangelical mind, on the subject of Catholicism and the papacy, reached its mature judgment with Luther and Calvin. There would seem to be little left to say. Oliver Ormerod's (d. 1626) volume, *The Picture of a Papist* (1606), is a series of dialogues between a Church of England minister, neither high church nor Puritan, and a Roman Catholic Recusant (a Catholic who refused to attend Anglican services). It was dedicated to Robert Cecil, earl of Salisbury and royal counselor, who directed the investigation and prosecution of the Catholics involved in the Gunpowder Plot of 1605.[12] The minister is pictured as learned, theologically astute, masterful, and loyally, perhaps blindly, supportive of the Protestant crown. His intellectual interests and skills are circumscribed by his polemical purposes. The recusant got little to say except to offer an occasional shocked protest, which sends the minister off on another polemical tirade. Ormerod's text is important because he is not a Puritan and Calvinist, and thereby shows just how wide and powerful is the stream of anti-Romanism in the English church.

There are several layers of intent. The political intention appears insofar as Ormerod is showing his devotion to the most important man in England next to the king and in effect becoming a publicist for Cecil—hoping perhaps for a return of support from his prospective patron who also happened to be the chancellor of the university in which Ormerod worked. The papists pose a serious danger to the civil order, to the safety of the king and to the government that Cecil protected. But Ormerod's intent is religious as well insofar as he wishes to expose heresy and refute it, and to bring the papists round to a better mind. Finally, the work is comparative insofar as he can show that papism is of pagan and Jewish inspiration, and bears comparison with the infamous "Turk" and their faith and religious practice (a charge common to the Protestant critique of Catholicism at the time).[13] He also recounts the sufferings of the conspirators and justifies the cruelty of their execution.[14] His purpose stated to Salisbury in the Dedication is to "estrange peoples minds from them (the papists), to alienate their affections, and to bringe them quite out of loue of their doctrine, and out of liking of their persons." He wants to turn the crowd against the Roman Catholic Church and to offset criticism of the crown and of Cecil for harsh judgment and the cruelty of the executions.

The fact that he recounts the trial and execution of six of the conspirators and not that of Henry Garnett, S.J., the only Jesuit charged, would place the earliest time of completion of the final version of the script in February 1606. The "Jesuites" come in for a beating throughout. One of the subtexts for the book might be to tar them again. For example, Robert Cardinal Bellarmine, a Jesuit and the "Archpapist," is quoted more than any Catholic author. But if so, then it is odd in the extreme that Ormerod makes no mention of Garnett at all, either his trial or execution. This would lead one to believe that the final copy may have been handed to the printer after the trial and execution of the six lay plotters and before the trial and execution of Fr. Garnett. Garnett was likely tried on March 28 and executed on May 3, 1606, while the others had been executed in January. By the book Ormerod makes himself part of the effort to "get the story out" from the government side. One also might suspect that the dialogues *sans* plot were ready for the printer when the plot was exposed and so Ormerod popped the plot into the script. He tells us nothing of the persecution of recusant Catholics which triggered the plot in the first place.

Ormerod supplies the same thematic content of the earlier and later anti-Roman polemics, but with somewhat different emphases. For example, although an account of opposed principles of salvation, Protestant grace, and Roman Catholic works is offered, it is not a major concern. There is far more in this work on idolatry in every facet of Catholic religious practice, more on the intellectual shallowness of Catholic beliefs (transubstantiation) than on salvation by faith alone through grace alone. He makes not so much a reformed as an Anglican case. In this sense, at least he leads directly on to Mayhew's sermon in two ways: by concentrating on idolatry and on the contradiction between transubstantiation and common sense.

When the minister arrives on the scene he finds the papist praying before a crucifix. Papists are Staurolatrians he informs us: they "crouche" to the "Cru-

cifixe." It is "idolatrie." The ancient councils and the fathers opposed worship
of images, and the scriptures condemn it. The minister smashes the crucifix,
citing Exodus 34:13 and Exodus 32:20. He says he is neither a pagan nor a
puritan, and even uses the sign of the cross himself in baptism, as it is not
superstitious to put us in mind of the cross of Christ. Papists also worship
statues of saints, turning Christianity into polytheism. The minister's comment: "O grosse! What a number of gods haue you?" Mary intercedes, merits,
and commands the Redeemer, shows mercy, and takes the role of Christ. So
they are gods. But the saints are dead and not here. The dead do not know the
"deedes of the liuing," and so cannot intercede for them.[15]

In *The Third Diologue* [sic],[16] the minister announces "great newes": Thomas Percie [sic] and "other Popish Gentlemen are discovered to haue contriued
to most horrible treason that euer entered into the hearts of men. They intended to massacre the king, the queen our fertile mother, and the olive plants,
the clergie, nobilitie, the councellors, and the grauve judges, . . .". He ends his
description of the plot and its intended effects with a plea for the conversion
of the recusant. The story of the plot is the official version drawn from the trial
records and repeated in the latest edition of the *Encyclopedia Britannica*. The
recusant responds that he will not convert because "your religion is a new
religion." The minister is not surprised: "It is no wonder to hear an hereticke
bragge of antiquitie, for it hath beene all the vsuall manner of heretickes in all
ages, to take vnto themslues the Chuch [sic], Scriptures, fathers, all antiquitie,
consent, continuance, and perpetuitie vnto the ende of the world."[17]

Once it is clear that Catholicism is a modified form of paganism, Ormerod
turns to the "semblances" between Catholics and Jews. The Catholics are like
the Nazirites because they mingle Jewish ceremonies with Christian religion.
He compares them to Pharisees.[18] Catholics are hypocrites, minding the little
things of the law and ignoring the great; they root in antiquity, count on works
for salvation, follow the traditions of men rather than the word of God, and
are legalists and sophists.[19] The Jews thought that the expositions of the "Rab-
bines" was authoritative—as Catholics do the pope's exposition of scripture.
"O horrible blasphemie! . . . To be plaine with you, had wee no other cause to
condemn you for heretickes; yet this one (me thinks) should be sufficient."[20]
Catholics are Jews as well as pagans. Then, in *The Fourth* [in fact, the Third]
*Diologue,* the papists are made out to be as bad or worse than the "Turkes."

The recusant gets to tell how the Gunpowder Plot was foiled.[21] The minister eloquently attributes the unthinkable crime of regicide to Catholics,
shown from scripture (David didn't kill Saul, after all). The recusant denies
that he had anything to do with it, and asks why he should be taxed with the
crime. Says the minister: "What though you be not [i.e., in this case]? A Scor-
pion you know hath his stinge within him, though hee doth not alwaies strike:
and a grounded Papist (I know) carrieth alwaies a woluish nature, which pre-
pares him euer to the spoyle, though hee neuer did hurt."[22] The recusant

continues the story of the plot. The minister then describes what he hopes will be the death of the traitor, looking forward to and perhaps preparing the reader for the description of the event.[23] All this allows the minister to denounce the Catholic plotters as "vile miscreants, machiavellians, blood-suckers, matchless villaines, dogged dogs, bloody-minded Joabs." The recusant tells him that he insults the pope, may be excommunicated, and then may be lawfully killed by "any Catholike." The minister responds: the whole history of the church rejects regicide, as it does the authority of the pope over princes, and even the authority of pope over bishops.[24] In fact, the pope takes the things that belong to God: he claims infinite knowledge and power, claims to be the cause of causes, the God of revenge, to be Lord God, Christ, feared as God, commander of angels, equal and even superior in authority to the scriptures, and to have the power to forgive sins, the power over the laws of God. Even worse, he claims to be God—he must then be "sonne of perdition and that aduersarie, prophecied of by Saint Paul, 2 Thess. 2." The minister will admit no reason to justify the "murther" of the king.[25] The central charge to be carried throughout the later English-speaking tradition is laid out:

> 1. That your religion bindeth you all to play the traytours, and to take vp armes against your countrey.
> 2. That the reason why you do not take up armes against your coun-
> try, is only becavse you haue not the power sufficient to match us:
> for had you sufficient power, your Romish Doctours would hold you
> inexcusable, if you did it not. You may therefore fitly be compared to
> serpents, which may bee handled, whilst the cold hath benummed
> them; but when they are warmed, they will hisse out their vene-
> mous poyson. My meaning is no mysterie: if you bee harboured a
> while longer in the bosome of the common wealth, you will in time
> get such warmth, & become of such a competent strength, as that
> you will be able to match us, if not overmatch us. But I doubt not,
> but that his Maiestie and the state will look to this betimes, and not
> nurse vppe Lyons whelps for their owne overthrowe . . .[26]

Are Catholics "Turkish"? Yes, there are twenty-five "semblances." For example, although the see of Rome was once "the eye of the west, and the anchor of true pietie," now it has fallen, like the other ancient patriarchies, into idolatry and apostasy "about the year of our Lord 607 . . . [when] . . . Boniface III [who was the first anti-Christian Bishop of Rome] take vnto himself the title of vniversal Bishop, and since then all his successours haue taken vnto them the same Antichristian title." This at the very time when Mahomet took over the Eastern churches, indicating, we are left to conclude, that Satan is at work! Saracens, too, were "traitours to the Emperor Heraclius, they are robbers and villaines, murtherers, cruel, heretickes, oppressors toward other religions, and so forth, like the popes." A six-page denunciation of the inquisition and description of its excruciating tortures of Protestants follows. "The Whore of Babylon is drunken with the blood of the Saints, and with the blood of the Martyrs of Jesus." The "Alcoran" is like the Romish tradition, adding to the scriptural revelation; the popes, like the Alcoran, are taken to be superior to the scriptures. At the end, after the twenty-fifth semblance, the recusant asks: are RCs worse than the Turks?[27]

> Yes, for there is (that I may vse his Maiesties words) no other Sect of Heretiques, not excepting Turke, Jewe, nor Pagan, no, not even those of Calicute [Hindus], who adore the Deuill, that maintaine by the groundes of their Religion, that it is lawfull, or rather Meritori-ous (as the Romish Catholickes call it) to murther Princes or people for the quarrell of Religion.[28]

Ormerod echoes a combination of religious and political animosity present from the very beginning of the Reform. The religious differences and political fears run through the literature to the present. The intimate tie-in of the religious and the political concerns and arguments is, if anything, intensified in the British Protestant tradition. Ormerod shows that the theological arguments are not the only ones, nor are theological concerns necessarily dominant. The Catholic Church is clearly a political threat that must be dealt with by political means. Although there is considerable sarcasm about Catholic beliefs and practice, the political motif is in control and the religious conviction of Luther and Calvin is modified by it. Second, there is a rush "through secondary to primary causes": this plot, in the contemporary view, was a Catholic plot rather than a plot hatched by a hotheaded and rather ungainly bunch of young Catholics. Third, the dominant and controlling theological criticism is the idolatry of Catholic practice and belief. Finally, note the twofold historical-comparative argument: Catholicism is an outgrowth of Judaism and Hellenistic paganism, and in essential features closely resembles Islam. The university disciplines comparative religion and comparative theology may have had their start in this fertile soil.

## Colonial Ministers: John Cotton and Jonathan Mayhew

John Cotton's death in 1652 ended an outstanding forty-year career as a Puritan teacher and preacher in old and New England.[29] Educated at Cambridge University under two Puritans, he became pastor in a well-to-do church in Boston, Lincolnshire, in 1612. He left that church and England when William Laud became archbishop of Canterbury in 1633 and shipped out to the Massachusetts Bay Colony. Laud was too much the high churchman and anti-Calvinist for Cotton, who must have anticipated severe restrictions on the congregational autonomy he regarded as essential for any authentic Christian church.

Appointed a teacher in Boston's first church on his arrival in 1633, Cotton was immediately among the leading men of the New England Puritan establishment. He must have been a talented preacher and teacher to have held two congregations for twenty years each. He proved influential in theology and church organization as well. His strong views on the latter are evident in *An exposition*. He made a clear and consistent congregationalist argument, and was strongly opposed to geographic, episcopal (both Roman and Anglican) diocesan organization inherited from medieval Christendom. In fact, he viewed such supracongregational organization as the chief evil afflicting the churches and, in the case of Rome, an instrument of the Antichrist. In addition, he contributed to the Cambridge Platform of 1648, especially in the matter of the "relation of saving grace" as a condition of full membership in the New England churches. Had he lived long enough, he probably would have had grave reservations about the Half-Way Covenant of 1656–59, a compromise that marked the end of the great American experiment with the public church as a community of saints.[30]

Cotton's particular view of the relationship between the civil magistry and the congregation, a hybrid offspring of medieval Christendom (I am sure he would be quite put out by this suggestion), brought him to stand against Roger Williams's demand for radical separation of church from the state and to stand just as firmly for the civil magistracy as enforcer of the purity of church doctrine and practice. In Williams, we have a thorough break with the ideal of Christendom, something even so radical an ecclesiologist as Cotton could not take in. For Cotton, secular power remained responsible for support of the church, financial but even to the exile or execution of the citizen. He clung to the magistrates' power to correct church abuses, but only at the call of the ministry, with no power over the church itself, its teaching and its life.[31]

Anne Hutchinson (d. 1643), a Cotton devotee in England, followed Cotton to Boston with her family. In 1635 she set up shop in her home as an increasingly influential lay teacher, inspiring others to protest against the preaching of the ministers. When she was accused of antinomian heresy, Cotton turned against her in her trial in 1637 and in 1638 agreed to her excommunication and exile, providing history with a perfect example of his unnoticed compromise of congregationalism with Christendom. He found it impossible in the shadow of the medieval notion to work out much more than the intimations of a distinction between church and state, and between church and civil society. Anne Hutchinson effectively made public what Cotton had taught her in England about the direct, unmediated presence of the Holy Ghost in the soul of the justified, but she had added a bit of pepper: she downplayed (or even eliminated, according to her accusers) the decisive role of the Puritan ministers in determining true doctrine and correct practice. Cotton could not in the end support direct revelation to the Christian soul from an unmediated God. A mediated revelation (scripture) and a mediating ministry stood side by side in

Cotton's theory of the church. He failed to note the Catholic undertones to his solution to the problem he helped to create when he opted for congregational autonomy coupled with state maintenance.

The myth of church decline, the demonic seizure of the church, and the revival of the authentic New Testament church marks Cotton's meditation on the book of Revelation:

> ... [The churches] had a time to be established by the Apostles, and such as they appointed: Afterward they grew to a dead frame. And as they had time of dying, that is to say of deformation, of Apostasy by the Catholicke Mother Church, so afterward they came to a new Reformation, such a Reformation as doth not only reforme the outward face of Government and Doctrine, but the inward frame of the Members of the church ... that they do arise to a lively Faith ...[32]

Nonetheless, it remained difficult to find a true Christian church in Christendom. So far as Cotton was concerned, there was little difference between episcopacy in the Church of England of which he was a (subversive) member and Catholic popery in respect to this ecclesiological impurity.[33] The Reformation did not end Satan's many instruments of perversion of the gospel.

As a Puritan, Cotton was interested in formulating doctrines in the course of preaching the Word of God. On the last pages of his commentary on Revelation 13, he does so:

> The Bishop of Rome exercises all the authority of the first Beast, that is, of the Roman visible Catholick church, he causeth all that dwell on the Earth to worship that church, he doth worke wonders, even to the fetching of fire from Heaven, and by his wonders procures all christian States to make an Image to the first Beast, and gives such life and power to the image of the Beast that it is able to speak, and it shall cause such as do not worship it to be put to death, and finally he leave an impression, or imprints a character upon all sorts of Christians, and will suffer none to enjoy spirituall or civill communion with them, unless such will receive either his mark, or his name, or the number of his name.[34]

The Beast in Revelation 13 is neither pagan Rome nor Rome under Christian emperors, although certainly Satan was behind them, too.[35] No, the first beast, the one who rises from the sea, is "the Roman Catholick visible Church," and the second beast, charged by Satan with the task of seducing all to worship the first beast, is the pope himself. The second beast had two horns: temporal and spiritual sovereignty, signifying the basic structural relation of church and state in medieval Christendom. The "wound" that marked the first beast is the barbarian invasions that many thought would be the end of Rome, but in 606

CE,[36] Boniface III was given universal jurisdiction and authority over all Christian churches by the emperor (the wound was "healed" and thus "amazed" everyone), and so the pope became the second, earth-born beast.[37] The whole world was his diocese! Universal dominion provides Cotton's clue. Satan tipped his hand by voiding the early church's, and Cotton's, congregational structure.

The first beast is the organized "Roman Catholick visible church": Bishops, archbishops, metropolitans, patriarchs, and then one, the pope. Cotton himself believed in no visible church aside from the local congregation. Any other church is invisible, formed by the people possessed of faith; the visible universal church is the church of the devil. Thus the doctrine, "The visible Catholick Roman Church is in the esteem of the holy Ghost a monstrous Beast." One might say that the second and third adjectives are as important to Cotton as the first, and that they in fact denominate the crucial historical instance of the practical and theological distortions (visibility/geographic extension tied to universality through the papacy) fostered by satanic power. "This is a Catholick Church of the Devil, but not of Christ."[38]

Cotton's problem is as much with ecclesiastical organization as with *Roman* organization. His objection to the unified organization includes not only imposed doctrine and religious practice, but also the papal domination of civil authority and its claim to the power to depose and set up kings, along with a corresponding immunity from all civil authority.[39] Cotton writes as if there are a visible secular realm and an invisible spiritual realm, carefully distinguished. The Roman Catholic view is otherwise: two perfect societies, both visible, one superior to the other and the secular obliged to recognize the prior and superior objectives of the sacred—the theory of medieval Christendom. Even when not explicitly mentioned, medieval Christendom is an ever-present and negative reality for Cotton. Palpable fear of its revival drives a lot of the worry about the Catholic Church, even though the Puritans seemed to have produced a modified version of it themselves in the New England Way.

> . . . [I]t [the doctrine of the church] may teach us how those Christian Protestant Churches wrong themselves that leave any footsteps of this [papal] government in their Churches: For that is part of the image of the beast; for the second beast, when he was advanced, he would have an image of the first beast, they must have Provinciall and Diocesan Churches, and National Churches, and carry I know not how many hundred congregations into one National Church, and there must be some Diocesan and Metropolitan church, and the rest must be inferior to that. Though this be not so great a monster as the great Beast, yet it is an image of this beast . . .[40]

Satan gave the Roman church power of signs and wonders, effectual sophistry, deceit and unrighteousness, and the power to make war on the saints;

authority over scripture, the consciences of men, and the treasury of the church, over kingdoms and commonwealths, over even the estate of the life to come.[41]

For Cotton as for Ormerod, the Catholic Church is the dark opposite of the gospel truth: Catholics worship not the reality but images; instead of the ministry of Christ you have doctrines of men; instead of justification by the righteousness of Christ, you have justification by works; instead of pardon of sin from Christ, you have it from the pope. "All things are in another forme, an Image of another forme set up, devised, contrary to what the word establisheth . . ." The charge that a Satanic Catholicism as the reverse of true Christianity makes psychological sense, every affirmative having its negative. Catholicism is a Christianity of fallen nature, could there be such a thing:

These foure things were all the matter of their Sermons, Vertue and vice, Heaven and Hell; if you be vertuous, then you shall go to Heaven; If you be vicious, then you must go to Hell: Now they would so convince men's consciences, and upon conviction binde the conscience under terror, as eternally shut out of Heaven, for want of vertue, which they had not; that indeed when these men's consciences are thus perplexed and wounded, here is a religion that finds them so many salves and medicines, as ease the power, but not remove the cause of the disease; that is, they set men a course; well, though you be vicious, and though Hell be dreadfull, yet Purgatory may ease you by prayer, and you may be dispensed with from going to Hell, especially by the Pope's pardon, or by your own works, by your confessions, by selfe-whippings and scourgings, or by going on a Pilgrimage, you may be discharged of this burden; This was very plausible to carnall reason, especially if they gave so much to such a Monastery, that they may offer so many Sacraments for them (for they look at the bread in the Lord's supper as a propitiatory Sacrament:) here were so many means to satisfy the consciences of those that were superstitious, as nothing could be devised to give better content to the spirits of men in those dayes: any man that knows it, shall finde it true, that when the conscience is terrified with the curse of Gods law, and never shewed the true way of fellowship with Christ, no man is so tender and conscionable in the performance of all duties as they: If you will have them kisse the Popes foot, or give so much to a Monastery; and by this means Hell shall be shut against them, and Purgatory discharged: But for the assurance of Salvation in Christ, they could not endure that; they that stood for that, they tell them, what, will you not have men doe good workes, away with that, faggot and halter for such Hereticks.[42]

What explains the success of the Roman Church? he asks. Its appeal to the natural person: for the eyes, images; for the ears, "curious musique"; for the smell, incense, and "sweet perfumes"; for taste, "many feasts full of luxury and ryot"; for the touch, the "toleration of Stews." That church appeals to natural reason: an implicit faith, that is believing in what the church believes rather than what scripture and the Holy Ghost teach the soul; progressive steps in repentance; obedience to the whole Law of God an easy achievement; pardon for money and bodily exercises; uncertainty of salvation; ecclesiastical order and unity. It appeals to natural conscience: works foreseen; redemption of all men alike; conversion by free will; perseverance by works; glorification by merits of work. The appeal of Satan to natural desire and reflection is the foundation of the evil empire of Roman Catholicism. So persuasive, so devilish, is this appeal that the Puritans' own ancestors were taken in by this for more than a thousand years.[43] Cotton's mastery of the sovereign freedom by which God gives the gift of salvation and of the *sola fide* enables him to deliver this profound criticism of the Catholic conception of Christian faith and practice.

No Christian person or true church could have a share in the Catholic Church (as one might have a share in the Anglican church?) because: (1) the Catholic faith is perverse from beginning to end; (2) Catholics put salvation by merit and grace in place of salvation by grace alone, a Covenant of Works in the place of a Covenant of Grace; (3) they worship creatures, "the Church of Rome is known to go a whoring after the worship of Saints, and Angels, and Images, and the great Beast mentioned in the text, and the Pope the head of it"; and (4) their repentance is the repentance of Judas flinging the coins down, and it leads to despair; they require contrition and satisfaction, both of which undermine true Christian faith.[44]

Cotton approaches verse 18, and the mysterious number 666, gingerly. Nowhere else is he so tentative. He has powerful convictions that the beasts are the church and the papacy. But he leaves the judgment of the meaning of the number to the reader and expresses his own "meditations as God hath suggested to men." The best he can do in support of his interpretation is to point to the fact that Pope Boniface,[45] the first official "universal bishop," added a sixth book of canons to the five already in existence, and so "maketh up a certain plat-form [*sic*] of direction for all matters of practice and manners in the discipline of the Church, and so it is a perfect number of all things to be done in the church, both for doctrine, worship, and government: so the Pope's Canons are summed up in his *Sextus* . . . the Lawes of the *Antichrist* . . ." He falls back upon his prejudice against universal church order to find a basis in the text for that very prejudice! ". . . but the truth is, the King hath power to make Laws to rule the Church, but it must be by the laws of Christ."[46]

Cotton is careful not to fall into obsession with numerology in his commentary. What he means to provide the reader with is an insight into the history of Christianity and the sources of evil. While there is nothing new in his commentary, he has a particularly sharp grasp of the power and distinctiveness of Catholic analogical imagination and the danger it poses to the Puritan dialectical imagination. Catholicism is the siren call of nature undermining the supernatural gift of Christian faith. Surely the congregational order that he favors decisively is important to his understanding of the Catholic Church, but more important yet is his objection to the imagination undisciplined by Scripture. The Catholic imagination skips through nature and history, and even through Judaism and paganism, finding by analogy traces of God here and there, snatching up the practices of unbelievers and even the godless political structure of the pagan empire, and imposes what it finds on the Christian faithful, while Protestant (Puritan) imagination accepts the discipline and limitations evident in sacred scripture.

Jonathan Mayhew's (1720–66) great-grandfather was among the original proprietors of Martha's Vineyard. His minister-father, Experience Mayhew, turned against Calvinism after the Great Awakening, and Jonathan's time at Harvard College inclined him to a rationalist, proto-unitarian version of Christianity. He became pastor at Boston's West Church in 1747. He espoused a three-proposition form of rational Christianity: that there is a natural difference between right and wrong, that "men" can naturally discern this difference, and that they have a natural obligation to do so. He was a dissenter politically, a critic of centralized civil government as well as church government, and was mentioned by John Adams as one of the earliest supporters of independence from England.[47] He had a bit of Cotton's fever when it came to local autonomy. Mayhew delivered the Dudlean Lecture in the Harvard Chapel in 1765. The series had been established to expose Catholicism to criticism.[48] Mayhew spoke on "the doctrine and practice of the church of Rome respecting the worship of the eucharist, saints and angels, pictures and images."[49]

At the Council of Trent (1545–62), Mayhew told his audience, the bishops taught that the Eucharist elements are to be accorded *latria*, the worship due to God alone. If they are wrong about transubstantiation, then they are guilty of idolatry. But they must be wrong:

> This doctrine is plainly absurd, self-repugnant, and impossible to be
> true, as any one that can be imagined. For what could be more so,
> than that bread and wine should be changed into the very body and
> blood of Christ? . . . [Besides the intrinsic absurdity,] this doctrine
> supposes also, that the same undivided body of Christ may be
> wholly on earth, and in ten million different places on earth, at the
> same time. . . . [that] Every apparent crumb of consecrated wafer,
> and each drop of consecrated wine, contains whole, intire [sic] Christ
> under that species; and yet, it is owned, there is but one Christ! Be-
> sides, this doctrine supposes, that when our Lord instituted the sup-

per, he took his whole body into his own hand, which was but a part of it; put himself into his own mouth, swallowed down his entire body into his stomach, and at the same time gave his body and blood to be wholly eaten and drunk by each of his apostles! Could the most fertile imagination invent grosser, more ridiculous, or more impious incongruities? The evidence of sense is the most certain, that we are capable of; and by this we know that transubstantiation is false.[50]

Charging that the priesthood imposed this on a superstitious, credulous humankind, Mayhew echoed the Enlightenment priestcraft charge as well as inherited Protestant polemic against the doctrine.[51] Like Ormerod, Mayhew saw Catholic belief and practice as idolatry clear and simple, identical to that of the "vulgar Pagans," falling short of the "more intelligent heathen . . ."?[52] However, unlike Ormerod and Cotton, Mayhew offers a perfectly naturalized and Satan-free explanation of the priestcraft and idolatry:

But worldly policy, as well as superstition, had some hand in establishing saint-worship. When Christian teachers became corrupt and worldly-minded, thro' the indiscrate [sic] zeal, or, perhaps, policy of Constantine the Great, they aimed more at increasing the number of nominal Christians, for secular ends, than that of real ones; or preserving their religion in its original purity and simplicity. And accordingly, observing how attached the Pagans were to the worship of their gods and demi-god [sic], to their magnificent temples, images, and the feasts kept in honor of their deities; the Christian leaders were for bringing them over, by imitating many of their customs. Then spacious churches were built, sumptiously adorned, and dedicated to the martyrs; pictures, images and altars were brought into use therein; and the formal invocation of saints encouraged. Thus Christians rivalled [sic], if not surpassed Pagans, in their own way, with a view to bring them over to the faith of Christ, at least to a profession of it. By which temporizing policy, as bishop Stillingfleet observes, christianity [sic] came at last to be little or nothing else but "reformed paganism," as to its external worship.[53]

Rome is, according to Mayhew, justly called "Babylon" because it slays the saints. This is no Satanic possession of the papacy as in Cotton nor a mystic reemergence of ancient Babylon, as later in Alexander Hyslop.[54] Although he displayed himself a diligent interpreter of scripture, he departed from Cotton's Manichean reading of Christian history.

But for him Rome is not only a threat to the Christian church. Mayhew turned to the political side of popery, bringing to it his suspicion of any governmental limitation of reason and rights, a limitation that he sees as intrinsic

to popery. Christendom is the enemy, whether Catholic or Protestant, as episcopacy and geographic order beyond the local church was the enemy to Cotton.
This is not a nativist conspiracy charge yet (the Irish and German Catholics
and their bishops hadn't arrived in force yet!), but it did provide grounds for
such a charge in the next century. Nor does Mayhew repeat the traditional
Protestant Satanic conspiracy theory.

> Detestable as the idolatry of the church of Rome is, there are other
> of her principles and practices, as has been intimated, which more
> immediately affect the peace and order of civil society, the honor of
> princes, and the liberty and common rights of mankind. Our contro-
> versy with her is not merely a religious one. It is not, on our part,
> only a defence of the worship of one God by one Mediator, in oppo-
> sition to that of a thousand demons and idols; of the authority of the
> sacred oracles [i.e., Scripture], in opposition to that of idle legends
> and traditions; and of sober reason in opposition to the grossest
> fanaticism: But [sic] a defence of our laws, liberties, and civil rights
> as men, in opposition to the proud claims and encroachments of ec-
> clesiastical persons, who under the pretext of religion, and saving
> mens [sic] souls, would engross all power and property to them-
> selves, and reduce us to the most abject slavery.[55]

Although Mayhew can field both theological and historical criticisms of
Roman practice in religious matters, those matters are "mere," while "laws,
liberties, and civil rights" must be protected against "ecclesiastical persons"
who would steal them. The supernatural myth has begun to produce its secularized twin, the enlightened democrat who fears Roman oppression. His
view of the Roman Catholic Church is in some respects in tune with his predecessors, although he broke with their doctrinal Calvinism and with their
Christian supernaturalism. The social and political objection was every bit as
sharp. Mayhew even worried about a Catholic resurgence in old England where
things in 1765 looked bad. "Popery is now making great strides . . . as great,
perhaps as it did in the reign either of Charles and James the second. . . .
Thousands of weak and wicked Protestants" are becoming Catholics. The Jesuits and priests are "very open and bold . . . , and even *popish bishops reside
there, and go about to exercise every part of their function, without offence*. . . .
Heaven only knows what the end of these things will be; the prospect is
alarming!" Agents of Rome are making proselytes in old England. God forbid
this should happen in New England![56] He had more than half a century to go
before his worries were met by the reality of the Catholic immigration.

The elements of the evangelical myth are well in place: declension and
demon possession. The myth enfolds not only the telling of Christian history
but politics as well, as it must. "Christendom" is the symbol for Catholics of

the ideal political order, and for Protestants of the dangers posed by the (feared) Catholic revival. The Protestant religious concerns are expressed in doctrinal argument and polemic, apocalyptic language, and inversion theories. The ammunition includes scripture, history and commonsense philosophical argument. We shall see those continuing, even as the context of the contest changes.

# 5

# The National Protest:
# Beginning in the Middle

## William Nevins and the Evangelical Outline

A contemporary of Morse and Beecher and their colleague in the
first wave of national no-popery, William Nevins (1797–1835) graduated from Yale University in 1816, and from Princeton Seminary in
1819. Ordained in 1820, he assumed the pastorate of the First Presbyterian Church of Baltimore and held it until his death in 1835. At
the beginning of the no-popery crusade, he wrote a series of essays
on the Catholic Church for the *New York Observer,* which were post-
humously collected in two volumes.[1] Remember that he was writing
in the midst of the first great outbreak of antipopery in the new nation, and in one of the leading no-popery newspapers, this one associated with Samuel Morse (Morse's brother was editor for a time).
Nevins concentrated on the failure of the Catholic Church to be a
Christian church. So far as he is concerned, it is not Christianity at
all, an opinion formally approved by the Presbyterian General Assembly over the next decade.

   Nevins's is a religious and theological critique, although not
without national cultural and political concern.[2] His problem with
Catholicism is that it has an unfettered religious imagination. The
grounds on which he objects to prayer to Mary and the saints, and
to the intercession of saints,[3] indicate the restraints placed on religious imagination by a certain kind of metaphysics and epistemology. He, of course, is neither a metaphysician nor an epistemologist
and so he points to the second commandment, the one most obviously concerned with restraining imagination, and to common

sense rather than to epistemology and metaphysics.[4] The Catholic "problem," and what makes it a different religion, is that the church puts no limit to uses of empirical imagination in religious life besides those set in the historical practice of the church, limits that are adjustable. Imagination carries the Catholic Church beyond the limits of Christianity. Here we have the beginnings of an intellectually interesting criticism of Catholicism, but Nevins was interested only in the church's violation of scriptural standards. In theological terms, Nevins addresses the issue of the proper way of speaking about and imagining God from the point of view of what David Tracy calls the dialectical imagination.[5]

Nevins was not a fine stylist (he's not Jonathan Edwards or William Ellery Channing), but he writes an informed column in accessible, sometimes even snappy prose. He was smart and well educated. He claimed to be a Calvinist, but he doesn't argue on distinctly Calvinist theological principles. The criticism followed the general reformation appeal to the scriptures and displayed a deep distaste for the Catholic way of doing things, especially when it adds to and departs from scripture. Even though his sense of humor and his sarcasm were occasionally wicked at the expense of Catholics, at least he had both. Morse and Beecher could not laugh or try to make their audience laugh at the Catholic way. To Beecher and Morse, it was no laughing matter. (None of them could laugh at their own religion for that matter, a gift reserved by God for Catholics, perhaps.) But Nevins did not think that Catholics were quite the threat Morse and Beecher supposed them to be. He did not accept Morse's Austrian conspiracy theory. Although his feelings were evidently quite strong, they did not reach the threshold of paranoia. The unscriptural, un-Christian nonsense of Catholic belief and practice is Nevins's interest.

We find in Nevins what we might call The Outline. The Outline is the evangelical myth organized in doctrinal rather than narrative categories, fit to appear as a tightly argued and properly ordered bill of particulars against Catholicism. American evangelical polemic against Catholic belief displays all the characteristics of a "tradition." The tradition imposes a table of contents and a supply of arguments that vary little from author to author, decade to decade, even century to century. It holds much of the present literature to the form and content of antebellum polemics. Nevins's *Thoughts* follow the logic of The Outline, with occasional columns devoted to ad hoc issues. For example, chapter 58, displaying his outrage at the dedication of St. Louis Cathedral, is in this respect anomalous. But the flow of Nevins's objections follows the rule of The Outline: The Catholic Church departs from biblical teaching and the rule of faith; Catholics fear the Bible; Catholics have an unbiblical understanding of sin; Catholics do not believe that the death of Jesus atones for all sin, nor do they believe in salvation by faith alone. They believe in infallibility of the church and in the papacy. Catholics practice idolatry and Mariolatry. They believe in seven sacraments rather than two ordinances; in transubstantiation and the sacrifice of the Mass; in penance and auricular confession; in purgatory and prayer for the dead; and in nonscriptural forms of life such as convents and monasteries and the religious life. They have adapted the priesthood of classical paganism. They persecute Protestants, desire to dominate the world religiously and aim to control the state.

The advantage of The Outline is that the use of it plants the author squarely in a tradition and in front of an audience. It lays out the order of address and relieves the author and the reader of the burden of thinking about the subject matter. Nevins follows The Outline closely but not slavishly. Eight of his columns are devoted to the subject of Catholic idolatry and thirty-one others repeat the standard objections to Catholic doctrine and practice. We are saved from numbing boredom only by his spritely style and willingness occasionally to tear off on a topic of special concern (the consecration of the St. Louis Cathedral, for example) or to tell a story.

Throughout the fifty-eight chapters, Nevins wrestled with Catholic diminishment of the Bible and concentrated on it in the first eight. The evangelical *sola Scriptura* is the basic Reformation doctrine and polemical norm against which other versions of Christianity are primarily measured, the lower blade of the evangelical critical scissors (the upper blade is *sola fides* and *sola gratia*). He titled his first chapter "The Rule of Faith." The Bible is enough, God is its author, it is addressed to people who will receive it and understand it as it was meant and written (it is "perspicuous," open to commonsense interpretation). Catholics oppose the Bible and the liberty of conscience taught in it. In the fourth chapter, he concludes that there is no papacy in the Bible, and its absence is especially notable in the letters of St. Peter who is supposed by Catholics to be the first pope of Rome but who obviously did not know it. In the fifth chapter, the charge is made that Catholics add to the Bible and even deny the Bible's most important teachings, namely justification by faith and regeneration. They cut the Ten Commandments to nine, dropping out the second, which forbids image-making as well as idolatry, and splitting the ninth to cover their exclusion of the second.

Instancing the attention paid by ministers to the publications of their adversaries, Nevins introduced the reader to John Hughes's *Christian's Guide to Heaven*. In this volume, Hughes, a Philadelphia priest who later became the archbishop of New York (1838), offered a standard Catholic challenge: Protestantism is a new religion that exists nowhere in the history of Christianity before Luther himself. Where has it been? Who taught it before Luther? Nevins's response is to the point: it was in Rome and Ephesus, for example. It is the Bible's own religion and the religion of the churches of the New Testament. And he counters: Where is Roman Catholicism in the Bible and in New Testament times? Why do New Testament authors know nothing of the doctrines and practices characteristic of Rome? On the dominance of Rome, true Christianity fled into the metaphorical desert and reappeared again at the time of the Reformation (The Myth). In fact, maintains Nevins, Catholicism is the new religion and Protestantism is the old religion of the New Testament reborn. The historical argument is as important to the polemic as is the biblical rule of faith. Each church appears bound to explain both itself and the other in terms of continuity and discontinuity. But the rule and history are not the only planks in Nevins's case.

A third plank is the idolatry that pervades Roman Catholicism at every level. The issue is addressed in eight chapters.[6] Like the worshipers of the Golden Calf and of "the host of heaven," and like "Hindoos," the pope "ascribes divine honors, and pays divine honors to a creature, even to a human being, a partaker in our mortality and sin!"[7] [65] Pope Gregory XVI's own words are the proof. In Pope his first encyclical letter, Gregory prays and urges prayer to Mary that she, "our Patroness and Protectress, may watch over us writing to you and lead our mind by her heavenly influence."[8] But worse yet: she "alone destroys heresies, who is our greatest hope, yea, THE ENTIRE GROUND OF OUR HOPE! . . . Now, just look at this? Did you ever hear anything like it?" This is no part of the religion of the scriptures (Psalms 121 and 123 are quoted) in which God is our hope and salvation. For Nevins, this is sufficient to prove the pope to be the Antichrist, overlooking Christ and saying of another being what can only be said of God.[9]

> I do really wonder that the Catholics continue to call their system Christianity. It is by a great misnomer it is so called. It is not the proper name for it at all. It should be called by some such name as Marianism, rather than Christianity. In Christianity the principal figure is Christ; but he is not the principle [sic] figure in the Catholic religion. Mary is. Catholics are not the disciples of Christ, but of Mary; she is their confidence and hope. . . . [S]he merits barely respectful remembrance. . . . No one thing is more susceptible of demonstration, less capable of denial, than that Roman Catholics render unto this creature that which is due to God alone, religious worship. . . . *Therefore they are idolaters.*[10]

Where Catholics claim that the saints are mediators only in a subordinate sense, they are in fact not mediators in any sense. The Bible doesn't make them mediators. Christ is the mediator, and Christians come to the Father by him. *"To* him we come immediately. Here we need no daysman." Christians pray to no other god than God. They do not worship creatures.[11]

> In looking over the Bible, the book which contains the religion of Protestants, and which, being older than the Roman Catholic religion, proves the seniority of Protestantism over Popery, I find no account of praying to saints. . . . Those writers say nothing about the *mother.* It is all about the *son.* What heretics Luke and the rest of

them were! How worthy of being excommunicated! Catholic books are full of the blessed Virgin. The Bible is all about Christ. There is the difference.[12]

Quoting from the medieval Catholic prayers to the Virgin, the Memorare and the Salve Regina, he comments: "Now, is it not a farce to call this Christianity? *It is a great deal more like atheism.* Here is an authorized Catholic prayer, in which there is no recognition of God whatever!" He quotes an act of consecration, commenting that one is being urged to be "entirely consecrated to the service of the Virgin. . . . Will any one, who has any regard for his character as an intelligent being, say that this is not idolatry?" He reiterates: he has proved idolatry in their own words. And then he goes on to "more specimens of Catholic idolatry," including Marian hymns, with the comment "We pass over [the Church's] absurdity and her intolerance, and plant ourselves on her idolatry. . . . The religion that is not of the Bible, and that scoffs at reason, must come to an end."[13]

> If there be any truth in phrenology, I judge that Catholics must have an organ of veneration very largely developed. There are no people, unless it be some Pagans, who are so inclined to worship. They worship almost every thing that comes in their way, with scarcely any discrimination. . . . Besides him [God], they must have a host of creatures, angels, saints, and what not as objects of adoration. Nor are they satisfied with these beings themselves. They must have visible representations of them to bow down unto, and worship. They want something to worship which they can see. . . . Here are Baltimore and Trent against Sinai . . .[14]

This is the reason the second commandment is dropped, even by Hughes in his list of sins to be examined by the penitent.[15] Catholics must have their images. He adds a bit of mockery, but mockery not far off the Catholic understanding of the practices that so upset Nevins. The confessor says to the penitent who has scruples about bowing down to images of the Virgin and saints:

> O, my child, you don't mean anything by it. You only use the image as a help to devotion. Your worship does not terminate on it. Your worship of it is only *relative*. Besides, you don't *adore* the image— you only venerate it and you only give *"due* honor and veneration" to images—nothing more than that. You should consider, my child, the distinction between adoration and veneration—and also between *latria* and *dulia.*[16]

So far as relics are concerned, if Catholics do not worship them, they come close to it (94). Hughes says the relics of saints are to be respected. What's the harm of that? But what is the use of it, what is the good of it? ". . . I cannot see how the spirit of devotion is to be promoted by contemplating St. Joseph's axe and saw, or the comb of the Virgin Mary, or even the finger of St. Ann. . . . All that can be said for them, is that they serve the cause of idolatry."[17]

Mediation was unquestionably the stone of scandal in Nevins's shoe. In chapters 40 and 41, he went on to auricular confession. Sin ought to be confessed, but why to a priest? Why not to the person offended? Why not to God? He made his essential theological objection:

> Nor can I see why we want more than one mediator between us and
> God. Why is not Christ enough? How admirably qualified he is for
> his work? With one nature that reaches up to God and another that
> reaches down to man, how excellently fitted he is to mediate for us!
> Do we want another between us and Christ? O no. Let the priest
> please not put himself in the way. Jesus says, "Come to me;" we
> want no human priest between us and our "great High Priest, that
> is passed into the heavens for us."[18]

The fundamental objection that Nevins raised was ecclesiological, but his understanding of revelation, redemption, regeneration, justification, and sanctification had little place for the church as a historical, mediating entity. The church could have no part in the forgiveness of sin for that has been accomplished in the death of Christ; no part in the distribution or application of pardon and grace except in the proclamation of the gospel. It cannot be in any sense a "cause," even an "instrumental" cause, of salvation. In this he differs most profoundly from the ecclesiology of Catholics.

Nevins bemoans the puerility of Catholicism, its childishness, its trifles and petty concerns. A missionary letter from a Catholic priest to the Austrian Leopold Society talks about the need for communion cups and wafers, rosaries and crucifixes. "Trumpery!" says Nevins:

> We have to bring before the *mind* of the sinner the great saving
> truth of Christ *crucified*; but they have only to put a little *crucifix* in
> his *hand*. I went, a short time ago, to visit a man under sentence of
> death, to talk to him about Christ and his death. I found him gazing
> intently on a little metallic image of Christ crucified, which a priest
> had left him. He seemed indifferent to all I said. The priest had *pre-
> pared* him.[19]

The priest had given the man what he thought the condemned man could use, an image to recall the death of Christ for his sins. But for Nevins the meaning of the gospel must be communicated only in words, for that is the medium by which God chose to reveal it. No passage in his book so well reveals the religious and theological chasm. Even Abraham could not cross it. Catholicism is a religion that took shape in a world of illiteracy, whereas Protestantism did so in a world of literacy, Catholicism the Christianity for the liturgical assembly and Protestantism the Christianity for reading, Catholicism the Christianity of imagery and symbolic action, Protestantism the Christianity of the mediating Word.

For all the fears expressed by Morse and Beecher about the advances reported in Roman Catholicism in the United States, Nevins differed from them in this one respect. He didn't agree with his colleagues' judgments that Catholicism will become the dominant religion:

> I confidently look forward to the overthrow of the Catholic religion;
> and I expect a great deal of the work of its destruction will be done
> by common sense. I have not the dread, which some have, that this
> religion is going to overrun our country, and rise to dominion here.
> There is too much common sense abroad in the length and breadth
> of the land to allow such a result. . . . You can never get a majority
> here to believe in contradiction of the five senses. They will stick to
> it that a thing is what they see and feel and taste it to be—in other
> words, that bread is bread.[20]

Of course, if common sense did prevail, Protestant Christianity would not fare any better. One might respond, "But dead is dead, isn't it? Resurrection violates any human version of common sense." Protestant Christianity is only marginally less looney than Catholic Christianity in terms of secular common sense, for example. But Nevins wrote when he could assume that the common sense of the general public would support his assertion.

Political and cultural worry dominated Morse and Beecher. Nevins tried, with success, to keep to religion. Sometimes he grafts nativism onto religious criticism. But there are two flags flying in *his* church as well as in the St. Louis Cathedral, although he would be loath to admit it: the United States is Protestant as a cultural fact and should be as a moral fact, in his context and assumption. In this he agrees with his fellow crusaders. Morse and Beecher talk politics and state their intention not to attack the Roman Catholic Church as a religious institution, but they fail as well. The reverse is the case with Nevins. He tried to assess the religion, but only and finally because the religion is alien to a unified Protestant culture. The questions and answers that drove them differ only slightly. Morse and Beecher ask: "What are those people doing *here*?" whereas Nevins asks: "What are those people *doing* here?" In neither approach should Catholics be here and be doing what Catholics do.

## The Great Debate

Although books, newspapers, and journals were the ordinary vehicles of conflict between Protestants and Catholics, and although the political arena and, sadly, the streets of American cities were the scenes of the sharpest and meanest meetings, the platform was perhaps the most fruitful, because it encouraged a degree of spontaneity brought on by vigorous back-and-forth exchange, even when not face-to-face.[21] While more than once it failed in this respect, it channeled anger, suspicion, and violence into language. The public debates were numerous, sometimes excruciatingly long and dull, occasionally funny, sometimes profound. They must have been a learning experience for those willing to listen. And they are American to the core! As with the all too brief presidential debates of our era, there was always hope for a glimpse of the man usually out of sight and of a truth behind party rhetoric. The problem with them, of course, is that they were only debates and not conversations; parties to the debate score points rather than unpack differences and share insights. One can expect the presentations to be contrived and aggressive. The issue was winning; no one won. I have chosen one very good example to discuss.[22]

Alexander Campbell (1788–1866) was born in Ireland, son of a Seceder Presbyterian minister, studied theology in Glasgow for ten months, and took his family to the United States in 1809. His father, Thomas, was already at work in the States, and already censured by Presbyterians for practicing open communion and for his anti-Calvinism. Unlike Presbyterian practice, immersion was for Thomas and Alexander the only correct form of baptism. The two stood against denominations and creeds, accepting all who confessed Jesus and were immersed. Alexander was dedicated to restoring "New Testament Christianity," an ideal construct free from accretions of history and denominational tradition, a church and a theology for the American frontier. The Bible was to rule the church. As Alexander put it, where the scriptures speak, the disciple should speak; where the scriptures are silent, the disciple must be silent as well. The Disciples of Christ or "Campbellites" stem from the Campbells' itinerant ministry in the "West." Alexander was founder and editor of *The Christian Baptist* and then of *The Millennial Harbinger* (from 1823 to 1866), and made the Disciples the fastest growing Protestant movement in the nineteenth century.[23] Much against his ideal of pure New Testament Christianity, the disciples quickly got capitalized and became another denomination. One could not ask for a better example of the American religious entrepreneur; his religion stood the test of time.

Like his colleagues in the hierarchy, John Hughes and John England, John Purcell (1783–1883) was an Irish immigrant. He studied at St. Mary's College in Emmitsburg, Maryland, and studied then in Paris, where he was ordained to the priesthood. He was professor at and president of St. Mary's College, and then bishop of Cincinnati (1833) for fifty years. When he arrived in the city there were fourteen priests; when he died, there were 480. He oversaw the building of over 450 churches, thirty schools, three colleges, three seminaries, and six hospitals, and saw the growth of ten communities of nuns and eight monastic orders. He was well served by the superior rhetorical skills and keen mind displayed in his debate with Alexander Campbell.

John England, bishop of Charleston, South Carolina, had addressed Congress in 1826. The Ursuline Convent and school in Charlestown was burned to the ground in 1834. John Hughes and John Breckinridge had had their debate in Philadelphia. Morse and Beecher had published their books. The Campbell-Purcell debate was held in February 1837 in a Baptist tabernacle in Cincinnati in response to Campbell's public challenge. It lasted eight days (Sabbath excepted), from morning to evening with presentations divided between hour-long statements and half-hour responses, with time out for lunch. They spoke in turn for approximately seven hours each day. Both men had trouble keeping to the point and moderators took them to task for wandering. Each often referred to the other as "my reverend friend" or "my esteemed colleague" although they had never met, and just as regularly tested the limits of that friendship and colleagueship, and of Christian charity itself. Although neither was a historian or even a theologian, both displayed remarkable book learning. Secretaries copied down the extemporaneous argument and, after the text had been checked by both men, a five-hundred-page transcript was published in book form. If one wants to check the pulse of the evangelical-Catholic relationship, this is the place to do it.

Campbell proposed for debate seven theses, six of them closely matching the Reformation "Outline." In order, his theses:

- deny that the Roman Catholic Church is a Christian church and find it to be apostate;
- reject Catholic claims to apostolic succession of their bishops; argue that the Catholic church is a confederation of sects with a single politicoreligious head rather than a union in a single faith;
- denominate the Roman church as the Babylon of John's Revelation, the Pope as the Man of Sin in Paul's letter to Thessalonika, and the papacy as youngest horn of the Beast in the Book of Daniel;
- denounce Catholic sacramental doctrine and practice as productive of immorality and injurious to society;
- deny that the Bible has relied on the Catholic Church for its canonical status and recognition of it as a divinely inspired work, and for its transmission through the middle ages to modern (Protestant) Christianity.
- And, finally, echo Cotton and Mayhew, Morse, and Beecher in the charge of incompatibility between the Catholic Church and American democratic institutions.[24]

For Campbell, Christianity is adequately and fully described and prescribed in the pages of the New Testament, and the church of the New Testament is the model for every age. For one who held that where the Bible is silent, Christians are silent, enough should have been said when he points out that the distinguishing beliefs and practices of the Catholic Church are nowhere to be found in the *sacra pagina*. He gave examples:

> . . . the Roman Catholic church of the nineteenth century, with her popes, her cardinals, her patriarchs, primates, metropolitans, archbishops, archdeacons, monks, friars, nuns, &c. &c teaching and preaching the use and worship of images, relics, penances, invocation of departed men and women, veneration for some being whom they call "the mother of God," teaching and preaching the doctrine of priestly absolution, auricular confession, purgatory, transubstantiation, extreme unction, &c. &c.[25]

Each item in Campbell's list of doctrines and practices specific to Catholicism is judged by the Word of God. The sins of Rome and Roman Catholics, and chiefly the immoral effects of her practice of auricular confession of sins to priests, of her distinction between mortal and venial sin, of her requisite of an antinatural celibacy for ordination, are all matters that tag along with the major focuses of Campbell's contribution to the debate. I will discuss some elements of the historical and political arguments.

The historical argument seems crucial for Campbell, for it occupies more space and generates more energy in the debate than the biblical, moral, and political arguments. Granted that there is no mention in the Bible of Our Lady of Guadalupe or of the papacy, this evangelical was drawn into the vortex of a nonbiblical question: how did this gigantic thing called Roman Catholicism and even Christendom come about, and how are we to explain it? If one is going to condemn Roman Catholicism (and a fortiori Eastern Orthodoxy) as unbiblical, needn't one account for the encumbering or even the disappearance of Christian faith for a millennium? Campbell left the safety of an ideally invulnerable biblical argument for the treacheries of history that, for better or worse, was a maze familiar to the Catholic apologist since Caesare Baronius answered Luther and the Centuriators. The two-edged sword of the past and historical investigation of it cut deeply into the antagonists on stage.

Once he concluded (a debate concludes at the outset!) that "Not one of these [Catholic dogmas] can be found in the Bible," Campbell immediately claimed that there was no pope or universal head of the church for the first six centuries. Even the great Gregory (590–604) was uneasy with the title "universal bishop"—at least when assumed by the patriarch of Constantinople. But his successor once removed, Boniface III, who ruled for only ten months in 607, gratefully received the title "universal bishop" from the tyrant emperor Phocas, and thus the claim of the bishops of Rome to special status and universal jurisdiction was formally recognized in the civil order.[26] Papal primacy over the entire church did not exist until that moment. A century and a half later, Pepin and Charlemagne gave the bishop of Rome the estate that made him "the supreme head of that politicoecclesiastical corporation called the Church of Rome."[27]

In fact, Campbell announced, the Roman Catholic Church did not exist until July 16, 1054, when the papal legate excommunicated Michael, patriarch of Constantinople, for maintaining that the Greek church was the only true church and for denying the validity of Western Eucharist and baptism. "If then, there be any truth in history, from that day the present sect of the church of Rome began its existence."[28] The real cause of the schism was the Roman claim that the pope was the universal father of Christendom. No doubt the bishops of Rome had been overreaching since the third century, but the Church of Rome, embodied in Bishop Purcell, began when the papal legate anathematized the patriarch of Constantinople. Although he does not argue as Cotton did that in 606 Satan entered and took possession of the church of Rome, he does make it plain that in the public and political order the entitlement of the papacy is to be found in a series of political acts and not in the truth of a religious claim that Peter was the first bishop of Rome.[29]

But where and how did the church or true Christian faith survive in this era of increasing darkness? Campbell must now meet Purcell's clever and obvious challenge: Where was the one, holy, apostolic church from which the Roman Catholic church apostatized, whether in 250, or 606, or 1054?[30] Where was that church with which Jesus promised to be "all days until the world ends" (Mt 28:20)? Campbell should have had, on Protestant grounds, no trouble in answering this. He might have said that there were always true Christians in the church who formed a true church spiritually even when Rome led the rest to hell. After all, Calvin, with great foresight, had preserved the possibility that the Church of Rome did not entirely destroy the Christian faith in its communion and Campbell could have left it at that.

But, instead, he stumbled badly. He needed to populate the true Christian church, to give it more than mere formal or ideal existence. He could not admit that people in communion with Rome could be Christians, and so he turned to those persons and movements who refused communion or who were excluded from it to uncover the historical root of Protestantism. He found "the Puritan strain" in the history of the church. He picked up the narrative of that strain with the bestowal of the papacy on the compromiser Pope Cornelius in 251, forcing the "Puritan" Novatian and his rigorist followers out of the Roman Church.[31] The Novatians, according to Campbell, were the first in a long list of Christian protest movements that carried true Christianity, the true gospel, through the centuries, among them Donatists, Paulicians, Cathari, Waldensians and, finally, the sixteenth-century reformers.[32] In Campbell's view, all of them suffered papal oppression. There had always been Protestants, ". . . a regular succession of those who have protested against the corruptions of the Roman church, and endeavored to hold fast the faith once delivered to

the saints, from the first schism in the year 250 AD to the present day . . ."[33]
The Centuriators of Magdeburg return![34]

Purcell responded:

> Luther repeatedly declared that he stood alone, that all antiquity was
> against him. Here are startling facts and no less startling admis-
> sions by sound Protestants. Will my friend insult this enlightened
> assembly by making up a monster-church, a very chimera, of all
> these sects, and give modern Protestants all the honors present and
> prospective of being *the tail of the beast?* I would counsel *him* not to
> dream of doing so, and *them* to look for more reputable religious an-
> cestors.[35]

Campbell continued to squabble over Gregory and Phocas and the title
"ecumenical father," and returned to the exegetical arguments surrounding
Matthew 16 and John 21, tugging at the biblical foundations of the Roman
claim of the original primacy of Peter, but he quickly gave up on the issue of
sainted predecessors to be discovered in movements that no Protestant theologian could regard as orthodox.

Purcell did return to the point, however. In his first presentation at 10 A.M.
on the morning after the Sabbath (January 16), by which time he must have
realized the extent of the wound Campbell had inflicted on his own case, he
demanded to know where was the one true church from which Rome apostatized in 250 C.E.—or at any other date. He got no answer, and the debate
moved on with a counterclaim by Campbell that the papacy lacked both biblical
and historical foundations. The heart of the Catholic position (the Catholic
myth) had been stated by Purcell in the speech opening Monday's exchange:
(1) Peter was made head by Christ, as proved from scripture (Mt 16 and John
21); (2) Peter had successors; and (3) the succession was to last till the end of
time. Both the tradition and the continuing Petrine ministry in the church
amount to a miracle attesting to the pope's apostolic succession. Historical
attestation of the succession is without exception for a thousand years.[36]

Each had trouble finding the other's wavelength. They relied on different
sets of historians, while trying to coopt one another's. They were not asking
common questions; they worked under remarkably different assumptions; they
simply defended current positions and so became perfect instances of the dominance of The Myth. At the moment Purcell was ahead on points by a bit; he
appeared to be smarter by a bit and able to keep to an issue better, and he was
a considerably better rhetorician. But neither at this point in the debate got
beyond the borders of his respective Myth.

When it turned out that Campbell could not gain a conclusive victory on
the thesis of historical apostasy, he continued his attack on the evidence that
the Roman bishop exercised or was recognized for exercising any peculiar
authority in the early centuries. All we have are later witnesses, he maintained,

none in the first two centuries. The "evidence" is a matter of ecclesiastical tradition issuing from interested parties, the victors in ecclesiastical disputes. So far as Campbell was concerned, history tells us nothing constructive about a papacy,[37] and when it tells anything at all Campbell was not edified. As Campbell recounted that long and sometimes very sad story, Purcell spent his time correcting the record. They even read *at length* from their favorite historians.[38]

They were matched point for point in Friday's, Saturday's, and Monday's debates on the apostate church and on the early history (or the lack of it) of the papacy. Campbell then opened Tuesday's argument (January 17) with the charge that the bishop had been "demolishing men of straw of his own creation," and misrepresenting him.[39] He pleaded for the bishop to stick to the point and answer the claims made. After painting one of his several sad stretches of papal history,[40] he summed up his case in four points that he thought he had proven and that Purcell had not cogently overthrown: (1) there is no scriptural warrant for a monarchical church; (2) it cannot be "ascertained that Peter was ever bishop of Rome"; (3) Christ gave no law of succession; (4) and even if he had, "a long continuance of monsters of crime" has destroyed the succession. "On what, now, rests Roman Catholicism?"[41] Of course, it rests on nothing sacred. He acknowledged not a single contribution to the life of the church on the part of any pope or the papacy as an institution.[42] The papal chair, he says, is the most corrupt and corrupting institution that ever stood on earth.

Purcell, in turn, reproved Campbell for his scattershot approach. How was he to answer attacks on every facet of Catholic faith? To him the essential issue was: "Did Christ establish an infallible tribunal to determine the meaning of scripture? If so, we are bound by its decisions. If not, the whole Catholic religion falls to the ground." But, Purcell adds, the scripture has it that "the church is the pillar and the ground of truth" and "I will be with you all days even to the end of the world."[43] In other words, the true church must have been there all along, or else Christ's word and the scriptures that repeat them are falsified. A true reform would have regarded morals, not a change in the church to which Christ has always been present and always will be, as he promised. Protestant morals have been low as well, or worse, as admitted by Luther, Melancton, Erasmus, and others. But why be shocked at immorality: "What is the world but the theater of falsehood and truth? A field of tares and wheat?" The papacy is off the moral hook, or Protestant church leaders are on it with the papacy.[45]

Two sharp and illuminating contrasts between evangelicals and Catholics appeared on the afternoon of Thursday, January 19. At 3 P.M., Campbell, in his disquisition on the independence of the Bible from the transmission of it by Catholics in medieval times (his fifth thesis), remarked: "The first, and characteristic difference, between the Protestant and the Roman Catholic, is this: the former believes the scriptures first, and the church afterwards; whereas, the latter believes the church first, and the scriptures afterwards."[46] Protestants do not need to believe in the Roman Church in order to believe in the scriptures which she had a hand in preserving. The Bible existed before the papacy and before even the Vulgate Latin version of the scriptures (c. 400 C.E.) "which is itself older than the church of Rome."[47]

Purcell responded by saying that the church precedes the Bible. Millions were Christians before the Bible was collected and determined to be scripture. Faith came from hearing, not reading. Catholics believe in the church first. "The Bible could not shed its blood to attest to its divine origin" as the martyrs did.[48] He agreed with Campbell, to put it in other words, that the Catholic Church is a liturgical (Campbell and other polemicists would say "ritual") church rather than a biblical church. Purcell, I suspect, also would agree that Catholicism is a Christianity that easily embraces illiterates, whereas Protestantism is a Christianity that demands literacy.

Campbell objected: the bishop is caught in a circle. The church approves the Bible and the Bible proves the church. When the bishop asked whether the Bible proves itself and answers no, he is mistaken. Does nature prove itself to be the work of God? Yes, and so the Bible proves itself to be the Word of God. Who collected the writings is irrelevant to their truth. The Bible, in other words, is the sole innerworldly mediator of God's saving truth and needs no church to interpret it.

And the second doctrine that divides Protestants and Catholics is the "main root of the whole papal superstition," namely *That the death of Christ is the great sin offering, and the only sin offering* is a cardinal doctrine of Protestantism."[49] Catholics, in Campbell's view, do not believe that the death of Christ is sufficient as a sin offering, and so purgatory is put in place to remove sin. Purgatory became the religious lever that has brought more money to Rome than any other. But in Protestant (i.e., biblical) teaching:

No human being has anything to give God; and therefore none can merit from him any thing. . . . Works of supererogation, auricular confession, masses for sins, transubstantiation, purgatory, with all the appurtenances thereto belonging, are the veriest ghosts of paganism—phantoms of infatuated reason, attempts against the dignity of God and the supremacy, as well as the true and proper divinity and dignity of his Son.

This superstition, this man of sin, stands with his two feet upon the two greatest lies in human history. He places his right foot on the first and his left foot on the second. Need I say that the former affirms *that the sacrifice of God's own Son is insufficient as a sin offering:* and that the latter teaches *that man can do more than his duty to God.*[50]

On these two heresies the Catholic Church became apostate. If Purcell would only meet him on these two issues all the rest of Roman practice will be undone and the church revealed as anti-Christian. Purcell responded with a charge that Campbell misrepresents Catholic teaching. Yes, Christ's sacrifice is sufficient, but God does not save us without involving us in the process. The sacraments (the Catholic religious "system") are the means by which God involves us in our salvation. And this is done by the church at the command of Christ.[51]

Campbell passed on to his final point: the profound incompatibility of Catholicism and democracy. It took nearly one hundred pages of print to reproduce a portion of the debate that took two days in oral argument, a testimony to its importance. Another testimony is the vehemence that accompanied it on both sides. By this point the enmity must have been palpable as the pretense of fellowship evaporated. The central conviction on Campbell's side was that the Catholic Church is the church of medieval political and social Christendom, and only by surrendering that self-conception can Catholicism exist in democratic (and Protestant) American culture. A surrender, however, is impossible, for the Catholic Church has made itself infallible and cannot correct its past. Campbell would turn out to have been correct in his analysis and incorrect about the church's ability to change on this point.

If the charge that the Catholic Church is not a Christian church can be taken as one bookend in this eight-day debate, the other is Campbell's analysis of the retrograde politics and social theory of the church. Although the theological and doctrinal arguments that lie between the bookends are important, from the illegitimate papacy to the pretensions of her sacramental teaching, these two hold Campbell's position together: the Catholic Church is not a Christian church and it is a threat to American freedoms. Americans heard this for three centuries, and they still do. When the sense of the Catholic political threat weakened in the latter half of the twentieth century, it became possible for the first time for evangelicals and Catholics to discuss, and not merely debate, the profound theological and religious issues that lie between them.[52]

Campbell opens the discussion:

> ... My last proposition [i.e., the Catholic church is anti-American]
> ... concerns him [i.e., Purcell] and his party more, than any other
> one of the seven. . . . I would emphatically tell him, the community
> expect him to discuss this subject above all the others. . . . Many who
> have no antipathy against Roman Catholics have some fears of
> them. I belong to that class. I have no antipathy: but I have my
> fears, . . . I do sincerely believe and think, that Roman Catholicism,
> in any country is detrimental to its interests and prosperity: and in a

republic, directly and positively tending every moment to its subversion. Such is my conviction. I avow it, that if possible, it may be removed. I always distinguish between a system and those who profess it,—between a creed and the people. . . . Let the public mind be disabused: for as present advised, Protestants generally think that civil liberty and the papacy are wholly incompatible with each other: and that the introduction of large numbers of Roman Catholics into this community, would inevitably subvert this government; and place us under a spiritual and political despotism, intolerant and cruel as those, which the see of Rome has established in every country on earth, where she has obtained a majority.[53]

Campbell and other Protestant Americans before him (and since) have been fearful, and they *have* had something to worry about. Authentic and official Catholic teaching held to the supremacy of the spiritual over the merely political, of church over state, of the necessity to curb heresy by state force if need be. This was no matter of inconsequential dogma but of historical practice as well. Campbell relied on a stream of documents from Rome, from the high Middle Ages to modern times. Cardinal Bellarmine, the intellectual architect of the Tridentine theory of papal primacy and universal jurisdiction, was a favorite of Protestant polemicists, but Campbell can list and quote from dozens of popes: Clement V, Clement VI, Boniface VIII, Leo X, Innocent IV, and Pius V. On Saturday morning he began the last day of debate with another list and a set of quotations, this time from Urban II, the council of Toledo, Innocent III, Leo IX, and Adrian I. He repeated the heart of his charge:

. . . for at least five centuries, the heads of the Roman church clearly and unambiguously taught that the spiritual sword was above the temporal, and that the vicar of Christ is by divine right Lord of thrones and all earthly things. This, I have no doubt, is the true doctrine of the immutable and infallible church of Rome! And certain it is, that it has never been disowned, or renounced, by a general council, the organ of infallibility. If the church of Rome be insusceptible of reformation, or infallible, it is proved to be essentially anti-American, and opposed to the genius of our institutions.[54]

The Holy Office of the Inquisition was hauled onto the stage. Hundreds of thousands suffered under it. He lists the number of its victims by nation, but the Roman church has perpetrated even wider horrors. Its victims, estimated by Protestant historians to have been as many as fifty to sixty-eight million, have been "sacrificed and devoured by this Moloch [the church]." Add to this the Index of Forbidden Books and the universal suppression of religious and political freedom in Catholic nations, and one gets the size of the problem anticipated by American Protestants in their own land.[55] Papal Rome is and always has been a persecuting government; she is essentially so, Campbell insisted.

He brought the charge home: all Catholic bishops swear in their oath of office "to persecute and oppose heretics and schismatics."[56] They swear loyalty to the Bishop of Rome. Bishop Purcell first swore allegiance to the United States and then to a foreign prince. Which is more binding? Campbell quoted the oath of American naturalization.[57] The conflict with the oath a bishop takes was obvious. How can anyone in good conscience take both oaths? The pope was a foreign potentate, with his own state, with claims to political as well as spiritual rule.

Campbell, no mean rhetorician at any point in the eight days, was perhaps most effective in this closing day. In a long and powerful passage he reiterated his challenge: the Catholic Council of Trent has decreed the condemnation of heretics and in its wake came blind obedience, intolerance, proscription, and persecution. Trent had not been undone by any later Catholic authority of comparable standing. No matter what individual bishops or groups of them may say to the contrary about this teaching, only a council can reverse Trent, something impossible in an infallible church. "The disavowal or the disclaiming of any priest or bishop in the Roman Catholic Church, is not worth more, and has no more authority, than mine."[58] Nothing John Purcell says, bishop though he is and sincere though he may be, can count on this question. "Rome" has spoken: the church is superior to the political order and claims authority over it; heresy is to be repressed wherever possible; the Catholic bishops must swear allegiance to the pope who is a foreign sovereign, and swear to oppress Protestants. No modern liberties are safe, no democratic nation can have civil peace with a powerful Catholic Church in it. The case is clearly and passionately made, as sharply as it has been in this literature.

Remarkably, Purcell did not appear to be flustered by this devastating historical attack. Surely he expected it. He told Campbell that there is no conflict of oaths, for the pope has no temporal sovereignty anywhere but in the papal states. The medieval arrangements have long since passed, and, as he hints, Christendom has come to an end.[59] He put persecution behind him by denying that his oath of office meant what Campbell took it to mean. And he was willing to match persecution for persecution:

My worthy opponent said, that he would only *touch* on persecution.
My friends, persecution has marked me for a victim in my native
land, and forced me to seek an Asylum [sic] in America, when I was
young and friendless! Persecution is there, in full operation at this
very hour. Scarcely a breeze comes across the ocean, without bringing on its wings, fresh tidings, of blood, shed under Protestant persecution—by ministers of the Protestant faith. Widows kneel there
in the blood of their own children; and because excess of grief has

made them maniacs, they drink that blood, and curse the authors of their misery. Is not this true? Does not the whole universe know and shudder at it?[60]

Finally, he asserted unconditionally that he recognizes no papal jurisdiction over the United States. In fact, he proclaimed that it cannot be church teaching for it appears nowhere in the first millennium of the church, and it has never been made a matter of church doctrine. As for Catholics and liberty, he said:

There is not such a people for liberty, on the globe, as Roman Catholics. Look nearer at home, at Maryland, where the CATHOLICS WERE THE FIRST THAT PROCLAIMED FREEDOM OF CONSCIENCE IN THE WESTERN HEMISPHERE!! LET THIS BE OUR ANSWER TO A THOUSAND SLANDERS.[61]

Neither of the "reverend friends" won or lost the debate. Both showed themselves men made for public life, certainly, each willing to risk a fall, each intent on respecting the other in public and failing to do so, each convinced of the truth of the great ecclesiological myth in which he lived his life. They argued forcefully the issues that divided them, but in the end neither refuted the other's position nor comprehended the other man's tight religious hold on the meaning of the church in history in any but negative terms. Not only was there no agreement reached even on small issues but also there was no curiosity and no sympathy. The Myth is there, controlling the debate, if one takes into account the difficulty of composing and reciting it in that atmosphere. All the doctrines and practices are brought into conflict and left unresolved, and each hears the other's story as a distortion of history as God knows it.

Although we have seen some of both and shall see more of Purcell later, recall at this point that there are two quite distinct arguments in Campbell's assault. The first is the Christian theological argument about the religious failures of the Catholic Church and the second is an argument about the threat Catholics pose to the *res publica Americana*. The first is argued in historical, doctrinal, moral, and apocalyptic languages. The second is an argument about freedom, cultural and political hegemony, and the fragility of a culture in the face of profound differences in religion—although the argument is not often framed in these terms. In Campbell they are two currents still in one stream—as in Cotton, Nevins, and Mayhew.


Excursus or Note on The Remish New Testament, Samuel Smith, the *Secreta Monita,* and the Jesuits

One of the features of the debate was the attempt by Campbell and Purcell to introduce evidence and educe support from a wide variety of published sources.

However, Purcell frequently objected to the authenticity of the sources used by Campbell. The use of spurious Catholic documents was a frequent occurrence in the literature I have been discussing, according to Catholic authors. For example, Campbell was likely familiar with the case of Maria Monk but avoided referring to that bit of fraud. He does, however, refer at some length to the *Secreta Monita Societatis Jesu*, a document from France "exposed" at the time of the Revolution there. It contained papal directions to Jesuits to subvert the civil order. It stands shoulder to shoulder with *The Protocols of the Elders of Zion*. Purcell objected and denounced it as "trash" from the sewers of Paris: "I pronounce it an infamous forgery." He claims it was a Jacobin attack on the ministers—"priests"—of all churches by an infidel.[62] Campbell also introduced Samuel Smith's synopsis and translation of the works of St. Alphonsus Liguori, the Catholic moral theologian.[63] Smith, who was editor of one of the least distinguished anti-Catholic periodicals of the time, claimed to be a former priest and made his living from his anti-Catholic publications and lectures. Purcell claimed that the synopsis and translation included insertions by Smith. Again, Campbell wanted to quote from the notes of the Catholic Rheims New Testament of 1582 in a version printed in New York in 1828. Purcell objected strongly on the grounds that what Campbell called the "Remish New Testament" was not a version of the Rheims New Testament but another counterfeit in the Protestant arsenal, a volume whose notes were exposed and condemned by the archbishop of Dublin and republished by a "caucus of parsons in New York . . . for the express purpose of vilifying the faith, and outraging the feelings of Catholics." Among the six "authenticators" of the accuracy of the notes were John Breckinridge and W. C. Brownlee, two Presbyterian pastors who were well-known anti-popery propagandists.[64] A comparison a research assistant, Kyle Rose, and I made of notes on Galatians, James, and Revelation 13 in Campbell's "Remish New Testament" and the Rheims New Testament of 1582 found no differences. On this document Campbell may have been in the right. Finally, Campbell cited the document excommunicating Fr. William Hogan, a Philadelphia priest who defied Bishop Kenrick during the trustee crisis in that diocese, cursing and damning Hogan, physical part by physical part. Purcell challenged the authenticity of the document (417–18). It was as much a fraud in his reckoning as Maria Monk's account of murder and sex in the convent and the *Secreta Monita*.[65] However, Campbell was correct about the terms *"persequar hereticos"* in the bishops' oath and Purcell was disingenuous in his interpretation of it, whether or not he would have acted on it.[66]

# 6

# Three Presbyterians and Three Congregationalists

John Hughes (1797–1864), Irish-born and American-educated bishop of New York, added to his twenty-five-year record of outspoken criticism of the no-popery campaign a provocative public address entitled "The Decline of Protestantism and Its Causes" (November 1850). Hughes had a restrained and intense preaching style, and was a man who commanded attention and was fitted for rough times.[1] He, as much or more than any Catholic leader in the nineteenth century, articulated the "present position of Catholics in America." He was a man of "views," and in this lecture to raise money for the Sisters of Mercy and their hostel for women, he delivered, in the words of his biographer, "a ruthless account of what he saw as the failure of the Reformation" and did so on the eve of his departure for Rome to receive the lamb's wool pallium of an archbishop from Pope Pius IX.

The Presbyterians

Nicholas Murray (1802–1861), also Irish-born, was a convert in his youth from his native Catholicism to the Presbyterian Church in New York. Later an exemplary pastor of the First Presbyterian Church of Elizabethtown, New Jersey, in 1847 Murray added a new avocation to his pastoral burdens, namely, writing open letters to Archbishop Hughes first published in the New York *Observer*. He became, in fact, the chief public antagonist of the archbishop, publishing under the *nom de plume* Kirwan. He authored three volumes of letters to Hughes and one to Roger Taney, the Catholic chief justice of the Supreme Court.[2] This evidence of his convictions and the attendant publicity may have had something to do with his election to be moderator of the General Assembly of the Presbyterian Church in 1849.[3] Murray was the logical person to answer to Hughes's address. He delivered his response in January 1851 in an equally sweeping lecture titled "The Decline of Popery and Its Causes." He expected and got a large audience for the lecture, as he had established himself the prime defender of the Protestant cause against the threat of Romanism and the chief of Hughes's many antagonists. His books reached hundreds of thousands of readers.

Despite his praise of Hughes's abilities in the very first letter, Murray despised Hughes as he despised the Roman Catholic Church. The closing paragraphs of the lecture reek with contempt, as do his letters. The structure of the argument is simple and familiar: Christianity was perverted by the Constantinian settlement, and grew worse as the centuries passed in both doctrine and polity. It was now weak. Protestantism, albeit admittedly not as successful as it might have been, advanced religion and civilization and by the middle of the nineteenth century it prospered. There are causes for the Catholic decline and the Protestant advance.

The first half of the essay is a rendition of "The Myth" of the corruption of the church.[4] The Christian faith was from the first simple and nonpolitical. But there was an apostasy. The Arian heresy excited enthusiasm for the divinity of Christ. Satan used that enthusiasm to corrupt Christianity through the rise of the papacy. The enthusiasm led to an inordinate devotion to the sacrament of the Last Supper and then to the medieval doctrine of transubstantiation. Relics of Christ such as the wood of the true cross led to idolatry. The cultivation of saints and saints' feast days led to the doctrine of relative worship (*dulia*), which in fact is adoration (*latria*), and to the doctrine of intercession. Add the demand for clerical celibacy, the forbidding of meat in special seasons, other forms of corporeal austerity, satisfaction for sin by human works and human merit, the distinction between venial and mortal sin, purgatory, and the treasury of merit at the disposal the church—the most profitable doctrine of popery. The practice of the Christian life and faith is thereby thoroughly corrupted:

> Thus did the devil, starting on the high wave of zeal and enthusiasm
> for the glory of Christ, build up the doctrinal Babel of popery, the
> foundation of which is laid in hell, whose top reaches unto heaven,
> and whose dark shadow has stretched from shore to shore.[5]

Roman doctrines are "the merest caricature of Christianity." The doctrine of the crucifixion of Christ has led to crosses as talismans and to "that most unmeaning of all mummeries, the mass, in which the tragedy of Calvary becomes an unmeaning and loathsome farce."

In the scriptures, the intercession of Christ as mediator is exclusive. But popery added Mary, Peter, Paul, and martyrs, virgins, widows, monks, bishops, and confessors, many of whom were "men of Belial," some of whom were ornaments of the church. "Of the true and only mediation of Jesus Christ, the millions of popery know as little as Chinamen."[6] Truth gave way to caricature. Murray managed to pack neatly into a lecture the essence of his long attack on Romanism, his former faith: its obvious weakness and its likely demise in modern situation is brought on by its insatiable need for money and its willingness to do what needs to be done to make money off the backs of the poor. Its compromising politics and its willingness to betray the gospel for money have lead to its present condition. The Catholic Church is, above all, the maw of its clergy, a money-making conspiracy. Whereas many of the Protestant critics attack the sacramental system as simoniacal, Murray fixed greed as the central feature of Roman Catholicism. His assessment of it is severe and even brutal. Of Hughes's response to Murray, I shall say more later.

Robert Breckinridge led the Presbyterian charge against the Catholic Church in the 1830s and 1840s shortly before Nicholas Murray decided to take on Archbishop Hughes. In 1835 the Presbyterian General Assembly picked him to head a committee on "The Prevalence of Popery in the West" and he responded with resolutions that denounced the Catholic Church as an apostate and announced that Protestant parents could not in conscience place their children in Catholic schools. In 1843 he helped found and then led the Society of the Friends of the Reformation, which used its funds to publish tracts and books against popery. In the same period he edited successive avatars of an antipopery journal, using the titles the *Baltimore Literary and Religious Magazine* and *Spirit of the XIX Century*.[7]

Like other no-popery authors Breckinridge had to exercise a bit of individual creativity, putting his own spin on the tradition if he was to keep his audience awake. It might be popish tyranny or idolatry or Mariolatry or pagan and Jewish heritage, or avarice (Murray's specialty), any one of the many possibilities that one's own experience and meditation presented and as the circumstances of one's time suggested. Catholicism, as most admitted, is a religion of a thousand facets. For this important sermon, the General Assembly's return from the problem of the New Light schism to the attack on popery, Breckinridge picked the *Rule of Faith*, the *sola scriptura* of the Reformers. The Protestant rule of faith is the scriptures and the individual conscience formed by them.

If the Bible is foundational to the existence of a true Christian church, then Rome cannot stand as a Christian church. Against the Bible, Rome teaches that divine worship is due to the Virgin, the host, the true cross; that veneration and even adoration is due to angels, departed saints and their relics, and to pictures and images. Against the Bible, Rome puts up a multitude of intercessors, the merit of good works, the seven sacraments, and the proposition that faith is not the only means of a sinner's justification. Against the Bible, Rome teaches that the transgression of her own commands is "heinous sin," whereas the transgression of many of God's commands is venial sin. Against the Bible, Rome teaches that men are regenerated by baptism, kept in a state of salvation by sacramental and ascetic practice and by indulgences. Rome tells us that there is a purgatory and the church can shorten our time in it. The Bible teaches that only Jesus Christ is "King and Lord of Zion," while Rome teaches that the pope is the vicar of Christ, reigning in his place, with gifts of infallible knowledge and extraordinary gifts of the Holy Ghost, and that this visible head must be obeyed and the church can enforce his will by the "power of both the temporal and spiritual sword."[8] The Bible teaches that the visible church has no other mission than to preserve and extend the revealed truth of God by means exclusively spiritual, exempt from every species of spiritual violence.[9]

The faiths are opposite in essential ways, but the Rule of Faith is the most basic. Where Protestantism holds to the Bible and to the Holy Spirit working in the hearts and minds of Christians, Rome interposes a church to tell the individual what the Bible means. We remember that Purcell insisted in the debate with Campbell that the basic issue between Protestants and Catholics is: Did Christ intend to set up an infallible church to determine the meaning of revelation? Breckinridge's version of it is this: "What is this rule, or measure, or law, by which we are to judge what things we ought to receive as revealed to us by God." Protestants and Romanists agree—the Bible is authentic, inspired, and uncorrupted:

> For it is never to be forgotten, that the perfect sufficiency of the
> Holy Scriptures to make men wise unto salvation, the absolute completeness of the power of God to entire exclusion of man's wisdom
> as the sure foundation of our faith, has been from the beginning,
> the universal testimony which martyrs have sealed with their blood
> [he cites Fox's *Acts*], the unanimous confession of every true Church
> of Jesus Christ, the very germ and heart's blood of the blessed reformation of the sixteenth century, and the clear, reiterated, and everliving assurance of God himself, by the mouths of all holy men who
> spake as they were moved by the Holy Ghost.[10]

But, said Breckinridge, Rome added to the ancient rule of faith, especially at Trent and in the creed of Pius IV of 1564, beliefs that differ from the creeds of all the reformed churches, the latter being in tune with the ancient creeds of the church. The Bible is interpreted by "the church." Who and what is that? It turns out to be the pope, who is "leagued with tyrants and fulminating curses against the sacred and indefeasible rights of human nature."[11] One must "promise and swear true obedience to the Roman Bishop, the successor of St. Peter, the prince of the Apostles and the Vicar of Jesus Christ." Popes, in other words, enter the rule of faith. The man who puts himself above the scripture usurps the Holy Scripture. The man who does that is the Antichrist.[12] In addition, no man can know whether any other man infallibly knows the meaning of the scripture. Finally, in the great mass of the popes over the twelve hundred years "since the apostasy began, the fewest have been men of blameless lives, and almost none have exhibited the genuine marks of true Christians."[13] Could these be vicars of Christ set up by God?

Then there are the Councils in the Roman rule. The Catholic must "profess and undoubtedly receive all things delivered, defined, and declared by the Sacred Canons and the General Councils, and particularly the Holy Council of Trent." "Councils infallible!" Breckinridge roared. "Councils in which the Holy Spirit did dwell! Beleaguered by strumpets, beset with fiddlers and buffoons, cursing God's truth, and leaving tracks strawed with bastards and dead men's bones!" but especially the Council of Trent, which had the audacity to anathematize those Christians who disagreed with Rome, Trent ". . . the final landmark, the last limit of his endurance with this great, bloody, drunken Babylon." Again, Catholic canon law (and all the constitutions and observances) "supercedes alike the codes of God and of the nations . . ." And, finally, the unanimous sense given to the Scriptures by the fathers is said to bind the church.[14]

Breckinridge offered a good contrast, brief and sharply made, between the two communities, continuing many elements of the tradition organized around the Rule. Alas, it is only a lecture/sermon and so not an adequate theological discussion of the rule and justification of the Protestant position on it. But the indictment was issued by a man who knew the differences and was able to organize them neatly, a fine example of a sermon called for by the General Assembly to be made in every congregation in order to combat Roman error. No one would come away confused about Rome's dilution of proper understanding of the role of the Bible in Christian life. No one hearing Breckinridge could be tempted to think that Rome was anything other than a creature of Hell.

James Henry Thornwell (1812–1862), professor at Columbia Seminary in South Carolina where he taught the history of Western philosophy and systematic theology, was a defender of states' rights and of slavery, and a founder of the Southern Presbyterian Church when the secession took place in 1860. Charles Hodge, himself the most able American renewer of the Calvinist heritage in the nineteenth century, regarded Thornwell as a "hyper-hyper-hyper Calvinist."

Thornwell wrote in an odd situation indeed. The General Assembly of 1845, under Thornwell's leadership, declared Catholic baptism invalid and the Catholic Church in no way a Christian church. In this it capped off its role in the fifteen-year American anti-Catholic campaign whose spokespersons often had been Presbyterian. In the words of Billington on the evangelical response to John Hughes's attempt to get state support for Catholic schools during these very years, "Nearly all of the Protestant denominations in the United States responded to this appeal but none with more enthusiasm than the Presbyterians whose heritage toward Rome fitted them to take full advantage of the excitement over the New York controversy."[15] Breckinridge's 1842 sermon opened the second phase, and it culminated in the 1845 decision. None of this is any way odd, but the conflict between Hodge and Thornwell over the Assembly's action is odd indeed. The most learned and intellectually vigorous Presbyterian theologian of the century was in deep disagreement with his Assembly and his fellow Calvinist theologian over the status of the Catholic Church. I would venture to say that Archbishop Hughes read of the squabble between the two with an unchristian amusement.

Hodge fought the Assembly decision in 1845 and published his criticism of it anonymously in the *Princeton Review* in 1845.[16] Hodge had argued in the Assembly and against the Assembly that the matter and form of Catholic baptism had not been so corrupted as to be invalid; that the marks of a true church are sufficiently present in the Catholic Church for its sacraments to be valid; and that even if it is not a true church, Protestants, including the Reformers themselves, have always believed that Catholic baptism is valid.

Why it took until 1851 for Thornwell's response to find print is a mystery. In it he argued in support of the Assembly's twofold decision: baptismal validity is taken up in a first article and the question of a true Christian church in a second. Although it includes some very strong language about the Roman Church at several points, this is a very good piece of theology, carefully controlled and generally temperate in the tone of the argument itself. Essentially the argument on sacramental validity is as follows:

1. The pure water (matter) is corrupted by the addition of the "holy oil" to it. Thus the Catholic baptism is not a washing, a sign of spiritual purification by the Holy Spirit. Rather, it is "part of the magical liturgy of Rome." Since oil corrupts the cleansing power of water, it is not baptismal water.

2. The Trinitarian language (form) is to be used to comply with the command of Christ by lawful ministers of the gospel. The words alone are not enough. Faith is required. A unitarian could not validly baptize even if he used the proper formula.[17]

3. Roman views on the covenant of grace are heretical and so they cannot intend to do what Christ commanded. The Catholics baptized are not taught to look beyond the signs to the signified, which is the action of the Holy Spirit. The entire sacramental theology of the Roman theologians is absurd. The Reformers condemned it universally. Right up to Robert Bellarmine, Catholic theologians taught that the sacraments are physical causes or mechanical instruments of grace. The act of pouring and reciting the formula causes grace as

its effect. Trent is clear on this, and so is Bellarmine.[18] A sacrament
not only signifies, it sanctifies, according to Bellarmine.[19] About the
Roman Catholic doctrine of sacramental causality he has these hard
words to say:

> Lying vanities, as they are, according to the teaching of the mother of
> harlots, they [the sacraments] are yet the Saviors to which millions of her
> deluded children cling for acceptance before God. They [her children]
> are accustomed to use nothing higher in the scale of excellence than
> empty pageantry of ceremonial pomp, or to dream of nothing better in
> the way of felicity than the solemn farce of sacerdotal benediction; their
> hopes are falsehood and their food is dust. Strangers to the true conci-
> sion of the heart, which they have experienced who worship God in the
> Spirit, rejoice in Christ Jesus and have no confidence in the flesh, the
> miserable votaries of Rome confound the emotions of mysterious awe,
> produced by the solemnities of a sensual worship, with reverence for
> God and the impressions of grace. Doomed to grope among the beggarly
> elements of earth, they regale the eye, the fancy and the ear; but the
> heart withers; imagination riots on imposing festivals and magnificent
> processions, symbols and ceremonies, libations and sacrifices; the suc-
> cessive stages of worship are like scenes of enchantment; but the gor-
> geous splendors of the liturgy, which famish the soul, while they delight
> the sense, are sad memorials of religion "lying in state surrounded with
> the silent pomp of death." The Holy Ghost has been supplanted by
> charms, and physical causes have usurped the province of supernatural
> grace.[20]

But the sacraments have no power of themselves—aside from the testimony of the Word. The shock is that Princeton (i.e., Hodge) should say that
the Roman and Calvinist views are the same.

> Rome's sacraments and our's [sic] belong to essentially different cat-
> egories. They are as wide apart as action and passion. When she
> baptizes, her water penetrates the soul, purges the conscience, and
> purifies the heart. When we baptize, we wash only the flesh, while
> our faith contemplates the covenant of God, and his unchanging
> faithfulness. Our baptism represents what the blood of the Redeemer,
> applied by the Eternal Spirit, performs upon the souls of the believ-
> ers. Rome's does the work itself. Our's is vain without the Holy
> Ghost. Rome's is all the Holy Ghost she needs.[21]

Rome vitiates the form by the dogma ex opere operato, changing the sacraments from means into laws or causes, a species of machinery. Thornwell
quotes Philipp Melanchthon (1497–1506), the colleague of Luther: "This opinion is pure Judaism, to suppose that we can be justified by a ceremony, without

a good motion of the heart—that is, without faith—and yet this impious and superstitious opinion, is taught with great authority in the whole kingdom of the Pope." And, of course, for Catholics the teaching of the church itself, not the opinion of the individual minister, is what counts for validity—so Arian Episcopalian ministers may validly baptize if they intend to do what the church wants while orthodox Catholic priests may not if they do not so intend. The creed of the church is the standard, and in this case it proves that the Presbyterian General Assembly and Catholics are not talking differently about the same thing (*res sacramenta*) but are talking about two different things: Presbyterians about a sacramental sign and Catholics about an act that causes saving grace.[22]

The latter point is the subject of the second article. The most conclusive proof that Roman baptism is not the same as Christ ordained is this: Christ ordained it as a sign and seal of *the covenant of grace*. Where that covenant is denied in essential elements, the sacraments are not administered or received. Baptism becomes an empty ceremony, a sign and a seal of nothing. The church must believe in the gospel for its baptism to be valid. Although one may call Roman Catholics Christian in the sociological sense, if the Church's gospel is not that of Christ her sacraments are invalid. She is anti-Christian in reality. Hodge thought that one is baptized a Christian by a papist, whereas in fact one is baptized a papist. Baptism puts one in a church with a non-Christian faith professed. So it is not Christianity distinct from Paganism, but popery distinct from Protestant Christianity. The Reformers knew this, and it constituted the heart of their protest.[23]

> And so the articles which make up the creed of a child of God, may enter into the profession of a papist, and yet the system, embraced by the one, be as widely different from the system of the other, as alcohol from sugar. The question in dispute is, whether the creed of Rome is a saving creed.[24]

Hodge's fallacy, according to Thornwell, was to think that the Catholic creed contains saving truths and so may save. But it is truth diluted and corrupted beyond saving. Yes, there may be children of God in "Babylon," but only because the Heavenly Father had their "attentions diverted from her monstrous conceptions." That Rome teaches "fatal, damnable heresy" was the judgment of the General Assembly, and that in fact she is apostate from the Christian faith. The issue was not whether Rome teaches enough true doctrine that one might be saved but whether she teaches enough error to damn the soul. She professes errors that cannot be professed without undercutting saving truth. Rome "denies the Blood" [atonement for sin and justification by grace alone] and teaches justification by works, a "false gospel." Rome believes that inherent righteousness is imparted by the sacrament, thus identifying justification and sanctification. No creed that teaches this is a saving creed.[25]

The Presbyterian line of the religious/theological criticism of the Catholic Church continued into the second half of the twentieth century in the work of evangelicals such as Loraine Boettner, John Armstrong, and R. C. Sproul.[26] On the other line, the political one laid down by Morse and Beecher, Catholicism is just as vigorously criticized in the twentieth century as a religion alien to democratic political and social values and practice. "This twentieth-century variety of nativism common to the secularized children of the evangelical movement (and to some evangelicals) is one that wishes to erase "illiberal" Catholicism, reaches the fullest form of expression in the work of Paul Blanshard after World War II. At this point, let us trace the religious critique represented by three nineteenth-century Congregationalists, at that time the "liberal" side of the evangelical spectrum, for the virulence of no-popery is not at all restricted to conservative evangelicals.

## The Congregationalists

Theodore Parker (1810–1860) as a young man had abandoned "the faith of our fathers" passed on by the New England Congregational tradition and embraced Unitarianism, a rationalized form of Congregationalism. Horace Bushnell, a vigorous evangelical Christian and contemporary of Parker, opened the door to a fresh theory of religious truth in his "Dissertation on Language," which later conservative evangelicals and fundamentalists called a road to modernism and unbelief. Noah Porter was a mid-nineteenth century exponent of a moralizing understanding of Christianity that some see as an important factor in the alienation of American institutions of higher learning from evangelical Protestantism. They are men whose theological positions have been abandoned by twentieth-century fundamentalists and neo-evangelicals but whose preeminence in the history of American evangelical Protestant thought can hardly be erased.

Parker must have infuriated and embarrassed every orthodox Christian in New England. In his short life he became an icon of liberal religion by denying the normative status of scripture and the divinity of Jesus, and by propounding the universality of religious truth. He rose to national prominence by supporting good causes, especially abolition, and by being an effective preacher and essayist. The short piece I consider here has the advantage of a compression of a view on the "apostate" wing of nineteenth-century Protestantism.[27]

In concert with ministerial intellectuals of his era, Parker judged Catholicism to be an authoritarian religion in an age of freedom. It "hates liberty in all its forms—free thought and free speech," he wrote. American Catholics at the time numbered less than two million, and in this sense the church was not a threat. But they were chiefly Irish and so enemies of "individual liberty in religion," unlike the Teutons "who have the strongest ethnological instinct for personal freedom." Catholics were pictured on a lower rung of the evolutionary ladder on the top rung of which stood the civilized, intelligent, and democratic Northern European—who appeared, in Thomas Nast's cartoons, tall, slim, and impeccably dressed. It required no particular form of the Christian faith to recognize the difference.

But the great problem presented by Catholics is the fact that their celibate masters determine how they live and act. In Parker's words:

> The Catholic worshiper is not to think, but to believe and obey; the
> priest not to reason and consider, but to proclaim and command;
> the voter not to enquire and examine, but to deposit his ballot as the
> ecclesiastical authority directs. The better religious orders do not
> visit America. The Jesuits, the most subtle enemies of humanity,
> come in abundance; some are known, others stealthily prowl about
> the land, all the more dangerous for their disguise. . . . No ten or
> forty Protestant ministers are a match for a combination of ten Jesu-
> its, bred to the business of deception, knowing no allegiance to
> Truth or Justice, consciously disregarding the Higher Law of God
> with the notorious maxim that "the end justifies the means," bound
> to their order by the most stringent oath, and devoted to the worst
> purposes of the Catholic Church. All these priests owe allegiance to
> a foreign head. It is not an American Church; it is Roman, not free,
> individual but despotic; nay, in its designs not so much human as
> merely papal.

Parker rehearsed the cant of common evangelical and nativist opinion of Roman Catholics, their clergy and the Jesuits. He foresaw political threats—especially to the public schools, the most consequential issue between American Catholics and Protestants in the nineteenth century. Parker bemoaned the fact that many do not recognize the threat, yet ends on a note that clashes with his distaste for all things Catholic. He enthusiastically (and perhaps ritually) welcomes Catholic immigrants:

> Let America be an asylum for the poor and the down-trodden of all
> lands; let the Irish ships, reeking with misery, land their human
> burdens in our harbors. The continent is wide enough for all. I re-
> joice that in America there is no national form of religion; let the
> Jew, the Chinese, Buddhist, the savage Indian, the Mormon, the
> Protestant, and the Catholic have free opportunity to be faithful each
> to his own conscience.

It is not hard to appreciate Parker's faith in America and his brand of American liberality, entirely absent the nativist exclusionary bent. No nativist would countenance a "let 'em all in" attitude. In this sense Parker is no nativist at all. It isn't the ethnic strangeness of the newcomers that bothers him, it is their supine acceptance of the religious, political, and intellectual tyranny of the Catholic clergy. Parker despises the Catholic mixture of hierarchy and tribalism, but he has more confidence than many of his countrymen in the power of the American landscape and ideal to digest these otherwise unpalatable morsels.

Horace Bushnell (1802–76) studied first law and then theology at Yale University, and later became the minister of North Congregational church in Hartford, Connecticut (1833–59). Conversion as young adult took him away from the legal profession to the podium of the anti-Calvinist Nathaniel Taylor at the Divinity School. Bushnell has often been called "the father of liberalism," no cheer to conservative evangelicals and reformed theologians. Emerson was more than happy in his Divinity School Address to toss Christian language overboard as offensive to human nature.[28] At the same time, Charles Hodge at Princeton argued constantly that Christian language was based on the propositional truths of the scriptures. With neither man could Bushnell agree. Considering all language to be metaphorical and a social phenomenon, he argued in his *Dissertation on Language* that the scriptural language provoked imagination and promoted insight rather than supplying propositions for a deductivist theological operation. Against revivalist ideologies of adult conversion, he emphasized the importance of Christian nurture in family and church community. He worked out a fascinating theory of the relation of nature and the supernatural as two sides of one system of providence. Some have put him up with Jonathan Edwards and Reinhold Niebuhr in impact on American theology.[29]

Bushnell wrote about Catholicism in three important essays. In *The Crisis of the Church* in 1835, he found American Protestantism confronting the obligation to civilize and Christianize the western states.[30] In the midst of the worry of evangelical preachers (Beecher) and others (Morse) about the danger of a papal takeover of the states from the Appalachians to the Mississippi valley, Bushnell wanted to find support for civilizing and Christianizing efforts while contributing a clarification to the public debate about the Catholic Church. Like Channing, Hodge, and Porter, he was no nativist, but he was an outspoken patriot, one might even say a chauvinist, and a believer in the sacramental bond between America and Protestant Christianity. In fact, his essays have more than a faint odor of Manifest Destiny. For Bushnell, the City on a Hill should become an American Christian Empire. In the path of empire stood slavery, infidelity, and Romanism, in that order of importance.

If less than the spread of slavery and infidelity,[31] Romanism was nonetheless a real threat. Perhaps from Morse and Beecher he heard of Roman "advances in a distant part of our country." Schlegel's Vienna lectures in 1828 proved to him ". . . that Romanism is the natural ally of absolutism."[32] Echoing Morse, Bushnell claimed that Austria's St. Leopold Foundation had flooded the western part of the country in the previous few years with six hundred nuns and Jesuits, and that Catholics spent $100,000 to spread popery. He, too, quoted Pope Gregory's encyclical of 1832, *Mirari Vos,* which vigorously condemned religious toleration, liberty of conscience, liberty of opinion, and liberty of the press. That there was a papal design on American institutions he does not doubt. The Catholic Church poured in immigrants and "Every one of them and their descendants are meant to be our enemies, and most of them probably will be."[33] And yet the American press sleeps, truckling to

> ... the Power that has ever opposed and still opposes the simplest ideas of liberty—the power which has filled the world for ages with fires and groans of torture Nay, it even trusts the Jesuits! whom it has ever been a standing maxim with all men to suspect and guard against. Alas, we have even been humbled to see our own American press, bent to the earth and fawning with flatteries and caresses [*sic*], that it might propitiate the votes of these alien enemies![34]

His theological liberalism was not an antidote to the simple pleasures of Protestant bias. With biases firmly in place, a decade later Bushnell raised Romanism a notch, to the second danger in the West. In *Barbarism the First Danger: A Discourse for the Home Missions,* the first problem is civilizing the West.[35] Romanism will only succeed if the effort to civilize fails:

> If you seem to struggle, in this matter of Romanism, with contrary convictions; to see reason in the alarms urged upon you so frequently, and yet feel it to be the greatest unreason to fear the prevalence here of a religion so distinctively opposite to our character and institutions; if you waver between a feeling of panic and a feeling of derision; if you are half frightened by the cry of Romanism, and half scorn it as a bugbear; you will be able to settle yourself into a sober and fixed opinion of the subject, when you perceive that we are in danger, first, of something far worse than Romanism, and through that of Romanism itself. OUR FIRST DANGER IS BARBARISM— Romanism is next. . . . Romanism will find us just where character leaves us. . . . For if we must have a wild race of nomads roaming over the vast western territories of our land—a race without education, law, manners or religion—we need not trouble ourselves farther on account of Romanism; for to such a people, Romanism, bad as it is, will come as a blessing.[36]

Those who think Romanism the great danger and those who think it no danger at all are mistaken. There are very accomplished Romanists; one can be socially advanced under it. But a freeminded people cannot be brought into the Roman church except if they first yield to superstition whose gate is opened by a loss of knowledge, social order, and religion, that is, barbarism. In some cases a person can surrender cultivation and reason, and be weary and get lost "in the mazes of fantastic speculation" and find himself a Catholic priest and so "fall a prey to their own delicate illusions, and drop into the Romish church to settle their peace. . . . Thus, over-cultivation may sometimes join hands at the church door with barbarism, both entering as fellow proselytes together."[37] But the only great danger is in a multiplication of persons who have no developed private judgment at all. Men must come to God through intelligence, or they will find a peculiar god through superstition. The Mormon Temple and city (Salt Lake?) prove just how bad things can get:

> Who could have thought it possible that a wretched and silly delu-
> sion, like that of the Mormons, could gather in its thousands of dis-
> ciples in this enlightened age, build a populous city, and erect a tem-
> ple, rivalling [sic] in grandeur, even that of the false prophet at
> Mecca? . . . It is vain to imagine that Romanism can find no affini-
> ties prepared among us. . . . Or if we persist in training a barbarous
> people for its use, let us indulge no regrets that Romanism gives
> them such a religion as they are capable of receiving.[38]

Romanism, like Mormonism, is a religion of superstition a step above barbarian paganism, surely preferable to paganism but by some leagues inferior to Protestant Christianity. Romanism can only attract the uneducated, the uncivilized, the barbarian.

Whereas in his first two essays on Catholicism Bushnell seems intent on pressing a measure of reason in the public discussion, the *Letter to His Holiness, Pope Gregory XVI*[39] (1846), is an anti-Roman broadside. It was prompted by a trip through the papal states and is little more than an expression of disapproval calculated to impress as well as inform his public and to insult the pope. He opened the letter by denying any respect for the papal office and the Catholic faith and closed with a warning (hardly needed!) that the pope is an old man facing death and judgment. In between he listed the horrors his trip had in store for him: papal despotism; clerical greed; saints' feast days that block economic progress; complete lack of interest in the truth; relics; infallibility, which he piously (and vainly) hopes is nauseating to the pope himself; celibacy, pageantry, *castrati*, collections of the fine arts, thrones borne aloft, statues being kissed, persecution of other Christians—what could any of this have to do with the apostle Peter? He is, of course, mainly correct. What indeed? The target is easy. The subject of the essay is outraged Protestant sensibility rather than papal rule. He is venting the passions of a self-righteous American.

We find in Bushnell a vigorous, if slightly refined and no less passionate, version of evangelical hatred of popery, but one that does not force him to believe that Rome poses an impending threat to the national, Protestant interest. He makes no theological attack and uses none of the standard apocalyptic imagery. His is a historicized, demythologized prejudice standing at the borders of Reformation and Enlightenment mythologies. Oddly enough, I have found

Bushnell's theories of language and Christian nurture far more compatible with Catholic theology than with those of his nineteenth-century colleagues— say, Thornwell and Hodge—and perhaps this accounts for the nontheological character of his criticism of it.[40] There is no more metaphorical or symbolic version of Christianity than Catholicism (and the equally ancient Orthodoxy). Still, while the hands are the hands of Esau, the voice remains the voice of Jacob. The profound American Protestant disdain for the papacy drives the man and the patriot, stopping short of nativist ethnicism and apocalyptic nightmares.

Noah Porter (1811–92), like Bushnell, studied with Nathaniel Taylor at Yale, but Porter got to marry Taylor's daughter Mary in 1836. After preaching in several Congregational churches over the next decade, in 1846 he became Clark Professor of Moral Theology and Metaphysics and Yale's president from 1871 to 1886. He led Yale away from clerical-doctrinal education toward "Christian character" education, a step on the now famous slippery slope to a secularized university sketched by George Marsden.[41] He resisted the elective system afoot at Harvard and nixed the use of Herbert Spenser's *Study of Sociology* as a college text.[42] He was a warm-hearted evangelical teacher and one of the outstanding religious philosophers of his time. He crosses our path in 1851 with the publication of a lengthy essay, *The Educational Systems of the Puritans and Jesuits Compared, a Premium Essay Written for the Society for the Promotion of Collegiate and Theological Education at the West.*[43]

Porter retells in forty of his ninety pages the history of the Society of Jesus, from Ignatius's founding in 1534 through its success in the Catholic Counter Reformation to its suppression in 1773 by Pope Clement XIV and its revival by Pope Pius VII in 1814, a short time after that pope's release from Napoleon's captivity. With the lengthy narrative Porter impresses on his readers that Jesuit education is the single largest factor in the recovery of Catholicism from what seemed to be the deadly blow delivered it by the Reformers. The Jesuits stopped the reform in its tracks, with no Protestant advances since 1550.[44] They did so by getting "personal influence over the youth of Europe, so as to be able to mold and use them at their will." The schools were staffed with highly skilled teachers, were severely religious, had a morally pure atmosphere, were devotionally rigid, applied an exacting discipline—and were free of charge to all comers, including Protestants![45] Jesuit education, in his view, was the strongest and most revealing expression of modern Catholicism, and the cause of the current American evangelical alarm.

To set up his initial comparison, Porter proposed that the Jesuit is the essential Catholic, whereas Puritan is the consistent Protestant. By "Puritan" he meant American evangelical Protestantism, primarily in New England. The Puritan is characterized by "freedom and independence . . . as obedience and dependence distinguish the Jesuit. . . . Hence he [the Puritan] is by nature a Reformer. He is intent upon changing old laws, old institutions, and old habits that they may meet new exigencies."[46] Porter took it for granted that the schools and colleges of the United States were Protestant, in which children had been taught to read the scriptures and be good citizens, as different from Romish-educated masses as marble is from limestone. If these schools ceased to exist so does Protestantism in its "freedom, its science and its religion."[47] So Puritan education is as essential to the freedom and progress of Americans as Jesuit is to Catholic control of their societies. Unlike Parker but very much like Bushnell, Porter identified Protestantism and American values.

Two basic contrasts are made by Porter. Puritans educate the masses. Jesuits consider this dangerous—they don't believe in popular education, and have never originated a project of education of the lower orders of society. And Puritan education is "earnestly religious," fitting students for the life to come. In the Puritan system all else is a means to the end of eternal life. Thus freedom and the independence of the sciences are prized, unlike the Jesuit's religion where every thought and every conclusion of science must be watched.[48] The Puritan favors democracy, the Jesuit despotism. Whatever the excellences the latter may achieve, it does so on the basis of despotism:

> It is a despotism far more dreadful than any civil or ecclesiastical system; for it takes into its iron grasp the intellect and soul of a living man. It seeks to crush and break in pieces the will which God gave him when he made him a person, and to mar and wrong the conscience, with which he has made him responsible to himself. . . . Its proudest results . . . are based upon a sin against the rights and freedom of the individual man.[49]

Yet (and here Porter lapsed into subjunctive and optative) the Puritan "may" surpass the Jesuit scholar in mental energy, ready tact, practical application, and continuing study. The product of Puritan schools will associate freely and cooperatively, on his own initiative. Jesuit education is like the French formal garden, while the Puritan is like the English garden where nature and grace conspire to harmony. The outcome of the one is erudition and of the other independent thought.[50]

> The Jesuit lives in the past, he adores and reverences the men and institutions that are gone by, with the blended enthusiasm of the scholar and the devotee. . . . The one system will train its pupils to investigate Truth. The other will discipline its scholars to defend opinions. The one will make philosophic thinkers, the other acute and skillful advocates. . . . The Jesuit will train erudite students, careful observers and admirable expounders of truths already received. The Protestant will be more likely to start a new theory, invent a new method, or make a new discovery.[51]

And they teach history differently, from different principles: "The Jesuit *dare* not teach the History of Freedom. . . . The history which he teaches, if true in its dates and events, must be false and sophistical in its philosophy. It must be steeped in sophistry—craven in its cowardice—or brazen with conscious lies."[52] They teach subjection in all things to the church. Whereas the end-in-view of Puritan education is eternal life, the end of Jesuit education is submission to the church (68–69):[53]

> To those who, like ourselves, look upon the Romish system as a system of dangerous and fatal error, as a monstrous incubus, stifling and oppressing the gospel of Christ, no place can be so dangerous to the young as a Jesuit college, every exercise of which is made to assume religious influence. With the most favorable judgment of this religious influence, it will be likely either to gain the pupil to the Catholic faith as a deluded devotee, or to harden him against all faith and feeling, as a hopeless unbeliever. The Jesuit denies to man the right training of his character. Nay, he denies to him a character at all; for he denies him the freedom and separate responsibility which are necessary to make a character possible.[54]

The basic charge throughout seems to be that the Catholic Church, with Jesuits in the vanguard, negates the humanity of its adherents, the key words being freedom and responsibility. All the Jesuit training and discipline in the world is no more than ". . . giv[ing] to the eyes a marvelous acuteness, in discerning objects on the floor of the dungeon . . ."[55] Jesuit education would make slaves of us all.

Porter exhibits throughout his essay an ambivalence that is only partially explained by the instincts of the scholar doing battle with the instincts of the bigot. His scholarship is suspect at the root, for he writes of what he knows little and attempts to persuade his readers to what he loves. In all fairness, he has done more than most of the American Protestants writing on Catholicism. He actually read a sympathetic history of the Society, and, *mirabile dictu,* envied their success and the excellence of the humanist education they impart. But it would have been an easy matter for him to have obtained copies of the *Spiritual Exercises,* the *Constitutions of the Society of Jesus,* and the *Ratio Studiorum* and read them himself. Surely in the darkened streets of New Haven he might well have stumbled over a hooded Jesuit scurrying home from a clandestine meeting whom he might have asked the purposes of the Society in its educational ventures. But he chose not to do so, or perhaps it did not occur to him. After all, the basic issues were settled long ago. What he did required little scholarship even by nineteenth-century American standards: he pitched a line torn from popular American Protestantism, puffing it up with the semblance of scholarship in the hope of making some money for the Western missions. Alas, neither the first nor the last theologian to do so, and at least he had the missions in mind!

The Jesuit, he tells us, as the "essential Catholic," bends young minds to the will of Rome. The will of Rome, of course, is to bend all minds to its own despotic purposes. The Jesuit is merely Rome's sharpest tool. The thesis at the center of Porter's charge is freedom to think for one's self, the highest American Protestant virtue, and Rome is its antithesis. Although there is nary a trace of the vicious ethnicism and xenophobia of the political and social nativists, and very little specifically religious criticism of the sort practiced by many evangelical anti-Catholic authors (very little of the myth), there remains in Porter's work the basic reformed perception that Protestantism means religious and personal freedom and that Romanism means mindlessness and spiritual slavery.[56] He, along with his fellow Congregationalists and theological liberals, indicate that basic suspicions are not modified by a move to the theological left, but what in fact begins with that move is the demythologization and the secularization of anti-Catholicism.

## Conclusion

The apocalyptic language of fear and denigration and the charges of gross sexual immorality make no appreciable appearance in the rhetorical persona of any of the six men, although the moral superiority of Protestantism is prominent in all of them. Although the reformation theological supposition (*lux ex tenebris*, the heart of the Reformation myth) remains in place for thinkers of both the Presbyterian and Congregational religious traditions and although all of them are apprehensive about dangers that Catholicism poses to Protestant America, the six diverge in their presentation of the danger. The Presbyterians' objections are primarily theological and remain in close contract with the original Calvinist impetus, perhaps because their respective audiences are Calvinist. The Congregationalists worry far more about the political and social dangers, perhaps because they are used to an Arminian audience. Like Morse, the Congregationalists concentrate on the national, cultural problem posed by the Catholic Church and much less on the religious and theological. Like Nevins, the Presbyterians stand with Reformation orthodoxy. Calvin is left far behind by Parker, Bushnell, and Porter, and theological liberalism already settled into their bones. None of the three Congregationalists had a significant theological objection to make; none rested his case on Roman apostasy or heterodoxy. Granted, Parker stood in a glass house when it came to heresy and apostasy, but it is notable that Bushnell and Porter made no argument on the issue of orthodoxy. Can we already see the emergence of two forms of Protestant critique in two more general tendencies of American Protestantism, those that will in the twentieth century come to be called mainline and neo-evangelical? I think so. We shall see more of it.

# 7

# Hard Evangelicals and the Apostate Church

The most important decision faced by American Evangelicals in the late twentieth century with regard to the Catholic Church was whether it was better to deal with it as an apostate church or a heretical church. If evangelicals choose to deal with the Catholic Church as an apostate church, there is very little more theological reflection left to do but there is evangelism to be done. If the church is an apostate, then her members must be converted to the Christian gospel lest they lose their souls, and the propaganda of the church and its growth must be checked. It is, in this case, the largest and most dangerous of the cults, all the more dangerous for its expert packaging of its pseudogospel in Christian terms. This option means a continuation of the historical assessment of the Catholic Church by most American evangelicals.

The second option is more complicated and requires a great deal more thought. If the "Romish Church" is a heretical church only, then one has to explain why one departs from the inherited judgment of apostasy, one must determine how and in what sense the Catholic Church is Christian and in what sense not, one must determine whether or not this or that Catholic is a Christian and deal with each accordingly, one must determine a strategy for dealing with the ambiguous and dangerous church which teaches an alloy of the Christian gospel without compromising with the heretical elements, one must be prepared to learn things about the church and about Catholics that one could not learn while maintaining the traditional stance. One must constantly discern and distinguish. One may be surprised, and one may even be tempted (she is the

Mother Church after all). Finally, and perhaps this is the trickiest problem of all, one must explain to one's fellow evangelicals who remain convinced of Rome's apostasy how one has changed one's mind on Rome without breaking fellowship with them.

Those who hold with the traditional judgment of apostasy I call "hard" evangelicals; those who have modified that judgment and are ready to act accordingly I call "soft"evangelicals. In this chapter I will review some recent examples of the "hard" evangelical option and, in the next chapter, trace the line of the "soft" evangelicals from the nineteenth through the twentieth centuries. The two lines met in public conflict over *Evangelicals and Catholic Together.*

## Loraine Boettner

Loraine Boettner (1901–90) received his Master's degree in theology at Princeton Seminary in 1929, at the time Princeton was making a transition from "the Old Princeton" theological tradition of A. A. Alexander and Charles Hodge to newer currents in methods and in theological options. J. Gresham. Machen (1881–1937)[1] withdrew from Princeton that year with several other conservatives, founding Westminister Theological Seminary near Philadelphia to keep the currents of "modernism" from eradicating orthodox Presbyterian ministerial training and Old Princetonian theological and biblical scholarship. Westminster is far more Boettner's theological home than Princeton, although he received his degree from the latter. He was also a member of the Orthodox Presbyterian Church founded by Machen in 1936 after his expulsion from the Presbyterian Church.[2] Boettner's book *Roman Catholicism,* first printed in 1962, had gone through twenty-seven printings and nearly 140,000 copies by 1989. It is still on the shelves of evangelical bookstores.[3]

Boettner published *Roman Catholicism* fifteen years after the first edition of Blanshard's *American Freedom and Catholic Power* (1947), four years after Blanshard's second edition (1958), two years after John Kennedy's election to the presidency (1960), and during the first session of the second Vatican Council (1962), which was effecting the most sweeping changes in the church since the Council of Trent (1545). Together the two books represent the high point in twentieth-century American Protestant criticism of the Catholic Church. Boettner relied on Blanshard's book, especially its sections on Catholic medical ethics and marriage, and thoroughly agreed with Blanshard's political criticism of the Church and the papacy.[4]

The framework as well as the content of his theological assessment is doctrinal rather than eschatological. The Antichrist and millennialism are entirely absent. His book is as much a secularization of the Protestant myth as is Blanshard's in this one respect. In addition, like Blanshard, he assigns a minor role to sexual charges against priests—both are more concerned with public policy than with private morals. The old Puritan concerns surface, however, in Boettner's chapter on the confessional, as we shall see. The nativist concern with the incompatibility of Catholicism and democracy is important to Boettner but the theological contrasts loom larger by far. Blanshard's objection to the Catholic Church is chiefly political and social, with a theology entombed in democratic/socialist idealism. Boettner's is a Protestant critique, with the politics in a prominent but still subordinate role. Blanshard's basic educational and philosophical suppositions are Deweyite Pragmatism, while Boettner's Christian language is Reformed evangelical.

The book follows the traditional Protestant Outline to a fault: chapter topics include the Church, the priesthood, the illegitimacy of tradition, Peter and Rome, the papacy, Mary, the Mass, the confessional, purgatory, infallibility, the sacrament of penance, indulgences, grace and works, ritualism, celibacy, marriage, parochial schools, the Roman Church's moral standards, and its persecution of non-Catholics. In most chapters he follows the traditional evangelical procedure: he presents the Catholic practice or belief, shows that it is not in the Bible or contradicts the teaching of the Bible, and then explores the history of the practice or belief showing its roots in paganism or Judaism, and finally compares it with Protestantism, showing Protestantism to be biblical Christianity. There are references to the second Vatican Council (1962–65) in footnotes and in the preface to the fifth edition (1989).[5]

The book stands out for several reasons: its comprehensive coverage, its organized presentation (it is a model of the tractarian literary form), and its consistent and clear conservative theology. Boettner has integrated historical and systematic arguments. He also weaves his comparison of Catholicism with paganism and Judaism into his historical narrative neatly, effectively, and persistently. The only significant drawback to the book as a specimen of no-popery is that, although it is better than most, it is much more of the same. Like Blanshard, Boettner is part of a long tradition, an ambiguous blessing as any thoughtful Catholic would know. Blanshard presents himself as if he discovered the danger posed by the Catholic Church, while Boettner happily places himself in the long line of those who have known of the danger for four centuries.

The Protestant myth is recited at the outset, parts of it reappear at crucial points in his narrative, and he ends with it.[6] The basic principles of evangelical Christianity are traced to Luther and Calvin and then to first-century Christianity. Protestantism is nothing else than a return to New Testament Christianity and the simplicity of the Apostolic church. The Reformation itself was a back-to-the-Bible movement, a return to apostolic Christianity. The Bible is the Word of God and so the sole authoritative rule of faith and practice. Any element of church life and belief that cannot be traced back to the New Testament is no essential part of Christianity. Protestantism, then, agrees on: (1) supremacy of the Bible; (2) justification by faith, not works; (3) the right of the individual to go directly to God apart from the mediation by any priest; (4) individual freedom of conscience; and (5) worship within the limits of the Bible.[7]

Answering the Catholic charge on the issue, Boettner made out that the differences between Protestant denominations are "for the most part exaggeration," and criticism of differences is "due largely to Rome's failure to understand what Protestantism really is."[8] Protestantism, in his view, is a unified protest against Roman corruptions. In addition, Protestantism has lead to the modern doctrines of freedom of religion, of conscience and of speech, and to the developments of the economies and politics of the Protestant nations. The United States is a Protestant nation: so also are Britain, Canada, Holland, Norway, Sweden, and Denmark, the most advanced and enlightened nations in the world, where people think and act for themselves. Protestantism leads to democracy and prosperity.

Between the early church and the Reform the popes controlled state and church in the Dark Ages, suppressing the laity and forbidding Bible reading, prying into marital life and public affairs, destroying resistance, keeping the Bible from the people, the very things it continued to do in Boettner's day in Spain, Portugal, Italy, and France. The papacy is in fact political rather than religious, a form of totalitarianism like Communism and Nazism. This echoes Blanshard's complaint. This is the unvarnished Catholicism, unlike that in the United States where it has had to adapt under the pressure of Protestantism. It must be seen as it was in medieval Europe and is in the Catholic nations where it currently has political as well as ecclesiastical control. There it becomes plain that the fruits of Romanism are poverty, ignorance, superstition, low moral standards, and intolerance.

The distinctive features of the Catholic Church were unknown in New Testament times and entered the church with the pagan influx beginning in the fourth century. Christianity became a Hellenistic mystery religion, and Gregory the Great (d. 604) founded the papal system.[9] A list of pagan features in Catholicism would begin in 300 A.D. with the introduction of prayers for the dead and include in chronological order: candles, veneration of angels, daily Mass, Mary as mother of God, clerical garb, last rights, purgatory, Latin imposed, prayer to Mary, pope title, kissing the pope's foot, the temporal power of the pope, worship of cross and images, holy water, worship of St. Joseph, cardinals, baptism of bells, canonization of saints, fasting during Lent, Mass as sacrifice, required celibacy, rosary, inquisition, sale of indulgences, transubstantiation, auricular confession, adoration of the host, the Bible forbidden to laymen and placed on index, the scapular invented, the communion cup forbidden to the laity, purgatory defined, seven sacraments affirmed, the Ave Maria as prayer, the Jesuits, tradition declared as source equal to the Bible, apocryphal books added by Trent, a papal creed imposed, the Immaculate Conception defined, Syllabus of Errors, papal infallibility defined, American public schools condemned, the Assumption of Mary defined, and Mary proclaimed Mother of the Church at the second Vatican Council. Add the superfluous and often antigospel practices: monks and nuns, monasteries and convents, forty days of Lent, Holy Week, Palm Sunday, Ash Wednesday, All Saints' Day, Candlemas, abstinence on Friday, incense, holy oil, palm, medals, charms, novenas, and others. The whole development of this peculiar form of "Christianity" culminates in the new doctrines of Mediatrix and Co-Redemptrix, wherein Mary has quite plainly become the fourth person of the Godhead.[10]

> There you have it—the melancholy evidence of Rome's steadily increasing departure from the Gospel, a departure so radical and far reaching at the present time that it has produced a drastically antievangelical church. . . . The real heretics are Roman Catholics themselves and the true orthodox are the evangelical Christians.[11]

How do we know that the Catholic "system" is not true Christianity? By comparing it with the Bible: Protestantism is identical with the truth of the New Testament, while Catholic accretions are false. But the nature of Romanism becomes evident in Latin America where, in every town of any size, heathenism and Romanism are woven into the pattern of life. Religious syncretism results in ignorance, poverty, superstition, illiteracy, suppression of religious freedom, and prostitution. In the United States the threat grows with the recent advances of Catholics in public life: dominance in the Democratic party for over thirty years (1928–60), and the election of a Catholic president. Of course, this advance needs explanation, for Boettner maintains that this is a Protestant and so a politically enlightened nation. The explanation is unregenerate human nature: "It can be assumed that Catholicism will remain popular as long as the majority of men remain unregenerate."[12]

Rome's failure to take the Bible seriously is, for Boettner, joined to an equally damaging flaw: Catholic practice and belief to a large extent originate in Hellenistic paganism and Judaism. Some examples follow.

## The Priesthood

Clericalism is an albatross on the neck of the Roman Church.[13] In a true Christian church Christ alone is Priest. There can be no second priest, no *alter Christus*, for his sacrificial death once for all ended the need for sacrifice. There is no New Testament priesthood. The priesthood has to do with ritual and sacrifice that have been abolished—except for the priesthood of believers who thereby have direct access to God. This true priesthood is a distinctive mark of the Protestant churches. Rome is in heresy on this point.[14]

> Through the use of spurious sacraments, the sacrifice of the mass, the confessional, indulgences, and other priestly instruments it in-

sists on keeping in place the curtain [in the temple] that God him-
self has removed. It continues to place fallible human priests, the
Virgin Mary and dead saints as mediators between the sinner and
God . . . absolutely unscriptural and unchristian.[15]

The crucial question is the source of these nonscriptural beliefs and practices. All pre-Christian religions had two common elements: a human priesthood and a salvation that was incomplete. Never-ending sacrifices failed to do
the job for pagans and for Jews, and so the sinful person was left to repair the
damage in the after-life. So also in Catholicism. Purgatory and Mass represent
a "radical perversion" of biblical Christianity, for they mean that Catholicism
has rejected the biblical doctrine of salvation by faith in the sacrificial death of
the Son of God, and has fallen back to a salvation by works common to paganism and Judaism.[16]

But how did the Romanists honeycomb the truth with paganism, and come
to have a "semi-pagan organization"? The answer is that "the illegitimate authority that Rome has given to uninspired tradition has produced the effect."
Rome displays ". . . the attitude which characterized the Pharisees and scribes,
who substituted a body of human teachings and made them equal to or even
superior to the Word of God."[17] Catholicism, like rabbinic Judaism, added to
the sacred scriptures an oral tradition partly codified in the documents of
popes, councils, and theologians. The refusal of Rome to allow the common
people to read the Bible allowed the symbiosis of Christianity with paganism
and Judaism. Had they been allowed to read, they would have been in possession of true Christianity and been able to recognize perversions of it.

Although modern political practice has changed, still Rome does not look
on it favorably. "Small wonder it is that ignorance, superstition, poverty, and
low moral conditions have been so characteristic of Roman Catholic countries."
Tyranny and biblical illiteracy, two marks of the Roman church, are traceable
to the ethos of pagan sacrificial practice that the Roman church absorbed and
the papacy imposed on others. The Bible makes Protestant Christians free,
progressive, and prosperous, while ritual binds Catholics to the practices of
classical pagan civilization.[18]

## The Papacy

The papacy, too, has nothing to do with the facts of the New Testament church,
and nothing to do with the historical Peter. The actual foundation and rise of
the papacy is not a complicated tale:

After the fourth century, when the Roman empire had fallen, the
bishops of Rome stepped into Caesar's shoes, took the pagan title of
Pontifex Maximus, the supreme high priest of the pagan Roman religion, sat down on Caesar's throne, and wrapped themselves in

Caesar's gaudy trappings. And that role they have continued ever since.[19]

"Pontiff" is the high priest (bridge builder) of pagan Roman religion, as the high priest of the Jerusalem temple was of Judaism. The pagan and Jewish unending sacrifice and their form of pontifical leadership led to the imposition of a sacrificial priesthood and a high priest on the Christian church. The imposition created the Roman Catholic Church. The popes have claimed to hold "upon this earth the place of God almighty . . . ruler of this world . . . Holy Father (blasphemy) . . . vicar of Christ," thus replacing the original early Christian practice, namely ". . . a democratic meeting of the ordained leaders of the churches judging matters according to God's word." The governance of the early church sounds suspiciously like a Presbyterian General Assembly.

Nor is there is much about Mary in the New Testament.[20] She arrived on the church scene after the veneration of martyrs and ascetics had begun. She was called "Mother of God" in the fifth century—but then it meant mother of the flesh of the human nature. The title was given to protect the reality of the human nature of Christ, but she was exalted to supernatural status as pagan Queen of Heaven, and as a result lost all reference to orthodox Christology.

> When we say that a woman is the mother of a person we mean that she gave birth to that person. But Mary certainly did not give birth to God, nor to Jesus Christ as the eternal Son of God. She was not the mother of our Lord's divinity, but only of his humanity. Instead, Christ, the second person of the blessed Trinity, has existed from all eternity, and was Mary's creator. Hence the term as used in the present day Roman Church must be rejected. . . . In the Roman Church Mary is to her worshippers [sic] what Christ is to us. She is the object of all religious affections, and the source whence all the blessings of salvation are sought and expected.[21]

Where did Marian piety and worship come from? Once again, the answer is simple. After 150 years of no devotion to Mary, the Christian church was flooded with pagans who transferred their goddess superstitions and devotions to Mary, the mother of Jesus. "Thousands of people who then entered the church brought with them the superstitions and devotions they had long given to Isis, Diana, Artemis, Aphrodite, and other goddesses, which were then conveniently transferred to Mary."[22]

## Confession

In talking about the sacrament of penance, Boettner immerses himself in one of the deepest of all the Protestant moral concerns about Catholic practice.[23] He sums up the long tradition: fear of intrusion into the individual's conscience; fear of nonfamilial and nonpublic power (What is my wife or daughter telling that man in that dark box and what is he whispering to her?); gender and sexual worries (How can a man listen to a woman's "private" thoughts without becoming sexually involved with her?); political, economic, and societal pressure from the confessor on behalf of the church hierarchy (you must vote for Al Smith, or I won't give you absolution, and you'll rot in hell!). Boettner once again echoes the literary tradition.

> Through the use of the confessional the priest has been able to pry into the conscience of each individual, so that no heretic might escape, and in the case of the faithful to gain entrance into the privacy of the domestic family circle. There is literally and in truth *no area* of life that is exempt from the scrutiny and supervision of the priest. "Knowledge is power," and that power can be wielded in many ways, to direct people along lines that will promote the church program, or for personal benefit of the priest himself. It is perfectly evident that the priest to whom a person has confessed his thoughts, desires, and every sinful action just as it occurred, has placed that person largely under his control. For some that means little less than slavery. This is particularly true of women and girls who have even destroyed their self-respect in so surrendering themselves to the priest. The result is a sense of shame, worry, and being at the mercy of the priest. Through the confessional Rome has been able to exercise an effective control not only over the family, but over political officials of every grade, teachers, doctors, lawyers, employers and employees, and indeed over all who submit to that discipline.[24]

To convey better the sordid aspects of the practice, Boettner calls on the books and pamphlets of former priests who describe their experience in hearing confessions, among them Lucien Vinet, *I Was a Priest,* and Charles Chiniquy, *The Priest, the Woman and the Confessional,* whose book is "the best available dealing with all phases of the confessional."[25] The former concludes "Poor Roman Catholic women!" after describing confessions of girls, young women, and married women. Chiniquy recounts putting "impure, immoral questions to women and girls . . . debasing, degraded, polluted" and so forth. "What a fraudulent, dishonest, futile, and unscriptural practice the operation of the confessional really is!" Boettner concludes.[26]

Jenny Franchot, in her review of the images of Catholicism in the literature of nineteenth-century American Protestants, suggests that in much American anti-Catholic and, in particular, anticonfessional propaganda, we find hints of the Protestant fears of sexual and economic encroachment on the patriarchal family, and worry about women on the loose engaging in unsupervised conversations with extrafamilial males. She writes:

> Because confession, according to anti-Catholic fictions, involved disclosing the repressed contents of the heart of bewitched Protestant

maidens, Protestants saw it as tantamount to illicit sexual inter-
course. "How terrible, my dear sister," explained a convent escapee
to women still outside the celibate enclosure of the convent, "is the
power of these men, who pry into the most secret recesses of our
hearts." Thus the encounter between the celibate priest and young
women in the hidden interior of the confessional was attacked as an
unavoidable occasion for seduction and sexual captivity because unsupervised talking . . . was itself seen as a surrogate sexual act. . . .
The convent's supposed invitation to leisure was typically represented in contradictory images of sexual license and mindless obedience, of a self both rampaging and passive that in both guises rejected republican and Protestant ideologies of self-government and
industriousness.[27]

The sacrament of penance is only the most evident perversion of biblical
Christianity leading to social degradation. Ritualistic worship accounts for the
power and influence the Church has over its own and others. For example, the
coronation of Pope John XXIII in 1958 on television: ". . . a purely man-made
religious display, ritualistic ceremony that is not even hinted at anywhere in
the Bible!" Romanism is a liturgical or ritual church, and as such it is a far
departure from the purity and simplicity of the Gospel, which spurs human
beings to progress.

The supposed blessing [of attendance at ceremony] is mysterious
and magical. . . . Romanism is in this respect a recrudescence of Judaism, and its ceremonialism stands much closer to Judaism than to
New Testament Christianity. It has the delight of the picture language of the ceremonies that were designed for the childhood of the
church, and it still is fascinated with the beauty of the temple and its
gorgeous ritual . . . most of the ritual and ceremonialism was taken
over from the pagan religion of ancient Rome. . . . Let Protestants
not be deceived by the outward splendor of Romanism. . . .
    Were the apostles to return to earth and enter a Roman Catholic
church, they would scarcely be able to distinguish between the pagan worship of idols that they knew and the present day practice of
kneeling before images, burning incense to them, kissing them,
praying to them, and carrying them in public processions. The Roman Church today is about as thoroughly given over to idolatry as
was the city of Athens when Paul visited there.[28]

The widest and best explanation that Boettner can offer for the existence
and the makeup of Roman Catholicism is that it is an historical amalgam of
paganism and Judaism. Its hierarchical structure is imperial Roman, its ritual
and spiritual practice is pagan and Jewish, its understanding of salvation is
Jewish works-righteousness, and its continued existence and appeal counts on

the sin-clouded nature of human being. He does not find a significant element of Christian faith in Catholicism.[29]

What cannot be explained by Catholicism's Jewish heritage is explained by the early church's assimilation of paganism:

> The condition of the present day Roman Church would seem to be in many ways similar to that of Judaism at the time of Christ. There was much truth in Judaism and there were many sincere believers among the people. But the priesthood was largely indifferent to the needs of the people, as were the ruling classes, the Pharisees and the Sadducees. Like the Roman priests, the Jewish priests withheld the Word of God from the people, and their chief concern was their own advancement. . . .
>
> The pagan priesthood, which was losing the battle in behalf of the old religion, readily sensed the trend of affairs and began to scheme as to how it too [millions of pagan laity were also invading] could share in those benefits. The result was that it too began to push into or infiltrate the church, at first cautiously, and then more openly and boldly. Some of the pagan temples were rededicated as Christian churches. This crafty, invading priesthood gathered to itself more and more power until it completely displaced the apostolic Christian ministry.[30]

The priesthood limited the laity's access to the Bible, and for a thousand years, from 476 to 1517, the struggle to liberate the Bible from the clutches of crafty priests went on unabated. Then

> . . . a large part of Christendom threw off the yoke of the priesthood and its elaborate ritual and returned to the simplicity of the first century apostolic church. The Roman Catholic priesthood was, therefore, nothing more or less than the pagan priesthood of ancient Rome which by skillful subterfuge had fastened itself upon the Christian church.[31]

The Roman priesthood is the old pagan priesthood. Liberalism and Modernism has done the same to the major Protestant denominations, replacing the Gospel of salvation with a social gospel, discarding the supernatural object of faith and hope. Romanism at its best is a "badly deformed type of Christianity" and when seen in its true form it is nothing more than "a gigantic business and political organization that merely uses religion as a cloak. . . .*It must, therefore, as a system, be judged to be a false church.*"[32] Still in print after forty years, Boettner's book summarizes the evangelical objections to Roman Catholic belief, polity, and practice, and the summary judgment of most of the evangelical tradition that the Catholic Church is not a Christian church, and is the product of a compromise by church leaders with paganism and Judaism.

## Cornelius Van Til

Van Til was in his prime when Boettner wrote on Catholicism. They were ministers in the same Orthodox Presbyterian Church. However, we should not confuse them. Cornelius Van Till (1895–1987) wrote an unusual theology, even among his conservative evangelical colleagues. One cannot claim that he is entirely representative of the group (in fact, he was highly critical of many of them), but he was sharply representative of the Reformation principles that motivate them all, and his criticism of his fellow evangelicals was based on the same Reformation principles as his evaluation of the Catholic Church. He was not a man to be accused of inconsistency. He was born in the Netherlands, emigrated to the United States at the age of ten, attended Calvin College, and then attended Princeton University, where he finished his doctoral studies in philosophy in 1927. He taught apologetics at Princeton Seminary 1928–29 and left there in 1929 at J. Gresham Machen's invitation to teach at the new Westminster Theological Seminary. He remained there as professor of apologetics until his retirement in 1972.[33] He was lecturing at Princeton when Loraine Boettner was a student. With Machen and others he stood against the tide of modernist apostasy in the churches and seminaries.

Van Til is important to this study because he was a consistent critic of Roman Catholic theology and was so clear in the formulation of his criticisms. Very little of the usual *religious* and political criticism enters his work, restrained as it was by his driving *theological* interests and intentions. He was temperamentally interested in the thought of others and not in their sins. The Outline of Catholic doctrines and the historically framed Protestant Myth are muted by his effort to frame a theological (systematic, in this case) explanation for the Reformed faith over against the faith of the Church of Rome. As hard as he was on Rome and its theologians, his critique of it took second place to his efforts to construct his unique apologetic for Christian faith. He was no anti-Roman crusader.

However, in many of the five hundred pieces of his published and unpublished works,[34] Roman Catholicism is an important pole in the theological dialectic he established early on in his career between Christian and other worldviews, in what he called his "presuppositional apologetics" (the Christian-Scriptural worldview must confront all other worldviews without a philosophical prolegomenon). Van Til was a Calvinist, and the major effort of his life was to spell out the presupposition of Calvinist Christianity, the scriptures, in contrast to a variety of its opponents, the Roman Catholic worldview as well the Enlightenment, modernity, modern Protestantism, dialectical theology (Karl Barth and Emil Brunner), and even neo-evangelicalism (the culture-mediating efforts of other evangelical theologians and philosophers).[35] For him there could only be one starting point for theological reflection, one source of it and one rule for it: the revelation of the triune God in Jesus Christ contained in the inspired and inerrant scripture. Anything less than that or other than that is an unacceptable compromise. With the scripture as presupposition and norm, autonomy became the enemy, the primal sin, the other starting point, source and rule. The Christian believer believes the scriptures and the rest do not, and they resist obedience to God's grace revealed in Christ through the scripture.

I shall look at two of his unpublished essays, one on St. Thomas and the other on a contemporary Thomist, Bernard Lonergan, to illustrate the objections he raised to Roman Catholic theology and to Catholicism itself.[36] Since the presupposition necessary to any Christian theology or philosophy is the inerrant scripture and that alone, every other foundation for Christian thought is illegitimate insofar as it departs from the scripture:

> There are only two kinds of people in the world, covenant-breakers and covenant-keepers. Covenant-breakers are such in all that they do and covenant-keepers are such in all that they do. Covenant-breakers make God in man's image, and covenant-keepers make man in God's image. This distinction, thus baldly stated, indicates the antithesis between the believer and the unbeliever in principle only.[37]

Philosophers are caught between alternative principles of continuity and discontinuity laid down in the pre-Socratic philosophers, a dilemma nicely balanced but not solved in Aristotle's principles of being (form and matter or actuality and potentiality), and again balanced but not solved in modern form by Kant's nature and freedom. Alas, St. Thomas and medieval Roman Catholic thought followed Aristotle, and in doing so attempted to reconcile what is irreconcilable, a commitment to scriptural revelation and a commitment to autonomous reason.[38]

> [Humankind in the Catholic view] . . . is not a covenant being that is always confronted with the revelation of God and always bound either to obey or not to obey God. There is in St. Thomas no room for this true Biblical existentialism which Calvin taught us. Calvin argued that no man can know himself without knowing himself also as a creature of God and that no man can observe the facts of nature and history round about him without seeing clearly manifested therein the all controlling and judging activity of this Creator God. Thomas starts from the abstract concept of *Being* and introduces the creator-creature distinction afterwards. . . . His philosophy and psychology thus make any true Christian theology impossible.[39]

St. Thomas admitted that the one and the many, or continuity and discontinuity, is in fact a problem whose answer lies in a philosophical investigation by human reason which can be answered by reason. His adaptation of Aristotelian hylomorphism in philosophy was his presupposition to theology. Fatal error, said Van Til, for the problem in the Scriptures is between grace and sin, not between form and matter, between one who understands him or herself as the God of Scripture does or is lost. Thomas steps outside the biblical revelation in naming and solving a problem, according to the categories of autonomous reason. But things decline yet further in the Catholic embrace of autonomy:

> There can therefore be no such thing [in the Catholic view] as a finished Bible. All reality is process and revelation too is in process. There can be no incarnation once for all in the past [for Catholics]. The meaning of a finished incarnation as an individual fact in history could never be made reasonable. The incarnation is a process continued in the church as the whole of human personality is in process of divinization. There could be no one fact at the beginning of history by which all men are influenced to the extent of being guilty as well as polluted. So there cannot be one finished fact in history by virtue of which men are made righteous and holy in principle. The distinction between justification and sanctification is practically wiped out. Or rather justification is virtually reduced to the process of sanctification and sanctification is virtually said to be elevation in the scale of being. . . . The idea of redemption is woven deep into the pattern of metaphysical being. How else could it be made acceptable to natural man?[40]

In other words, the historical fall and redemption, the story told in the Scriptures, is logically invalidated and abandoned when one adopts a "science of Being as being." This was not merely a slip on St. Thomas's part; it is a basic flaw in the Roman Catholic worldview. Thomas merely replicated on a theological level what the Catholic Church is on the historical. That church was originally constituted by a compromise between the scripture and Greek culture. Although abstract (necessarily so, since it is theoretic), the criticism should make a Catholic thinker uncomfortable. Van Til struck home cleanly, and did so without insult. He disagreed in the strongest possible terms with the Roman Catholic position, yet he did not demean it.

Twenty-five years later, he turned to his contemporary, the Jesuit methodologist Bernard Lonergan, and found St. Thomas *redivivus*.[41] After a thirty-page summary of Lonergan's thought on human subjectivity and theological method, Van Til remarks:

> As a Christian philosopher Lonergan joins with non-Christian philosophers in a common effort at self-analysis and in a common effort of finding the presuppositions which make human experience intelligible. . . . Lonergan does not pretend to be able to say a syllable

about the Self without, at once, relating it to the cosmos. He knows
the self in a way similar to the way the Greeks, particularly in the
way Aristotle knows the self, i.e. by the idea of the analogy of being,
i.e. by the idea of the correlativity of the idea of abstract chance to
the idea of abstract timeless being. The "essentialism" of St. Thomas was built on the same idea.[42]

The idea, of course, is Greek not Christian. Lonergan makes the same
mistake as St. Thomas did, adopting not only the Aristotelian synthesis of St.
Thomas but adding to it the Kantian problematic of nature and freedom, as
well as the host of non-Christian philosophical notions spawned by the philosophers of modernity. The result? Lonergan's position implies that:

> The church must not proclaim the Christ that Paul preached to the
> Greeks. When Paul required the Greeks to repent in terms of the
> story of creation, of the resurrection and the coming judgment, the
> Greeks were, in Lonergan's view, right in refusing to listen to him.
> When Paul went on to tell the Greeks that wisdom, the wisdom
> based on human autonomy, had been shown to be "foolishness"
> with God the Greeks were right in turning from him with disdain.
> There cannot have been a creation, a resurrection and a judgment
> such as Paul proclaimed.
>
> Of course Lonergan, as well as St. Thomas and the Roman
> Catholic philosophers in general, does not put the relation of Chris-
> tianity and philosophy in this way. It is of the essence of the Roman
> Catholic philosophy of history as a whole that it seeks to synthesize
> the Greek and the Christian positions. But such a synthesis is artifi-
> cial at its center. What is more serious is that it is destructive of the
> gospel of God's saving grace to men. Instead of challenging the nat-
> ural man to repent the Roman Catholic synthesis establishes him in
> his notion that he is not a creature of God who has sinned against
> his maker and therefore is rightfully under the wrath of God as he
> walks the way of death in this life toward final death hereafter. In
> teaching a theology that is consonant with a philosophy such as that
> of Lonergan the mother Church today, together with neo-orthodox
> Protestants, leaves men where they are, i.e. without God and with-
> out hope in the world.[43]

A devastating criticism, if valid, and one that applies to every form of
mediating theology. Lonergan and Roman Catholicism ("the mother church"
may be either sarcastic or ironic) are not Christian in the full sense, and cannot
preach or teach the full gospel of grace and election as it is taught in Scripture.[44]
At very least, the secular foundation is implicitly a denial of the gospel's truth.
Lonergan would be disturbed by the charge and would call Van Til's under-

standing a misunderstanding—as would the many other Catholic thinkers whom Van Til reviewed similarly. But it should be noted that Van Til does not miss entirely, for in contrast with his own image of the scripture as the proper foundation for theology, Lonergan in the very first sentence of his *Method in Theology* writes that "A theology mediates between a cultural matrix and the significance and role of a religion in that matrix." For Van Til, theology preaches the scriptural story to the culture, and Van Til knows exactly what the difference is between himself and Lonergan on the matter.

For our purposes, we must note that Van Til's principled criticism of Catholic theology parallels the historical and doctrinal criticism of other American evangelicals (Reformed and otherwise), as well as capturing the meaning of the Myth: Catholicism is at bottom, as a practiced religion and a doctrine, a fatal compromise with paganism, and not fully, if at all, Christian. The "living church," as Van Til puts it, medieval, modern, and contemporary, has snatched away the right of believers to take the scriptures as the norm, has canonized that denial in both doctrine and law, and has replaced the scriptures with its own interpretation. It has compromised scripture by relying on autonomous (pagan) reason in theology and it has accepted faith as a "process" such that the Catholic Church implicitly (at least) denies the historical, one-for-all nature of redemption, so echoing Greek myth and thought. In doing so, Van Til advances his own version of those Protestant critics who postulate a corruption of the early church and its cooption into a paganized imperial church whose rites, doctrines, and structures are all impositions of pagan forms on the congregations of Christians in the third and fourth centuries, the beginning of the "apostasy of the church." Roman Catholicism is not biblical Christianity, as St. Thomas and Lonergan were not Christian theologians, as Hans Kung and David Tracy are not. All of them are examples of the Catholic "both/and" of analogical imagination, and Van Til a near perfect example of the "either/or" of dialectical imagination.[45]

## Evangelicals and Catholics Apart

The evangelical signers of the 1993 document *Evangelicals and Catholics Together: The Christian Mission in the Third Millennium* declared that (some) Roman Catholics may be considered "brothers and sisters in Christ." When they declared that [some] Catholics and evangelicals share the belief that "we are justified by grace through faith because of Christ . . ." and that "all who accept Christ as Lord and Savior are brothers and sisters in Christ," they shocked many of their fellow evangelicals. Although the signers admitted areas of deep disagreement between Catholics and evangelicals and that many of "these differences may never be resolved short of the Kingdom Come," they were convinced that the disagreements should not keep Catholic and evangelical Christians from joining hands in opposing "what opposes Christ and His cause." I will discuss *ECT* in the next chapter—it is an important document in the history of the relationship—but what concerns me here are the objections raised to the document, for the objections add up to a reaffirmation of the old evangelical charge of Catholic apostasy.

The reaction to *ECT* was swift and electric. In short order, TV evangelists raised a cry, evangelical journals published essays and editorials, and leading theologians had book-length assessments on the book shelves. The critics charged that the gospel had been compromised by the evangelical signers. In specific terms, the critics maintained that there is in fact no agreement between evangelicals and Catholics on the meaning of justification and no agreement on the nature of faith. In more general terms, the critics raised the specter of a wholesale betrayal of the Reformation itself. Finally, the critics made it clear that in their view the Catholic Church in the post–Vatican II era was in no relevant way an improvement over the Catholic Church of the Council of Trent. In fact, some maintain, it is less a Christian church now than in the sixteenth century, when Catholics were at least required to believe in the Bible and the Creeds.

Several respected evangelical theologians wrote a set of responses collected by John Armstrong into a volume entitled *Roman Catholicism: Evangelical Protestants Analyze What Divides and Unites Us.*[46] In that volume, W. Robert Godfrey, a church historian at Westminster Seminary in California, contributed an illuminating review of John Calvin's three documents on the Roman Church.[47] The Reformation, he maintained, was not over issues of Roman morals but about Christian doctrines and practice. At its heart were five prime theological concerns: (1) the Bible is the only religious authority; (2) pure worship as God commanded in scripture; (3) justification by faith in the imputed righteousness of Christ; (4) the two biblical sacraments; and (5) the true pastoral teaching office for the church. Rome corrupted all five and remains corrupt in all of them. What, he asks, would Calvin say today about Rome?

> He would surely conclude that Rome is worse off today than it was
> in the sixteenth century. The Word of God is compromised not only
> by church traditions but also by the corrosive criticism of its reliabil-
> ity. Worship has become even more syncretistic. Justification still
> rests on human cooperation, but it is often understood in a univer-
> salistic sense. The sacraments, after Vatican II, may be administered
> somewhat more simply, but they continue to be understood in an
> idolatrous and magical manner. The church continues to insist on
> the authority of its pope and traditions.[48]

Like Godfrey, Robert B. Stimple taught at Westminster Seminary in California and once taught at Westminster in Philadelphia. A systematic theologian, he was a serious student of contemporary Catholic theology.[49] His point is that Catholicism is fundamentally compromised by the desire to be "fully modern in terms of post-Enlightenment theology." The crucial event was Pope John XXIII, the Council, and its updating agenda (*aggiornamento*). At the Council, the Church turned to the Enlightenment principle of autonomy. As a result, the most basic Christian terms and doctrines are up for grabs: nature of God and of humanity, the fall, sin and divinely revealed law, salvation, the Savior and his work, incarnation, resurrection and life everlasting.[50] Catholic theologians have done in a few decades what liberal Protestants did over two centuries. "Theological *pluralism* (now moving increasingly toward recognition of the validity of religious pluralism) is today the clearest fact of theological life in the Roman Catholic Church."[51] The differences between theologians in the mainline Protestant churches and the Catholic Church have ceased to matter very much. The "most important insight of modern Roman Catholic theology" according to them is the historicity of all human statements, including the Bible. The old Roman problem is still there, redoubled: if not the Bible, then what is the *norma normans non normata* by which we can determine which of the many interpretations of church teaching and Christian life is correct, which is to be believed? "Our question, however, must be: Does it [the contemporary pluralism] allow any room for true certitude and full assurance? This was the tremendous problem the Reformers had with the theology of the Roman church, and the problem continues with the same force for Rome today."[52]

All Catholic theologians agree today that there is no new revealed teaching outside scripture, no "constitutive tradition." This might look like an improvement over Trent. But it is not. Stimple holds that:

> . . . Roman Catholic theology today is, in its leading representatives, a consciously post-Enlightenment theology, the basic presuppositions and concerns of which are the same as those that have motivated Protestant theology is modern times. We have now seen this eloquently reflected in the theology of the most influential Roman Catholic theologian of the twentieth century, Karl Rahner. Because modern Roman Catholic theology has imbibed the ethos and spirit of modernity in this century, it is imperative that evangelicals recognize the influence of this spirit and respond more accurately and faithfully to the present situation as it really is. The most significant historic theological affirmations, even those we once agreed upon . . . are no longer a basis for agreement. . . . [E]very doctrine of our historic Christian faith has been challenged; therefore we must gird up our minds if we are to respond adequately.[53]

Strimple's audience is the theologically literate evangelical, while John Ankerberg addresses evangelicals in general. In *Protestants and Catholics, Do They Now Agree?*[54] he and John Weldon return to The Outline in their table of contents and to the Protestant Myth in an appendix.[55] Like Dave Hunt, for whom they show reverence, Ankerberg and Weldon revive many of the traditional evangelical themes, but in short order they get to their objection to *ECT*:[56]

> ... Many leaders on both sides have hailed this important document as a historical event—even as the most historic event since the Reformation. What was agreed to by both sides? Throughout this document a major new assumption was made. ... The Evangelicals agreed that all Roman Catholics are genuine Christians, and the Roman Catholics agreed that all Evangelicals are genuine Christians.[57] ... But if this is really true, why is it that scholars from both sides ever since the Reformation have refused to recognize the other as genuine Christians? The claim that all who accept Christ are brothers and sisters in Christ begs the big question "How does a person get in Christ?" ... Historically, Evangelicals have held that the only way a person gets in Christ is by admitting that he is a sinner and placing his total trust in Christ's atoning work for him. If he does not do this, he is not in Christ and, therefore, not a genuine Christian. ... So how can Roman Catholics be considered "in Christ" if they continue to deny the only basis for coming to be in Christ— justification by grace through faith alone? Those who signed this document do not tell us. They just start from the false premise that all Catholics are "in Christ."[58]

Nor for Ankerberg and Weldon are there two different ways of being Christian—on every significant issue the Roman Catholic position opposes the gospel and true Christianity. In the past 450 years of disagreement, the Catholic positions have not changed. The *ECT* agreement is not real. Its affirmations are ambiguous and imprecise, for evangelicals and Catholics do not mean the same thing by the basic terms. The statements are unsupported by scripture or supported by distorted scripture. The main doctrine separating Catholics and evangelicals—justification by faith—is not dealt with clearly. Ankerberg quotes G. C. Berkouwer's *The Conflict with Rome*: "For it is not only a different doctrine that causes the separation, but a different practice, and fundamentally a different sense of life."[59] Roman Catholicism is not only not the true church, it is not even a Christian religion. "Thus, millions of Catholics today think they are Christians when, in fact, they are Catholics."[60] Is Roman Catholicism Christian? In a nutshell, there are so many ways in which Catholicism is not biblical that it is logically impossible to classify it as a Christian religion.

## The Apostate Church

Apostasy is not the same as heresy. A heretic denies an important doctrine. An apostate abandons the basic beliefs of his or her community and takes on another set of basic beliefs. Catholics historically have regarded Protestants as heretics. The list of anathemas pronounced at the Council of Trent (1563) marked Protestants as heretics; in 1965 the Vatican II bishops refer to them as separated brethren and anathema is not hinted.[61] American Protestants (with some important exceptions discussed in the next chapter) branded the Catholic Church an apostate church, while sometimes admitting that individual Catholics may be Christians and saved. Catholics as a rule, willing members of a church that has denied the gospel, are lost. They, like other non-Christians, are in desperate need of conversion. On this side of the evangelical tradition, theological judgment followed that of Luther and Calvin. It is far from uncommon in evangelical literature today.

The apostasy of the Catholic Church was articulated by Protestants in several ways, finding its most lurid expression in the apocalyptic tradition begun by the Reformers: the church is the Whore and the pope is the Antichrist. Although now largely abandoned as a literary form by evangelical intellectuals, it remains an active part of popular evangelical anti-Catholic propaganda. The judgment of apostasy is carried as well in the continued use of the Outline, which lists Christian doctrines and practices denied by the Roman church as well as the distortions and perversions of the Pauline gospel affirmed by true Christian churches. And it remains as well in the Myth, which tells the story of the decline and fall of the Christian church in late antiquity and the preservation and rebirth of the true Christian church, *lux ex tenebris,* in the sixteenth.

The gospel that the Catholic church has definitively denied is that a Christian becomes such by faith alone through Christ alone by grace alone according to the inerrant word of scripture. The Reformation material and formal principles are so distorted by the Roman church that it can only be branded apostate. The hard evangelicals still regard the Catholic Church as an apostate body, the only possible relationship to which is preaching the saving gospel and subsequent conversion. An agenda of conversation with Catholics is in fact an agenda of preaching to lost souls.

But the soft evangelicals judge the Catholic Church to be an heretical church worth talking with and working with for common ends, and tend to regard the Catholics with whom they converse as "anonymous evangelicals." They do not think that the Catholic Church has unqualifiedly rejected the gospel; rather, they think that Catholics and their church truly but far from adequately express their faith in ways that partially meet the criteria of the scriptures—as they would think of other (Arminian) Protestant bodies. The crucial turn of the National Association of Evangelicals toward culture-healing and vigorous inter-Christian dialogue embraced Catholics and their leaders. The next chapter takes up the effort of some evangelicals who, over the past two centuries, attempted to moderate the hard evangelical line.

# 8

# Soft Evangelicals and the Heretical Church

Understanding the Catholic Church as positively related to the Pauline gospel of free grace, as in some sense a Christian church, is no easy task given Reformation principles. That many conservative evangelicals today cannot manage it should be no surprise; that some have is the surprise. But an opening for such a view is also part of the American evangelical tradition, a tiny crack in the rhetorical wall of hard judgment that was taken advantage of a decade ago by the evangelical signers of *ECT*. I want now to follow a lead through the nineteenth and the twentieth centuries, looking especially at figures representative of the very Reformed tradition that has historically judged Rome to be an apostate church. But first we turn to one not regarded as part of that tradition at all, one who left Calvin far behind and Christian orthodoxy with him, who nonetheless, like Theodore Parker, is genuinely representative of the American Enlightenment, but who, unlike Parker, still claimed to be a Christian.

William Ellery Channing (1780–1842), pastor of the Federal Street Church in Boston, has been described as shy, uncompromisingly honest and courageous, gentle, generous, and reflective, and is surely one of the finest writers of the English language in a New England tradition replete with fine writers.[1] His chief affliction was his unbending belief in common sense, and it made a Unitarian of him. He sometimes meant by common sense what any Bostonian on Nob Hill would regard as reasonable, especially in matters of religion. It did take nearly a century to get from Charles Chauncy's commonsensical rejection of the enthusiasms of the Great Awakening to Channing's sweeping rejection of Trinitarian doctrine, but the descent from Chauncy's distaste for religious enthusiasm through Jonathan Mayhew's Christian moralism to Channing's Unitarianism seems to me direct. His common sense may have been a source of scandal to his fellow evangelicals, but, as we shall see, it proved a godsend to Catholics.

Channing addressed the "great question" of Catholicism twice, once in 1836 in a letter to the editor of The Western Messenger (Kentucky) and then again in 1841 in a lecture delivered in the First Unitarian Church of Philadelphia.[2] The former is an occasional piece penned in answer to the editor's request for a formal essay that Channing did not have time to write but which request he could not bring himself to refuse entirely. The latter is far more a formal piece of writing, which evidently took a lot of authorial concentration.

When the editor of The Western Messenger, in his brief introduction to the letter, remarked that "the view of Catholicism given here seems to us very original and striking," he well might have added "given the vituperative tone and blanket condemnations recently in print on the subject." Channing's essays are models of civility when compared with the books of Nevins, Beecher, and Morse. He even went so far as to admit that the "good city of Boston . . . among all its virtues . . . does not abound in a tolerant spirit." This he knew well, for his fellow minister, Lyman Beecher, had recently been preaching against the Catholic Church, providing fuel for the mob's destruction of the Ursuline sisters' convent and school. Channing chided the public criers against popery for committing a "pious fraud" in order to attract "distinction and funds." It is impossible to think he meant anyone other than Beecher himself. He went on to criticize the Protestant denominational leadership:

> Most Protestant sects are built on the Papal foundation. Their creeds
> and excommunications embody the grand idea of Infallibility as
> truly as the decrees of Trent, and the Vatican; and if people must
> choose between different infallibilities, there is much to incline
> them to that of Rome. This has age, the majority of votes, more dar-
> ing assumptions, and bolder denunciation on its side. The popes of
> our different sects are certainly less imposing to the imagination
> than the pope at Rome.[3]

Disagreeing with his younger colleague Theodore Parker, he regarded the Catholic Church as not a very formidable threat in his time. It was crippled by its attack on progress and innovation. "It takes its stand in the Past, and this generation are [sic] living in the future." Its doctrines appear ignorant to the intelligent, it denies the rights of enquiry; it rejects the congregation's right to choose its ministers when election is the essence of modern institutions; it clings to a clerical aristocracy when the world turns republican; the world reads and the church still forbids the scriptures. Its memory seems not to come down lower than the middle ages: ". . . Catholicism belongs to what may be called the dogmatical age of Christianity."[4] What counts decisively against the

Catholic Church's survival in this age ("How sure then is its fall!"), is that genuine religion is a spirit and not a dogma, a spirit evident in the life and teaching of Christ. The great foe of the "Romish church" is "human nature waking up to a consciousness of its power. . . . I look to the ineradicable, ever-unfolding principles of human nature, for the victory over all superstitions." He shared the mad optimism of the age of Enlightenment, undone a hundred years later by stupendous wars and the murder of Jews.

But even Catholicism itself, he thought, was changing: "The silent reform spreading in the very bosom of Catholicism, is as important as the reformation of the sixteenth century, and is in truth more effectual."[5] Its flaw is its opposition to the progress of humankind, its strength is its flexibility toward the modes and moods of spiritual yearning. It has, in effect, something for everyone, from the beauty of its ritual to its ascetic practices. Protestantism, he admitted, has a similar appeal through its great variety of sects, with Episcopalianism leading as "Catholicism improved."[6]

If the alarms against Rome going up in his time are both overstated and ineffectual, and part of a "pious fraud," then how should Catholicism best be opposed?

> I know but one way. Spread just, natural, ennobling views of religion. Lift men above Catholicism by showing them the great spiritual purpose of Christianity. Violence will avail nothing. Romanism cannot be burnt down, like the convent at Charlestown. That outrage bound every Catholic faster to his church, and attracted to it the sympathies of the good. Neither is popery to be subdued by virulence and abuse. The priest can call as hard names as the protestant [sic] pastor. Neither do I think that anything is to be gained by borrowing from the Catholic church her forms and similar means of influence.[7]

In a word, only Enlightenment will do it. And that enlightenment has come to many, for Channing recognizes "true disciples of the common master" in all communities. In fact, "Catholicism boasts some of the best and greatest names in history . . ."[8] Channing was no less critical of his Protestant colleagues than he was of the Roman church, and even harbored hope for her improvement.

A year before he died, Channing spoke in the Unitarian church in Philadelphia, in a "discourse" that covered the bases of his ecclesiology and laid out a good bit of his soteriology as well. Titled simply "The Church," its burden was to justify in theological terms his long war on sectarianism in Protestantism. Sectarianism is the enemy, while the Catholic Church is but one instance of it. Channing had, in his "Letter on Catholicism," made this objection to sectarianism the centerpiece of his comments on the Catholic Church and drew out in rhetorical shorthand its implications for Protestant belief and practice. In Philadelphia he spelled out a notion of the church that is, on the one hand, in continuity with the Reformation notion of the invisible church but, on the other hand, a church so invisible that it would void Protestant as well as Roman Catholic belief in an historical church with claims to a true as opposed to an heretical doctrine. For the church is not doctrinal in its aim but spiritual, a sharing of the spirit of Christ, not an historical, properly organized body of orthodox believers engaged in correct practice. The spiritual church is indeed catholic, that is, found wherever there are Christians in spirit no matter their ecclesiastical connections, their doctrines, and their practices.

The church as it exists is a natural entity, the outcome of the socializing instincts of human beings. The church is spiritual, and outcome of the spirit of Christ in the souls of human beings. Choose the church that best fits your needs and temperament, he urged, but always belong to the spiritual church. The latter is necessary for salvation, while the former is at best an aid or means to it. Here we run into the transcendentalist view that the reality of the church is found in individual souls rather than in a community, a "body of Christ," an identifiable people, the latter existing only by virtue of the former:

> What I wish is, that we should learn to regard ourselves as members of a vast spiritual community, as joint-heirs and fellow worshippers, with a goodly company of Christian heroes who have gone before us, instead of immuring ourselves in particular churches. . . . I have spoken of the Roman Catholic church. My great objection to this communion is, that it has fallen peculiarly into the error which I am laboring to expose in this discourse, that it has attached idolatrous importance to the institution of the church, that it virtually exalts this above Christ's spirit, above inward sanctity. Its other errors are of inferior importance. . . . The grand error of Roman Catholicism is its narrow church spirit, its blind sectarianism, it exclusion of virtuous, pious men from God's favor because they cannot eat, drink, or pray according to certain prescribed rites. Romanism has to learn that nothing but the inward life is great and good in the sight of the Omniscient, and that all who cherish this are members of Christ's body. Romanism is anything but what it boasts to be, the universal church. I am too much a Catholic to enlist under its banner. I belong to the universal church; nothing shall separate me from it.[9]

Although "other errors" are pronounced of "inferior importance," Channing came back to a few of them in short order: The objection to "reifying the spirit" into a "true church" is quite specific and sharply put:

> Now I meet precisely this difficulty in the doctrine [the necessity of sacraments], that God bestows his Holy Spirit on those who receive bread and wine, or flesh and blood, or a form of outward benedic-

tion or baptism, or any other outward ministration, from the hands
or lips of certain privileged ministers or priests. It is the most glorious act and manifestation of God's power and love to impart enlightening, quickening, purifying influences to the immortal soul.
To imagine that these descend in connection with certain words,
signs, or outward rites, administered by a frail, fellow-creature, and
are withheld or abridged in the absence of such rites, seems, at first,
an insult to his wisdom and goodness; seems to bring down his
pure, infinite throne to set arbitrary limits to his highest agency, and
to assimilate his worship to that of false gods.[10]

To imagine, then, that God acts in an historical community with a divinely
established order as Catholics do; to imagine that God's grace is "bestowed"
through the ministrations of a priestly caste as Catholics do, is to violate the
"spirit" or the immediacy of God's presence to each individual soul. Although
he admits that the "spirit has found a home" in the Catholic church, it cannot
be *the* home, nor can its way by *the* way—but then, neither can any other
human community "have" the spirit as a possession to bestow, nor could any
way be *the* way. God's grace is not controlled by magic and Christian rites are
not charms. For Channing, the church's foundation is nature and the sacraments' mode of operation is commonsensical; Catholics accept neither proposition.

What Channing accomplished here, in accord with his "liberal" evangelicalism (if we may classify him so at all) is to criticize the Catholic Church and
the anti-Catholic Protestant churches by a single standard that neither could
accept: the church is a spiritual reality raised up by the Spirit of God and never
to be identified with any historical institutionalized version of it. One might
reply that Channing's view is ecclesiological Docetism, verging on Gnosticism,
and the outcome of Channing's Unitarian heresy. By contrast, there is an eerie
similarity between his notion of the spiritual reality of the church and that of
the century's most able defender of reformed orthodoxy. The root of Channing's notion of the church runs down into the Reformation itself. In fact, as
a Catholic counterargument would run, Channing stood close to the end of
the Reformation's logical track.

Standing at the other end of the theological spectrum, Charles Hodge
(1797–1878) was the foremost Presbyterian theologian of the nineteenth century. He failed, some scholars say, to retrieve the Calvinist orthodoxy he loved,
but as a matter of fact he did not fail. He most certainly was no epigone of
Calvin. He was the greatest systematic theologian Princeton Seminary produced, and set the high standards for and much of the content of the "Princeton
theology" which has been so important as a model for twentieth-century conservative evangelical theology.[11] Alas, his theoretical explanation of the verbal
inspiration of the original autographs of the scriptures is considered the the-

ological background of what is sometimes called fundamentalist literalism, and so he often is dismissed by liberal Protestant scholars. His masterpiece, *Systematic Theology*,[12] remains in print after a century and is read to this day in many evangelical seminaries. In my view, he does not deserve either obscurity or the condescension of liberals.[13] Unlike Channing, Hodge was an orthodox Christian; like Channing, he condemned sectarianism. And each, in his particular way, belonged to the "spiritual" Catholic Church.

Hodge was educated at Princeton College and in Germany, and returned to teach at Princeton Seminary from 1822 to 1878. In addition to the three-volume systematics he wrote late in life, he edited the *Biblical Repertory and Princeton Review* for several decades and therein published hundreds of critical assessments of and comments on classical and contemporary theological texts. No one of significance escaped his eye or his pen. Of the men I have discussed, he was historically and theologically the most able, a man of vigorous and informed opinions and few prejudices, with a strong leaning against having his mind made up for him by others no matter their orthodox credentials, a man of the church unmoved by the mob. For liberals of the Parker-Channing tendency and for those following the lead of softened Calvinism of Nathaniel Taylor and Horace Bushnell, Hodge had a constant stream of hard words, something one would expect of the champion of Reformed orthodoxy. Moreover, he refused to give in to the undiscriminating anti-Catholicism of his Presbyterian contemporaries, and that is what interests us here.

In 1845 the Old School Presbyterian General Assembly pronounced that the Roman church was not a Christian church and that its baptism, therefore, could not be considered valid.[14] Hodge didn't have a vote that year, but he was there and stood to debate the issue with James Henley Thornwell, the other prominent Presbyterian theologian of the day. Hodge lost the vote, 169 to 8. Six of the eight signed a minority report agreeing with the majority that Rome was an apostate church but disagreeing that thereby her baptism was invalid. It was difficult for them, and for Hodge, to imagine that Luther and Calvin had not been validly baptized. For many of the other voters, however, the lack of valid baptism may not have been a significant issue—one is saved *sola fide*, after all. Thornwell himself seemed to have overlooked this tiny irony in his argument for the invalidity of Romish baptism.

Hodge alone was willing to consider the Catholic Church a part of the true church in spite of her many flaws and errors. In fact, in his responses to the Assembly's position, he went so far as to charge that the Assembly itself was guilty of "Catholicizing tendencies" in its exclusion of the Catholic Church and its refusal to recognize Roman baptism. After all, was it not Rome that initially insisted that no one outside the "true church" could be saved? In another delicious piece of irony, he charged that his fellow Presbyterians were taking a Roman tack. The General Assembly was as Roman as the pope. It was guilty of making the church equivalent to an external organization and a particular way of doing things, and of demanding more than the apostolic faith for membership in the true church.

But, maintained Hodge, those who profess the gospel and the true religion were Christian churches, no matter how they are externally ordered. No matter how much Rome had added over the centuries, no matter that Rome mistakenly made the organized church itself and its ministerial forms essential to the church, Rome did teach what was need to be saved: faith, the scriptures, the doctrines of the creeds. Hodge himself accomplished a very neat bit of theological dialectic: he took the principle of free and unmediated grace and faith, used it to criticize Rome and the American Protestant consensus against Rome, and then used it to bring the Roman Catholic Church into the catholic church. Logically, his move is close to Channing's.

In 1868, as part of the preparation for the Vatican Council, Pius IX wrote a general letter of invitation to Protestant churches to send representatives.[15] As one might have predicted, the letter invited all those who do not profess the true faith or belong to the true church to return to it. The General Assembly asked Charles Hodge to respond in its name, a curious choice given Hodge's unbending opposition in the Assembly of 1845.[16] Hodge informed His Holiness that the General Assembly recognized as Christians and members of the visible church all who profess the Christian faith. He implied that the Assembly recognized even Catholics who professed that faith as members of the true church. His final words in this brief letter are these: "We love all those who love Our Lord Jesus Christ in sincerity. We regard as Christian brethren all who worship, love, and obey him as their God and Savior."[17] But Pope Pius and his church, he noted, did not reciprocate. At the Council of Trent the Catholic Church had "excommunicated and pronounced cursed" all who depart from her teaching, and so cast out the reformers and their descendants. How, still excommunicated and accursed, could the descendants attend a Council? It seemed perfectly plain to Hodge that the pope requested not only their presence but their submission, and that all the suppositions and exclusionary canons of Trent were still in effect. In spite of that, unlike the probable response of other rabidly anti-Catholic Presbyterians, Hodge took the letter of Pius IX seriously and answered it responsibly. His letter merited no papal answer, a signal of the utter lack of papal interest in Protestant opinion.

While I am not interested here in the theological arguments advanced for and against the Assembly's resolution and in the heated exchanges in print afterward—the discussion of Thornwell in the previous chapter covers this— I am concerned to point up Hodge's basic critique of Catholicism and his *modus operandi* in its regard. In Hodge's view Rome had made "externals" essential to salvation, when the scriptures made only grace and faith (i.e., "internals") essential to salvation. She added to the teachings of the scriptures, and is justly tarred with these "corruptions." Hodge was not disagreeing with the Reformers in this matter, and in fact thought he was more faithful to the

Reformers than were many of his Presbyterian colleagues. Nor was he backing off in a fit of ecumenical dizziness from any of the Reformed tradition's hard judgments on Roman heresy.[18] The thing to note is that his argument was *theological*, in no sense submissive to the current nativist motives, without a hint of apocalyptic frenzy, and with no use of the common symbolic epithets. But note as well that the theological principle is *decisive*, namely, that what establishes a Christian as a Christian is an unmediated gift of God's grace and personal faith to which no ecclesiastical organization, minister, or act is essential. It is this basic evangelical conviction that ties Hodge and Channing together, and both of them with most of the evangelical critique of Roman Catholicism. It is odd, is it not, that among leading ministerial and theological figures in the nineteenth century, Channing and Hodge, men from opposite ends of the confessional spectrum, should stand together in recognizing this, and in doing so stand against the tsunami of nineteenth-century Protestant anti-Catholicism insofar as it refused to recognize that Catholics are Christians? They both recognized the Catholic Church as a "true" if "impure" church, both arraigned their Protestant colleagues for the Catholic mistake, and they both denied that any particular organizational form of Christianity was uniquely Christian or necessary to salvation. They refused to join the nativists or the apocalypticists. There was none of Morse and Beecher in them, and very little of Breckinridge and Thornwell. Channing and Hodge did, albeit in quite different theological contexts, hold to evangelical views on faith, freedom, the immediacy of God's grace, antihierarchism, antisacramentalism, and demythologized versions of other Reformation charges. They also refused to chant the Myth. They each sorted through the Catholic problem as an intellectual problem, a genuine theological problem that cannot be settled by singing an old song. Neither of them repeat the items listed in the table of contents of the typical anti-Catholic religious tract. As befits intellectuals they pared the contents down to the nub issues.

In general, they and most of the critics are deeply distressed that the leaders of the Roman church (the lower clergy as well as the hierarchy) exercise the authority they do and that the ministers of the church dare to claim an exclusive mediatorial and hermeneutical role in Christian life. The Catholic leaders hold all the deeds to property, open and close all the doors, define all the doctrines, make and change all the rules, and act as if they and their people must have a loyalty to a church organization that transcends nation-state and approximates a spiritual empire in a world of nation-states. The leaders are not elected, they are not accountable to their members or even to the sacred text, they cannot be wrong in what they teach, and they cannot be impeached, all deeply offensive to Protestants and republicans. This was perceived neither as solely a political or solely a religious problem, and so the criticism is at once secular and sacred.

William Ellery Channing and Charles Hodge especially, by tempering the profound hostility of the religious criticism by other American evangelicals, showed that theologically nuanced criticism is possible and that genuine theological debate (and even dialogue) might occur when conditions change. That is exactly what has happened in the last quarter of the twentieth century. Conditions changed, a more focused critique emerged with its roots in the theology rather than the polemic of the Reformation, and the evangelical leadership argued over whether the lion had lost its teeth and claws and will join the lamb for a vegetarian repast.

## Other Princetonians

While remaining theologically critical of the Roman Church, Hodge backed off from the judgment of his fellow Presbyterians that Rome was not to be accounted a "true" church. He certainly agreed that it was "impure" in doctrine and practice (and so was his church, he would add!), but looked on the Roman church with a quite different, indeed "conciliatory," attitude. Mark Reynolds remarks that Hodge's strategy was ". . . to negotiate between what he perceived as the uncharitable position and narrow prejudice of his Presbyterian co-religionists and the exclusivity of Roman Catholics by reducing the church to those who professed the gospel."[19] Reynolds claims, in fact, that "Hodge was the only significant non high-church American theologian of his period who maintained that the Roman Catholic church was a Christian church."[20]

Hodge did have successors in the view. Two important "Old Princetonians" of a later generation echoed Hodge's transformation of the received Calvinist judgment and attitude. J. Gresham Machen (1881–1937) and Samuel Craig (1874–1960) were each deeply involved in the Presbyterian turmoil in the 1920s and 1930s. Craig, the editor of *The Presbyterian* and founding editor of the first *Christianity Today* and an ally of Machen in the struggle to save the Presbyterian Church U.S.A. from modernism, served for a while on the Board of Trustees of Machen's Westminster Theological Seminary founded in 1929.[21] When Machen, stripped of his ministerial status in 1936, led in the establishment of the Orthodox Presbyterian Church in 1936, Craig remained in the Presbyterian Church U.S.A. to fight for the orthodox cause. Both of them exhibit a distinctively moderate assessment of Roman Catholicism.

Mark Van Doren once remarked that a classic is a book that remains in print. Machen's *Christianity and Liberalism* remains in print after seventy-five years and deserves to be so.[22] Perhaps the best theological broadside of the twentieth century by an American Christian thinker, it exposed liberal-modernist Protestant theology as a new religion rather than a legitimate modern version of Christian faith.[23] In doing so he drew lines for his and succeeding generations of orthodox and liberal Protestants. He framed the religious significance of religious modernism as sharply and unforgettably as did Pope

Pius X for Roman Catholics in *Pascendi dominici gregis*.[24] Intent on illustrating the significance of the gap between Christianity and liberalism in the churches, Machen pointed out some of the most serious disagreements between churches: Lutherans and Reformed on the Eucharist, Anglicans and Reformed on apostolic succession and ministry, Arminians and Calvinists on grace and freedom. None of these, in his view, reaches the depth of the difference between orthodox Christians and liberals in all the denominations, for liberals are not Christians at all. Turning to the Catholic Church he remarks:

> Far more serious still is the division between the Church of Rome and evangelical Protestantism in all its forms. Yet how great is the common heritage which unites the Roman Catholic Church, with its maintenance of the authority of Holy Scripture and with its acceptance of the great early creeds, to devout Protestants today! We would not indeed obscure the difference which divides us from Rome. The gulf is indeed profound. But profound as it is, it seems almost trifling compared to the abyss which stands between us and many ministers of our own Church. The Church of Rome may represent a perversion of the Christian religion; but naturalistic liberalism is not Christianity at all.[25]

This is not to say that Machen looked forward to a resumption of communion between Presbyterians and Romanists. Nearly a century after Machen's comment they are still far from a common Eucharistic table and common missionary activity,[26] and theologians of his Orthodox Presbyterian Church remain among the Catholic Church's outspoken critics. He would not look kindly on a common table with Lutherans, Anglicans, and Methodists, precisely because of those differences in doctrines. But it appears that, as with these other churches, Catholics, in spite of their doctrinal and practical "perversions," remain in the Christian camp in view of their scriptural and creedal orthodoxy. In some sense that Machen did not clarify further, the Catholic Church remains Christian, heretical but not apostate. Modernists were apostate, but not the Catholic Church. To use Hodge's terms, it is a "true Church" even if an "impure" one. In addition, in the preface to the second edition of his exegetical masterpiece, *The Virgin Birth of Christ*, when he expresses gratitude for favorable reviews of it by Catholic scholars, he goes on to record his "high estimate of the Roman Catholic Church; and he rejoices greatly in the important contributions made by Roman Catholic scholars to the subject dealt with in the present book," a remark much in the spirit of Hodge and not at all the spirit of a Van Til, or a Godfrey or a Strimple, all of whom share in the institutional and theological tradition of Hodge and Machen.[27]

Craig, an old friend and close ally of Machen, read an essay at a seminar of the General Assembly of the Presbyterian Church U.S.A. in 1938, just two years after his refusal to join with Machen in the new Orthodox Presbyterian

Church (at first called the Presbyterian Church in America) and a year after Machen's unfortunate death.[28] He was out to inform his hearers and readers that, in view of the critical battle with the forces of modernism in the churches and liberalism in the society at large, something was occurring in the Catholic Church that Presbyterians concerned with orthodoxy ought to take note of and, even further, ought to look on with hope for a common front against a common enemy. Like the evangelical authors of *ECT* over half a century later, he saw that the new battle was not around the issues that engaged the Reformers, as important then and now as those issues are, but around issues in which Catholic and Protestant theology have a common stake:

> . . . even if we regard Roman Catholics as anti-Christians, as many of our fathers did, they nonetheless constitute an entity that refuses to be ignored. It does not seem to me, however, that we should so regard them. I have no sympathy with those who apologize for the Reformation. On all the more important points that were at issue in the sixteenth century between Rome on the one hand and Wittenberg and Geneva on the other I am as unalterably opposed to Rome as were our fathers; yet as matters stand today I cannot but regard them, to a large extent at least, as friends and allies as over against an enemy that would eradicate Christianity, root and branch.[29]

The attractive side of the revival of Neo-Scholasticism or Neo-Thomism for Protestants was its intellectual heft as a systematically expressed metaphysical worldview. Disagreeing with Van Til's hope for a presuppositionless Christian theology, Craig pointed out that a worldview is something that Protestants lacked as Calvinism receded. He disagreed as well with some estimates of the Reformation by his predecessors and contemporaries when he wrote:

> Genuine Protestantism, however—Protestantism as it has found expression in such historic creeds as the Augsburg Confession, the Canons of the Synod of Dort, the Heidelberg Catechism, and the Westminster Confession of Faith—is what it claims to be—the *reformation* of an old, not the erection from the foundation of a new, life and world view. Consequently there is a basic similarity between the historic Protestant and the Roman Catholic life and world views. Protestantism modified the Roman Catholic view but preserved its basic structure intact. As Herman Bavink rightly said, in his book, "The Philosophy of Revelation," Luther, Zwingli, and Calvin "in their view of the world and life, sin and grace, heaven and hell, Church and State, faith and knowledge, were children of the Middle Ages and revealed this fact at every point of their activity as Reformers."[30]

Not only is the enemy of evangelical Protestantism's enemy a friend but also, in this case, the former enemies have a common heritage to support a new friendship. Fully aware of the liabilities of Roman belief and practice and so of the likely liabilities of Neo-Scholastic thought, nonetheless he finds the agreements solid foundation for common action against secularism. He, like Hodge, recognizes Catholics as Christians:

> I suspect that when the whole company of the redeemed join for the first time in the great jubilation many Roman Catholics will be surprised at the number of Protestants present, and many Protestants will be surprised at the number of Roman Catholics present.[31]

A quite different judgment of the Catholic Church ran through the thinking and feeling of Hodge, Machen, and Craig from the judgment and feeling that run though the great pile of literature and equally great number of authors represented in the previous chapter. Not all American evangelical Protestants, not all the orthodox and the Calvinists, see Rome as the Beast and the Whore, an apostate church without any of the faith and belief of the apostolic church. Not all agreed with Van Til, another friend of Machen and perhaps of Craig, that Roman Catholicism and its theology are mortally flawed by compromise with ancient and modern forms of paganism. Perhaps the Whore is after all just a heretic.

## The National Association of Evangelicals

The nineteenth-century Evangelical Alliance was absorbed and replaced by the Federal Council of Churches (1908) in which the concerns of conservatives were marginalized.[32] The World's Christian Fundamentals Association (1919) took a stab at rounding up the disorganized conservatives, but made very little progress. But the New England Fellowship (1931), a cooperative organization of conservative evangelicals working for a revival in that corner of the vineyard, had considerable success in the 1930s.[33] It was not a church union, it was a para-church service organization under the leadership of lay evangelist Elwin Wright who spurred a new effort of conservative Protestants to achieve a national public voice and platform. Very successful in his own evangelism by the mid-1930s, Wright, himself from the holiness tradition, began to call on fundamentalist leaders around the nation, speaking with them about the need for some organ of united action.

In 1942, under the leadership of Wright and his young friend Harold Ockenga, a graduate of Machen's Westminister Theological Seminary and pastor of the Park Street Congregational Church in Boston, about two hundred evangelicals (they would have been called fundamentalists then) met in St. Louis to decide whether an organization of orthodox Protestants was needed

to strengthen the evangelical presence on the national scene. At this first meeting, called the National Conference for United Action among Evangelicals
(held April 7, 1942, at the Coronado Hotel in St. Louis), included Baptists,
Presbyterians, independents, holiness Wesleyans, Pentecostals, Southern Baptists, southern Presbyterians, Missouri Synod Lutherans, Mennonite Brethren
and other peace churches, Scandinavian Evangelical Free churches, Scandinavian Evangelical Covenant churches, and Dutch Reformed and Christian
Reformed churches. Not all eventually joined, but they showed up at the initial
meeting.[34]

The assembly reacted positively, indeed joyously, to the proposal and a
second assembly met the following year in Chicago. Once again, the leaders
(now elected) evoked a positive response. The organization was named the
National Association of Evangelicals (NAE) and was founded to represent the
culturally and politically marginalized, doctrinally conservative Protestants, in
ways similar to the public representation afforded mainstream ("liberal" or
"modernist") Protestants by the Federal (later World) Council of Churches. It
was not a church or a representative council of churches but, rather, an association of like-minded individuals.

The organization that emerged had a rocky start. It had trouble from the
right, for the separatist fundamentalists would abide neither its tolerance of
liberal churches nor its inclusion of charismatic Christians. It failed to receive
the support from Machen's successors in the Orthodox Presbyterian Church.
It had trouble from the left, for the liberal churches that then occupied the
high cultural and political ground branded it a fundamentalist coalition. It got
a cold shoulder from the Southern Baptist Convention because the Convention
had all the interchurch services and public representation it needed from its
own organization. The NAE failed to interest some of the larger evangelical
church bodies even when their members joined it. But after a sputtering start
it weathered the storms expected in a tradition with powerful separatist tendencies and a decided leaning to the congregational "independency" so prized
by John Cotton in the seventeenth century, and within five years the NAE
numbered 750,000 members. A few years later, the NAE was an influential
para-church service organization that spawned in short order the National Religious Broadcasters, the Evangelical Theological Society, the Evangelical Press
Association, the World Evangelical Fellowship, the National Sunday School
Association, the Evangelical Foreign Missions Association, and a revival of
Samuel Craig's popular journal *Christianity Today*.[35]

No-popery is a common inheritance of American Protestants, liberal as
well as conservative. A series of articles in the liberal *Christian Century* in these
years illustrate this.[36] Harold Fey charged in eight essays that the Catholic
bishops meant to take over the culture, if not the country. Reinhold Niebuhr
and Paul Tillich, the leading public liberal theologians of the period, were as
critical of the Catholic Church as was Cornelius Van Til of the conservative

Westminister Theological Seminary faculty. Fundamentalists, however, wore their anti-Catholicism on their sleeve in ways that would embarrass their moderate and liberal brethren. You would not catch Niebuhr or Tillich calling the pope "The Man of Sin." Their diction was secular and theological rather than biblical and apocalyptic. But for the fundamentalist leaders of the 1920s and 1930s (and for many to this day) the pope remained "the Man of Sin" and the Antichrist and the Catholic Church was still the "Whore" or the "Beast," the center of Satan's conspiracy and an engine of Last Day persecution of true Christians. The fundamentalist men (and women) were the heirs of evangelical enmity toward the Catholic Church and they were ideological parents of many of those who met in Chicago. The meeting was momentous for other reasons, but it affords us another look at the many hued orthodox Protestant attitude toward the Roman Catholic Church.

Harold Ockenga was president of the NAE, temporary at its first and elected at its second assembly. He delivered keynote addresses at both. He exhibited in both an acute sense of national crisis whose only solution was a new awakening of Americans and of the American cultural and political soul, a revival. In his first address he set the context for an attempt to unify orthodox Christians by pointing to the "amazing growth" and the increased power of the Catholic Church and its urban leaders, and by bemoaning the spread of "that terrible octopus of [Protestant] liberalism" whose organ, the Federal Council of Churches, had "a monopoly on government relations to Protestantism." Finally, he conjured up the threat of secularism and its attendant vices. Romanism touched people's "sense of isolation and impotency." So strong was this need to end isolation that Protestant pastors were turning to imitation: "the ceremonialism of an empty cross; the formalism of a sacramental religion has been substituted for preaching. You hear men talking about reinstating five or six sacraments in the church instead of two."[37]

"I believe," he said the following year, "that the United States of America has been assigned a destiny comparable to that of ancient Israel which was favored, preserved, endowed, guided and used of God," thus shedding the ambiguity of many other fundamentalists about the standing of America in God's plan. The spiritual crisis of the civilization was evident to him in materialist philosophy, the naturalistic exclusion of God from the public culture, and soulless education. Already that crisis had evoked "the Catholic revival" in which people "are turning to the one source today which gives an external authority and claims to mediate between the soul and the absolute, namely Roman Catholicism. Though it may be by ritual and sacraments, nevertheless it has an appeal unto the minds of men."[38] With the renewal promised by the founding of the NAE, orthodox Protestants would be able to match "the Eucharistic Congresses of Romanism" with meetings "containing the dynamic of the great spirit of the evangelical revival."

He was followed to the podium by John W. Bradbury, who reiterated the crisis and the disadvantage that the Protestant groups suffer in facing it—they lacked Catholicism's unity and they had no common voice in American culture. Ecumenical Protestants (the Federal Council of Churches) seemed to have forgotten what the Reformation stood for in contrast to the Roman Catholic Church. Organic unity (the Catholic sort) was not a desire of evangelicals. Their unity would be built on a common orthodox faith and biblical principles rather than on "ecclesiastical hegemony in which the conscience of the individual believer would be stultified and in which discipline would take the place of persuasion." Bradbury played the constitution of the NAE off against the Roman hierarchical structure. The NAE would be, like true Christianity, a "spiritual democracy." It would refuse membership for any group that wanted a union of church and state, resist all [Roman] attempts to garner tax money for the parochial schools, and oppose the "continued existence of the American Embassy to the Vatican." The head of Federal Council of Churches approved the arrangement of a personal representative of the president to the Vatican and thus betrayed American Protestantism. The point is made in the first product of the Resolutions Committee opposing the recognition of the Vatican as a violation of the constitutional principle of separation.[39]

The Catholic Church is viewed as another denomination, large and pushy, with an unacceptable political agenda. Its points of attraction in the crisis are not Christian (hierarchy and ritual). It presents a threat, along with modernist Protestantism and secularism. But note what is *not* mentioned by the children of the fundamentalists: apostasy and Satanic inspiration. The apocalyptic form of discourse is not part of the vocabulary. Granted that by conscious intention these meetings and the NAE that resulted from it were to be free of polemic while retaining the right to criticize, the restraint shown toward Catholicism markedly contrasts with the lack of it in their fundamentalist forebears and many of the groups and individuals who made up its membership. This is a fact of some import in the future of relations between evangelicals and Catholics.

What I find here—and this is a proposal rather than a conclusion—is an important change in conservative Protestant self-understanding. Separatism is no longer to be a principal constituent of orthodox Protestantism. The culture is to be engaged, not only through preaching but also through cooperative and constructive criticism. Again, in principle if not immediately in act, evangelical Protestantism opened itself to exchange and mutual criticism. It reentered the American civic and cultural arena after decades of isolation. This much was recognized clearly by Carpenter. But it also set a path toward an encounter with the other eight-hundred-pound gorilla in the American religious neighborhood. That encounter would be unlike the tribal wars of the past, for the NAE already had in place a self-chosen stand that dammed the easy flow of hatred and bigotry and that embraced argument and tough love. Cooperation, even conversation, with Catholics was theoretically possible. There was no overt signal that the founders knew what was implied in their decision to change the relationship of conservative Protestants to American culture *with respect to the Catholic Church,* but decide they did. The NAE was a sign of a large scale, if very gradual and contested, transformation of relations between the two forms of Christianity. It would be another twenty years before the Catholic Church took a step of this magnitude on the same issue, and fifty years before the writing of *ECT.*

## Vatican II: Berkouwer and Wells

Shortly before Pope John called the second Vatican Council, a book by the Dutch evangelical theologian G. C. Berkouwer (1903–96) was translated and published in English,[40] and had, I suspect, a large influence on evangelicals in the United States. Gerrit Berkouwer was a professor in the Free University of Amsterdam, founded by Abraham Kuyper and home to Herman Bavinck, both of whom were and are highly regarded by American Reformed theologians of Calvinist persuasion and Dutch heritage. The latter men were formative influences on Berkouwer, and all three were known to be tough controversialists and highly critical of Roman Catholicism—as one would expect from heirs of John Calvin.[41] Both of Berkouwer's books, however, are unusual. Unlike Van Til, who also owed a debt to Kuyper and Bavinck in their polemical method, Berkouwer made efforts to restrain the dialectic and the polemic. Where Van Til thought he discharged his duty as a theologian by counterposing the Reformation and Trent, Aquinas and Calvin, Berkouwer tried to understand with sympathy the positions of those he wished to engage. Engagement was a large step beyond dialectical confrontation. Perhaps he did not have Van Til in mind when he wrote this, but the shoe fits: "The trouble with the fear of dialogue is that the alternative is monologue."[42] Van Til's dialogue amounted to reading the enemy's books, while Berkouwer met "the mother Church" in her own kitchen.

Berkouwer accepted Pope John XXIII's invitation to be an official observer at Vatican II, to sit in the observers' box, to attend all public debates, and to mingle with bishops and theologians over coffee during the sessions and at meals after them. Before the Council ended he published a second book, as erudite and even more fascinating than the first. The second was an analysis of the first two sessions (1962–63), especially of their implications for the inner life of the Catholic Church and for relations to evangelical churches. What we have with the two books is one of the most valuable comments by Protestants on Roman Catholicism in the twentieth century, a comment that could not have been made by a Van Til or perhaps even a Karl Barth. Remaining completely faithful to the Reformation's *sola Scriptura,* he criticized Rome's insistence on the role of the Roman and episcopal magisterium in the supposed normative interpretation of it:

It is in this area that Berkouwer raised his most serious complaint against Roman Catholic theology. In his *Conflict with Rome,* the Dutch edition of which was published in 1945, he pointed out that the Roman Catholic dependence on two sources of authority—scripture and tradition—often relegates scripture to the background. Berkouwer later viewed the developments of the second Vatican Council as promising because there was a shift away from the reliance on two authorities. Nonetheless, he wrote in *The Second Vatican Council and the New Catholicism* that the central problem still remained. For whenever church tradition serves to guarantee the interpretation of scripture, it acts as an *a priori* authority that bypasses the need for living faith.[43]

And so the Reformation charge is reiterated, but in a new context of criticism. In the book on the Council we find a judicious reflection on the problems confronting a Protestant at the Council as well as on Catholic problems exposed at the Council. He asks himself and his Protestant reader: Is this an open door to new perspectives on the gospel or the old call to return to Rome? Is it genuinely ecumenical (unity sought) or another proclamation of unity already there in the Roman church? Are Catholics dominated by certainty that they are the true church and that their doctrine is unchangeable?[44] Can Catholics only talk of "separated brethren" or can they recognize separated churches? This is the big problem in ecumenism: after all, personal relations may change in the ecumenical situation, but what of this deep *religious* conviction of Catholics about their church that can admit of only one true church?

And if it is true that there is significant change, what is the challenge to Protestants? The personal alienation of the old anti-Catholicism creates caricatures and fights them. It cannot make a contribution to a renewed discussion of the Reformation-Rome argument, for it cannot be objective. The polemicist's fear of loss of the Reformed faith or compromise of it makes conversation impossible.

But the division remains serious, and there *are* deep theological differences.[45] The issue before the Council is: how shall we understand the Church of Christ? Berkouwer recounts the Catholic struggle over "the mystery of the church," from Pius XII's encyclical "The Body of Christ" (*Mystici Corporis*) in 1943 to the Council's discussion of "The People of God" which led to *Lumen Gentium* in 1964.[46] In twenty years, the Catholic view changed from an exclusive ecclesiology to an inclusive one, and because some of the sins of the church are recognized by its leaders, the old lines between evangelicals and Rome were blurred. On its side can the Catholic Church any longer demand the unconditional surrender of other Christians once the tug between a genuine humility and the exclusiveness that runs through Roman history is felt?[47] The old cry is: the leopard cannot change its spots. In fact, at the Council ". . . a more serious attempt is made than has ever been made before to come to grips with the problem created by the Church's claim to be the only ark and the fact that many outside are not drowned in the floods of divine judgment" (197). In the past the church was seen as one, unified *visible* body. What now? The problem is summed up this way: How can you recognize others as genuine Christians and yet say that their churches are not genuine churches?[48]

These are deep tensions that Berkouwer recognized within the Catholic Church in 1962–63. "And the core of Rome's problems in its relation to other churches still lies in its own pretensions of being the Church established by Christ and maintained under the government of His Vicar at Rome." In other words, the Church is wrestling with its own Myth. What could be more difficult? Berkouwer warns: "We would be doing the Roman Church an injustice if we did not take its problem in this complicated situation with utter and sympathetic seriousness."[49]

Berkouwer's trenchant yet kindly critique, as it was called by Van Til,[50] was echoed in the work of David Wells. A professor of theology at Trinity Evangelical Divinity School and later at Gordon-Conwell Seminary, Wells took up the second Vatican Council in a short book, *Revolution in Rome*.[51] He, too, recognized the seriousness of the changes in the Catholic Church, but from a quite different evangelical perspective. In his book, even the guarded optimism of Berkouwer is muted; in fact, one might say that Wells raised an alarm on the sources and direction of the change. Berkouwer saw an opening of a formerly closed Catholic ecclesiology. Wells, in 1972, in the aftermath of the Council, notes a continuing conflict between old and new theologies that clouds the identity of Catholicism, with the new in the ascendency but of doubtful Christian validity. In fact, he saw more Christianity in the old Tridentine partners in polemic.

The crucial fact in the Council and its aftermath, in Wells's view, is that the Catholic Church is changing. The myth of unchangeability, undermined by Johann Moehler (d. 1838) and John Henry Newman (d. 1890) a century earlier, collapsed at the Council under the ministrations of Catholicism's "new theologians." The documents themselves are evidently compromises between different factions, which he terms old theology and new theology, or conservative and progressive Catholicism. Generally, the old theology is what Protestants would recognize as the Catholicism canonized at the Council of Trent (1563) and at the first Vatican Council (1869). Its prime characteristic is an exclusivist insistence that the Roman Catholic Church is the only true church and that membership in it is necessary to salvation. The new theology, by contrast, is inclusivist, open to the presence of the Spirit in the secular world and in other churches and religions. The new theology, he thinks, was in the ascendency at the Council (1962–65) and during the reign of Paul VI (1963–78). He concludes (prematurely, it now seems!) that the papacy's power is on the wane and the future belongs to bishops, people, and progressive theologians:

The future is not in the hands of the conservatives and even less under the control of Pope Paul VI. . . . The future of Roman Catholicism depends on the outcome of the struggle between the people
and the Pope. . . . the theology of the Counter Reformation will not
again be an option. That the future will see a progressive Catholic
theology is not really in debate; what is undecided is *how* progressive
it will be.[52]

What is important to evangelical Protestants is the shift from the combination of scripture and tradition to a new combination of scripture and inner
experience. The objectivity and sole normative status of the scripture has not
been improved among Catholics in that switch. It sounds to Wells as if the
Church has affirmed a version of "progressive revelation," while evangelicals
restrict revelation to the written Word of God. The new Catholic theologians
find God and salvation in the secular order and opt for the salvation of all
people, even atheists and those practicing non-Christian religions, repudiating
the call of Jesus to make disciples of all.[53] The Council, not far behind its
theologians, endorsed horizontal as distinct from vertical eschatology, that is,
salvation inside the historical process rather than a salvation that transcends
history. All this, of course, is secular anthropology rather than Christian theology, and it recalls Marxist themes to Wells.[54]

The new Catholic theologians also plump for divinization à la Eastern
Orthodoxy, deification rather than justification. Behind this is the thought form
of neo-Platonism and what Wells, recalling Van Til, denominates "the philosophy of Being." This theology focuses on the incarnation rather than on atonement and the cross, Bethlehem rather than Calvary. In this view, the person is
organically joined to the divine life loosed in humankind in the incarnation.[55]
As consistent as this may be with the old Roman doctrine of sacraments and
of the church as mediator, Catholics now are caught up in the flow of gradual
secularization of church and doctrine.

For the new Catholics, the membership in the Catholic Church is no longer
necessary to salvation. Human beings are "anonymous Christians." The world
been turned into the church and salvation is not only available but also effective
there. Wells noted in 1972 that tension between the old exclusivist and the new
inclusivist Catholicisms had not yet been resolved. But, one might suggest,
should it be resolved in favor of inclusivism, then the Catholic Church's hold
on the Christian gospel will have been weakened even further. Catholicism's
new universalism contrasts starkly with orthodox evangelical Christianity. The
contrast between the Reformers and Tridentine Catholicism was sharp:

Faith [in the old Catholicism] was defined as assent to what the
*Church* taught; salvation consisted in receiving the sacraments
which the *Church* offered; Christianity had become identified with

what the *Church* was. In each case, the Church assumed a primary
role that should only have been secondary.

For the Reformers, Christianity was not identical with the Church. The
Church was not an end in itself; it was only a means to an end. The end that
it should have served was the spiritual life of its members, the corporate life
of their fellowship. When the Church lost sight of its essentially pastoral and
subservient role, it lost sight of its biblical mandate. And when this happened,
the power of the Church grew at the expense of genuine Christianity. The
confusion between means and ends in regard to the Church was really what
the Reformation was all about.[56]

But now, he remarks, Catholics are dropping the mediation of Christ
through the Church and finding a new "Christ" in the world and its history.
This seems to worry Wells, and his worry about the progressives is a clue. Not
only is his treatment of the Council and Catholicism respectful, it is irenic.
One would guess that he thinks that the Catholic Church is a Christian church
but a deeply flawed one under threat of a rising tide of secularization. It would
be hard to explain his interest and effort otherwise. The Catholic Church is not
pictured as an enemy, but a community struggling over its traditional (some
orthodox?) beliefs. Although Wells thinks its tradition contains many objectionable elements that obscure its devotion to the gospel of Christ, he does not
convey a judgment that it is an (not to say *the*) apostate church. Wells, with
Berkouwer behind him, sets a new tone to evangelical-Catholic relations. The
Reformation is there, the doctrinal criticism is there, but the polemic is muted,
apocalyptic is absent, and the cry of apostasy does not appear. And there are
no cavorting priests and nuns. What is next?

## The Soft Evangelicals and the Heretical Church

The issue—that is, is the Roman Catholic Church an apostate church and so
not a Christian church, or it is, like the mainline Protestant churches, an
heretical church—is old and is not nearly settled for evangelicals. If it is an
apostate church, it is anti-Christian and must be classified among the sects. If
there are true Christians to be found in it, one may accept them as brothers
and sisters in Christ, even though the vast majority of Catholics need the gospel
preached to them. After all, particular church membership does not go a long
way toward settling whether a person is a Christian or not in the view of
evangelicals. If the Roman church is heretical, yet has not abandoned "the
gospel," one may deal with the Roman church as one may deal with other
Christian churches with which many conservative evangelicals disagree—as
one may deal with Lutheran or Baptist churches which maintain the gospel of

faith and grace. They are true Christian churches who are simply wrongheaded in one or another doctrine or practice. They are true even if not pure churches.

The traditional and apparently still widespread view of evangelicals is that the Roman Church is not a Christian church and, so say the "hard" evangelicals, should not be granted any sign of acceptance or fellowship. For these evangelicals, Rome definitively condemned the gospel of faith and grace at the Council of Trent and thus formally became an apostate church. However, some have held, with Charles Hodge, that enough of Christian truth remains there and the baptismal ordinance is sufficiently well observed, that true Christians and even true Christian churches, are to be found in the Roman communion. While the structure and practice is that of Esau, the faith and life may be that of Jacob. This is reason enough to extend recognition and fellowship to the Catholics who are Christians. To hard evangelicals, however, only an 'ecumaniac' without Reformation principles, would accept fellowship with the Roman Catholic Church as such. While some Catholics are Christians, they are so in spite of membership in that church rather than because of it. In the normal course of events Christian faith cannot survive Romanization, and so one is especially suspicious of the Christian faith of those Catholic leaders who serve Roman interests.

Among the factors that have impelled the search for a new relationship between evangelicals and Catholics are the evangelical loss of cultural hegemony and the experience of cultural displacement all too familiar to American Catholics, the regretted loss of the mainline church bodies during the modernist crisis, the founding of the National Association of Evangelicals, the profound changes in the Roman Catholic Church at the second Vatican Council—in particular, the end of its official romance with medieval Christendom and the modification of its ecclesiological exclusivism—and the marked success of the last three popes of the twentieth century in putting the Catholic Church in the forefront of the public quest for human rights and democratic process. Each of these fed a new way of doing business with American culture in the two communities and so created a demand for a new way of doing business with each other. The spark of the new relationship is the culture war of the last decades of the millennium, centered on the judicially recognized constitutional right to abortion. Neither evangelicals or Catholics could see this as anything other than a monstrous betrayal of social responsibility and morality on the part of the American leadership. Evangelicals and Catholics found each other in the same trench, fighting the deadly fruit of a secularizing culture.

After a year of consultation, fifteen evangelical and Catholic leaders signed the document *Evangelicals and Catholic Together: The Christian Mission in the Third Millennium* (commonly called *ECT I*),[57] and in short order they were joined by twenty-five others. Seven priests (among them three Jesuits, one of them now a cardinal), two bishops (one a Jesuit, another now a cardinal archbishop) and one archbishop (now a cardinal), one cardinal (now deceased), and nine Catholic laypersons were among the Catholics approving, along with twenty evangelical leaders of mixed clerical and lay status and varying institutional and church affiliation. Over a year later a second document, "The Gift of Salvation" (commonly called *ECT II*), meant to continue the dialogue and to answer criticism of the first, was issued by eighteen evangelicals and fifteen Catholics, most of them signers of the first document.[58] A note of confusion and intense dissatisfaction appeared in the evangelical camp immediately after the issuance of *ECT I*. Even granting all that is cited in the document in favor of a renewed conversation, how, its astonished evangelical critics asked, could such a conversation take place with those who continue to deny the rightness of the basic Reformation claims, to reject the Pauline gospel, and to practice a religion whose distinctive marks have no roots in true Christianity?

Some thought that *ECT I* could be best understood as a political move by conservative activists on both sides of the ecclesiastical divide.[59] Committed to victory in the "culture wars" so much the preoccupation of conservative religionists, especially evangelicals and Catholics, since the *Roe v Wade* decision of the Supreme Court in 1973, the signers wanted to side-step inherited enmity and doctrinal polemics to promote the reentry of "orthodox" as distinct from "liberal" Christians into what one of the Catholic leaders called "the naked public square."[60] They wanted open cooperation (they already had informal cooperation) on a list of moral and social issues. In fact, most of the print in *ECT I* was taken up with spelling out those issues for readers. The authors were driven by a common faith in Christ to "contend together" against relativism, anti-intellectualism, nihilism (the three perhaps summed up as "postmodernism"), denials of religious freedom, excessively intrusive government, abortion, euthanasia, eugenics, exclusion of morality in public education ("the promotion of moral equivalence between the normative and the deviant"), the lack of parental choice in schooling, pornography, the celebration of violence, sexual depravity and anti-religious bigotry in the media, and, finally, "militant Islam."[61] They "contend" for a "free society, including a vibrant market economy," a renewed appreciation of Western culture versus the anti-Western bias of multiculturalism, "the irreplaceable role of mediating structures in society," and the prudent use of American power in defense of democracy, and, "where prudent and possible," human rights and religious freedom.

But in order to provide a specifically Christian platform for this cooperation, the authors had to say that the signers, supporters, and cooperators were at least putatively Christian, thus assuring that the "culture war" remained a *Christian* struggle against secularism.[62] The objectives listed are not themselves distinctively Christian, and could be bound together for evangelicals as matters falling under "common grace" and for Catholics under "natural law."[63] But the signers wanted to make a public declaration that they regarded one another as Christian brothers and sisters, and so they pried open Pandora's Box of *odia theologica* once again and they got what the evangelical signers must have anticipated, vigorous opposition among their fellow evangelicals, many of whom were stunned to find dedicated papists such as Richard Neuhaus and Avery Dulles, S.J., being called brothers and sisters in Christ.

The common mission the signers would embark upon rests on a common faith: "The mission that we embrace together is the necessary consequence of the faith we affirm together. . . . We affirm together that we are justified by grace through faith because of Christ. . . . All who accept Christ as Lord and Savior are brothers and sisters in Christ. Evangelicals and Catholics are brothers and sisters in Christ. . . . However imperfect our communion with one another, however deep our disagreements with one another, we recognize that there is but one church of Christ. There is one church because there is one Christ and the church is his body."[64] They repeat their common orthodox faith by reciting the Apostles' Creed. Distortions must be "cleared away," along with "misunderstandings, misrepresentations, and caricatures of one another." The genuine differences are deep, and the authors list them in a ten point version of the Outline, and they conclude:

> On these questions, and other questions implied by them, Evangelicals hold that the Catholic Church has gone beyond Scripture, adding teachings and practices that detract from or compromise the Gospel of God's saving grace in Christ. Catholics, in turn, hold that such teachings and practices are grounded in Scripture and belong to the fullness of God's revelation. Their rejection, Catholics say, results in a truncated and reduced understanding the Christian reality [*sic*]. Again, we cannot resolve these disputes here. . . . As we are bound together by Christ and his cause, so we are bound together in contending against all that opposes Christ and his cause.

Step one, then, is to affirm a shared Christian faith. Step two is to declare a common enemy in a struggle for the soul of American culture. Step three is to declare a common witness in the struggle: the saving power of Christ. These were steps already taken by evangelicals in the founding of the NAE, in which partisan (denominational) differences were set aside for the sake of a revival of American Christianity. But in order to bear a common witness, a fourth step is required for cooperation between evangelicals and Catholics. Just as both sides were alarmed at unchristian public policy and antichristian culture, Catholic leaders were dismayed (to put the matter mildly) at a steady and some would say huge leakage of Catholics to evangelical churches in North and South America in the second half of the twentiet century.[65] The deepest religious and theological convictions of evangelicals for centuries impelled them not merely to denounce Rome as an apostate church but to mount missions to save the benighted Catholics. As the sponsors spoke and signed, the United States, England, and Ireland were dotted with organizations whose mission was to convert Catholics to true Christianity.[66] The prized scalps were (and remain) convert priests and nuns. What is to be done about this problem for the sake of a unified witness in a secular culture?[67] If it can fairly be said that the evangelical signers stepped into deep water when they decided to call the Roman Catholic participants brothers and sisters in Christ, they went over their heads when they attempted (or seemed) to put limits to "sheep stealing."

Calling this a "serious tension between Evangelicals and Catholics" and preserving some balance by calling attention to "attempts to win converts from one another's folds," they adapt the familiar liberal notion of "different ways of being Christian" in "different forms of authentic discipleship" to a new use. Catholics and evangelical Protestants have not till the present recognized their respective forms of life as legitimate. As we have seen for evangelicals, and will see for Catholics, quite the opposite is the case. Yet, in *ECT I*:

> We condemn the practice of recruiting people from another commu-
> nity for purposes of denominational or institutional aggrandize-
> ment. . . . [W]e as Evangelicals and Catholics affirm that opportunity
> and means for growth in Christian discipleship are available in our
> several communities. . . . It is neither theologically legitimate nor a
> prudent use of resources for one Christian community to proselytize
> among active adherents of another Christian community.

Three problems leap from the pages of *ECT I*. Can it be said by consistent evangelicals that consistent Roman Catholics are Christians? The answer from the evangelical perspective must rest on some version of the *sola fide, sola gratia,* and *sola scriptura,* else the Reformation and Protestantism has lost its point. Second, what is that common faith on the basis of which evangelicals and Catholics may work together, as distinct from common human concerns and values? Third, how is it possible, given the nature of evangelical faith and its historical critique of Catholicism, that evangelicals could cease to evangelize not just the loosely affiliated Catholics but especially the strongly affiliated Catholics who, by the very reason of that affiliation, are most in danger of losing their immortal souls?

*ECT II,* "The Gift of Salvation," issued a year after *ECT I,* was an attempt to clarify the agreement on a common faith reached in *ECT I.*[68] The signers accept in common the atoning sacrificial death of Christ; justification by faith and not by good works or merit; God's gift of salvation pure and simple, and not in any way a human achievement; the fact that baptism visibly incorporates a person into the community of faith; and that as a consequence of faith and baptism one is bound to live "the law of love in obedience to Jesus"; and what a Catholic would call the "moral certainty" of an eternal future. Finally, they believe in common that they are bound to witness to, to evangelize, "everyone everywhere." "Evangelicals must speak the gospel to Catholics and Catholics to Evangelicals, always speaking the truth in love." Again, they list the hard doctrinal questions that remain unsettled. Nonetheless, they conclude:

> As Evangelicals who thank God for the heritage of the Reformation
> and affirm with conviction its classic confessions, as Catholics who
> are conscientiously faithful to the teaching of the Catholic Church,
> and as disciples together of the Lord Jesus Christ who recognize our
> debt to our Christian forebears and our obligations to our contem-
> poraries and those who will come after us, we affirm our unity in
> the gospel that we have here professed. In our continuing discus-
> sions we seek no unity other than unity in the truth.

The affirmations of *ECT II* seem a reiteration of *ECT I* and not a significant step in the clarification of the problems presented by *ECT I*. True, they have answered the question of evangelizing one another with what appears to be a blanket approval of it and so take a step back from *ECT I* contrary to the concerns enunciated by the Catholic bishops and the pope. But on the equally crucial question of the *sola fide* and *sola gratia* there is no advance theologically. In other words, it may be true as the signers write that "we understand that what we here affirm is in agreement with what the Reformation traditions have meant by justification by faith alone (sola fide)," it still remains a mystery to many evangelicals and myself that "faithful Catholics" could mean and sign that. Reservations aside, however, *ECT* is at very least a large step in opening communication where before there was little but polemic, and a call for un-derstanding where there was suspicion and denunciation. Whether the Roman Catholic Church is a Christian church and whether committed Catholics can be considered Christians are now questions once again before the evangelical community.

I turn now to the question Catholics have historically put and continue to put to evangelicals: Can the communities of evangelical heritage be considered Christian churches?

# PART III

# Peter Speaks of Paul

# 9

# The Nineteenth-Century Bishops and Anti-Catholicism

The basic lines of *political* anti-Catholicism articulated by Morse and Beecher in the 1830s continued through the nineteenth and twentieth centuries to the purified (i.e., secular) version in Blanshard: Catholic hierarchism is tyranny and so a threat to democracy. As Americans we must resist it, the political critics said. This is a religious/theological argument as well as a political one, for it strikes directly at Catholic ecclesiology, and so Catholic theological apologists had to deal with it. The political attacks largely disappeared, perhaps entering a period of quiescence, after its latest apogee in the work of Paul Blanshard (1948), since the election of John Kennedy to the presidency (1960), and since the second Vatican Council (1962–65). So also pornographic and apocalyptic forms of religious anti-Catholicism have been sidelined.

The Roman version of Christianity is an easy target, however, for, among the many versions of Christianity, the Roman Catholic Church most retains the look and feel of medieval Christendom. When I mentioned to a Quaker couple that I thought that American anti-Catholicism had at last run its course, they cautioned me that it likely had not. When I asked them why they suspected it survives, they said that they doubted that Protestants and other Americans will ever be able to understand how any adult could belong to a church structured and run like the Catholic Church. Similarly, a Protestant student who had worked for six years in the St. Louis University historical theology program commented on graduating that she could never belong to the Catholic Church because Catholics are not free to think. Anecdotal evidence does not take us far, of course, but it can help to pinpoint the continuance of the perception that Christendom thrives within the Catholic Church. The nub of the matter is that Catholics are not full participants in the democratic experiment, nor are they free to do their own religious thinking. In this chapter I will look at some Catholic responses to the more virulent historical forms of expression of this common perception.

The basic lines of the *theological* argument and the Reformation myth retold by Nevins and Campbell, and so comprehensively presented by Boettner, amounts to the Catholic abandonment of the gospel of Christ. The newer theological material on faith and works is a rehearsal of inherited Reform rhetoric by Sproul, Armstrong, Ankerberg, McCarthy, and others, the critics of *Evangelicals and Catholic Together* (1993). Protestant apologists from Calvinist and free church backgrounds afflicted with the congregational and separatist impulses maintain that the Vatican Council changed nothing basic in Roman theology of the church and justification, and that the American cultural crisis is not an adequate reason for evangelicals to mix with the leaders of an apostate church on a theological level. Even those soft evangelicals who signed *ECT* prefer to talk about the Christian faith and life of some Catholics rather than of the Christian faith and life of the Catholic Church or of Catholics as a community. Biblical Christians remain uncomfortable with the Catholic Church and have quite varying degrees of patience with Roman error. I will review the Catholic responses of Bishop England, Archbishops Purcell and Hughes, and Cardinal Gibbons to some of the religious as well as the political criticisms.

## The Pastoral Letters

The pastoral letters of the American Catholic bishops in the nineteenth century, usually issued at the close of the provincial councils of bishops (1829, 1833, 1837, 1840, 1843, 1846, and 1849) and later of plenary councils (1852, 1866, and 1884), reflect the conversations among the bishops meeting in Baltimore for as long as two weeks at a clip.[1] They are written to the clergy and laity in the name of all the bishops. Although not transcripts of the meetings of the bishops, they do tell the historian, as they told the Catholics who at the time read them, what the bishops thought important about current church life. For example, in the nineteenth century, they typically contained comments about the shortage of priests and invariably urged Catholics to read scripture and reflect on it as the Word of God. Evangelicals might be surprised at the latter and the constant quoting of and references to the scriptures. As most of my discussion in this chapter utilizes the apologetics of individual bishops and concerns their theological conceptions of the church and her enemies, it may be well at the outset to get some sense of how deeply the body of Catholic leaders was affected by the events and the wave of anti-Catholic publication and action of the nativist period. Although only one among a number of items on their agendas, it is a matter of pain and resentment, and something, they say, which must be met with a vigorous response without hatred or ill-will. Although the startling quality in much Protestant polemic is the intensity of the hatred of all things Catholic, the startling thing about the official Catholic public response is the control of negative emotion. We shall see instances in which the control slips, but overall the Catholics kept their head. This may be as much a matter of customs of Catholic speech as it is of calm of spirit of individual Catholic bishops, but it is a fact nonetheless.

The steady growth of the Church is revealed in the numbers of episcopal signatures to these letters. The first letter is written by John Carroll, the first and only bishop in 1792; the last in the nineteenth century is signed by James Cardinal Gibbons, archbishop of Baltimore in 1884 in the name of fourteen archbishops and sixty bishops, in a time span in which the Catholic population had increased from less than fifty thousand to more than ten million.[2] The first, by Bishop Carroll in 1792, is free of the least allusion to anti-Catholicism. The last by Archbishop Gibbons in 1884 is briefly concerned to explain that the declaration of papal infallibility by the Vatican Council in 1870 does not change the purely religious character of the pope's leadership of the Church, that is, that the pope has no pretensions to political power or leadership, and that the Catholic Church in America is not hostile to the nation's "principles and institutions."[3] But neither that letter nor the letter of 1866, at the close of the Civil War, show explicit concern with American anti-Catholicism, although nativism and evangelical polemics flourished in the period after the war. Between 1829 and the Civil War, as one would expect, these public letters display a high level of concern with anti-Catholicism among the many problems that faced the bishops, and show the worry of a growing but still young and vulnerable church to the rampant enmity in the religious and political community surrounding her. What to the young church is a serious threat, to an older, larger, and more mature church is a matter of inconvenience that can be taken for granted as a chronic sore in American society. One might be thrown by Morse, but Josiah Strong is more of the same. The bishops in the mid-nineteenth century addressed a challenge. I look now at their preoccupations.

Baltimore's Archbishop John Whitfield, successor to John Carroll in 1814, called the conference in 1829 and, the Catholic historian Peter Guilday tells us, Bishop John England of Charleston, South Carolina, wrote its two letters, one to the laity and one to the clergy.[4] In the first of the two, after discussion of the growth of the church, the need of priests, the responsibilities of parents for the Christian education of their children, and before discussions of Holy Scripture, the unity of the church, the problems of trusteeism, the obligation of attendance at Mass and the threat of indifference to religious truth in a society in which, happily, religious freedom is guaranteed, Bishop England took up "Attacks on the Faith." What concerned him was literature that misrepresented the church's life and teaching, which exerted influence over "good men" and "virtuous women," and that reached "from the very highest place in the land to all its remotest borders," exhibiting Catholics "as what we are not, and . . . maintaining what we detest." Even children found in their books falsification of Catholic teaching, practice, and institutions. He pled for publications by Catholics refuting what was charged, and books for children that were free of attacks on the church.[5]

In 1833, England bemoaned:

> . . . a spirit exhibited by some of the conductors of the press, engaged in the interests of those brethren separated from our communion, which has, within a few years, become more unkind and unjust in our regard. Not only do they assail us and our institutions in a style of vituperation and offence, misrepresent our tenets, vilify our practices, repeat the hundred times refuted calumnies of days of angry and bitter contention in other lands, but they have even denounced you and us as enemies to the liberties of the republic, and have openly proclaimed the fanciful necessity of not only obstructing our progress, but of using their best efforts to extirpate our religion; and for this purpose they have collected large sums of money.[6]

The words sum up neatly the content of decades Protestant anti-Catholic rhetoric. His advice to the Catholic people: "heed them not . . . whilst you serve your God with fidelity."

In 1837 the tone became urgent: the very first item in the letter is "Persecution of the Church." John England, again the author, noted that "the misrepresentation and persecution to which you and we have been exposed since our last council" has been given "blazing notoriety." The bishops were filled with regret, as well as with feelings that they hoped to restrain. The national community was injured and its communion with God interrupted by violations of tolerance. Close to ten pages in a letter of forty are devoted to a discussion of nativist attacks, primarily narration of the burning of the Ursuline convent in Charlestown on August 11, 1834, and its legal and political aftermath, and the 1836 publication of Maria Monk's bogus memoir of life in the convent in Montreal, the sad tale of its composition by New York ministers, and the sadder tale of Monk's fate.[7] The bishops were fully aware of both stories and made sure that their readers were as well. But once again the bishops felt it necessary to defend themselves against charges of disloyalty:

> We owe no religious allegiance to any State in this Union, nor to its general government . . . [our fellow citizens and] we, by our constitutional principles, are free to give this ecclesiastical supremacy to whom we please, or to refuse it to everyone, if we so think proper:

but, they and we owe civil allegiance to the several States in which
we reside, and also, to our general government. When, therefore,
using our undoubted right, we acknowledge the spiritual and ecclesiastical supremacy of the chief bishop of our universal church . . .
[w]e do not thereby forfeit our claim to the civil and political protection of the commonwealth; for, we do not detract from the allegiance to which our temporal governments are plainly entitled, and
which we cheerfully give; nor do we acknowledge any civil or political supremacy, or power over us in any foreign potentate or power,
though that potentate might be the chief pastor of our church.[8]

The bishops were fighting a war on several fronts: religious, civil, legal,
and political. Distortions of church doctrine and history were joined by physical
violence and pornographic renderings of Catholic religious life. Arguments
over salvation by faith or works and papal authority were complicated, and
perhaps even rendered marginal, by questions of political loyalty and images
of randy priests and compliant nuns traversing tunnels between convents and
rectories and cavorting in the convent basements. The morality of public discourse was, according to the bishops, undermined.

Nothing is more surely calculated for the destruction of that purity
which is the soul of virtue, than the perusal of lascivious tales; and
never did the most unprincipled author compile any work more foul
in this respect, than the productions of our assailants, and never
was there exhibited a more voracious appetite for mischievous ali-
ment than that which they have unfortunately excited. With what
avidity have not the numerous and heavy editions of those immod-
est fictions been taken up, disseminated through the country, pur-
chased and introduced in the name of religion amongst the aged
and young of both sexes, in every state and territory of our Union?[9]

England was once again—and, for the last time—the author of the letter
of 1840 (he died in 1842) There is but a brief mention of the fact that the state
of Massachusetts had not indemnified the "diocess" [sic] of Boston for the
destruction of the convent and school, but England is happy to report no increase in public attacks "by religious teachers high in the estimation of some
of our fellow citizens" (possibly a reference to Maria Monk's New York Presbyterian handlers). He also mentions a lessening of the violence of attacks in
the religious press and in the pulpit.[10] Perhaps Archbishop Samuel Eccleston
took it on himself to write the letter of 1843, for England's tone, style, and
range of concerns are absent. And, as Guilday comments:

There is absent from its pages any forewarning of the terrible outbreak against the Catholic faith which was to occur the following
Spring. Rather do the prelates appear to ignore the signs of the com-

ing storm, and to confine themselves to questions of education, temperance and divorce, with a passing reference to the Oxford Movement.[11]

More surprisingly, in the letter of 1846 only an illusion to "the artifices
employed to impede the progress of our holy religion by designing and interested men" can be found. On the tumultuous events of the 1844 church burn-
ings and killings in Philadelphia and the threat of the nativist riots in New
York and elsewhere, the bishops apparently decided to refrain from comment.
In a brief letter they wrote on other church concerns and dedicate the church
in the United States to "the special patronage of the Holy Mother of God" who
is called on to "obtain for us grace and salvation through the mediation of her
Son, the one mediator," something that would not endear the church to its
evangelical critics.[12]

The councils of 1852, 1866, and 1884 follow the same path, wrestling with
the momentous events of the time, including the Civil War and its effects and
ignoring anti-Catholicism as they ignored both slavery and emancipation.
These later councils display considerable concern for the definition of the
dogma of the Immaculate Conception, the increasingly unfortunate political
situation of Pope Pius IX and the struggle over the status of the "Patrimony
of St. Peter" (i.e., the papal states), and the Vatican Council's definition of papal
infallibility (1869), all issues that fed anti-Catholic propaganda. It would seem
that no amount of propaganda would again call for public attention from the
bishops.

After England, Purcell and Hughes presented themselves as champions
of the church, the burden could be carried by theologians, historians, and the
educated laity. Although the bishops, individually and collectively, showed no
hesitation in addressing public issues, nativism was behind them and for conversation behind closed doors. They passed up the nativism of the age of Josiah
Strong and the conquest Cuba and the Philippine Islands (1876–98), the revival
of the Ku Klux Klan and the campaign of Al Smith (1920–28), and the period
from Paul Blanshard to John Kennedy (1948–60). The hierarchy's concern
would not reappear until the late twentieth century, and then it would be in
an entirely different context, namely, the movement of large numbers of alienated Catholics to evangelical churches.

## John England

The first bishop of Charleston was consecrated in St. Finbar's Church in Cork,
Ireland, in 1820. As a young priest he had shown himself to be a very capable
public proponent of the church in calling for the exclusion of British government's role in the appointment of Irish bishops. His new diocese comprised

the states of North Carolina, South Carolina, and Georgia, and there were three priests and five thousand Catholics in the entire area. He spent so much time on the road tending to his flock that his metropolitan bishop (Baltimore) chided him for it. Slave owners were annoyed by his concern for slaves and his desire to open a school for them. He bothered his brother bishops by his support for national synods and for a quasi-republican form of national church government, by writing a constitution for his diocese meant to ameliorate the challenges to episcopal authority by lay trustees, and by his attempts to mediate trustees disputes in other dioceses. He served once as papal delegate to the church in Haiti (1833). He founded, wrote, and edited the weekly *United States Catholic Miscellany* from 1822 until his death in 1842. When he spoke to Congress in 1826 he was one month from receiving his citizenship papers.

From the 1820s to the 1840s and the rise of John Hughes to the See of New York, England was the chief apologist for the Catholic Church in the United States. He quickly and firmly grasped the principles of mixed republican and democratic social and political organization of the United States, and the benefits to the Catholic Church of the separation of the church and state in the American system of government. Peter Clarke commented:

> John England was the first theoretician of the separation of Church and state and freedom of religion. He greatly influenced the young American Church in its acceptance and involvement in American constitutional democracy and contributed to a trend that would lead the universal Church to replace the older ideal of union of Church and state with John England's ideal of a free Church in a free society.[13]

In England's practice, Clarke's comment is exemplified by England's "Constitution of the Roman Catholic Church, of the Diocess [*sic*] of Charleston," Title II,

3. We do not believe that our Lord Jesus Christ gave to the civil or temporal governments of states, empires, kingdoms, or nations, any authority in or over spiritual or ecclesiastical concerns.
4. We do not believe that our Lord Jesus Christ gave to the rulers of his church, as such, any authority in or over the civil or temporal concerns of states, empires, kingdoms, or nations.
5. We do not believe that our Lord Jesus Christ hath appointed any special or particular mode of civil or temporal government for mankind, so that men should be bound by the divine law to adopt or prefer one mode of civil or temporal government to any other.[14]

England's formulation of these propositions in the negative is odd in an official Catholic document. Typically, I think, they would be framed positively, affirming what the diocese does believe. Moreover, although one might expect such a clear statement to diffuse any worries on the part of his countrymen, they would have known, had they read it, that England's constitution sounded a peculiar note for a Roman Catholic document. But many must have read his next—and this time national—statement. I will concentrate here on his Discourse before Congress (1826), in which he offered congressmen an explanation of the Roman Catholic Church in terms of the apprehensions and misinterpretations of it by some of his fellow citizens.[15] Although the public task was a common one for nineteenth-century bishops and England fills it with competence and due public modesty and affection, he foresaw a greater task yet and a larger problem. A decade before Morse and Beecher ignited the first great public assault on the church's threat to the American republic, England took on the relationship between church and state, far in advance of the current Catholic thinking on the subject, even by his fellow bishops. On this latter issue he set a standard with which the Vatican leadership of the church as a whole and even elements of the American church would not be entirely comfortable until the second Vatican Council in 1962–65.

Invited by some friends in Congress and speaking with the permission of the Protestant chaplain, he recognized the "extreme delicacy" of his position as representative of a minority. He expressed his hesitation to speak freely and feared some unintentional slight to the feelings of his hearers. He also knew that he must speak of the Catholic Church, yet, obliged to lay the groundwork for a discussion of the "peculiarities" of his own religion, he first had to address "the general principle of our religion (i.e. Christianity)." And so he launched into an oration on natural religion and the duties of "men" to God and one another by virtue of their creation and common humanity.[16]

But on to the political worries of 1826! Within ten years, Maria Monk, Samuel Morse, Lyman Beecher, William Nevins, and Alexander Campbell would bring to the attention of the American public the peculiarities of the Catholic Church in belief and practice, and her arrogant and exclusivist understanding of her role in the salvation of the world, but they also would force questions of the incompatibility of the constitution of the Catholic Church with any form of social and political life that prized freedom and the rights of religious conscience. Within twenty years, the Nativist crusade would be in full swing.

The issue was not invented by the nativists in 1836, and it was not new to John England and the congressmen in 1826. Fear of popery entered the colonies with the first immigrants, and had a first round during the war between the French Catholic settlements in Canada and the northern colonies (1756–63), and in the tensions that led to it. Sydney Ahlstrom notes of the war: "The long French and Indian Wars from beginning to end involved a hostile Roman Catholic presence in various areas, and they left an enduring legacy of heightened anti-Catholic animosity among colonial Americans."[17] In the New England tensions between British and French that preceded the outbreak of war, Jonathan Edwards found a sign that the Beast was stirring, and during the war Jonathan Mayhew saw a threat to liberty from the Catholic Church. The wars of nations were wars of religions for three hundred years before England spoke, and so he and those who followed after in the Nativist crusade were picking up well-used cudgels. England here lays out a Catholic response that no Catholic apologist would substantially improve on. No one would make the case more clearly and more directly. He raises three questions in the voice of a worried citizen, and answers them:

(1) "If the infallible tribunal, which you profess yourself bound to obey, should command you to overturn our government, and tell you that it is the will of God to have it new modeled, will you be bound to obey it?"[18] Remember, Bishop England is within a few short weeks of taking the oath of allegiance to the American political community. No, he says, we are not bound to obey it, and he recognizes no such authority in his church:

> I would not allow to the Pope or to any bishop of our Church, out-
> side this Union, the smallest interference with the humblest vote at
> our most insignificant ballot-box. . . . You [i.e., Congress] have no
> power to interfere with my religious rights; the tribunal of the
> Church has no power to interfere with my civil rights. . . . It must
> hence be apparent, that any idea of the Roman Catholics of these
> republics being in any way under the influence of any foreign eccle-
> siastical power, or indeed of any Church authority, in the exercise of
> their civil rights is a serious mistake. There is no class of our fellow-
> citizens more free to think and to act for themselves on the subject
> of our rights than we are; and I believe that there is not any portion
> of the American family more jealous of foreign influence, or more
> ready to resist it.[19]

(2) Is not the Catholic Church aristocratic and despotic in its principles, and so ". . . its spirit opposed to that of republicanism"? But, said England, "the vast majority of republican States and republican patriots have been, and even now are, Roman Catholic." The church has no teaching on what sort of government people may establish. "Upon this God has left us free to make our own selection." The principle is boldly stated. Alas, England would not convince the critics of the church, for several reasons.

While it should have been clear even then that the church, in spite of some clouded instances and provocative texts,[20] is not much up to overthrowing governments, there is the large area of public policy that the church has an interest in and continues to influence. Education, for example, will shortly become a key concern of the church's leaders and England's colleagues and successors. About the church's interest in policy, England says nothing.

Moreover, the critics often regard statements by individual Catholics, theologians, and even bishops to be inconsequential and even disingenuous to this extent: no one but a council or a pope can commit the Church to any principle or any course of action. Anyone pretending to do so is deceiving himself and others. Bishop England's protestations in favor of the separation of jurisdictions are mere wind from this perspective. The critics will go on saying: "But the Roman documents say differently." The Roman documents in the course of the nineteenth century will continue to support the critics' suspicions.

(3) The critics may ask: "But is it not a tenet of our church, that we must persecute all those who differ from us? Has not our religion been propagated by the firebrand and the sword? . . . and in the code of our infallible church have we not canons of persecution which we are conscientiously bound to obey and to enforce?" Said England in response:

> It is no doctrine of the Roman Catholic Church; I do not know that
> it is the doctrine of any Church calling itself Christian; but, unfortu-
> nately, I know it has been practiced by some Roman Catholics, and
> it has been practiced in every Church which accused her of having
> had recourse thereto. I would then say it was taught by no Church;
> it has been practiced in all.[21]

He knew that religious liberty and persecution was sure to be the thickest part of any debate, and he spent the largest number of lines on it. Rather than report on the historical argument with regard to the fourth Lateran Council and the papal power of deposition of monarchs, interesting as those topics may be, I return to one point in his response that proves to be of special importance for the future of evangelicals and Catholics, what I would call "nascent histor-ical consciousness," a perspective on the past more common in the twentieth century than the nineteenth, but still hard to come by and even harder to define. To make his point he calls on Henry Hallam, a British Protestant his-torian of the Middle Ages:[22]

> We are now arrived at the place where we may easily find the origin
> and the extent of the papal power of deposing sovereigns and of ab-
> solving subjects from their oaths of allegiance. To judge properly of
> the facts, we must know their special circumstances, not their mere
> outline. The circumstances of Christendom were then widely differ-
> ent from those in which we are now placed. Europe was then under
> the feudal system. I have seldom found a writer, not a Catholic,
> who, in treating of that age and that system, has been accurate,
> and who has not done us very serious injustice. But a friend of
> mine, who is a respectable member of your honorable body, has led
> me to read Hallam's account of it; and I must say that I have sel-
> dom met with so much candor and, what I call, so much truth.

From reading his statement of that system it will be plainly seen
that there existed amongst the Christian potentates a sort of federation, in which they bound themselves by certain regulations, and to
the observance of those they were held not merely by their oaths,
but by various penalties. Sometimes they consented that the penalty
should be the loss of their station. . . . They were, however, all members of one Church, of which the Pope was the head, and in this
respect their common father; and by universal consent it was regulated that he should examine, ascertain the fact, proclaim it, and declare its consequences. Thus he did in reality possess the power of
deposing monarchs, and of absolving their subjects from oaths of
fealty. . . . He governed the Church by divine right, he deposed kings
and absolved subjects from their allegiance by human concession.
. . . It is not then a doctrine of our Church that the Pope has been
divinely commissioned either to depose kings or to interfere with re-
publics, or to absolve subjects of the former from their allegiance, or
interfere with the civil concerns of the latter. . . . [S]ome divines were
found who endeavored to prove that what originated in voluntary
concession of States and monarchs was derived from divine institution. . . . Neither will any person attempt to establish an analogy between our federation and that of feudalism, to argue that the Pope
can do amongst us what he did amongst European potentates under
circumstances widely different.[23]

Some Roman theologians of the time would not have agreed with Bishop
England's blunt statement of the limits to papal authority, as evangelicals would
be quick to point out, but that is beside the point.[24] The case was made, not
repudiated, and carried forward by other American Catholic apologists. For our
purposes, the more important point is England's forceful introduction of the
difference of "circumstances" and the difference of "ages" between the medieval and the modern into the interpretation of "that" age in "this" one. He is,
of course, talking about the papacy and of the Catholic Church changing from
age to age. The notion of change in the interaction between church and the
civil order eliminates to a significant degree the abstract and deductive conclusions of the papal maximalists and Protestant critics by which the papacy and
the Roman church are seen as ever the same, incapable of change and adaptation without inauthenticity on one side and falsification or deviousness on
the other.

England and Purcell, who followed and quoted him in this matter, were
perfectly sure that their fellow citizens and the leaders of their nation had
nothing to fear from Rome and from the presence of Roman Catholics in their
midst—with the same sort of certainty that Al Smith one hundred years and
John Kennedy 140 years later were to display before their Protestant critics and

the nation. Smith and Kennedy were not historical scholars of any sort, they were politicians and storytellers who "told it as they saw it," without scholarly nuance. They had no need of recourse to historical consciousness, and no historical interest in the hard cases that lay between Protestant polemicists and Catholic apologists.[25]

But England, and Purcell and Kenrick in his wake, obviously knew those cases and had to break free of them as setting the eternal law of the relations between the Roman church and the state. They had to leave off the "classical consciousness" that the past provided the ideal to which each age after it must conform or prove itself barbarian, and take on the "historical consciousness" in which each age is seen to work out its own ideals and norms, many in continuity with the past and many distinct from those admired in the past. These new men in a new nation saw nothing desirable about a restoration of the "golden age" of medieval Christendom. Although they may have sometimes felt that the thirteenth was "the greatest of centuries," they evidently did not hanker for it.[26] They also opened the path to a later reconsideration by an American theologian, John Courtney Murray, of the common Roman "thesis" that the union of church and state remains the normal and ideal relation even when it cannot be established.[27] American Catholics quickly came to the conclusion that theirs was the normal situation, and the traditional Roman "thesis" on the matter was the peculiar one.

At this point England turns to

> ... the essential distinction between the Roman Catholic Church and every other. ... The doctrine which, as a prelate of that Church, and from my own conscientious conviction, I preach, differs very widely indeed from what is generally professed and acted upon by the great majority of our citizens, and by a vast portion of the re-spectable and enlightened assemblage which surrounds me. ... And here let me assure you that if, in the course of my observations, any expression should escape from me that may appear calculated to wound the feelings of those from whom I differ, it is not my atten-tion to assail, to insult, or to give pain; and that I may be pardoned for what will be in truth an inconsiderate expression, not intended to offend. ... My kindest friends, my most intimate acquaintance, they whom I do and ought to esteem and respect, are at variance with my creed; and yet it does not and shall not destroy our affec-tion.[28]

Mellow as England sounds, sensitive to the feelings and convictions of his audience, he was ready to tell them what Catholicism is in short order. Here he dealt with an audience which is doubtless curious, surely in some part hostile to his church, yet has not attacked him or it. And so he took the high road of preemptive penitence for even the slightest of unintentional slights.

The first Catholic priest to address his country's legislators, he shall close rather than open wounds—while telling his church's story forcefully, needless to say.

Again he mentioned the minority status of the Catholic Church and spread a bit of unction on his hearers. Understandable, for he was about to lay out for them the traditional Catholic response to the Protestant view of the church and the scriptures that had echoed down the corridors of three centuries—with an addition of the special concern of American evangelicals, the incompatibility between Catholicism and American republican government and social democracy. I shall follow England's presentation, thus leaving me free to attend to the particular emphases of his successors rather than their general adherence to the course of the Catholic apologetic. I shall pick up England's sensitivity to the American situation as well. As we pass by his material, we should be conscious of what we do *not* find there. He addresses himself exclusively to *historical* argument rather than to the substantive *theological* positions of the Reformers, for example, justification by faith alone. Insofar as he engages here in theology, it is ecclesiology, or theory of the church, that he set forth. This forum called for political, not theological, argument. For our purposes, I shall restate England's argument in a few brief propositions, using his own words when convenient:[29]

1. "It is a fact that our Blessed Redeemer did not write His communications; it is equally certain that He neither gave a command nor a commission to have them written. It is a fact that His religion was fully and extensively established before any part of the Scriptures of our new law was committed to writing. We therefore believe it to be evident that our religion was not established by the dissemination of writings."

2. Rather, the Lord committed his message to some witnesses who were to tell others what he said, what he commanded, "what he positively instituted, and for what purpose, and what were to be the consequences."

3. "The witnesses ordained others as "fellow-witnesses, extended to them the power of commission" so that there would be teachers in every city."

4. "These scattered witnesses taught the same thing in all places, and distinguished themselves from those who taught novelties and separated themselves from the great body." Division over the commission to teach existed "almost at the very origin of the Christian Church."

5. "Those books [i.e., those which would comprise the New Testament] had a limited circulation amongst the Christians in some places, but highly as they were valued, they were not looked upon as the exclusive evidence of the doctrine of the Redeemer, and the very fact,

which is, of course, incontestable, that a vast quantity of what we all receive now as his doctrine is not contained in them, but was subsequently written, renders it impossible for any of us to assume this principle." In other words, there was no New Testament in the formative two centuries of the Christian church, an historical proposition which, if it stands, would present large problems for the common evangelical picture of "biblical Christianity."[30] As it is difficult for evangelicals to imagine a Christianity without the Bible, and a printed Bible with universal distribution, so it is difficult for Catholics to imagine a Christianity restricted to the text, and even more to the printed text. Once again, is it the book or the church that is the primary medium of the Christian revelation? In fact, if England's Catholic argument is correct, it would negate the possibility of a return to biblical Christianity in an early church which did not possess a Christian Bible.

6. Well, then, how was an enquirer in those bookless days to know what God revealed, how tell truth from error? The "common rule of evidence arising from testimony would have been sufficient. . . . Examine the witnesses fully as to the fact, and, if the vast majority, under proper circumstances, will agree in the testimony, it is evidence of truth." This is in fact what history tells us happened in the churches.

7. Although the Apostles died in the first century, a "tribunal of witnesses" survived and grew in the form of the successors to Peter and the Apostles. The same system continued in the second century—only after three centuries was there a New Testament and it was selected and the list closed by consultation among the inheritors of the apostolic mantle. "And our belief is, that the mode of ascertaining the doctrine of truth originally was, and continued to be, from the testimony of that tribunal, rather than by the mere testimony of those books."

8. What would be the authority of those books without the living witness? None. For if documents are introduced into a court, only a witness can establish their authenticity: "a document flung upon the table of a court lies there without any use, until it is made useful by testimony beside itself." Read this and believe it, the witnesses said, and skip that! Why? Because these books embody what we have all believed back to the Apostles themselves. "We say, that when the great majority of the bishops united with their head, the Bishop of Rome, who succeeds to Peter, thus concur in their testimony, it is evidence of truth; we will infallibly come to a certain knowledge of what God has revealed. This is our doctrine of the infallibility of the Church."[31]

9. "Thus, the decisions of our councils are the exhibition of the original revelation, not the expression of adopted opinions."

The argument turns on questions of historical fact; for example, did the Apostles appoint successors, are bishops of the Catholic Church those successors, did Peter go to Rome and lead that church or any other church, and did the bishop of Rome succeed Peter? What is the evidence for all of this? And I raise these questions, as they have been raised since the Reformation, without alluding to contemporary conflicts over what Jesus said and did in historical fact. There is something other than historical fact filling the interstices between the facts we do know with greater or lesser probability. It is that tightly knit whole composed of historical facts and of their relations, transfused by divine intention, that make up the Catholic myth of Christian origins. Deny the divine will, call into question some of the historical facts and refill the interstices, and one might make another narrative hypothetically as plausible or mythically as satisfying.[32]

England presented Congress with a neat outline of the Catholic understanding of the construction of the church. The "facts," even were they beyond question historically, need to be glued together by divine purpose. The narrative is not "mere history" of an institution but is the history of God and grace told by Catholics who have found both in their community and who cannot otherwise understand its existence than as an act of God and an unwarranted gift. Some of the congressmen seated before him knew the other myth, as Luther and the Centuriators of Magdeburg told it. The Reformation had reformed the Catholic myth, but England was able to rehearse the old one in this strange new land. It was quite a day for an immigrant and his cherished church.


## John Purcell

Like John England, John Purcell (1800–83) was born in Ireland, emigrated to the United States at the age of eighteen, entered St. Mary's College in Emmitsburg, Md., shortly after, and was ordained in Paris in 1827. He taught at St. Mary's College and became its president (1829–33), then was appointed bishop of the church in Cincinnati and later its archbishop (1833–83). He saw the same sort of astounding growth that Bishop Francis Kenrick did in Philadelphia and Bishop John Hughes did in New York City in numbers of Catholics, church institutions, religious communities, parishes, and schools. Along with Hughes, Purcell was an outspoken defender of Archbishop Gaetano Bedini, the first representative of a pope to tour the American Catholic Church (1853). In spite of the public uproar over Bedini's visit, Purcell invited Bedini to the diocese of Cincinnati and faced down a mob of protestors at the cathedral church. He supported the total abstinence movement (may God forgive him), rallied Catholic support for Lincoln's war to save the union, and took a firm public stand against slavery, the latter an unusual thing among American Catholics. With several other influential American churchmen, Peter Kenrick of St. Louis among them, Purcell was an "inopportunist" at Vatican I and left before the final vote on papal infallibility.[33]

Purcell accepted Alexander Campbell's challenge to a weeklong debate in January 1837. The debate was structured on seven questions put by Campbell, and ranged across the broad expanse of evangelical-Catholic differences in doctrine. Several of them we touched on in chapter 5. The issue I wish to notice here follows closely on Bishop England's intention to counter public opinion on Catholic views of the relationship between the Catholic Church and American democracy. Purcell did not take a step back from England's distinction between the proper spheres of each, a distinction aimed at calming Protestant fears of a dominant Catholic majority but, perhaps more important, at lending Catholic support to "the American experiment" and thus assuring the church of freedom for its own religious mission. Purcell ceded nothing to Campbell in the course of the seven-day debate, least of all on the question of church and state.

Campbell appealed to the putatively deep suspicions of his audience that the Catholic Church and democracy were incompatible, and Purcell set out to deny his allegations. Purcell's problem was to explain why the leaders of the church, the popes in particular, could take one stand in medieval European politics and another in modern democratic politics. Campbell's charge was simple enough: Catholics as citizens are not the source of the threat to democracy, but the papacy's dogmatic claims to universal political sovereignty and its ugly history of political persecution of dissenters renders them so.[34]

He then quoted the oath taken by bishops upon their installation.[35] In addition to the promise made by every bishop to "persecute heretics," it says that the bishop will visit Rome, report on the state of the diocese, and keep the church's property, avoiding "alienation" of it.[36] Campbell regarded this as casting suspicion on Purcell's devotion to his country. How can one hold allegiance to a foreign sovereign and to the Constitution and way of life of the American republic, he asked. As to the oath, Purcell simply denied Campbell's interpretation of it: "My ecclesiastical oath is of a purely spiritual nature. The only oath of allegiance, of a temporal character, which I have ever taken, was to the United States. The two oaths cannot be incompatible."[37]

But Campbell's primary suspicion rested on the history of the papacy—a history of despotism, a history known to all educated citizens in his time. And, second, Campbell knew that the Roman church never changes, and this matter of the superiority of the spiritual over the temporal had already been settled in formal church teaching. No matter what Purcell had to say on the matter, Protestant Americans had to keep their eyes on the documents:

. . . Trent fully established, adopted, and re-promulgated these decrees [of the fourth Lateran council and Innocent III], and they are,
at this moment, in full force at Rome. Until, then, a general council
is called, and makes fallible the decisions of the great Lateran council; such is, and must be the dictum and belief of the Roman church;
and, as I judge, there will never be another general council, this will
ever be the doctrine of papal Rome, till the day of her death. Is this,
I emphatically ask, the genius and spirit of republican America?[38]

For his fear of Catholics Campbell gets no sympathy from Purcell: "I was
about to say: 'Poor baby, do not be so afraid: do not be such a coward: shake
off those old woman's fears about raw head and bloody bones, and be more
manly.'" George Washington was not afraid of us, says Purcell. Look at Lafayette, Kosciuko, William Tell, the Republic of Venice, the Republic of San Ma-
rino, and take heart.

But the documents! What about the documents and the history? Campbell
quoted Urban II, the council of Toledo, Innocent III, Leo IX, and Adrian I on
the power to absolve people of their allegiance to kings. He repeated the heart
of his charge:

. . . The gentleman is under his "Holy Lord, the pope." I am not a
foreigner in this sense. But still better, I am the father of a family:
my children are native Americans: and through these I am more a
kin (sic) to the great American family than he can ever be. Without
perjury or apostasy from his office, he can never have a wife, nor
family. He is a stranger to those near and holy relations. He has no
country—no home. He lives and he must die under the command
of foreign superiors; and they may, by authority or promotion, remove him to Europe or Asia at pleasure. For these and other reasons I am identified with Protestant America, and I claim a relation
here to which his heart shall ever be a stranger.[39]

Purcell denied that the oath of a bishop recognizes a temporal sovereignty
of the bishop of Rome. Then on to the deposing power of the popes—Purcell
declared that he would not defend it in Cincinnati and would not defend it in
Rome. "The see of Rome is as the sun and center of the system, to which all
the planets, revolving in beauteous harmony, tend. . . . But like the planets, we
are not absorbed by it. We know its excellence, its usefulness, its destination,
its limits." He quoted a theology textbook (Bouvier) from his days of study with
the Sulpician fathers in Paris, showing that it is common Catholic doctrine
that "the pope has no right, direct or indirect, by any divine commission, to
the temporalities of kings or other Christians."[40] The power of deposition was
first claimed in the tenth century, "a thousand years too late" to rank as a

doctrine. The general councils never made the power an article of faith, and the text itself is found in none of the early manuscript copies.[41] In other words, Purcell argued that (1) one cannot make a doctrine out of a history and (2) the doctrine has not been declared such.

Purcell quoted at length John England's Address to Congress.[42] The Lateran Council was talking about the Albigensians, a very specific case not a doctrinal rule or definition. It was an act of excommunication of those who denied the faith. A council of the civil lords made its own stand clear on the matter, and later copyists included that, adding it to the canon of the council. But, argued Purcell, this did not to apply to the circumstances of Campbell's own time: "The circumstances of Christendom were then widely different from those in which we are now placed," an admission that implies that we are no longer in the culture of Christendom. The essence of the church is not what Campbell and his Catholic counterparts, the papal ultramontanists, took it to be, namely, that every act of a pope displays and proves a power of the papacy.

All at once we are thrown into a different intellectual context from the one supposed by Campbell. John England and Purcell recognized the "end of Christendom" that has become commonplace among Catholics only since the end of the second Vatican Council: feudal Christendom, Catholic Christendom is gone, and the pope no longer has the authority ceded to him by Catholic rulers in the medieval period. Why? Because nations no longer cede it, peoples no longer cede it to him. The culture of Christendom evaporated under the pressures of the Reformation and the rise of the nation-states. England, as we mentioned, referred to the Protestant historian Hallam, who viewed the medieval system is as a federation in which the monarchs agreed that their "common father" had the right to depose when circumstances required it.[43] Purcell read to the audience the following words of England:

> Thus he did in reality possess the power of deposing monarchs, and of absolving their subjects from oaths of fealty, but only those monarchs who were members of that federation, and in the cases legally provided for, and by their concession, not by divine right, and during the term of that federation and the existence of his commission. He governed the church by divine right, he deposed kings and absolved subjects from the allegiance by human concession. I preach the doctrines of my church by divine right, but I preach from this spot not by that right, but by the permission of others. . . . Neither will any person attempt to establish an analogy between our federation and that of feudalism, to argue that the pope can do amongst us what he did amongst European potentates under circumstances widely different.[44]

Answering Campbell's charge that he evaded the political implications for Americans of the deposing power claimed by the pope, and evaded an explanation of the oath of a bishop, which would lead to Catholic persecution of Protestants (*persequar et impugnabo, salvo meo ordine*), Purcell said:

> Here is the fullest, the clearest, the most unequivocal disavowal, of the doctrine of the pope's deposing power. The Catholics do not believe he has any such power. We would be among the first to oppose him in its exercise; and we would be neither heretics nor bad Catholics; and we each of us bishops swear the very words of the oath: '*Persequar et impugnabo, salvo meo ordine,*' in the sense specified, which is the only true sense, the assumption of any such power by the pope, or the pope for the assumption of any such power. FOR TEN CENTURIES THIS POWER WAS NEVER CLAIMED BY ANY POPE. IT CAN THEREFORE, BE NO PART OF CATHOLIC DOCTRINE. IT HAS NOT GAINED ONE FOOT OF LAND FOR THE POPE. IT IS NOT ANYWHERE BELIEVED, OR ACTED UPON, IN THE CATHOLIC CHURCH. NOR SHOULD IT BE, AT THIS LATE DATE, ESTABLISHED, IF ANY MAN COULD BE FOUND TO MAKE THE ATTEMPT. Let these go before the American people, as the real principle of Catholics concerning the power of the pope. And if we must pronounce a judgment on the past, let it be remembered, that when the pope did use this power, it was *when appealed to as a common father,* and in favor of the oppressed. We should go back, in spirit, to former times, when we undertake to judge them. We should understand the condition of society at the period; we should know the circumstances, general and particular, which controlled and influenced the great events recorded in history. We should not quarrel with our ancestors, because they did not possess the knowledge which we possess; not flatter ourselves that we are vastly their betters, because of these adventitious advantages; while they manifestly surpass us in others of greater value, to the Christian, the moralist, the artist. They had the substance of good things; we seem to be content with the shadow of them. The very efforts now being made by fanatical preachers, and petitioners to congress, to proscribe Roman Catholics, clearly show that we are far behind them in regard for the truth, and the exercise of toleration. Let it never be forgotten, *what the sect was, of what religion the men were, who first petitioned congress, in this free country, to restrict, or, to use a more appropriate word, to abolish liberty of conscience, and to form a Christian party in politics.* They were not Roman Catholics.[45]

Is Purcell's answer, following on England, another incipient insight into the End of Christendom? Remarkably, yes! And more. The bishops understood not only that circumstances change (and so Christendom as a fact goes the way of the feudal ideal—and feudalism was once an ideal, too), but that the church changes with the changed circumstances. What was once ceded to be a power of the pope is not eternally a power of the papacy, not a doctrine of the faith. Everyone from Campbell to Boettner knew as well that Christendom had perished, and quite possibly had their own half conscious dreams of reconstituting it as a Christian America, but they were convinced in their waking hours that the Catholic Church, essentially the church of Christendom, roamed the earth looking for cultures to devour like the noonday demon seeking souls. The immense row raised by the nineteenth century popes over the modern world and modernity must have sounded to all, Christian and secular, like a demand for a return to Christendom—and they were not wrong entirely. The popes themselves were trapped in the rhetoric of a bygone era, and the ideal of one true church in one just society.

What are we to make of this now common insight—that a phase of Western culture has passed? For one thing, Christianity survives cultural collapse and its own stupidity and sin. Not only did it survive the collapse of classical culture but also it survived the passing of feudal culture. It even survived its own tumultuous period of reform, the Protestant reform and the Catholic reform. As classical civilization ended, Christendom arose; when feudal culture ended, Christendom weakened and Christianity blossomed. New forms of Christianity arose, at first several "reformed" versions and then the Tridentine Catholic version. Whereas the Catholic version of Christianity clung most closely and openly to the ideal of Christendom and its hierarchical and sacramental universe, it formally surrendered its ideal of political and cultural hegemony at the second Vatican Council.

Now the modern world is ending, when it was still possible for Catholics to dream of one church. When modernity ends, what then? Christianity in the post-Christian age now often announced by prophets and dissident Christians? Catholicism in a post-Christian age? Yes, and Protestantism, and ecumenism with its slices of union and cooperative action, are clearly the answer. History sometimes takes on the glow of metaphysical fact and becomes something that we must face. How on the theological level can Christians make sense of it? How shall the Catholic Church handle differences that will not go away, differences of doctrine and practice, and even more deeply, permanent and different "ecclesial bodies" that claim to be churches of Christ? England and Purcell had no clue. Their strength was to think how the Catholic Church would survive in a Protestant and republican culture, and they came on an incipient historical consciousness to accomplish survival intellectually. And how shall evangelical Protestants handle the fact that Catholic Christianity has survived and is not the playpen of Satan, any more or less than they themselves are? Was not Satan on the loose in the loins of Luther as he turned the Anabaptists over to the mercy of the princes, and in the indomitable mind of Calvin as Michael Servetus was executed by the Geneva Council in 1553? Such a question does not appear on the horizon of Campbell and the others who preceded and followed him. To them, it sufficed to destroy the Catholic Myth and to tell the still-new story, *lux ex tenebris*. That story, to them, is without moral shadow.

# 10

# John Hughes and Kirwan
# in New York

John Hughes (1797–1864) was, as they used to say, a man of parts.
More a public intellectual and a controversialist than a scholar, he
began his battles with Protestants as a young priest in Philadelphia,
where he played a practical joke on one of the leading anti-Catholic
sheets of the day, and perhaps of any day, *The Protestant* (later subti-
tled *The Expositor of Popery*).[1] In 1829, Hughes submitted a half-
dozen antipopery letters under the pseudonym "Cranmer," to the
New York paper where they were published. He thereupon announced anonymously in the New York Catholic newspaper, *The
Truth Teller*, that the author was in fact a Catholic satirizing Protestant antipopery. The revelation caused an uproar among the ministers who sponsored *The Protestant*, who in their turn embarrassed
the editor of *The Truth Teller* by accusing him of the trick.

Hughes was an intelligent and aggressive man, not ambitious
so much as determined in his love of the church and dedicated to its
service, impressed with the public role and responsibility of a
bishop, and utterly convinced of the divinely established apostolic
foundation and the monarchical character of the Catholic episcopate.
He was, from the beginning of his clerical career to its last days, a
formidable figure. The immigrant Catholics of New York could not
have had a stauncher defender, nor Ireland a more attentive exiled
son.

As bishop of New York (1838–64), Hughes led the Catholic
campaign to secure public funding for the Catholic schools and, as a
consequence, was taken by Protestants to be the chief enemy of
public education, which was only then beginning its century-long

emancipation from de facto Protestant control. The impact of the school controversy on the non-Catholic American public cannot be overestimated when explaining the nativist rise to public power in the 1840s and 1850s. Hughes provided leadership in efforts to secure public funds with an intensity not displayed by a Catholic bishop before or since.[2]

He also was the leading opponent of the nativist movement in New York. The oft-told story (told by Catholics, at least) of his communication with the nativist mayor of New York may be apocryphal but it is worth repeating. Nativist riots had resulted in the burning of several Catholic churches and a convent in Philadelphia and the death of a dozen nativist rioters there, and threatened to engulf New York.

> Rumors grew that a delegation [of nativists] was bringing northward the enshrined flag "trampled upon by Irish Papists." A City Hall Park demonstration was being planned by nativists for the occasion. John Hughes planned an extra issue of *Freeman's Journal* admonishing Catholics to stay away from public meetings. He also called on the municipal authorities and bluntly warned them: "If a single Catholic Church is burned in New York, the city will become a second Moscow." The lame duck Mayor Robert Morris asked him: "Are you afraid that some of your Churches will be burned?" "No, sir," Hughes countered, "but I am afraid that some of yours will be burned. We can protect our own. I come to warn you for your own good."

Hughes had stationed armed Catholics around every Catholic church in the city. The nativist mayor-elect called off the rally. Tension continued and minor clashes were reported, including the assault on a Sister of Charity who was called a "Papist bitch" and slapped in the face.[3] But the Catholic churches in New York did not suffer as the churches of Philadelphia had, thanks to Hughes's strong defense.

But there was another Irish immigrant of decidedly different views. Nicholas Murray (1802–61),[4] like Hughes, arrived in New York a penniless Catholic teenager. In short order he found a sponsor, a Protestant pastor of the city, and became a Presbyterian. In Hughes's years as the controversial leader of New York Catholics, Murray was pastor of the Presbyterian church in Elizabethtown, New Jersey. Dr. Murray was a rhetorical and intellectual match for Hughes, and must have had a good deal more time on his hands in Elizabethtown than did the New York bishop who pastored a flock scattered around the entire state of New York. Murray took to his study in 1850 to expose popery in series of essays addressed as letters to the bishop, by then the most prominent Catholic priest in the country. Murray published his letters initially in the New York *Observer*, in which Morse had warmed a seat for him a decade earlier, and then collected the letters for the Presbyterian Board of Publications in Philadelphia.

They were printed in 1851. According to his friend and biographer, Samuel Prime:

> More than a hundred thousand copies were soon in circulation; and,
> adding to this number those that were circulated in the newspapers,
> we shall make up an aggregate scarcely exceeded by any publication
> of the day. And it is certainly safe and just to say that no writings on
> the Roman Catholic question have excited so much attention since
> the Reformation, or have been so widely read by the masses of the
> people.[5]

Hughes ignored the pseudonymous author of the letters, but he did publish nine essays on topics of importance to dispute with Protestants in the *Freeman's Journal,* under the general title "The Importance of Being in Communion with Christ's One Holy, Catholic and Apostolic Church."[6] When Murray was revealed to be the author of the Kirwan letters (then grown to two journal series and two volumes), Hughes felt the need to respond and did so in *Kirwan Unmasked.*[7]

Murray portrayed himself as having some respect for Hughes as a controversialist. He undoubtedly was familiar with Hughes's substantial published exchange with his fellow Presbyterian pastor, John Breckenridge.[8] But Murray had unrelieved contempt for the Catholic Church, and thinly disguised contempt for Hughes himself. These were the motives in charge of his attempt at theological criticism. He was convinced that the Catholic Church was a case of organized sheep-shearing, in which the Catholic clergy stripped the poor and illiterate peasants (Irish, in his own experience) of whatever pittance they had by means of anti-Christian Roman rituals and beliefs. His contempt for the priesthood would still bewilder and offend a Catholic a century and a half after it was penned. Imagine, then, the feelings of Hughes when he read passage after passage of this sort and realized its extensive public circulation:

> And if Absenteeism, and sub-letting, and the tithe system do much
> to impoverish the [Irish] people, Popery does yet more. It meets
> them at the cradle, and dogs them to the grave, and beyond it, with
> its demands for money. When the child is baptized, the priest must
> have money. When the mother is churched, the priest must have
> money. When the boy is confirmed, the bishop must have money.
> When he goes to confession, the priest must have money. When he
> partakes of the Eucharist, the priest must have money. When visited
> in sickness, the priest must have money. If he wants a charm
> against sickness or the witches, he must pay for it money. When he
> is buried, his friends must pay money. After mass is said over his
> remains, a plate is placed on the coffin, and the people collected to-
> gether on the occasion are expected to deposit their contribution on

the plate. Then the priest pockets the money, and the people take the body to the grave. And then, however good the person, his soul has gone to Purgatory; and however bad, his soul may have stopped there. And then comes the money for prayers and masses for deliverance from purgatory, which prayers and masses are continued as long as the money continues to be paid. Now when we remember that seven out of the nine millions of the people of Ireland are papists, and of the most bigoted stamp; and that this horse-leech process of collecting money, whose ceaseless cry is "give, give," is in operation in every parish; and that as far as possible every individual is subjected to it, can we wonder that its noble-hearted, noble-minded people are everywhere hewers of wood and drawers of water? Shame, shame upon your church, that it treats a people so confiding and faithful so basely! Shame, shame upon it, that it does so little to elevate a people that contribute so freely to its support! O, Popery, thou has debased my country—thou hast impoverished its people—thou has enslaved its mind! . . .

My dear sir, your religion is for the benefit of the priest, and not that of the people. Its object is not to spread light, but darkness,—not to advance civilization but to retard it,—not to elevate but to depress man, that he may more readily be brought under your influence.[9]

The passage is far from unusual. It is a tissue extending through the entire series. Indeed, it belongs to a tradition of its own: the Reformation and Enlightenment cry of "priestcraft."[10] Murray spiced it up with a generous sprinkling of narrative from his Irish youth—drunken, arrogant, and ignorant priests; fawning, ignorant peasants; orgiastic Mary-worship, scenes of ritual masochism; roads dotted with saint-idols and holy wells; contrasts of Catholic clergy with the enlightened and compassionate ministers of Scotland; contrasts of poverty-stricken Catholic countries with the prosperous and happy Protestant lands; a drumbeat of contempt and the repeated exposure of every Catholic doctrine to sarcasm and "the light of common sense" (bread and wine, after all, are bread and wine, and what you see is what you get, no matter what the priest declares!).

There is far more going on in Nicholas Murray than in the rigorous theological criticism mounted by his contemporary Presbyterian, the Princeton theologian Charles Hodge, whose inherited Calvinist anti-Catholicism was broad as Murray's—but nowhere so deep. Much of the steamiest of the centuries old anti-Catholic polemic arises from fear and a touch of paranoia. Not so Murray. Murray does not seem afraid in the least. The spice Murray added to the Calvinist stew is different. At her most charitable, a reader might suggest the need of the convert to paint his past black; at worst, one can find in Murray the working of treason's subterranean guilt. Hughes caught it, bit into it, and clung to it like a pug to a postman's leg.

In addition to contempt for the priesthood, Murray made yet another mistake: he feigned respect for Hughes's intellect, and used it to challenge the sincerity of Hughes's Catholicism. He concludes his fourth letter:

> And permit me to say, my dear sir, in reference to yourself, that I have too high a regard for your intelligence to admit for a moment that you believe in the absurd doctrines which your church teaches. Like the ancient priests of Egypt, you must have one class of opinions for the people, and another for yourself. Will you say this is harsh and uncharitable? None knows better than yourself that history affirms it of popes, cardinals, and bishops that have lived before you. On no other ground can I possible account for your remaining an hour in the Roman Catholic Church.[11]

Why would Murray address letters to a "too intelligent" man who could not possibly believe in this oppressive religion, who was at the same time a man so corrupt as to pretend to believe? Of course, Murray only appeared to address them to Hughes. He "sent" them to the readers of *The Observer*. The internal contradiction in Murray's composition, an address that revealed Murray's own insincerity and public posing, was the hook on which Hughes hung his response:

> By what right, sir, did you assume that I am not sincere in the profession of the Catholic faith? And if you did assume it, by what rule of hypocrisy and falsehood did you stultify yourself by professing respect for my character? You could find the premises of such a false and uncharitable conclusion only in your heart, or mine. To mine you have no access, and you should have been cautious in proclaiming such discoveries as could have been derived, only by analogy, from your own.
>
> I believe the truth of the doctrines taught by the Holy Catholic Church, as firmly as I do my own existence. Nay more, I believe that, as containing the fulness of divine revelation, it is the only true Church on the earth—although many Catholic doctrines are found floating about as opinions in the religious atmosphere of Protestantism. This is my profession of faith, of the sincerity of which the Almighty is my witness; and I am not aware that I have ever given you, or any other human being, reason to infer, by word or action, that I believed otherwise.
>
> I must decline, therefore, the tender of *your* respect for my character. But I would not have you on that account to regard me as an enemy. On the contrary, I would be your friend; and my highest

proof of this which you have left it in my power to offer, is the sincere declaration that, as a fellow-being, you have my pity—and best
wishes withal.[12]

In the exchange, we find a sample of the dysfunction threaded throughout
the evangelical-Catholic controversy. Try as either side might, and they did not
try very hard, suspicion of motives, and verbal and logical trickery, prevail, and
trust in the honesty of the other party, hope of reconciliation and desire of
forgiveness are all absent, as in a decayed marriage in which partners are locked
in mutual rejection. These men may have been good Christians, but they were
good haters as well. The immense labor of each side in the mines of history
and theology is obviated by the unbroken stream of self-justification, personal
wounds, and heaped-up communal antagonism. Get over it! one might say,
but one might as well command a mountain to move. Even faith could not
move this one.

Hughes skips through Kirwan, easily finding slips and overt and covert
contradictions, a bit of insincerity here and a lot of rhetorical over-kill there.
The sauciness of his youth had fled him. He had no intention of entering a
disputation with a man who despised him and his faith before he had picked
up the pen, and whom no words, no plea, no logical or historical argument
could move. He addressed Murray and the public with fierce resolve and no
diplomacy, responding with sarcasm and invective, and with the hand of the
pastor who knows the tricks sick souls play on themselves. But he does not
write as the shepherd seeking a lost sheep, nor as a public figure trying to
meet criticism calmly:

> . . . sir, no genuine Irishman would attempt to justify his act by rea-
> sons which, in the order of time, occur to his mind thirty years after
> the act had been performed—as you have done. A genuine Irish-
> man would consent to be laughed at, and would join in the laugh
> with right good humor, rather than attempt the trick of reversing the
> wheel of time, and assigning the reasons of 1847 as the motives of
> his conduct in 1820. . . .
>
> The reasons assigned in your recent letters, may or may not be
> good reasons, but whether good or bad, they had nothing to do with
> *your* change of religion. You *blundered* out of the Church and into
> infidelity, without knowing why or wherefore—and your reasons are
> all out of date.
>
> Now, dear "Kirwan," we are told in logic, that, of two proposi-
> tions which mutually contradict each other, *one* must be *false*. If your
> mind was "a perfect blank as to all religious instruction," as you as-
> sure us it was (p.30), how could you have had "reasons that induced
> you to leave the Church?" [sic]—(p.11). Have you forgotten in the
> one page, what you had affirmed in the other? . . . Why, sir, your

own great stand-by, "common sense," revolts at the insult of religious "reasons" offered from a mind which, as to religious instruction is a "perfect blank!!" [sic][13]

Hughes, in six letters over some seventy pages, never veered from his
course: to expose the shallowness of mind and spirit that had produced the
Kirwan letters:

> . . . I doubt whether Christendom could furnish one other instance
> of such mental nudity—and utter destitution of all Christian knowl-
> edge.
> And now, forsooth, YOUR "Reasons" for leaving the Church!
> What reasons? The experience of reasons in such a mind, on such a
> subject, was a metaphysical impossibility.[14]

And then there is the Catholic Irishman talking to the Irishman who became Protestant, tweaking the latter's bad conscience:

> If circumstances had not placed you in a *false position*, I think you
> would feel proud of the poverty which you inherited from your Irish
> parents; for it is the most incontestable evidence that your Catholic
> ancestors were "true men," in their generation. If they had been un-
> principled hypocrites, capable of betraying their conscience and their
> God, at almost any period within the last three hundred years, they
> might have renounced their religion, and pocketed the bribe which
> the Gospel, as "by law established," had set apart as the recompense
> of apostasy from their Catholic faith. They supposed that their pos-
> terity would be worthy of them; they supposed that *one* Esau, selling
> his birthright for a mess of pottage, was enough in the history of
> our race; they submitted to be plundered of their earthly goods; they
> submitted to be deprived of education; the cruel edict of ignorance
> thus enacted against them, was a *Protestant* edict; they submitted to
> its penalties; but, on the other hand, they asserted the right and su-
> periority of glorious *principle* over base and mercenary *interest;* they
> proved that the material tyrant cannot vanquish the immaterial and
> immortal mind; they bore and defied his torture, while they writhed
> under it; they spurned and repelled his offered bribe of apostasy,
> whilst to human view it was the only alternative between them and
> ignorance, poverty, starvation, and death. But they welcomed all
> sooner than betray principle or violate conscience.[15]

Of course, Murray had done quite the opposite. Hughes took easy advantage of Murray's mistake of "weaving in your own biography, your own personality, as the woof of your polemical web."[16] He could have dealt with the
arguments for Protestant and against Catholic Christianity (the web), but Mur-

ray offered him an escape (the woof) from that fruitless task. Hughes had
slashed at the web nearly twenty years before in his disputation with John
Breckenridge, and he must have known just how fruitless that effort was.
Hughes jumped at Murray's mistake of joining his personal history to his low
polemics. Murray's audience was primarily Protestants, although he addressed
the first two series to Hughes and the part of the third to "Roman Catholics."
He cared not a fig to speak to or with Hughes. Hughes spoke to Murray as
Murray had to him, and slapped him for his impertinence and his hypocrisy.

But Hughes spoke to Catholics as well, letting them know that their own
fidelity echoed that of their ancestors, and that Murray's apostasy was not just
any old sin of momentary human weakness (like drunkenness or fornication)
but a contemptible abandonment of parents and principle for social and material gain. Magdalen and Peter repented, while Judas died of shame by his
own hand. Hughes was fully aware of what Murray was doing. Murray would
bear personal witness that his apostasy was a conversion to gospel truth, but
Hughes would show it to be something other:

> You will observe that I have not pretended to defend a single Catho-
> lic doctrine from your course and profane invective,—that I have
> not raised the question with you as to whether those doctrines are
> true or false; that I have confined myself to watching narrowly the
> state of your mind, your motives and movements, as described by
> yourself, until I saw you clearly beyond the bounds of the Catholic
> church and landed in the cold, dark regions of infidelity. . . . Allow
> me, in the mean time, to suggest the only plausible, natural, and
> satisfactory reason for the important event in regard to which you
> have taken such superfluous pains to enlighten the public. . . . You
> attracted the charitable notice of certain Presbyterian patrons. In the
> intentions of their benevolence toward you, your renunciation of
> Popery was a condition either already accomplished or necessarily
> implied as a *sine qua non* of your education. Now what could be
> more natural, under these circumstances, than that you should be-
> come a Protestant, after the fashion of training provided, and the
> creed professed by your patrons? If in all this your conscience ap-
> proved of what you friends recommended, so much the better for
> you. . . . You wish me to dispute with you on matters of general con-
> troversy. I must beg leave to decline the proposed honor. I cannot
> consent to dispute with any man for whom I feel no respect, and
> therefore I can enter into no controversy with you; especially until
> you have extricated yourself from the inconsistencies and self-
> contradictions pointed out in this review. . . . You suggest "the infer-
> ence that I am a devil."—(p. 64.) You proclaim "your high respect
> for me."—(p. 75.) Now, sir, I entertain no respect for any man, espe-

cially a *Minister of the Gospel,* who can cherish and avow "his high respect" for "a devil," even by inference.[17]

Although Hughes believed that such a rebuke was earned, could he have for a moment believed it would be effective, either for Murray or for the public? Hughes, his biographer maintained, made a mistake in replying at all. I would venture that there were many delighted New York Irish Catholics, lay and clerical, in the days after his letters were published. But Hughes's anger, righteous though it be, led him to waste an opportunity to take a higher road than Murray had. Murray feigned a high opinion of Hughes, but Hughes feigned nothing, matching contempt for contempt.

For himself, Murray jumped at the opportunity Hughes had handed back to him. In September 1948, he responded in a third series of public letters, taking up the issues of the priority of the Bible over the church, the lack of any evidence for Petrine leadership of the early churches, and the absurdities to which Catholic notions of authority and infallibility lead Catholics such as Hughes. Hughes's anger merely confirms what Murray knew all along:

> I have long ago concluded that the scaly hide of the Beast was impervious to reason and argumentation, and that the time has come for Wit and Ridicule and Caricature to empty upon the monster their quiver of arrows. There are some things too absurd to waste reason upon; there is a point beyond which to reason is to cast pearls before swine, and where we must answer fools according to their folly. . . . If I were all you say of me, and as much beyond that as that is beyond the truth, that would not prove the absurdities of Romanism—that would not prove that you can create God [i.e., in the consecration of bread and wine], and forgive sin [in the confessional],—or that your religion is anything else than a peacock religion, which has nothing useful or attractive about it save its glittering plumage. . . . The person who raises himself to station, name, and influence, is worthy of double honor; but in case such a person should rise from the cabbage garden to a mitre, he ought to know that the line of conduct which would not particularly dishonor the hoe or the spade, would reflect no enduring reputation upon the crook and the crosier.[18]

Alluding to Hughes's involvement in professional gardening before entering the seminary, Murray had what he must have regarded as the last word in this public debacle from which neither man emerged unscarred. After he had finished with Hughes in nine chapters of the third series, he appended a chapter entitled "An Appeal to All Roman Catholics," summing up his moral criticism of the Catholic Church and appealing to his Catholic readers to turn away from Rome:

I here assert before heaven and earth, that you are grievously imposed upon by your priests—that for the sake of your money they
daily practice upon you impositions such as should brand them as
imposters—that they traffic in souls, and make a gain of godliness,
and that instead of your veneration they are worthy only of your rejection. . . . Popery is the religion of children, of low civilization—
Christianity is the religion of men, and of high civilization. Dare to
be Christians. Your attachment to popery only benefits the priest;
Christianity will enrich yourselves. Dare to be Christians. The night
is far spent; the day is at hand. O be children of the day. Fear God,
and then the wrath of the priest inspires no more terror than do the
gentle whisperings of the evening zephyr.[19]

Anyone who might accept at face value Murray's charge that Hughes sunk
to "personalities," because he had nothing to say to the issues in the conflict,
will be illumined by Hughes's public exchange with Breckenridge and even by
the nine journal articles in which he responded to Kirwan without engaging
in dispute with a pseudonym.[20] Although a good bit more high-strung than
either England or Purcell, Hughes was as capable as they of mounting an
intellectual defense of the Catholic faith on such standard topics as the rule of
faith, and faith and good works. Once Kirwan was revealed to be Murray, in
fact and not in fiction a fellow Irishman and a former Catholic, he did not take
the high road. Hughes decided he had enough of those "arrows" piercing his
"scaley hide" and would empty his own quiver. In cool hindsight a reader is
likely to find that Hughes accomplished at least this: he made it clear that
Murray was not a reflective scholar or public intellectual or even a Christian
who wanted a conversation—he was a man with an ax to grind, whatever its
mysterious source. Hughes had more important things to accomplish than to
attempt an intellectual answer to Murray's rabid attacks. He drove a stake
through Murray's heart, and Murray kept right on talking.

The exchange is important, not because it adds any theological or philosophical depth to the Great Controversy but precisely because it did not. Here
we see two apparently high-minded men who took religion and citizenship
seriously but who could not speak to one another or to the public without
displaying the *odium theologicum* for which this age-old battle is famous. Perhaps it is difficult now to place one's self in the psychic shoes of Murray and
Hughes as they sat in their studies composing these letters—what must they
have thought and felt in addition to what the letters, controlled by the needs
of composition and publication, display? Was it hatred, anger, resentment,
aggression? Not fear, surely. But the effort to understand these two is necessary,
for the *odium theologicum* remains and in fact thrives in some precincts of the
conservative evangelical and fundamentalist movement, and Catholics who
know of it remain not just mystified but deeply offended by it. Murray's charges

and his judgments, as well as his disdain, did not go to a New Jersey graveyard with him in 1861.[21] We see in the exchange between Murray and Hughes the path that should not be taken: high-minded men, low road. We are fortunate that they left a record of the heat generated by such a confrontation, low though it may have been.


## The Decline of Protestantism

The struggle did not end with Murray's three series and Hughes's responses in *The Freeman's Journal* and his *Kirwan Unmasked*. Although Hughes never addressed Murray again, he pressed the Catholic case before the ink dried in the controversy with him, and, predictably, tempted Murray to another response. In November 1850, a he delivered a lecture in what is now called "Old St. Patrick's," his cathedral church on Mott Street.[22] He titled it "The Decline of Protestantism and Its Causes." It provides us with another side of the controversy in addition to the defenses of Catholic doctrines and exoneration of the charges against the church. Here we find Hughes trying to explain how Protestantism came to be, what it is, and how it fares, and to do this in Catholic perspective. In other words, Hughes gives us an additional part of the Catholic myth. To the dramatic explanation of its own identity (the essential element of any myth), Hughes adds the story of "the other," the schismatic and the heretic. In "the civilized world at the present day" there are "two denominations," Catholic and Protestant. The first is *the* original Christian church. How did the second get there and how has it been doing?

This is how it happened, according to the archbishop. "Protestantism began in 1517."[23] It started with one man against the whole of a united Christendom. The new doctrine spread quickly supported by political ambition and popular discontent. In northern Europe it met resistence only on "the western borders ... the Irish nation ..." Within fifty years it held "every inch of ground, of which it is in possession today."[24] It took over what Catholics had spent a thousand years building, a civilization and its institutions, and so "reaped where it had never sown." It took churches that it has never since been able to fill. It set out to introduce a pure and perfect religion, one that could substitute for the "apostate church." It meant to convert both pagan nations and Catholic nations, and it meant to preserve itself. It failed to do either. It reached its full extent in 1567 and its borders hadn't moved since. Since then, it has declined in health and influence. Why?

First, there is the problem of defining this hydra-headed movement. Hughes takes a stab at something he regards as impossible in specifics:

> Protestantism is a general term, indicating that an individual accepting it explicitly protests against the Catholic Church in the first in-

stance, but implicitly against all human authority; and claims on the other hand, the right of taking the Holy Scriptures, reading them for himself, and taking the meaning and light which they reflect upon his mind as the religion of Christ.[25]

Protestantism in its three original historical forms has within itself the "seeds of its own dissolution": it tends to rationalism and infidelity. It began by selecting the elements of true Christianity, "this and this, no; and this and this, yes." Even its clinging to elements of the ancient (Catholic) Christian faith, Protestantism could not arrest its internal and essential ambiguity. It opposed authority and celebrated individual freedom to determine what the gospel means, and so began its slide to its sad, nineteenth-century state: "How great has been its decline on the side of Latitudinarianism!"[26]

In Europe, "Rationalism has taken the place of Protestantism, although men still claim the name, from the meaning and purport of which they have so widely departed."[27] In Germany, the Trinity has been banned from the pulpits. In Switzerland, Rousseau has taken the place of Calvin. Calvin the Trinitarian would be laughed at in Geneva in Hughes's day. In France, German rationalism has conquered the Protestants. In Sweden, only the ghost of Christianity remains in empty state churches. In England, Protestant by name, the movement "appears to be utterly unconscious of what really constitutes its religious life and mission."[28] Protestantism has proved itself unable to preserve the Christian faith, and, "if you look for anything like the propagation of Protestantism in the Catholic or Pagan world, you look in vain." It converts not the pagans or the Catholics, and its own adherents become infidels or turn to the old faith.[29]

And so the declension of Protestantism is in two opposite directions, as the positive or negative principle prevails—the negatives all rushing off, every one in his own way, and the positives all gathering towards a Catholic centre, under the influence of a prudence that dare not reject divine authority. Here is the test point of Protestantism; and here it is made manifest that, in its very birth, it inherited the seeds of death and dissolution, so as to destroy the very possibility of its self-preservation or self-propagation. . . . [The preacher] preaches Protestantism when he preaches against the divinity of Christ,—when he preaches against the miracles, against original sin, or against the atonement; and in all this he is warranted by the negative element in the very constitution of the system of which he forms a part—so that Protestantism has no check upon him. If he preaches error, what right has any authority on earth to rebuke him?[30]

All of its attempts to provide a substitute authority through creeds and confessions are destined to fail. It has no institutional point of authority, and so it turns to state establishment from the outset, and without the authority of the state it shatters. It is a "state slave from the very first hour of its existence." Christ established a church to continue his teaching, they say, but for fifteen hundred years, it was in process of failure, and they had to renew it. But now that they have, "[t]here is no heart in it, no intellect, no comprehensive or comprehensible body of principles, by which men could be brought into religious and harmonious association with one another."[31]

What about that "City upon a Hill," New England? "A land of Socinians—a land of infidelity." In the Puritan pulpits erected to preach the divinity of Christ we now have preaching against it. We have Miller and his Adventists, Joseph Smith and his Mormons.[32] ". . . Protestantism has declined, is declining, and is destined to decline; and probably before the end of a century from the day [November 10, 1860], there will remain of it throughout the civilized world but a spectacle of the wreck of what had been Protestantism."[33]

This is the Tridentine Catholic comment, in the midst of its own story, on the fate of the branch that separates itself from the true vine. As it has been with the heretics of history, so shall it be with the children of the Reformation. The true church goes on while the broken branch withers. Granted that Hughes at this point in the nativist controversy may have been flying a bit high, still what he said of Protestantism is undoubtedly what he believed in sober reflection, and the history of the church he served provided him with grounds for his hope.

# II

# James Gibbons of Baltimore

Born in 1834, James Gibbons returned to Ireland with his family in 1837. Barely was the ink dry in the controversy between Hughes and Murray when James Gibbons's family reentered the United States in New Orleans in 1853.[1] Gibbons entered the Baltimore seminary and was ordained by Francis Patrick Kenrick in 1861. His ecclesiastical rise was swift and sure. Martin J. Spalding, Kenrick's successor, made Gibbons his secretary in 1865. He was a bishop by 1868, the youngest in the world at that time. He also was the youngest bishop at Vatican I, where, unlike some of his American elders, he voted for the dogma of papal infallibility. He was named bishop of Richmond, Virginia, in 1872.[2] In 1877, at the age of forty, he became the archbishop of Baltimore with the right of succession to James Roosevelt Bailey (Bailey died that year), and reigned over forty years. He was named to the college of cardinals in 1887.

His first sermon after his elevation to the college of cardinals took place in the church of Santa Maria in Trastevere. It was an enthusiastic and characteristic praise of the United States and its political principles. He was the acknowledged leader of a group of bishops, among them Archbishop John Ireland of Minneapolis and St. Paul, who banded to found the Catholic University of America over the objections of Archbishop John Corrigan of New York and the Jesuits. He managed to stop a Roman condemnation of the Knights of Labor and the political theorist Henry George. Gibbons's participation in the World Parliament of Religions in 1893 upset the papal delegate to the United States, Francesco Satolli, causing Gibbons to shift his political weight to the more ecumenically reserved American bishops. Leo XIII's *Testem benevolentiae* (1899) was one in a series of blows to Gibbons and the so-called Americanizers.[3] But Gibbons's stature grew in spite of the Americanist problem, especially in non-Catholic circles, including a close friendship with President Theodore Roosevelt. In the course of his episcopacy he published five books, and became the primary public voice of the Roman Catholic Church in America. In terms of his attitude toward the church's life in American democracy, he stood in the tradition of the founding bishop of Baltimore, John Carroll. "Like Carroll, he was tireless in his praise of American virtues, institutions, and principles. And like Carroll he could interpret Roman directives broadly or ignore them altogether."[4]

In 1960, when Loraine Boettner composed his encyclopedic piece of evangelical anti-Catholicism, he could count on a four-hundred-year tradition of literary organization of the objectionable features of *Roman Catholicism*.[5] But, so, too, could Gibbons count on the persistence of The Protestant Outline and its Catholic respondents. Boettner and Gibbons could count on each other. A century apart they danced together, so to speak. A dance works only if the partners know what to expect of each other, and these two men did. The settled framework and the rote arguments allow for little creativity and only a limited influence of passing circumstances, but the door is ajar for both. Audiences grow and change, threats are felt more now and less then, a blow struck here is ineffective there, a concession on one point can be made up on another, historical research advances here and there, a certain style counts more now than then, "reason" and "reasons" differ from time to time in their presentation and weight, perception of a weakness in opponents intensifies, the intellectual penetration of authors differ, and, not least of all, the publishers' evaluation of markets vary. In the face of these even the most formal minuet will adjust its step.

For our purposes it is the continuities that count: both men knew just what the issues are that divide them and their traditions. So close is their knowledge of the issues that they could easily exchange tables of contents with a minimum effect, a modest editorial adjustment on their composition. We might switch authors and we would have the same books. Long before Boettner, long before Gibbons, the evangelical-Catholic table of contents had been fixed.

Unlike Hughes and Purcell, Gibbons writes his own book. He is not provoked by a scurrilous Murray or trapped by the irregular sallies of a Campbell. Gibbons's *Faith of Our Fathers*, an apologetic work meant on the surface for an American Protestant audience rather than a catechism meant for Catholics, is clearly shaped by the evangelical attacks on his church. If it were meant for the instruction of his own flock—as was the nearly contemporaneous *Catechism of the Third Plenary Council of Baltimore* (1885)—it would have been addressed to Catholics and dealt with instruction in doctrines Catholics were thought to be in need of. The evangelical criticism would be less in evidence. But the direct address to American Protestants in its very first words ("My Dear

Reader:—Perhaps this is the first time in your life that you have handled a
book in which the doctrines of the Catholic Church are expounded by one of
her own sons.") does not preclude the book's falling into the hands of Catholics.
In fact, the book is an armory for Catholics. The distribution of the text in over
two million copies is unintelligible if we understand it to be solely aimed at
Protestants. This is as well a medium of instruction of Catholics in the conduct
of apologetic wars, in "how to answer complaints and fears" and "why are we
right and they wrong." It is a book, not of polemic (though there are certainly
elements of that) but of educational apologetics meant to explain to "fair-
minded readers" how Catholics are Christians, how in fact they are the best
Christians of all (i.e., members of the true church), how they are misunderstood and how they should be understood, and how they are just as good
Americans as anybody else. This sort of instruction was needed as much by
American Catholics as Protestants.

Gibbons was defending the Catholic Church as Hughes and Purcell and
England did before him. There is none of Purcell's humor here, none of
Hughes's sarcasm and testiness, but a great deal of England's directness, calm,
and appeal to fairness. It is easy to see why Gibbons was so successful as a
bishop and the chief spokesperson for the American church. He didn't give
an inch in his convictions, but his convictions never pulled him into nastiness
and rarely into caricature (the Reformers do *not* come off well here!). He
wanted to answer criticisms but he was not out to clobber his opponents with
any weapon that comes to hand. This is the high road of public exchange that
does not ignore legitimate complaints, but that does not accept them with head
hung low in a false ecumenical humility. His opponents are wrong, and he is
not out to learn from them. As Hughes did, Gibbons wants Protestants to join
the one true church and he tries to argue them into it, but he is not seeking
the good graces of his cultural superiors. He is a leader seeking tolerance and
understanding at the very least, and converts at the best.

It may strike the reader as odd that Boettner's attack in 1960 contains no
chapter on "The Bible and The Church"—as Gibbons's table of contents does.
That seems from the evangelical perspective to be the heart of the matter. And
it is, so much so that Boettner doesn't need a chapter on the issue, and Gibbons
does. Boettner doesn't need a chapter because the evangelical principle of the
Bible over the church pervades every chapter. Asserting the lynchpin of the
Protestant myth, Boettner asserts on the first page of his 450–page treatise on
the failures of the Catholic version of Christianity that the failures are everywhere measured by one rule:

> But the basic principle and common system of doctrine taught by
> these Reformers and by the evangelical churches ever since go back
> to the New Testament and to the first century Christian church.
> Protestantism as it emerged in the sixteenth century was not the be-

ginning of something new, but a return to Bible Christianity and to
the simplicity of the Apostolic church from which the Roman
Church had long since departed.

The positive and formal principle of this system is that the Bible
is the Word of God and therefore the authoritative rule of faith and
practice. Its negative principle is that any element of doctrine or
practice in the church which cannot be traced back to the New Testament is no essential part of Christianity.[6]

After this, the operation is simple. Boettner opens each chapter with a
comparison of the Catholic belief or practice with the appropriate biblical texts.
Boettner's table is organized by what is nonbiblical, and so both distinctive and
objectionable, in Roman Catholicism. Its sins are measured by the Rule, and,
although its sins are many, some stand out in their blatant and consequential
violation of biblical principle: the priority Catholics accord to the church and
tradition over the Bible, and the unbiblical notions of priesthood and papacy.[7]
From these spring most of the evils of the Catholic Church. And these must
be met in any Catholic response.[8]

There are a few things about Gibbons's book that are surprising. First of
all, there is not even a mention of the chief subject of public battle in the first
half of the nineteenth century, the public schools and the Catholic schools, no
chapter, no footnote, no entry in the index.[9] From Gibbons one would not know
there was a problem. Second, there are only a few offhand allusions to typical
evangelical charges about immorality of the Catholic clergy. Perhaps Gibbons
felt no obligation to respond to them. Third, there is no defense of what evangelicals call Catholic "works righteousness," or the view that what one does
can in some way determine one's status in heaven. Rather than devoting a
section to the problem of faith and good works, Gibbons assumes that there
is no problem. Perhaps, with other Catholics, he assumes that faith and works
quite properly interpenetrate in the Catholic salvational schema, that neither
faith alone nor works alone make any religious sense, and that there are such
difficulties with the Protestant interpretation of Paul on the issue that it can
be ignored. Gibbons rarely got "philosophical" in this text, and an argument
over faith and works quickly calls for serious philosophical theology, not to say
exegesis of the Christian scriptures. Whereas he hit other controverted issues
head on, this difference, so important to evangelicals theologically, barely registered with Gibbons.[10]

We turn first to Gibbons's argument on the marks of the true church, the
church and Bible, and the papacy. If one gets it straight on these, the Catholic
apologist argues, the evangelical sore points about saints, the Virgin, purgatory,
the sacraments, and so on, will fall into perspective. He jumps in three pages
over the doctrines of the Trinity, the Incarnation, and the death and resurrection
of Jesus, and the founding of the church to what will occupy him for the

following 124 pages, namely the marks, or those essential characteristics by which "any fair-minded reader" will recognize the "true Church."

*Unity* means "that members of the true Church must be united in the belief of the same doctrines of revelation and in the acknowledgment of the authority of the same pastors," not one without the other. Jesus, the biblical text tells us, founded *a church* on the Rock, not "conflicting denominations."[11] Neither the Bible nor common sense sanctions doctrinal or organizational anarchy:

> With all due respect to my dissenting brethren, truth compels me to say that this unity of doctrine and government is not to be found in Protestant sects, taken collectively or separately. That the various Protestant denominations differ from one another not only in minor details but in most essential principles of faith, is evident to everyone conversant with the doctrines of the different Creeds. The multiplicity of sects in this country, with their mutual recriminations, is the scandal of Christianity, and the greatest obstacle to the conversion of the heathen.[12]

We find Christian unity nowhere but in the Catholic Church, in both doctrine and government. The notion of a "free church," congregational or presbyterian polity, or that there should or could be two churches, is repugnant to a Catholic understanding of the Body of Christ.

*Holiness* of its members Gibbons tells his reader is the objective of the existence of the Catholic Church and the reason for its sacramental life and teaching. Catholics often aren't holy, he admits, but holiness remains the point of their life in the Church. So bad did the "corruptions of morals" become in the sixteenth century that a "sweeping reformation" of life outside and inside "the sanctuary" was called for.

> But how was this reformation of morals to be effected? Was it to be accomplished by a force operating inside the Church, or outside? I answer that the proper way of carrying out this reformation was by battling against iniquity within the Church; for there was not a single weapon which men could use in waging war with vice outside the Church, which they could not wield with more effective power when fighting under the authority of the Church. The true weapons of an Apostle, at all times, have been personal virtue, prayer, preaching, and the Sacraments. Every genuine reformer had those weapons at his disposal. . . . How do Luther and Calvin, and Zuinglius and Knox, and Henry VIII, compare with these genuine and saintly reformers[13] both as to their moral character and the fruits of their labors? The private lives of these pseudo-reformers were stained by cruelty, rapine, and licentiousness; and as a result of their propagan-

dism, history records civil wars, and bloodshed, and bitter religious
strife, and the dismemberment of Christianity into a thousand sects.
. . . They sanctioned rebellion by undermining the principle of authority.

What an opportunity they lost of earning for themselves immortal honors from God and man! If, instead of raising the standard of
revolt, they had waged war upon their own passions, and fought
with Catholic reformers against impiety, they would be hailed as
true soldiers of the cross.[14]

The Reformers, then, did not act as good Christians. They were revolutionaries.
They were driven into heresy and schism by their passions. Insofar as they
were unholy, they compromised the holiness and the unity of the Church.
Christian virtue could not have such an effect. The Reformation, then, was not
simply an issue of correct doctrine and practice; it was an event that revealed
its sinful nature in the fear, anger and disobedience, psychological weaknesses—and lust—of its leaders.

*Catholicity* denotes the fact that the Church, like none other, "is defused
over every nation of the globe, and counts her children among all tribes and
peoples and tongues of the earth."[15] Only the Catholic Church claims this title
for only "she" has fulfilled the command of Jesus to teach all nations. She
numbered in Gibbons day three hundred million, twice the number of Christians outside her fold, east and west.[16]

With *Apostolicity* we reach the top step in Catholic anti-Reformation apologetics. We may hope and believe that the church is one, holy and catholic,
but it had better be apostolic. Apostolicity is a matter of inner-historical fact,
open to demonstration in the Catholic understanding of the matter, and to
Protestant challenge. On the demonstration and elucidation of this mark hang
the authority, perpetuity, and infallibility of the church, and these set the context
for the peculiar Catholic claims for the bishop of Rome.

As far as Gibbons was concerned, the claim requires that the church must
be able to display doctrinal and ministerial identity with the Twelve, and pass
on to negate the claims of any other church to Apostolicity.[17] This he manages
in a chapter of less than ten full pages. In this complicated task, he settles for
"some examples," further theological-historical claims, and quotations from a
few "early Fathers," namely Tertullian and Augustine. Like John England, Gibbons merely sketches the support for the claim.

The apostolicity of doctrine is "proved" by listing in a column ten examples
of apostolic doctrines "which are in all respects identical with those of the first
teachers of the Gospel." He then listed in a second column the Catholic belief
or practice and finally in a third column the beliefs and practices, or the lack
of thereof, of the Protestant churches. The primacy of Peter, the infallibility of
the apostolic church, the practice of fasting, the Pauline exclusion of women

from preaching, the sacrament of confirmation by laying on of hands, the real presence of Christ in the Eucharistic elements, ecclesial forgiveness of sins, the anointing of the sick and dying, the indissolubility of marriage, and counsel of virginity and celibacy are all shown to be apostolic by a verse or two from the New Testament. In the third column we find that Protestant churches deny the primacy, repudiate infallibility, ignore fasting as an ecclesial practice, allow women to preach (Methodists et al.), deny the sacramentality of confirmation, condemn the doctrine of the real presence as idolatrous, deny that the minister can forgive sin, refuse to anoint the sick, allow divorce and remarriage, and slight the virtue of perpetual chastity.

He moved on to the ministerial family tree:

> To show that the Catholic Church is the only lineal descendant of the Apostles it is sufficient to demonstrate that she alone can trace her pedigree, generation after generation, to the Apostles, while the origin of all other Christian communities can be referred to a comparatively modern date.[18]

The sixteenth-century reformers were late arrivals on the scene of Christian church founding. Of the twenty he listed, the earliest (Anabaptists) can be dated to 1521 and the latest (New School Presbyterian) to 1840, all of them ". . . fifteen hundred years too late to have any pretensions to be called the Apostolic Church." The Catholic Church was founded by Jesus himself in the year 33 A.D.[19] The evangelicals would respond that an apostolic church in any age or place is marked as such by preaching and teaching the doctrine of the Bible, by enacting the "ordinances" commanded by Jesus in the New Testament, and by practicing discipline over members' moral life (the latter a special favorite of the Puritans). But Gibbons would have none of this, nicely carved as it is to cover the Protestant lack of linear, historical apostolicity. The supposition of the evangelical schema is that while a corrupt Catholic Church dominated the public stage there was an "invisible church" in every age gathered around the Bible. Says Gibbons:

> Your concealment, indeed, was so complete that no man can tell, to this day, where you lay hidden for sixteen centuries. . . . It is equally vain to tell me that you were allied in faith to various Christian sects that went out from the Catholic Church from age to age; for these sects proclaimed doctrines diametrically opposed to one another, and the true church must be one in faith.[20]

No, Gibbons and the Catholics had something else in mind than an invisible or spiritual continuity. In the Catholic notion, as Gibbons has it, the historical link to the apostolic church is quite visible: the episcopal appointment of the American bishops by the current bishop of Rome, Pius IX, roots them all in succession to ". . . Peter, the first Bishop of Rome, the Prince of the

Apostles and Vicar of Christ."[21] This was the way the early Fathers determined the apostolicity of doctrines when confronted by sectarians, that is, by giving catalogues of the bishops of Rome on the orthodoxy of whose teaching all could count. Apostolic means the commission traceable to an Apostle or an "apostolic man" who was in communion with the Apostles (thus, Mark or Luke would do, if one wanted to make the argument individual in its linkage). As a closer, Gibbons quoted Augustine to the Donatists:

> Come to us, brethren, if you wish to be engrafted in the vine. We
> are afflicted in beholding you lying cut off from it. Count over the
> Bishops from the very See of St. Peter, and mark, in this list of Fa-
> thers, how one succeeded the other. This is the rock against which
> the proud gates of hell do not prevail.[22]

Gibbons adds to the classical marks of the true church two more, Perpetuity and Infallible Authority. Both are implied in Apostolicity. *Perpetuity* does not mean to Gibbons that Christianity or the Christian faith or Christian faithful will exist in one form or another in every age, but that the Church, in its full integrity as a visible community with its essential institutions, has existed and, by the promise of Christ, will exist through all ages. So, if we did not have the church yesterday at noon or on any day at any time, we do not have the church with which Jesus promised to be until the last day. The gates of hell will then have prevailed.[23]

But has the church been here? Gibbons lists the times when it might seem to have been on the edge of extinction: the persecution and the catacombs, the barbarian invasions, the effects of the work of the great heresiarchs Arius, Nestorius, and Eutyches, the periods of Islamic expansion, the "religious revolution of the sixteenth century," the Enlightenment and the political revolutions of the eighteenth and nineteenth centuries. In fact, there is a parallel between the Reformation and Arianism:

> Both schisms originated with Priests impatient of the yoke of the
> Gospel, fond of novelty and ambitious of notoriety. Both were
> nursed and sustained by the reigning Powers, and were augmented
> by large accessions of proselytes. Both spread for awhile with the ir-
> resistible force of a violent hurricane, till its fury was spent. Both
> subsequently became subdivided into various bodies. The extinction
> of Protestantism would complete the parallel. . . .
>
> In this connection a remark of De Maistre is worth quoting: "If
> Protestantism bears always the same name, though its belief has
> been perpetually shifting, it is because its name is purely negative
> and means only the denial of Catholicity, so that the less it believes,
> and the more it protests, the more consistently Protestant it will be.
> Since, then, its name becomes continually truer, it must subsist un-

til it perishes, just as an ulcer disappears with the last atom of the flesh which it has been eating away."[24]

He did not have to quote that passage, telling as it is. He made his point in the first strongly enough: Protestantism is as much a distortion and curse on the true church as was Arianism. DeMaistre's image is revolting, and the thought it reflects follows the harsh analysis of Hughes in "The Decline of Protestantism." But so it was in the imaginations of Catholic leaders: Protestantism is an ulcer eating away its own flesh. Even in the otherwise quiet and sensitive soul of a great American Catholic bishop there lurks such an image! Gibbons goes on:

> But similar causes will produce similar results. As both revolutions were the offspring of rebellion; as both have been marked by the same vigorous youth; the same precocious manhood, the same premature decay and dismemberment of parts; so we are not rash in predicting that the dissolution which long since visited the former is destined, sooner or later, to overtake the latter. But the Catholic Church, because she is the work of God, is always "renewing her strength, like the eagle's."

Who or what can breach her gates? The kings of the earth? They have been her enemies from the beginning, from the Caesars to Bismark. Some rival religious body? The great heretics tried it. Perhaps the fall of the papal states just six years before (1870)? But they have fallen before and she has survived. Perhaps modern technology? She has turned inventions in the past to her own use. Surely the intellectual advances and arts of the nineteenth century? She has always been the patron of the arts and has founded the great universities of Europe. Then it must be the spread of political liberty that will do her in! Hardly, for she clearly thrives on the political liberty she has found in the United States, the homeland of liberty. She is the church of Christ. If hell cannot break her, culture and politics will not. The Catholic Church is here to stay, by the promise of Jesus himself.

If the church is both apostolic and perpetual by the will and promise of Christ surely she must also be *infallible*. This favorite target of evangelical critics was, just a few years before Gibbons wrote, reemphasized by the dogmatic definition of the first Vatican Council. Gibbons was one of the Council Fathers who voted for the definition.[25] At this point, he argues for the infallibility of the church itself. Only after he has set the priority between the church and the Bible will he take on papal infallibility.[26] The claim of papal jurisdiction rests on Matthew 16:18, but the infallibility of the church (which is the necessary condition for the infallibility of the one who can speak for the church) rests on the commission of the church by Christ to preach the gospel (Mt 28:19, 20; John 20:21; Mk 15:16; Acts 1:8), on the promise of Jesus to be with the Church to the last day (Mt 28:20), and on the dominical blessing on those who hear the disciples and curse upon those who do not (Mt 10:14, 15; Mt 18:17; Mk 16:16; Lk 10:16):

> ... we see, on the one hand, that the Apostles and their successors have received full powers to announce the Gospel; and on the other, that their hearers are obliged to listen with docility and to obey not merely by an external compliance but also by an internal assent of the intellect. If, therefore, the Catholic Church could preach error, would not God Himself be responsible for the error?[27]

And so the mutually conditioning doctrines: if there is to be faith and the certainty it implies, there must be a corresponding infallibility; if there is infallibility, then faith can possess its object [divine and saving truth] with confidence. "There can be no faith in the hearer unless there is unerring authority in the speaker."[28] Jesus promised to be with them all days, every day until the end, and he promised to guard them from error. He has done both, primarily by being with the teachers of the church. Never once have the pastors of the Catholic Church ceased to teach what has been taught or contradicted what has been proclaimed, claims to the contrary notwithstanding. In fact, if one contradiction were to be found, the entire Catholic package would come unwrapped.[29] But that has not and will not happen, and so if his reader were to join the church Gibbons could say to him or her:

> You are a part of that universal Communion which has no "High Church" and "Low Church;" no "New School" and "Old School," for you belong to the School which is "ever ancient and ever new." You enjoy that profound peace and tranquility which springs from the conscious possession of the whole truth.[30]

Many converts to Roman Catholicism were and are to this day powerfully drawn to the certainty that the infallibility of the Catholic Church offers, as Gibbons well knew.[31] But what of the Bible in this dialectic of faith and infallibility? Isn't the Bible also infallible? For Gibbons, the church is the teacher, and the Bible is "the great depository of the Word of God" of which the church is the "divinely appointed Custodian and Interpreter."[32] The crucial point for Gibbons was how this revelation given to the Apostles was meant to be communicated to "those who have not seen." He echos John England:

> But when our Redeemer abolished the Old Law and established His Church, did he intend that his Gospel should be disseminated by the circulation of the Bible, or by the living voice of His disciples? This is a vital question. I answer most emphatically, that it was by preaching alone that he intended to convert the nations, and by preaching alone they were converted. No nation has ever yet been

converted by the agency of Bible Associations. . . . Jesus Himself
never wrote a line of Scripture. He never once commanded His
Apostles to write a word, or even to circulate the Scriptures already
existing. . . . The Apostles are never reported to have circulated a single volume of the Holy Scripture, but "they going forth, *preached* everywhere, the Lord cooperating with them" (Mk 16:20).

Thus we see that in the Old and the New Dispensation the people were to be guided by a living authority, and not by the private
interpretation of the Scriptures.

Indeed, until the religious revolution of the sixteenth century it
was a thing unheard of from the beginning of the world, that people
should be governed by the dead letter of the law either in civil or
ecclesiastical affairs. How are your civil affairs regulated in this
State, for instance? Certainly not in accordance with your personal
interpretation of the laws of Virginia, but in accordance with the decisions which are rendered by the constituted judges of the State.

Now, what the civil code is to the citizen, the Scripture is to the
Christian. The Word of God, as well as the civil law, must have an
interpreter, by whose decision we are obliged to abide.[33]

England spoke of "the Tribunal." Protestants talk of an inerrant Bible (Gibbons himself did not use the phrase), but the apostles and their successor were
commissioned to preach and teach, not to print and distribute Bibles.[34] Protestants proclaim "The Bible, and the Bible only, must be your guide," yet they
build churches and schools, they preach and catechize—as did the early
church.[35] They don't just hand out Bibles. The first generations of Christians
lived and died without the Bible, and for fourteen hundred years the people
heard, and did not read, the scriptures. Gibbons estimates that there were "but
a few hundred copies" in the Christian world and more could not have been
available until the invention of printing in the fifteenth century.[36] It is an anachronism to require as divine will what cannot in fact be accomplished in the
absence of printing and literacy. The Bible when subject to individual interpretation produces chaos. Protestantism proposes what could not have been,
and still for the most part, cannot be realized. "But even if the Bible were at
all times accessible to everyone, how many millions exist in every age and
country, not excepting our own age of boasted enlightenment, who are not
accessible to the Bible because they are not capable of reading the Word of
God! Hence, the doctrine of private interpretation would render many men's
salvation not only difficult, but impossible."[37] Add to the problem of illiteracy
and the fact that the Bible "is full of obscurities and difficulties not only for
the illiterate, but even for the learned":

Does not the conduct of the Reformers conclusively show the utter
folly of interpreting the Scriptures by private judgment? As soon as

they rejected the oracle of the Church, and set up their own private judgment as the highest standard of authority they could hardly agree among themselves on the meaning of a single important text. The Bible became in their hands a complete Babel. . . . No one can deny that these divisions in the Christian family are traceable to the assumption of the right to private judgment. Every new-fledged divine, with a superficial education, imagines that he has received a call from heaven to inaugurate a new religion, and he is ambitious of handing down his fame to posterity by stamping his name on a new sect. And every one of these champions of modern creeds appeals to the unchanging Bible in support of his ever-changing doctrines.[38]

Examples of heretical and contradictory interpretations among Protestants follow: Trinitarianism and Unitarianism, the denial of the divinity of Jesus, infant baptism and its rejection, two sacraments and none, eternal hell and universalism, predictions of the date of the end of the world and equally confident resetting of it when it does not occur, and Mormon arguments for a biblical basis of polygamy. In sum:

We must, therefore, conclude that the Scriptures *alone* cannot be a sufficient guide and rule of faith because they cannot, at any time, be within the reach of every inquirer; because they are not of themselves clear and intelligible even in matters of the highest importance, and because they do not contain all the truths necessary for salvation.[39]

Finally, he must answer the charge that the Catholic Church is opposed to the reading of the scriptures:[40]

The Catholic Church the enemy of the Bible! Good God! What monstrous ingratitude! What base calumny is contained in that assertion! As well you might accuse the Virgin Mother of trying to crush the Infant Savior at her breast as to accuse the Church, our Mother, of attempting to crush out of existence the Word of God. . . . For fifteen centuries the Church was the sole guardian and depository of the Bible, and, if she really feared that sacred Book, who was to prevent her, during that long period, from tearing it to shreds and scattering it to the winds?[41]

The divergence between evangelical and Catholic apologists on the Bible, its role and its use, are immense. It is hard to imagine that, when they talk of each other, they are talking of the same history and of the same people. It is equally hard to imagine that, in the presence of the historical work that has been done on the medieval and modern church in the past century by both

Protestant and Catholic scholars, the immensity of difference on this issue can continue, but in some evangelical circles it does.

The myths seem indestructible. Two distinct and, in some ways at least, contradictory accounts of the Christian life exist, each powered by the belief that it tells the true story of God's dealing with humanity, each rejecting the other and incapable of assimilating it, unable to explain the other in any but negative and pejorative terms. No wonder that Gibbons is bothered by and dismissive of the tale told by biblical Christians, for it took centuries to formulate and hone the Catholic myth that, long holding the field in the West, was suddenly confronted with a new story, the heart of which was concocted in those few moments when Luther realized that his protest would fail utterly if he tried to ground it in the old Catholic story. Appeals to a council wouldn't work, although that might have provided a bit of room in the old story for his reformist instincts and plans. No, he needed a new foundation, a new rule other than the Tribunal, the apostolic college. That implied a new story—and he tossed the old one aside. John Hughes pointed out that the expansion of Protestantism to its geographic limit took about half a century. But the Protestant myth exploded on Europe in a much briefer time. Four hundred years later, neither side had much changed the geography, and the myths were still in place, pitched against one another as St. Michael the archangel and Satan, each seeking to exile the enemy from heaven (Rev. 12:7).

In the next four chapters (IX–XII), Gibbons fills out his Catholic tale: the primacy of Peter over the first church and the consequent supremacy and the infallibility of the popes, along with the necessity of their political independence if their spiritual jurisdiction is to be exercised as Christ intended it to be. From Gibbons's perspective, the primacy of Peter over the other apostles and over the apostolic church is evidenced in scripture and in the practice of the early church. He claims a precedent in salvation history in the primacy of the high priest of Judaism, for Catholics an important bit of structural continuity and for evangelicals a telling compromise of the Pauline gospel. The analogies to the family and the secular community are there to be called on: each needs a single head if chaos is to be avoided. The absence of a single head promotes the "weakness and dissension" evident among Protestants, while its salutary effects are evident in the "admirable unity" of the Catholic Church.

Did Christ appoint such a head of His Church? There is "abundant evidence" in the New Testament that he did, at least for those "who read the Scriptures with the single eye of pure intention."[42] Matthew 16, John 21, and Acts 1–15 are among the texts on which Gibbons comments. He refutes objections that Peter was rebuked by Jesus, that Peter was rebuked by Paul, that Peter's supremacy conflicts with the supremacy of Christ, and that Peter did not live and die in Rome. The first three objections are answered by exegesis of the very texts that give rise to them, and the last by the weight of the testimony of early witnesses, from Clement to Jerome, and by the agreement of many Protestants such as Calvin and Grotius that Peter was indeed in Rome. In fact, Gibbons says, "no historical fact will escape the shafts of incredulity if Peter's residence and glorious martyrdom are called into question."[43]

"The Church did not die with Peter," writes Gibbons, and so the church's need for central leadership continued and in fact increased as the church grew. The essential pastoral work of Peter is inherited by his successors, the very same scriptural and theological arguments that support Peter's primacy count for the supremacy of the popes.[44] In addition, there is "incontestable historical evidence, that the Popes have always, from the days of the Apostles, continued to exercise supreme jurisdiction not only in the Western Church until the Reformation, but also throughout the Eastern Church until the Great Schism of the ninth century."[45] The bishop of Rome was the court of last appeal from the first century onward. Among the appellants he lists: Corinth to Pope Clement (c. 100); the churches of the East to Pope St. Victor (d. 198); Cyprian to Cornelius (d. 253) and Stephen (d. 257); the patriarch of Alexandria to Dionysus I (d. 432); Athanasius to Julius I (d. 352); Basil to Damasus I (384); John Chrysostom to Innocent (d. 417); Cyril to Celestine (d. 432); and so forth.

Moreover, the Fathers of the first five centuries without exception "with one voice, pay homage to the Bishops of Rome as their superiors." In addition, they called, presided at (through delegates), and confirmed the eight ecumenical councils of the whole church, as if nothing could be law without the approval of the bishops of Rome.[46] "Is this not a striking illustration of the Primacy?" he asks.

Finally, every nation that has come into the church "has received the light of faith from missionaries who were either especially commissioned by the See of Rome or sent by Bishops in open communion with that See. This historical fact admits of no exception," including the nations from which American's Protestants have come.". . . [Y]ou," he says, "are indebted to the Church of Rome for your knowledge of Christianity."[47]

Now, these are impressive arguments for persons who expect that God works in our history through institutions and continuously (i.e., Catholics like myself), while they are quite unimpressive for those who expect God to challenge and even uproot "merely human traditions" (i.e., Protestants). The latter can only find compromise and deadening routinization of the Gospel in the growing ecclesiastical and papal tradition. Trust in the line of apostolic succession and its evidences gave Catholics divine life, but they were choking weeds to evangelicals, and evangelicals would respond to Gibbons with a list of the sins and growing arrogance of the bishops of Rome. In Gibbons's perspective, instances of rejection of divinely underwritten church office from Arius to Luther are understood as moral failure but by Protestant critics as brave resistance to papal tyranny. Well-tutored and justified suspicion in men such as Nevins, Campbell, Murray, and Thornwell make Gibbons's clear, well-ordered, and simple reading of church history, even at its most persuasive, incredible.[48]

For such as these Catholic moral theologians invented the category "invincible ignorance," to render such benighted men still subject to salvation under the mercy of God. Gibbons must have known that, although he could hope for some converts, he also would get a stony reaction from Protestant readers as he plowed ahead through the proofs for the infallibility of the popes (recently defined) and arguments that the papal states (recently seized) guarantee papal independence of control by the nation-states.[49]

I have stayed close to what is most important in Gibbons's book to the ongoing but backhanded exchange between nineteenth-century American Catholics and evangelicals, namely, the church and the papacy. Gibbons goes on to run the gamut of Protestant issues, from saints to celibacy. But not much more is to learned there for our purposes, for Gibbons's basic position on the mediational nature of the church remains at the bottom of all he has to say about sacraments and religious practice.

For both Catholics and evangelicals, things changed in the twentieth century. Both the council and the emergence of the new evangelical movement in the United States, the internationalization of the evangelical faith, and the assumption of a leading moral voice and evangelizing stance by the popes after Vatican II, among other things, have brought American Catholics and evangelicals into a significantly closer relationship. *ECT I* and *II* are the evident signs of this realignment. Whereas in these documents the divergence of ecclesiological and spiritual doctrines remains profound, there are nonetheless changes to be noted in the way Catholics understand biblical Christianity. Doctrines may have remained constant but perspectives and contexts have changed. It is to the last quarter of the twentieth century and its Catholic responses to the evangelical resurgence that I now turn.

# 12

# What Have Catholic Theologians Made of Biblical Christianity?

## Terminology Again

Tangles of language sometimes require interim commonsense solutions.[1] As mentioned in chapter 1, the terms *evangelical* and *fundamentalist* are in a seemingly never-ending whirl of redefinition. Evidence for this state of affairs is found in the Catholic literature of the late twentieth century. Nineteenth-century Catholics had little use for adjectives when they used the term *Protestant*. For them, whether you were a Bible-toting frontier Campbellite or a genteel New England transcendentalist, you were a Protestant. This is no longer the case for anyone interested in the thickets of American Christianity, Protestant and Catholic.[2] The Catholic religious and theological literature typically uses the term *fundamentalism,* and only sometimes *evangelicalism,* but they seemed to use fundamentalism in a broader sense than currently used by scholars of American evangelicalism. For these earlier Catholic authors, fundamentalism seems to include all evangelical Christians. The Catholic bishops added to fundamentalism the term *biblical Christianity,* and do not use the term *evangelical*—although they now have to do so after the signing of *ECT I* and *II,* which canonize a new Catholic usage. The bishops seemed to know that there is more to the threat they wish to address than what is commonly meant by a tight usage of the term *fundamentalism.* Biblical Christianity covers what they mean, the tens of millions of evangelicals beyond the fundamentalist label. Even the media, in their commonsensical grasp of the complexities, are aware that there are Protestants who are not evangelicals, and evangelicals who are not fundamentalists, and Catholics who are evangelicals but not Protestants, and even Catholics who are fundamentalists (in some usages) but not evangelical or Protestant. To add the confusion, Vatican sources have used the term *cults* and *new religions,* and seem to refer at least in part to forms of Latin American evangelical Christianity, as we shall see.

My commonsense solution to this conundrum is to use the term *biblical Christianity,* in part because it is broad enough to cover all the evangelical Christians, from the nineteenth and twentieth centuries, and to include those American Christians (but not Catholics!) called fundamentalist. But I also use the term because it provides me a neat contrast with liturgical Christianity.[3] What I mean by the term is this: biblical Christianity is that form of Christian practice and belief that finds its basis, its limits, and its primary content in the Bible, in which community life and worship are organized around and in conscious imitation of the forms provided in the Bible. The element of the historical heirs of the sixteenth-century Reformation that I hesitate to put under the category biblical Christianity (and I apologize if any of them find this offensive) are those who show the marks of historical consciousness in their approach to the Bible and those communities that have managed by tradition or recent decision to couple the Bible with the intricate hermeneutics of a worshiping community (i.e., the liturgical assembly). For the latter groups of Protestants the Bible either may not mean what it says or does not say everything. Roman Catholics, Anglicans, many Lutherans, and most assuredly the Orthodox Churches, to varying degrees in each case, place the Bible in the context of a historical worshiping community and do not tend to take it outside the worshiping community for definitive individual interpretation.[4] For biblical Christianity, the Bible constitutes Christianity; for liturgical Christianity the Bible is the book used in common worship of a community, and there is more to Christianity than the Bible, namely the community itself.

## Sorting Out the Literature

A new Catholic reaction to American biblical Christianity began in the wake of the political and cultural resurgence of evangelicalism marked publicly by the election of Jimmy Carter in 1976. The Catholic anti-Protestantism of the centuries prior to Vatican II made no significant distinction between mainline and evangelical Protestantism, and so in twentieth-century America no particular distinction set off evangelicalism from Protestantism in general. A change occurred when Vatican II fueled the already smoldering Catholic theological interest in the achievements of Protestant theologians, and so in both popular and scholarly publication, study and dialogue replaced the wariness of pre–Vatican II days. But in 1976 it became clear to the American Catholic public that there was another Protestantism in addition to newfound ecumenical friends, one that is not very friendly at all, that was having its effect in politics and, above all, opposed Catholic belief and practice. As the ecumenical dialogue with mainline Protestantism grew, it set off evangelicals and fundamentalists more and more sharply from the rest of the Protestants. There are Protestants, there are Bible Christians, and the latter are distinguished by their continuing criticism of the Roman Catholic Church.

Between 1976 (the Year of the Evangelicals) and 1992 (the year before *ETC*), over eighty essays were published in Catholic periodicals, ranging from scholarly analyses in journals aimed at pastors and intellectuals to articles and columns in the national Catholic weekly press; over thirty of those essays appeared in journal issues dedicated entirely to fundamentalism; five general readership monographs and one collection of scholarly essays on fundamentalism were published by Catholic theologians; and there were at least five public statements by American bishops on biblical Christianity and one document issued by the Vatican that touches directly on Catholic attitudes toward "sects and new religions." Although not massive (it would be outweighed considerably by the Catholic literature on church reform and on peace and justice questions), it is significant. In terms of popular publications for Catholics, it replaces the earlier Catholic literature on mainline Protestantism. In my terms, then, and in that fifteen-year period, there was a modest wave of Catholic publication concerned with biblical Christianity or "fundamentalism," as it typically was called.

Sorting out the literature on the basis of its reactions poses a problem. A good deal of the literature is commonsense history and description, replete with predictable doctrinal contrasts that are accurate as far as they go, but that are of very little theological interest and value. It gets interesting when particular theological insights flash, when the common is put uncommonly, when strategies of response are developed and promoted, when particularly abysmal ignorance is displayed, and when the canons of a methodical theology and even Christian virtue are violated. But how do we approach such a complex, if not especially profound, literature with something of a modicum of discrimination and justice? I put three ordering questions to it, as a whole and individual pieces.

1. Is the literature intellectually serious and responsible? Does it exhibit a wish to understand? What questions are being raised and what relevant questions are not? What unquestioned suppositions are at work? Is it evenhanded? Does it represent an affirmation, a reshaping, a replacement of older intellectual attitudes and convictions? Is there anything of note going on intellectually?

2. Insofar as the literature is pastoral (most, if not all, of this literature

is such), is it pastorally responsible? What are its goals and are they worthy? What are the strategies of response adopted and urged, and are they worthy? Are there problems of justice and charity?

3. What does the literature reveal about the authors and their concerns about the present condition of the Catholic Church? Does the literature reveal currents of unsettlement or conflict? Anxiety? Fear? Resentment? Bad conscience? Attitudes of superiority? Double consciousness—the manipulation of the overt (ecclesially external) subject matter for other covert (ecclesially internal) objectives?

I use these questions to address three different sorts of the literature: first, the periodical literature ranging from academic/pastoral journals to newspapers; second, five books that more amply display Catholic attitudes (out of modesty I shall skip the collection of essays I have edited).[5] In the next chapter I address six pieces of literature that serve as a sample of the response of the Roman Catholic hierarchy. Finally, at the end of the next chapter, I shall attempt a characterization of the literature as a whole.

## Periodical Literature

Of the some eighty essays that have been written by Catholics on "fundamentalism" since 1976, none is to be found in a Catholic scholarly journal.[6] Not one of the essays has biblical Christians among its intended readers. Fewer than a handful seem to envisage scholars among their readers, and most are written for Catholics engaged in ministry and the theologically literate lay audience, and for the readers of the weekly Catholic press.

Although many of the essays are well informed, they are so by virtue of familiarity with secondary literature. Few reveal any direct acquaintance with the primary literature of evangelical and fundamentalist history and doctrine.[7] As a whole, the literature makes plain the fact that Catholic intellectuals are not in the slightest interested in biblical Christianity as a phenomenon in its own right, but only insofar as it poses a "pastoral problem." All of the literature, in other words, has a pastoral as distinct from an academic interest, and so a close reading of evangelical histories such as those of Marsden, Noll, and Hatch, and mainline Protestant anti-fundamentalist polemic (James Barr's books), and works of American Studies scholarship (Ernest Sandeen) will do.[8]

The most evident distinction in the literature is between those essays that seek to inform Catholics on the belief and practice of biblical Christians and to contrast it with Catholic belief and practice, leaving the critique of it muted and indirect, and those essays in which a direct argument against biblical Christianity is mounted. Those in the latter class typically attempt to explain "fundamentalism," its attractiveness and its growth, as an aberration of the age, whereas the former typically attempts to set up comparisons that will lead to a clarified commitment to Catholicism. Nearly all of the literature explicitly or implicitly regards biblical Christianity as a radically incomplete, not to say "false" Christianity (there are some exceptions), as inadequate or distorted. When reaching for an explanation of the global expansion of evangelical Christianity, many of the essays link American fundamentalism to a perceived rise of religious fundamentalism worldwide, and some link it with what they call Roman Catholic fundamentalism.

Although many of the essays are pastorally serious, very few of them are academically serious, getting beyond the commonplace in areas such as biblical hermeneutics and ecclesiology. They mean to report and give advice, but not to open up questions or establish new questions and research possibilities. Whereas some raise serious questions about current Catholic practice, none raise questions about fundamentalism, which lead to more inquiry. Only a few are irenic (and fewer yet ironic!); a good number appeal to Catholics to ponder the lessons for the Catholic Church arising from the conversions of "millions" of Catholics to fundamentalist churches, and these sometimes offer critical reflections on the current state of the Catholic Church, favoring the defection of Catholics. Because a report on the contents of over eighty essays is out of the question, I shall discuss a few representative pieces and relegate comparable pieces to footnotes.

## Scholars for a Theological Audience

To Brigid Frein's "Fundamentalism and Narrative Approaches to the Gospels,"[9] an essay on hermeneutical possibilities, there is appended a bibliography that is long on works on critical hermeneutical theory and short on works by fundamentalists and evangelicals. She refers to two collections of essays by evangelical and fundamentalist hermeneuticists,[10] and her chief source for the fundamentalist approach is the "Chicago Statement on Biblical Hermeneutics," printed in the collection of essays by Radmacher and Preus. The essay is a careful and respectful contrast of the two approaches, including the presuppositions, methods, and goals of the two. The two share certain characteristics. Both take the gospels as unified compositions rather than compilations of previously independent units; both are primarily concerned with the general reader's understanding of the text rather than with an audience of technicians of historical-critical method; and both have a lack of confidence in historical method's ability to shed light on the meaning of the text.

But the approaches collide irreparably on several counts: inerrancy, the unity of the Bible as a whole, and the goals of interpretation (the intention of the individual author versus the openness of the text to multiple interpretations that go beyond the intention of the author): narrative "... approaches are at odds with the fundamentalist doctrines of exact historicity and of the mono-significance of the text and ... cannot be used as a way of avoiding the difficulties of historical critical approaches."[11] The essay is aimed at an audience not only of theological interest but also of some theoretic sophistication. She treats fundamentalism as a hermeneutical option and in no way as a competing religious movement. Her criticism of it moves with the same deliberation as it might had she been addressing the limits and glories of Marxist literary criticism.[12]

Clifford G. Kossel writes in the conservative journal, *Communio*.[13] Aimed at Roman Catholic intellectuals, the essay promotes a mutually critical and constructive engagement of the Moral Majority, a fundamentalist political organization, by Catholic conservatives. Whereas the approaches to politics by the two religious communities may differ, there remain significant features in common. There are fundamentals, after all, of the Christian faith that are nonnegotiable and are expressed in the creeds of the church and that can serve as the basis for cooperation. But there are differences as well that need attention, namely ". . . ecclesial unity and the relationship of Christianity to culture."[14]

Catholic ecclesial unity is built on the Eucharist, which constitutes the body of Christ; the Eucharist along with the formal teaching Magisterium allows Catholics a gradualist and open attitude toward cultural change. The Catholic struggles over the direction of culture and its implications for faith

> are not carried out without a great deal of controversy about the boundaries of orthodoxy and about the strategies employed. Nor is it without some confusion, shock, pain, and losses. But the Eucharist goes on and the Magisterium stands, the two centers of the whirlwind. . . . [But] it is difficult to understand how a group which apparently has no inherent principles to prevent religious fragmentation can supply a public philosophy to put brakes on the individualist-pluralist tendencies in our society.[15]

Thus, the argument of Isaac Hecker and, more recently, of Richard Neuhaus, is revived[16]—Catholicism has the ability to provide a public philosophy, while the Moral Majority (fundamentalists) cannot appeal to the broad public (they can argue publicly only on biblical grounds) and divides the world between "good guys" and "bad guys." The Catholic retention of the natural law argument and a universal appeal to reason, and its ability to stand back critically from capitalist economic theory and national interest politics, make its contribution to the public debate firmer and steadier.

But fundamentalism has its gifts to bring. First, there is its emphasis on the importance of education of the young at the very time Catholic schools have been decreasing; second, the fundamentalists are setting the example in their activist role in politics for the sake of Christian values. In sum:

> Catholics, then, have reason to applaud the active participation of the Evangelicals in the political process and to support several of

their positions. On the religious plane Evangelicals do not seem very open to ecumenical moves, but they may be ready for some advances in the social and political areas. Certainly we must be honest about our differences, but Catholics might contribute to the broadening of their perspectives and a toning down of their more abrasive (and counter-productive) tactics. And Evangelicals might communicate to us some of their vigor and enthusiasm—as well as their skills in organization and in the use of electronic media.[17]

The author sees practical avenues of cooperation without fudging the profound differences in ecclesiology and culture. The essay is a model of constructive criticism, entirely without antifundamentalist ranting, polemic, and stereotyping.[18]

Roy Barkley, an "orthodox" and "loyal" Catholic (thus distinguishing himself from liberal and presumably heterodox Catholics such as me) and member of the Fellowship of Catholic Scholars, is an author, editor, and scholar of Middle English who is a convert to the Catholic Church from "hardbitten Fundamentalism."[19] In the wake of the *America* special issue in 1986, Barkley wanted to set the record straight on what fundamentalism is, why Catholics join the movement, and what to do about it:

The authors [of the essays in *America*] consider themselves an intellectual in-group and speak with the condescending evasion that Fundamentalist attitudes are too simpleminded to argue against. Furthermore, they fuse Catholicism with mainline Protestantism, a juncture which yields bogus ecumenism and a bemused revulsion to Fundamentalist proselytizing. There, one suspects, is the rub: the centrifugalist Church is flinging droves of Catholics to Fundamentalist communions which, though theologically confused, are still capable of winning converts, a capacity increasingly moribund among mainline groups. The prospect of the "American" Church casting out modern Fundamentalism by the use of Modernism . . . is scarcely less hopeful than the attempt to cast out Beelzebub in his own name.[20]

The problem with fundamentalism is not, as liberals claim, its biblical literalism—on selected texts Catholics are as literal as they and they are as "symbolic" as Catholic exegetes!—but biblical *legalism*, a fault corresponding to Catholic legalist tendencies. Barkley joins other Catholics in the claim that the Bible is the book of the church as the expression of the church's truth and the locus of its learning. The difference is ecclesiological, and profound, but that is the difference between Catholics and all Protestants, and between "loyal" and "dissenting" Catholics, the latter having joined the Protestant camp on the matter. Protestants and liberal Catholics do not believe that the Holy Spirit guides the church, and do believe that the Holy Spirit speaks finally in individuals. Thus, Protestantism including fundamentalists and now Catholic dissenters and liberals constitute Barkley's "centrifugal church."

But, Barkley maintains, loyal Catholics and fundamentalists have in common at least a belief in the sinfulness of the world so evidently displayed in the host of "social issues" confronting us. In addition, their attitudes toward scripture are "vastly preferable to the 'rationalistic prejudices' that vitiate much modern exegesis."[21] Again, its problem is not literalism but the legalism arising from a text torn out of its ecclesial interpretative matrix, its "tradition." Fundamentalism's problem is that it is Protestant, in its centrifugalism as well as its anti-Catholicism.

Catholics leave the church because its modernist elements have undercut the church's ability to provide a reasonable certitude of the truths of faith, and have substituted for it self-worship and subjectivism. What the church needs in order to stem the tide toward fundamentalism is a reaffirmation of its identity. Finally, his strategy for dealing with fundamentalists face to face echoes that suggested by Karl Keating, another "orthodox" Catholic: do not duck the important arguments, argue quietly and with conviction, stick with the priority of the church, express the *whole* teaching of the church, and "fear no threats; and trust God for the harvest."[22]

Barkley's is among the best of the Catholic essays of the period preceding *ECT*: clear and accurate in its presentation of fundamentalist positions, direct and tough in its criticism of those positions, realistic and charitable in its estimate of the fundamentalist strengths and weakness, and just in its contrasts of fundamentalism with Catholic doctrine and culture. One could hardly ask more, except perhaps a more nuanced and charitable judgment of Catholic liberals and mainline Protestants!

### For the General Catholic Public

The popular Catholic press (monthly and weekly magazines and national and diocesan weekly newspapers) present us with a decidedly mixed bag of Catholic responses. First, there are essays that respond to fundamentalism with something more than concern and something less than magisterial calm, and of these I shall discuss two very briefly. Then there are five examples of essays that, although obviously concerned with the "fundamentalist challenge," take it all quite calmly and judiciously, and offer a strategy of response-by-contrast. Essays of these two sorts are samples of the body of periodical literature, and reflect attitudes that can be found mixed in all of it.

Mary Ann Walsh, R.S.M., in "Fundamentalists Give the Bible a Bad Name,"[23] uses a few horror stories of fundamentalist incursion to set up a review of the weaknesses of American Catholicism, and accounts for the defection to fundamentalism in terms of those weaknesses. She does so for a general Catholic readership. Fundamentalism is scored as "anti-intellectual . . . closed," unable to handle issues of literary form and historicity of the biblical narrative, and pushy and intrusive. Catholics, by contrast, are vulnerable to conversion for several reasons, among them: poor education in the Bible, a shallow spiritual life, absence of knowledge of their heritage, a weakened sense of identity, an atrophied sense of community, and poor preaching.[24] The answer to the problem is clear: "Teach people how to read the Bible," help them intensify spiritual life and clarify their identity, and improve their community life. The statement of the problem, the analysis of the causes, and the suggested remedies are all typical of the Catholic literature.

Richard Chilson, whose book is discussed later, contributed to the *America* special issue on fundamentalism.[25] Reversing the nativist charge against the Catholic Church, Chilson maintains that "the fundamentalist threat in our country is more real than the Communist threat ever was, yet little is being done in response," Chilson launches into a critical listing of "fundamentalist perversions": its gospel is a version of the American dream rather than a representation of the gospel of Jesus; its understanding of conversion is inadequate to the facts of Christian experience which reveal it to be ". . . a lifelong process of discernment, change and growth nurtured in authentic community"; it abstracts the Bible from the church; compassion for the sinner is available only at the price of conversion; and it stands against the doctrine of the goodness of creation. Chilson calls on Catholics to "mount a massive response to the Fundamentalist threat. It is time to give time, money, talent and energy to face an enemy that openly threatens in the public media to bury us."[26]

The list of essays that are meant to inform Catholics about fundamentalist doctrine and practice and to set up contrasts between Catholic and fundamentalist doctrine and practice is long. The aim is pastoral education and retention, which aim it shares with nearly all the Catholic literature. Here we have essays that could serve as the opening statements in a theological dialogue and argument.[27]

Thomas Coskren and two of the previously mentioned authors (Walsh and Chilson) are in the trenches of the proselytizing wars, the college campuses.[28] But Coskren, at Rutgers University, writes a seriously reflective piece on adolescent fundamentalism, catching both the appeal of Bible study to college-age Catholics and the shortcomings of such study, and scoring the lack of a sense of Catholic identity among the young, which allows them a move toward such groups. He confesses that he himself, after all his training and his experience as a theology teacher in college, was unprepared "for the emotional power generated by small groups concentrating on the Bible in the shared intimacy of dorm rooms." It has led him to the conviction that Catholics have neglected the power of the liturgically unadorned Word. He, too, lists weak preaching and badly understood liturgical practice, as well as ignorance of the history of the Catholic faith, as faults of contemporary Catholicism—but, above all else, the "power of the Word" experienced raw and the failure of Catholic communal experience accounts for the loss of young Catholics.

Francis X. Cleary, S.J., may have been the earliest Catholic essayist to take note of what most of them look on as the "fundamentalist challenge"—although he does not call it that. Cleary was at the time a professor of biblical studies at St. Louis University. He wrote a series of essays for *Universitas*, the alumni journal of the university.[29] Sharply aware of the post–Vatican II turn in Catholic exegesis from ahistorical and apologetic to historical and literary critical methods, and at the same time aware of the attraction of fundamentalist Bible study groups for adult Catholics, Cleary in his first piece sketches the development of historical investigation among Catholic New Testament scholars from the time of Pius XII. In the second essay he sketches the conservative reaction in Rome on the eve of the council, attempting to repudiate and eliminate the "new criticism," and criticism's eventual victory in the council document of the phrase "religious truth" as distinct from historical and scientific information as the proper subject matter of inerrancy.[30]

In the third and last essay, Cleary recounts the story of fundamentalism in early twentieth-century America, and adds that the consequential distinction between fundamentalism and Catholicism is not methods of exegesis but ecclesiology: for Catholics, the Bible is the book of the church, and the church in its concrete historical existence and practice is the sacrament of the Risen Lord. He ends the series with this commonsensical observation, apparently meant to defuse a more negative reaction to fundamentalists on the part of Catholics:

> Fundamentalist Christians are often unfairly judged. All too often it
> is an insensitive, pushy, self-righteous minority who are encoun-
> tered by outsiders. Many live a deeply committed religious life, their
> local community an enviable source of strength, of warm fellowship
> and practical example, for daily living.[31]

The restraint shown by Cleary was echoed by American Catholicism's premier biblical scholar, Raymond Brown. His comments on fundamentalism are few.[32] In his popular book on the bible, *Responses to 101 Questions on the Bible*, Brown addressed a series of four questions dealing directly with fundamentalism. He distinguished the correct claim of fundamentalists that Christianity has fundamental doctrines from what he regards as its fundamental mistake: "I applaud some of the doctrinal stress of fundamentalists but disagree thoroughly with the method they employ. In my judgment, a literalist reading of the Bible is intellectually indefensible and is quite unnecessary for the defense of the basic Christian doctrines."[33]

The two points in Brown's discussion that are relevant to this inquiry are (1) his analysis of the Catholic problem with fundamentalism, and (2) what to do about it. The advice to some degree is common enough among Catholic authors: don't argue over individual texts, for the real issues are much larger (e.g., the very nature of the Bible); don't think they are fools or ignorant, for they are often "extremely intelligent," well informed in archeology and languages, with well-developed apologetic arguments; don't try to convert them too suddenly, for they may lose their faith altogether. Like nearly all of our authors, Brown recognized the serious institutional failures of Catholicism with regard to the Bible and Bible education, of clergy as well as laity. In fact, he maintained that only significant improvement in biblical education and in media use by Catholics, joined by mainline Protestants, will be able to slow the advance of fundamentalism. He also made the usual plea for smaller and more intense Catholic communities: "We may have to break those parishes down, at least functionally, into smaller groups."[34] Finally, he admitted as well that our liturgical language is far less vivid than fundamentalist language about the love of Jesus, and called for more preaching of that love.[35]

His explanation for the current (1981) problem was not so typical of his fellow commentators. He roots the problem between Catholics and fundamentalists in cultural and practical order rather than in individual and social psychology. There is not a hint that there is anything pathological or offensive about fundamentalists. He cites three factors to explain the new confrontation. First, in the 1960s, Catholics began to move en masse into the Sun/Bible Belt, and so into the culture of fundamentalism; second, the media explosion of the same period made popular Bible preaching available to Catholics in the Snow Belt as well as in the Sun Belt; and, third, Catholics left their cultural ghetto in the same period and entered the American economic and social mainstream whose religious *lingua franca* is the Bible rather than the Catholic devotional tradition. The innate attraction of the Bible for all Christians, once it has been discovered, plus the lack of serious biblical education of Catholics and attractive preaching, occasioned the peculiar contact of Catholics with these "new" Protestants. What is noteworthy about Brown's discussion is that the grounds for his explanation remained sociocultural, and the blame was not pinned on fundamentalist aggressive proselytizing. The thorny issue is discussed with Brown's usual magisterial calm and devotion to objectivity.

Leonard Foley, in "Catholics and Fundamentalists: We Agree and Disagree," is concerned to inform a general readership of the history and nature of American fundamentalism.[36] He traces the history, laying stress on the relationship between fundamentalism and evangelicalism, and confesses that fundamentalism is by no means a simple thing. His criticisms of fundamentalism are typical. He then sets up several point of contrast (inerrancy, inspiration, hermeneutics), and ends with some advice on response to fundamentalists. We agree on much but disagree on premises. Don't argue biblical texts, but do take fundamentalism as a personal, social, and pastoral concern. Foley does not mean that *fundamentalism* is a problem, as many Catholics do. Foley means that we, Catholics and fundamentalists, share problems and concerns. We are all bound in common to preach the gospel; we all share the same upsetting social and economic conditions that need transformation; we all need to stop straining gnats (six days of creation) and swallowing camels (frightful social conditions). We do disagree, but:

> . . . we must give both the evangelicals and fundamentalists great credit for their zeal, spirit, enthusiasm, dedication (if not their militancy). Perhaps the most telling criticism a fundamentalist can give (some) Catholic communities was tersely put. . . . "You Catholics ain't got no *soul.*"

*Commonweal,* a weekly journal of theology and culture for left-leaning Catholics, published two essays by John Garvey, one asserting the claim that secular humanism is a fundamentalism and the other finding something good to say about Jimmy Swaggart. Garvey's problem with modern and contemporary culture is its smugness and intolerance, its assumption of rightness and its privatization of every opposed point of view. This, of course is a standard critique of modernism in the age of postmodernism, and is common among Catholics, right and left. The intolerance of the fundamentalist right is balanced by the intolerance of the humanist left:

> Secular humanists and fundamentalists deserve one another. . . . They are equally intolerant. Because liberal intolerance pretends to understand, it is not as obvious as fundamentalist intolerance, which thinks it understands the only thing that matters, and to hell (literally) with anyone with any other point of view. But secular humanist intolerance is clear enough. . . . What is incredible is the assumption that religious people indoctrinate, and secular humanists guide people toward truth.[37]

In a cultural situation of this sort, in which the public voice of religion and of value is silenced by Enlightenment prejudice, and when it is clear that the offensiveness of fundamentalists pales before the horrors worked on human beings by the offspring of the Enlightenment, even fundamentalism has its role:

> Fundamentalists are responding—stupidly, all thumbs—to this situation, which really is a threat in many ways. Right wing Christians may be a little like the canaries coal miners used to take into the mines with them, because they were the first to be affected by poison gas.[38]

So Jimmy Swaggart, whose ignorance is appalling, has his saving grace:

> The man really is pig-ignorant, as stupid about the limitations of his own very recent version of old-time religion as a man could be and

still be able to get dressed in the morning and tie his own shoes. I remember hearing him one morning talk about the dying of a famous atheist, and I couldn't remember ever having heard of Voll Terry, and then I realized that he meant Voltaire. . . . He is wrong about a lot of things, terribly wrong, but he seems to be a man who thinks that the Bible is true, and that what can be found in it is meant to transform us. This is the claim which embarrasses us, or part of us. . . . They come close to the truth, to the fact that there are moments in our lives when we really must make choices that are just as simple and demanding, and finally saving as the ones these preachers rant and rave about.[39]

Of course, the vulnerability of the left-leaning Catholic is on the side of Enlightenment privatization and relativism, and Garvey and a journal such as *Commonweal* must be on guard about it and about attacks on it from the Catholic right, and so Garvey is putting some distance between himself and the failures of the Enlightenment marked out so sharply in two hundred years of Catholic dissent from it and its excesses. American evangelicals arrived at an anti-Enlightenment critique a century after Catholics did. But it is not easy to compliment the right, Catholic and Protestant, for taking a stand where the left wavers, and when the right is so extraordinarily unappealing. Garvey cannot bring himself to that compliment unequivocally.

There is a point in the Catholic literature at which the term fundamentalism shifts denotation, and a new epithet in Catholic politics is born. Catholic liberals began to call Catholic conservatives "fundamentalists," and to make stabs at interpreting their post–Vatican II enemies in the church under that term.[40] The theologian Gabriel Daly, an Irish priest and historian, at the seventy-fifth anniversary of the American Academy in 1984, in his comments on the Catholic struggle with modernity, wrote:

Integralism was the form in which Catholic fundamentalism expressed itself. . . . Integralism, like other kinds of fundamentalism, is more a state of mind than a corpus of beliefs. It is a *way* of approaching those truths which are perceived to lie at the heart of one's religious faith.[41]

Daly returned to his usage at the end of his wise and generous comments on the struggle of the Catholic Church against the demons of the Enlightenment, a struggle that he regarded as necessary and yet badly waged by the leaders of the church. He offered a piece of advice to liberal Catholics and others, unfortunately unheeded: "The instinct to entertain and where possible to respond positively to the truth in the positions of others should extend also (if unilaterally) to fundamentalism. An attitude of academic contempt achieves nothing."[42] Daly recognized that fundamentalism (integralism in the Catholic case) preserves a Dionysian element in religious life, which a church often loses in its close encounter with modernity:

> The sensible rationality of Apollonian religion somehow fails to sat-
> isfy the deeper receptors of religious symbol in the human psyche.
> The Kantian ideal of "religion within the limits of reason" is in the
> end the most unreasonable aim of all, because it neglects an ele-
> ment in human nature which is both necessary to spiritual health
> and impervious to the censorship of reason [i.e., mysticism]. . . . Dio-
> nysus always strikes back—which is only another way of expressing
> the New Testament conviction that the Spirit breathes where he
> wills.[43]

What for Daly was a category in the clarification of religious stands and an element in an explanation of the Catholic integralist movement became something else entirely in the hands of American liberal Catholics. They de-fended themselves and their recently fragile theological hegemony against the attacks of contemporary Catholic inheritors of the integralist mantle. Along with a frequent use of the epithet "fundamentalist," which for a Catholic is rarely if ever only descriptive, one finds a remarkably harsh attack on the Prot-estant and Catholic right in terms of psychological analysis and, in some cases, the language of disease.

Amateur psychological analysis occurs frequently in the academic and lib-eral essays of Catholics (and others) on fundamentalism.[44] The American Cath-olic Bishops, as we shall see, find explanations for the fundamentalist appeal to Catholics in individual and social psychology. But there are several pieces that are dominated by their appeal to psychological and even medical catego-ries. For Patrick Arnold, S.J., Catholic fundamentalism, as any fundamental-ism, is not a religious movement at all, but a political, social, and cultural reaction to change that can only be explained in psychological terms:

> Psychological studies describe its strongest adherents as "authoritar-
> ian personalities": individuals who feel threatened in a world of con-
> spiring evil forces, who think in simplistic and stereotypical terms
> and who are attracted to authoritarian and moralistic answers to
> their problems. . . . The Catholic community was not to prove en-
> tirely immune from this disease. In the past few years, indications
> have grown that the fundamentalist virus is mutating and beginning
> to produce Catholic symptoms. That this neo-orthodox movement is
> an illness, and not a genuine reform, is first of all suggested by its
> affinities with the contemporary problems afflicting Islam, Judaism,
> and Protestantism. At least five unhealthy characteristics are visible
> within the movements threatening all these religions.[45]

Fundamentalism, Catholic and otherwise, is an emotional movement whose root is fear and anger at cultural change, always religiously divisive, taking flight into myths of the Golden Age, obsessed with issues of authority and obedience, and usually linked with rightist political movements. Finally, this "religious disease" is unconcerned with Jesus and what concerned Him, and is "bereft of any spirituality, preferring instead either partisan political topics or subjects of a largely intramural, ecclesiastical nature."[46]

Jacques Weber, S.J., directly addresses the problem of Catholic fundamentalism,[47] and includes some remarkably condescending descriptions, taken in part from Damien Kraus:

> As Catholic, the fundamentalist is more often concerned with doctrinal and moral simplicism [sic] than with biblical fundamentalism, though this also can be part of the mind-set. The Catholic fundamentalist craves the simple and the absolutely certain; he is intolerant of doubt, of doctrinal development, of developmental stages of faith, and of an ongoing search for the truth. He is reductionistic in his theology and antagonistic toward Catholic pluralism.[48]

The stereotyping here reaches depths of absurdity matched only by the crudity of Arnold's medical metaphors. Weber wants to make use of Gordon Alport's work on childhood and adult faith, and Bernard Lonergan's theory of conversions (intellectual, moral, and religious) to "place" what James Hitchcock prefers to call "activist conservative Catholicism."[49] He concludes:

> It is my observation and experience that Catholic fundamentalism as described above seriously truncates and blocks ecclesial conversion, intellectual conversion, and wholistic moral conversion. It also creates "serious deformations" in the area of religious conversion (to the holy) and Christian conversion (to Christ), causing a distorted view of the holy and of the humanity of Jesus and his teaching.
>
> I suggest that one caught in the mind-set of Catholic fundamentalism will have a distorted view of the holy and of one's own human nature and, therefore, of Christ incarnate. The Catholic fundamentalist would, I suggest, rate low in all aspects of the conversion process. I further suggest that the fundamentalist mind-set seriously inhibits the passage from infantile or childhood faith to adult faith.[50]

It is hard to imagine the loss to the dignity and decency of Catholic theology displayed in such paragraphs, to its methodological good sense, and to a proper interpretation of the important work of Bernard Lonergan, who made his suggestions on the various conversions *not for the analysis of enemies but for self-understanding!*[51] Weber uses Lonergan's "conversions" as a checklist for psychological and spiritual health, a club for battle with his fundamentalist enemy. He ends his essay with an adventitious homily on our complementarity in a single church, informing us that "we are the body of Christ"! Weber matches the worst of anti-Catholic polemic, low blow for low blow.

Another low point is reached by John O'Donohue, W.F., in two articles in the *African Ecclesial Review*.[52] The first is interesting as an example of the kind of interchange that takes place between Catholic liberals and conservatives, for it is a response to an article on authority and freedom published by *Opus Dei* that O'Donohue considers a perversion and that he criticizes with classic modernist and liberal appeals to religious experience (with the appeal I would agree, although I find the particular argumentation vacuous).[53]

The second essay better fits my purpose. This one is directed to a more general analysis of fundamentalism, which at the very outset is characterized as a "demand for absolute certitude in religion" that is traced to "a failure to outgrow the infant's craving for security."[54] The body of the essay is devoted to explication of this claim. The immediate enemy remains *Opus Dei* and the Catholic right ("ecclesiastical fundamentalism," although "biblical fundamentalism" takes its lumps as well. The latter is "an obsessive demand for an inhuman certainty . . . most easily explained as a desire to return to infantile security which, however, the adult must shed if he or she is to grow." The disease is adequately met only by the invitation to "grow up, painful and even agonizing though this process must always be." He appeals to Marx and Freud in support of his position that fundamentalism ". . . offers illusory psychological security . . . [in] false and illusory religion" for the poor as well as the "psychologically handicapped."[55]

Finally, Jesus is called in to witness that in the current argument between ". . . 'Fundamentalists' and 'Liberals', we would find that the legalistic Pharisees, for whom the Mosaic Law and the 'immemorial traditions' were the ultimate tests of truth and ethical righteousness, were fundamentalists, while Jesus, who proclaimed that the Sabbath was made for man, was a liberal." We are brought to the conclusion, then, that fundamentalism is a "radical human failure . . . an intellectual failure . . . [and] a moral failure . . ." as well as ". . . an enemy of human progress . . . the source of insoluble human conflicts . . . [and] the destruction of all authentic religion."[56]

This essay is an example of psychological reductionism and of effects of the liberal blinders on empirical observation and theological judgment. The only question that fundamentalism raises for these authors is how to get rid of it, and the most that one can say about its effect on them as scholars is that it clearly creates no serious intellectual problem, not to say curiosity, and calls forth the most distasteful of metaphors and similes, vicious stereotyping, and expressions of self-righteous wrath. Dare we suggest, then, that liberal religion is "emotional," at least on occasions when its presuppositions are challenged?

Jesuit Thomas E. Clarke's essay "Fundamentalism and Prejudice" could have been better titled "Fundamentalism, Liberalism, and Prejudice" and might well have been read by Arnold, O'Donohue, and others.[57] Recognizing the psychological mechanism of projection of the Shadow, and aware of the theological shortcomings of fundamentalism, Clarke will not settle for the easy slide into liberal attacks on fundamentalism:

> A certain forensic violence then begins to characterize the field of ecumenical relationships. Healthy conflict yields to sterile polemic, or to what is worse, the contemptuous ignoring of the adversary as unworthy of serious attention. As one who is more prone to liberalism than to fundamentalism, I have to acknowledge that this dynamic seems to obtain in both parties to the quarrel. . . . Liberals are no less prone to "inordinate attachments" and to the resulting prejudices than are fundamentalists. In a way, the spiritual snares of liberalism are the more insidious for being less blatant. The liberal does not differ from the fundamentalist in being free from anxiety or from the absolutizing tendency. . . . The peculiarly liberal form of idolatry is to canonize the endless quest for truth, to absolutize the value of doubt and to find safe shelter in keeping an open mind.[58]

Hence, Clarke delivers a moral message to the learned and holy despisers of fundamentalism: people in glass houses shouldn't throw stones. The shortcoming of Clarke's essay is that it covers only one of the oppositions to fundamentalist Protestantism, namely, Catholic liberalism. But the crucial opposition is between fundamentalism and Catholicism itself, and it is to this pair that Clarke's essay needs to attend.

## Special Issues of Periodicals

Four American Catholic journals thought fundamentalists bothersome enough to print issues entirely or chiefly devoted to them: *Catholic Charismatic* (1979), *The New Catholic World* (1985), *America* (1987), and *The New Theology Review* (1988). I shall make some comments on the issues as wholes rather than review each piece in each (some have been mentioned earlier), singling out a few of the best and the worst, and taking them in chronological order.

The *Catholic Charismatic* (1979) is the organ of the more moderate wing of the charismatic movement in the church; its counterpart, *The New Covenant*, is the voice of the Ann Arbor national service committee of the Catholic Charismatic Renewal. The moderate wing publishes materials by Catholics who do not belong to the movement, among them scripture scholars and theologians who could not otherwise find ready access to the right-wing cousins. The early date on the *Catholic Charismatic* issue suggests that the charismatics were among the first to register the attractiveness of fundamentalism for Catholics.

Perhaps the charismatic movement's emphasis on a second birth in the Holy Spirit and on Bible study and pentecostal worship phenomena left them vulnerable to the appeal of evangelicalism.

The issue carried short essays by George MacRae, S.J., and John Haughey, S.J., both of which are theological critiques of fundamentalism.[59] The first faulted its refusal to accept the humanity of the Bible and so its implicit rejection of the Incarnation, and the second found that it rejected the analogical character of our knowledge of God and the limitations of all human knowledge, including our knowledge of God. Both were typical of Catholic commentary on fundamentalism. Richard Rohr, O.F.M., contributed an excellent meditation on the Marian mystery as a key to incarnational and sacramental Christianity,[60] offering an example of the explication of the *res catholica* in the face of Protestant and Catholic legalism. Bill O'Brien and Barbara O'Reilly, in separate pieces, worried about the growth of fundamentalist attitudes among Catholic charismatic groups, especially in "covenant communities,"[61] while Juan Hinojosa detailed the history of biblical fundamentalism and suggests a psychological reading of its "attitude."[62]

The *New Catholic World* (1985), in its editorial introduction, linked Protestant and Catholic fundamentalism and proclaimed its desire "to show our respect for Fundamentalism as a deeply sincere form of Christian commitment, while frankly facing and even criticizing many aspects that are unacceptable to a true Catholic vision of faith."[63] The hope was partially fulfilled when, in its opening essay, Edward Dobson, one-time faculty member at Jerry Falwell's Liberty University and coauthor with him of *The Fundamentalist Phenomenon*, fashioned a history and *apologia* of the American fundamentalist movement in the early and mid-twentieth century.[64]

Dobson's portrait was followed by Thomas Stransky's contrast of fundamentalist and Catholic teaching, expressing the dangers of psychological explanations of it, yet accepting a softened version of that explanation as basic: "Struggling to find a firm footing in life; longing to break through the bewildering variety of religious/moral/amoral claims which are offered through the media; searching for a buttress against social instabilities and demographic dislocations, so many look for the clear, absolute, not-to-be-disputed word."[65] Yet in the end Stransky wanted Catholics to examine their conscience on their loss of a "passion for truth," which is easy to find in fundamentalists.[66]

Eugene LaVerdiere explains what a Catholic might mean by "being born again" (it is a departure, not an arrival).[67] Brian E. Curley, in "Fundamentalism and Its Challenge to Catholic Religious Education,"[68] attacked fundamentalism rather than answer its challenge: it is anti-incarnational, confrontational, antidialogic, escapist. The piece belongs with Arnold and O'Donohue for its psychological reductionism, but its ignorance surpassed theirs by far. The collection ended with the essays by Thomas Coskren and Richard Chilson, the latter a brief version of the introductory chapter to his book.[69]

The editorial heading the collection of articles in the special issue of *America* (1986) repeated the most frequent of Catholic comments: fundamentalism offers "quick and easy solutions to complicated questions of life and belief."[70] Martin Marty, a leading church historian who has written extensively on fundamentalism, once again made his case against the common misunderstandings of fundamentalism, arguing that fundamentalism is a "truly modern movement," that it is not conservative despite its devotion to certain classic themes of orthodoxy, that it is historically eclectic, that is possesses "astonishing" cultural adaptability and a "multiplex consciousness" carrying ". . . apparently conflicting signals without necessary disruption of psychic health."[71] On the frequently practiced psychological reduction, Marty commented: "To see Fundamentalists as pathological is in many cases a problem of the observer's spectacles." Attempting to place fundamentalism among the many movements reacting to change in the modern world, Marty pleaded for care in the judgments we make:

> Fundamentalists do not only organize to gain political power or to demonstrate aspects of modernity. They believe in Christ crucified and risen, and they gladly testify to the experience of Christ in their born-again lives. But they are also parts of social movements that their neighbors and fellow citizens have to understand if they are to coexist creatively in civil and religious life.[72]

Marty was followed by Archbishop John F. Whealon's brief comment summarizing the contents of the bishops' letter (see later for comments), and Thomas Stahel interviewed auxiliary Bishop Cuquejo of Asuncion, Paraguay, on the growth of "sects" in Paraguay. John Catoir, director of The Christophers,[73] strings out some anecdotes and statistics meant to warn Catholics, including a charge that "a lot of child abuse [is] taking place among Fundamentalists . . ." and a report that Catholics are contributing about $60 million a year to television preachers. Richard Chilson's essay was reviewed earlier, and his book is commented on later. Alan Deck, S.J., writes on the worries of American Catholic bishops about the numbers of Hispanic Catholics who have defected to fundamentalist churches and makes suggestions on how to tighten up Catholic communities of Hispanics. William Dinges, professor at Catholic University of America, writes a careful analysis of the Vatican statement on sects, cults, and new religious movements, among the best pieces in the Catholic literature of the last two decades.[74]

*New Theology Review: An American Catholic Journal for Ministry*, was edited by Robert J. Schreiter, C.P.P.S., a faculty member of the Chicago Theological Union, who opens his collection with a warning against reductionist explanations of fundamentalism:

> Most attempts to explain the American fundamentalist phenomenon have been reductionist in nature. Some critics maintain that it is pri-

marily a psychological reaction to the ambiguities of modernity. Others see it as a form of theological ignorance. Still other consider it as related to a socio-economic class that feels itself left out of the mainstream. But therapies, rational debates, and reform programs do not seem to loosen fundamentalism's grip on the heart and minds of people who are not necessarily frightened, uneducated or socially deprived. Reductionist strategies seem to get religious leaders nowhere in combating fundamentalism. . . . fundamentalism must be understood in its own right and within its own context, and not simply as an anxious reaction to the mainstream movements in the dominant culture. Fundamentalism is a major pastoral problem in the United States. It is a complex phenomenon that cannot be reduced to a psychological diagnosis, a theological error or a single social analysis.[75]

The essays that follow kept carefully to this guideline (or perhaps the guideline emerged from the essays). To open, Dominic Monti, O.F.M., of the Washington Theological Union, wrote a straightforward and balanced survey of the origins and development of American fundamentalism, relying on secondary sources.[76] In perhaps the best single piece on fundamentalism by a Roman Catholic theologian, Zachary Hayes, O.F.M., presented, analyzed, and criticized dispensational premillennialism.[77] He read Darby and Scofield, catching their own "canon within the canon." The explanation of the technicalities of dispensationalism is clear and accurate. His criticism was vigorous and well rounded, and almost entirely theological and not at all psychological. He explained it with Timothy Weber as an assertion of the final intelligibility and goodness of an opaque and mean human history, but raised the further question: Why does this particular affirmation of intelligibility and goodness have strong appeal to some and not to others?

But why do some people seem to be satisfied only with clear knowledge of the future, while others seem to be willing to live with a hope that thrives in the face of ignorance concerning the specifics of history? Are we here confronted with two different forms of religious consciousness?[78]

One might suggest that we are facing two quite different understandings of human consciousness and of human knowledge, and perhaps the same sort of dispositional leanings that account for general stances of liberalism and conservatism. What to make of them, however, is a mystery, and so also the fact that some switch readily from one to another. I still cannot account for the fact that, although there are Republicans I like, I do not like Republicans and would allow very few indeed into my family circle. And Republicans only head the long list that seems to be based on a mixture of ideological, affectional, religious, and ethnic predisposition. Tribal bonds are not tied by blood alone.

Gabriel Fackre, a professor of evangelical theology at Andover-Newton Theological School, offered a theological analysis and evaluation of fundamentalist doctrines, with helpful distinctions at the outset among varieties of fundamentalists.[79] Spirituality and eschatology are the doctrinal threads he follows to the conclusion that hope is the driving force of fundamentalism:

Whatever one might think of the hermeneutics of scripture here employed, or the doctrinal specifics concerning the end-time, political apocalyptic fundamentalism constitutes a "theology of hope" for multitudes. All the elements recommended by the Moltmanns and Schillebeeckxes of ecumenical Christianity reappear here: (1) human suffering as the contextual question to which the Good News must speak; (2) the focus on the future as the reference point for the gospel; (3) Christ's resurrection as the warrant for hope; And (4) a doctrine of "hope in action" that disavows escapism and mobilizes the faithful for social change.[80]

Theodore Ross, S.J., ended the issue with an essay on Catholic integralism, "Catholicism and Fundamentalism," carrying on the association of the Catholic right with fundamentalism.[81] He traced the "unfortunate" history of integralism, in which it was elevated to the norm for Catholic theology for a century, and catalogued its theological faults: its opposition to historical study of the Bible; its identification of truth with its own theology, one school among many; its identification of authentic Catholic practice with one historical period of that practice. Although the history of integralism as a movement as well as an apologetic deserves as much sympathy and nuance as does the history of fundamentalism, Ross delivers a fair enough sketch of it in an essay that is decisively in the negative.

The interpretation and criticism of fundamentalist eschatology and spirituality by Hayes and Fackre are insightful. When Fackre charged fundamentalism with "simplistic absolutisms" and "quick-fix ideologies," one has the sense that the criticism is as fair as the presentation and evaluation. Perhaps in part because Fackre is not a Catholic, and has a firsthand experience with fundamentalism, he produces the most theological stimulating essay on Protestant fundamentalism to be found in the Catholic literature. Hayes shows just how good a serious Catholic theological critique of an "alien" theological world can be when it is not driven by the immediate concern with "sheep-stealing." The essays by Zachary Hayes and Gabriel Fackre, then, make this special issue (the first) of the *New Theology Review* the most valuable of the four.

## Books

The five books by Catholics echo concerns, themes, and arguments of the periodical literature. They all regarded fundamentalism as a threat to Catholics, and judge it to be intellectually, spiritually, and doctrinally inadequate. All five were written for Catholics; all are defensive (only one is genuinely offensive!); and all set out to enlighten Catholics on what fundamentalism is, and how it arose and why it prospers (the comment on the history is cursory), what its central affirmations are and how these contrast with Roman Catholic doctrines and current scholarly views. All five seem written because large numbers of Catholics are attracted to fundamentalist belief and practice. All regard fundamentalist anti-Catholicism as both abhorrent and groundless. They attempt to refute fundamentalist doctrines where these depart from Catholic teaching. They are pastoral rather than scholarly, although two are written by established scholars. None can be counted as a work of scholarship, although the authors are educated, intellectually able, and even sophisticated. All were driven by the pastoral as distinct from any intellectual challenge that fundamentalism posed. All were at least minimally restrained, avoiding attacks on individuals and concentrating on teachings and worldviews, and all are directly argumentative. They all agreed that "irenicism" and "ecumenism" have little or no place between Catholics and fundamentalists, but pinned the blame for that on the fundamentalists (Catholics, it seems, will now talk to anybody!). All regard fundamentalists as Christians (at least there is no explicit argument mounted that they are not), mistaken though they may be. None displays any interest whatever in fundamentalism as a valuable subject matter for study in its own right, and none expends any effort in making distinctions among evangelicals. For them all, it appears, the term fundamentalism means biblical Christianity. I will discuss four of them.[82]

The peculiarity of Anthony Gilles's book, *Fundamentalism: What Every Catholic Should Know*,[83] is its pleasant narrative style. Gilles grew up in the Bible Belt, and is able to take a friendly and bemused look at his neighbors' religion. Whereas his objective is to provide Catholics with a response to common fundamentalist charges and to contrast Catholic doctrines with its teachings, he does so in a folksy style laced with stories of his family's encounters with fundamentalists and with some humor.

Gilles was able at the outset to provide a balance to his list of "common fundamentalist tendencies" (not good!) by adding a shorter list of "fundamentalist good points."[84] The former include most of the standard Catholic criticisms: fundamentalists are legalists, docetists, reifiers of the Divine Mystery, ignorant historically, uncritical individualists, and dualists (i.e., they are pessimists on human nature and pay little attention to the creative as distinct from redemptive divine activity). But there is another side: their devotion to the Bible should make Catholics blush; they are typically on a serious quest for holiness in a world that cares little for that; they take moral choice seriously in a world of moral relativism.

Richard Chilson, whom we met earlier, is a Paulist campus minister. His *Full Christianity: A Catholic Response to Fundamental Questions*,[85] in its body, answered fifty questions derived from fundamentalist-Catholic differences gathered under five topic headings: (1) Scripture, Authority, and Revelation; (2) Jesus Christ; (3) The Church; (4) Christian Life; and (5) Other Questions. In the preface, he pointed to the rising tide of fundamentalism on campuses. The Navigators, the Campus Crusade for Christ, and the Inter-Varsity Christian Fellowship are listed as perpetrators. Fundamentalism is placed in direct line with "classical Protestant themes," while his answers rest on a "Catholic vision" now embraced by mainline Protestants and their scholars as well as Roman Catholics. Once again we can feel the post-Reformation ecclesiastical ground shifting under our feet. Protestant liberalism has manifestly failed to solve the problem created for Christianity by "the modern world," and so we are left with these alternatives, fundamentalism and "the Catholic vision." Only "Catholicism" in this broadened, post–Vatican II sense, has clung to the fullness of Christian faith and only it remains in dialogue with the modern world.

In the introduction, the two visions are contrasted.[86] Catholicism is inclusive, culturally creative, optimistic, incarnational, and sacramental. Fundamentalism, by contrast, is exclusive, culturally reactive, pessimistic, oriented toward the doctrine of atonement, and fixed on the verbal. These are taken to be worldviews underlying doctrines, and so the specific doctrines are interpreted against the background of the worldview. In general, the book is a moderate to liberal Catholic response, with some stereotyping on the author's part but it is not an angry response. Fundamentalist positions, however, are presented sketchily and dismissed out of hand.

Karl Keating is a lawyer and a layman in the church of San Diego, where he heads a national organization called Catholic Answers, Inc. The organization publishes and distributes a monthly paper and pamphlets on religious topics and tapes of debates and lectures and maintains a Web site. Keating talks publicly in a variety of contexts, including parish and diocesan meetings, debates with fundamentalist speakers in their own churches, and is available for consultation to other Catholic organizations. He is well known and is respected in conservative evangelical circles, both for the strength of his convictions and his knowledge of the Bible, fundamentalism, and Catholicism.

His book, *Catholicism and Fundamentalism*,[87] is the most substantial and interesting of the lot. Keating knows fundamentalism and fundamentalist literature, especially its anti-Catholic variety, thoroughly. Second, the book is well organized to serve his very clear purposes, and he proceeded dispassionately and unerringly to accomplish them. Third, it represents an intellectual and public style of Catholicism that was out of tune with the Catholic academic-theological mainstream (represented, say, by the College Theology Society, the Catholic Theological Society of America, or the Catholic Biblical Association) but was quite in tune with more conservative Catholic elements (for example, the Fellowship of Catholic Scholars) and with the tendencies of much of popular conservative evangelical apologetics. The style is that of public debate over the truth of religious claims. To read Keating is to reenter the world of Catholic apologetics, which seemed to have slipped beneath the surface of Catholic discourse with the emergence of Vatican II's ecumenical style. As fundamentalists slip easily into the clothes of traditional Protestant anti-Catholicism, so Keating is at home in the world of Hillaire Belloc, G. K. Chesterton, and Frank Sheed. It is the world of British Catholic "in-your-face" response to Protestant nonsense that had a determinative effect on American Catholic education and culture in the first half of this century.

The book is well written, and, given the methodological premises of apologetical theology, very effective. Although Keating shows little of the wit of the English Catholic authors and controversialists whom he admires, he knows how to take an argument apart. There is no impatience here, no liberal petulance indicating that he would prefer to be doing something else, no dismissal of or disrespect for fundamentalists. He is calmly sure, however, that fundamentalism is doctrinally and theologically flawed, that Catholics make a serious mistake in converting to it, and that the only way to staunch the current wound is to display the good sense that Catholicism makes and the incoherence of fundamentalism.

Keating thinks that fundamentalist doctrine must be refuted rather than explained away, and that unless Catholics care about "the truth" as much as fundamentalists profess to, no amount of psychologizing or babbling on about the difficulties of the age or even turning up the affective thermometer of Catholic congregations will stop the bleeding. Catholics must be willing to argue doctrine and history with conviction as well as knowledge.

Eight chapters (125 pages) provided a survey of anti-Catholic fundamentalist landscape, from the work of the "godfather" of mid-century fundamentalist bigotry, Lorraine Boettner, to the conversionary antics and pamphleteering of the fringe anti-Catholics, Tony Alamo, and Jack Chick. Thirteen chapters (180 pages) presented and refuted the chief fundamentalist charges against Catholic doctrine and practice, from the inspiration and role of the scriptures to the "facts" about the Inquisition. This section is a handbook of responses to fundamentalist attacks. One chapter describes how one should deal with the fundamentalists one is sure to meet, and a last chapter reviews scholarly, especially historical, literature useful in apologetic learning and debate.

The Catholic scholarly literature Keating relies on, like the style and technique of apologetic debate, is drawn from the previous era of Roman Catholic thought and language. Even the literature that is dated after that period is, for the most part, reprinted or by authors whose formation and primary work is preconciliar. That, of course, is an option rather than a flaw, and will surely work for many Catholics, as it just as surely will not for others. Keating had no place for any of the mainstream-to-left scholarship and theology that dominated the American Catholic scene after the council. This is understandable, as it would not have served his purposes and it may account for some of the very weaknesses of the church that make evangelical inroads possible.

Catholic theologians, professors, and teachers no longer commonly mount apologetic arguments. They do not, for example, take the Bible as a historical text that gives evidence that Jesus, the miracle worker, meant to establish an infallible church whose witness in turn establishes the inspiration of the scriptures, which in turn gives evidence that he is the Divine Son.[88] The Catholic theologians no longer argue with Protestants whose subjectivist argument for the verification of the inspiration and inerrancy of scripture was formulated so well by Charles Hodge a century and a half ago.[89] Catholic scholastic apologetics disappeared as did the mainline Protestant version, and we are now unfamiliar and uneasy with apologetics in both forms of Christianity. But evangelical theologians and Karl Keating are not. As long as the Protestant rationalism and anti-Catholic bias live in fundamentalist apologetics, its counterpart, neoscholastic apologetics, may be needed in Catholicism.[90]

About many things Keating was correct, among them a view of fundamentalism that supports his efforts at respectful apologetic argument. In the midst of his discussion of the background of the argument, he wrote:

> Many Catholics who have written about fundamentalism misunderstand it. They psychologize it into a mass of emotional contradictions. They accept the view of the popular press that fundamentalism is not a matter of theology but of pathology. A man subscribes to the fundamentalist position, it is said, because he is ashamed of being poor, or because the priest or minister at his previous church mistreated him and he is out for revenge or for consoling pats on the back. He does not accept fundamentalism the way an enlightened liberal accepts liberalism, with consideration and forethought. Some critics come perilously close to concluding that any fundamentalist is a loon. Granted, some are—but so are some Catholics and more than a few secularists. . . . Whatever forces might have steered a man to fundamentalism in the first place—and it must be granted that emotional factors play a part, as they do in most conversions, no matter the direction—he remains a fundamentalist for doctrinal reasons. He might have left his previous church out of anger or frustration, [but] . . . as important as those factors might be they were not the reason he converted. His conversion had to do with doctrines.[91]

It is this conviction that grounded Keating's option for apologetic argument. He knew that if fundamentalism is loony, so are we all. If fundamentalism would rightly distinguish itself from the rest of us in an argument over doctrine, then questions about what *really* happened and what *really* is the case in the Christian claim will be essential to relations between religious communities and individuals. Although this inclination to argue is on the surface of some of the antifundamentalist Catholic literature and supposed by much of it, Keating's book has the decided advantage over most Catholics of not losing sight for a moment of the historical suppositions and essential doctrinalism of Catholic Christianity and of evangelicalism in general. Neither tradition preaches metaphysics or social theory, they proclaim what they regard as fact.

Keating's conviction that fundamentalism is a doctrine rather than a psychological disease is directly contradicted by Thomas F. O'Meara, a professor of historical and systematic theology at the University of Notre Dame. His book, *Fundamentalism: A Catholic Perspective*,[92] broadened the discussion of American Protestant fundamentalism to include manifestations of fundamentalism in the Catholic Church, and made a vigorous and direct claim that fundamentalism is primarily a psychological problem as well as the "great threat to Roman Catholicism in the United States in the period following Vatican II."[93]

In the first half of his book, O'Meara discusses what he means by fundamentalism, how it exists in Catholicism as well as Protestantism, and a "new ecumenism" between Protestant and Catholic fundamentalists. In the second half, he interprets fundamentalism as a psychological distortion brought on by anxiety experienced in rapid social change. He then presents four Catholic critics of fundamentalism,[94] and sets up a theological contrast of fundamentalism with Catholicism, making the case that they are "polar opposites" as interpretations of Christianity.

O'Meara's contrast was not between doctrines or specific practices, although he has a great deal to say about both throughout the book. In his view, the important differences are in theology, psychology, and culture, in what it means to be human and a citizen of the Kingdom. Like Chilson, O'Meara places the Catholic "vision" at the center, between theological liberalism, on one hand, which fades into secularism and fundamentalism, on the other, which identifies God with an object(s). Taking over Richard McBrien's phenomenology of Catholicism,[95] he finds Catholicism to be a religion of sacramentalism, mediation, and communion. Fundamentalism denies all three: "Christian Fundamentalism is *an interpretation of Christianity in which a charismatic leader locates with easy certitude in chosen words, doctrines, and practices the miraculous actions of a strict God saving an elite from an evil world*".[96] For Catholicism, God is loving creator and redeemer, human life can be trusted, human beings are usually not sinful and dangerous, and the loving God is present in the "ordinary" ways of human beings and makes himself available in sacramental, communal, and historical mediation.

Fundamentalism, by contrast, has a god [*sic*] who is an unpredictable trickster, a magician, a god of anger and fear, and their human beings are tricky, corrupt, untrustworthy, and ugly. Fundamentalists demand the extraordinary (the miraculous), they narrow salvation and are generous in condemnation, they are enthusiastic for a violent end to history, and they are humorless. Fundamentalism is "somewhat world-hating," and "a tribal religion from the past."[97]

O'Meara's argument against fundamentalism was bold in its psychologization. He was not content merely to stigmatize fundamentalism as a psychological aberration, but he argued that this is the way it ought to be approached. Although not "contemptuous of the people who find good things in it," nonetheless "if we want to understand this movement with its various branches, we cannot stay with the Bible but need to reach the aspects of faith and psychology which lie beneath this attitude to scripture."[98] It is the relentless pursuit of the psychology of fundamentalism that sets his work apart from that of his fellow Catholics, although many, including the bishops, take regular and brief steps into individual and social psychology. Although he told his readers that "psychology is not the author's field, and the following insights do not claim to be theoretically or scientifically verified," he nonetheless claimed a validity for them arising from his twenty years' experience in seminaries and universities, his experience with fundamentalists of various sorts, and his own theology of nature and grace. The latter demands that he pay attention to the psychology of a theological or religious position. Thus, he put himself in the curious position of making an analysis of a sort he was not qualified to offer, yet insisting that it is an accurate portrait.

The basic thesis of the analysis was that change produces anxiety, and that the flight from anxiety can involve a distortion of the human psyche.[99] Such change characterizes contemporary America, and the result is an increase in the incidence and appeal of fundamentalism, the signs of which are elitism, the desire for certitude, anxiety before diversity and change, rigidity, compulsive behavior, and anger. The portrait was painted at some length in the fourth chapter, "the psychology of fundamentalism," but was not confined there. It pervaded the book.[100] So pervasive was it, in fact, that it overshadowed and perhaps in the end even undercut his hope to present a convincing contrast of the two religious and theological worlds.

For the portrait violates a methodological directive commonly held among scholars of religion and theologians, namely, a rejection of psychological reduction: you must not do unto others what you would not have done unto you. That precept was hard-won in the world of the study of religion as well as in the relations between religious communities and between their theologians. We are familiar with the caricature, indeed the parody, of Catholicism easily erected on the same principles of analysis followed by O'Meara. We are left by him with a psychological counterpart to the fundamentalist apocalyptic caricatures of Catholicism, and the drumbeat of political fear that the Catholic laity are sheep in the hands of a manipulative priesthood.[101]

Finally, perhaps in order to avoid criticizing individuals, O'Meara wrote in a code that makes it very difficult to know to what he was responding. For example, in sketching the "new ecumenism" that unites Protestant and Catholic fundamentalists in common effort to shape contemporary Catholicism to their liking (a conspiracy which is *prima facie* unlikely), we are left guessing at his specific meaning: "neo-conservative political theorists" may mean Michael Novak and George Weigel; "Protestants . . . who might become mentors of the Catholic Church today" might be Richard John Neuhaus who, at the time of writing, had not yet become a Catholic; "antiquarians fascinated by the ritual and organization of the Catholic Church" might be Anglo-Catholics who have entered or profess interest in entering the church; but, then again, they might not. There follows a section reprimanding the "outsider" or "tourist" for misunderstanding Catholicism, and a warning to "recent converts" who have "a shallow or skewed understanding of Catholicism," yet are not identified.[102] In addition to finding it impossible to identify the "new ecumenists," it is equally impossible to know just what his worry about the "new ecumenism" was. Did he think that the interdenominational right wing of American Christianity was combining or conspiring to make life difficult for Catholic moderates and liberals? O'Meara lapsed into the papal habit of avoiding specification of his enemies and leaving it to waves of interpreters to figure it out and apply it. He has created a piece of literature the adequate interpretation of which calls for a practiced apocalypticist![103]

All of these books remain intensely practical and do not become theoretic or scholarly. Even when they are written by scholars, they display no interest in fundamentalism, fundamentalist thought and practice, or in fundamentalists themselves, except insofar as they impinge on Catholics and the Catholic Church. We cannot say, then, that there is a Catholic scholarship of fundamentalism evident in monographs.

# 13

# Bishops Again and the Vatican

To put the statements of American bishops on fundamentalism in perspective, one has only to recall the years of preparation and consultation, and then the waves of subsequent reaction and analysis, to their statements on war and peace and on the American economy.[1] By way of contrast, in 1987 a small committee of the National Conference of Catholic Bishops (NCCB), including three archbishops and three auxiliary bishops (two of the six trained scripture scholars), composed and approved "A Pastoral Statement for Catholics on Biblical Fundamentalism." This received little public attention.

The letter was addressed to "our Catholic brothers and sisters who may be attracted to Biblical Fundamentalism without realizing its serious weaknesses . . . to remind our faithful of the fullness of Christianity that God has provided in the Catholic Church." The letter offered no attempt to analyze fundamentalism theologically or historically but treated it as a "general approach to life which is typified by unyielding adherence to rigid doctrinal and ideological positions." The letter's criticism of fundamentalism was threefold: fundamentalist biblicism eliminates the church from Christianity; it ignores the historicity of the Bible itself, distorts the meaning of the Catholic doctrine of inerrancy, and ends in a hermeneutical leap from the Bible to contemporary life; and it offers simple and confident answers to complex questions:

> The appeal is evident for the Catholic young adult or teenager—one whose family background may be troubled; who is struggling with life, morality and religion; whose Catholic

education may have been seriously inadequate in the fundamentals of doctrine, the Bible, prayer life and sacramental living; whose cate-chetical formation may have been inadequate in presenting the full Catholic traditions and teaching authority. For such a person, the ap-peal of finding *the* answer in a devout, studious, prayerful, warm, Bible-quoting class is easy to understand. But the ultimate problem with such Fundamentalism is that it can only give a limited number of answers and cannot present those answers on balance, because it does not have Christ's teaching church, nor even an understanding of how the Bible originally came to be written and collected in the sacred canon or official list of inspired books.[2]

The opening attack on fundamentalism as a psychological attitude of ri-gidity and as primarily a problem for the immature and uncertain youth vitiates the letter's brief presentation of a contrast between fundamentalist and Cath-olic doctrines, leaving the reader with the impression (once again) that the bishops' responsibility is exhausted by a warning and a simple contrast. The saving grace of the letter was its admission that "the Catholic Church in the past did not encourage bible study as much as she could have" and that there is currently need for better homilies, warmer liturgical atmosphere, and greater familiarity with the Bible through parish study and faith-sharing groups.

The bishops of Alabama and Mississippi on June 29, 1989, issued their own letter, "Toward Your Happiness: Catholicism and Fundamentalism, A Contrast."[3] It opened with a review of the economic, political, and cultural grounds for the uncertainty and confusion current in American life, a confu-sion to which even the Catholic Church seems liable. The bishops made out the present as a season of opportunity and promise ("After all, the same age that produced Kohemeni produced Mother Teresa of Calcutta."). But the bish-ops saw that fundamentalism offers Catholics "a false security." From an essay by Bill J. Leonard, a Baptist historian, they took a sketch of the origins of the fundamentalist movement, and reached the conclusion that "the fundamen-talists were looking for simple solutions to the increasingly complex problems of life."

Positions deemed common among fundamentalists are scored by the bish-ops. The fundamentalists have an unreasonable certainty about the meaning of scripture texts regardless of context; a simplistic certainty of salvation in-stantaneously achieved; a sense of personal security that identifies God's way with "the American way," namely, with rugged individualism and self-sufficiency; and an intimacy with God that excludes others (i.e., the church). At the end, the bishops added a fifth doctrine, dualism of the world and the kingdom, which they apparently drew from fundamentalist apocalypticism, and contrasted it with Catholic cultural incarnationalism.[4]

The familiar Catholic teaching on these matters was put forth: one cannot understand even the existence of the scriptures much less interpret them apart from the church that determined the canon to begin with. Again, while many American values are to be cherished by Christians, others must be rejected as "exaggerated and selfish." Finally, the incarnation implies commitment to this world, to its peace and well-being, as well as to the world to come. The function of Christian faith—and of the Bible within the church—is to provide hope and direction as the Christian community makes its way through history. Catholics do not despair of the world and flee to God, *solus cum solo*. They celebrate the gifts of creation and redemption ". . . with unparalleled joy. That is why the Eucharist, the greatest sign of our unity in sharing God's life, is the sun and center of our lives."

The bishops ended with a set of recommendations to the church meant to help Catholics avoid "the temptations and dangers of fundamentalism and at the same time discover that confidence and hope to which the Lord calls all true disciples": Bible reading and study; improved preaching; transformation of parishes into "communities of God's love" through Cursillo, charismatic prayer groups, retreat movements, and social ministry. Beware, they say, for "we will not find peace and joy in a simplistic manipulation of biblical texts or in some instantaneous and emotional religious experience." Rather, Christians will find the yoke of discipleship in the world. Once again, as in the case of the NCCB letter, these bishops located the problem in the age and in false teaching that has a surface attraction, and once again they called for changes in Catholic practice to counter that attraction. Once again, they offered a contrast of true doctrine to false.

Bishop John Liebrecht of Springfield and Cape Girardeau (Missouri), on November 8, 1988, wrote a letter to his flock entitled "Sharing God's Life Together: Being Catholic in the Bible Belt."[5] It is the longest and most interesting of the episcopal documents. It is animated, I think, by a quite different spirit and adopts a markedly different strategy from those of his brother bishops. He opens by expressing his admiration for the faith of his non-Catholic neighbors and writes to explain Catholic belief to his own people who may sometimes find their neighbors' religious language "confusing . . . frightening or irritating," and does so by offering a reflection on "the kinds of questions and issues we encounter among our neighbors." He then writes successive sections on the topics of salvation, the church, worship and prayer, mission and hierarchical authority, the Holy Spirit, the Bible and tradition, and Mary, thereby following closely the list of topics ever-present in evangelical criticism of the Catholic Church. I will take the first as an example of the strategy pursued in the others.

When a Catholic is asked "Are you saved?" he or she is often shaken, first because Catholics are not used to talking easily about their religious life and, second, because Catholics do not speak about it in these terms. The question is aimed at a very specific sort of religious experience, "being born again," in which we are "confronted" by God and "surrendered to him." The bishop hopes that every Catholic has had such experiences of Christ and of the presence of God in life. He himself has had several, and they are blessings. But the Catholic doctrine of salvation is broader. It is not the work of a moment but of a lifetime of our gradual entry into God's life, not only of God's entry into ours. "Catholics have peak religious experiences in life, but 'being saved' [in Catholic terms] is not such a singular peak experience. It is a life-long process of growing in the gifts God gives us."

This section of the letter, and those that follow, amount to a "mystagogical catechesis," an introduction to the fuller meaning of the Christian faith rather than an attack on the weaknesses of others. Unquestionably there are contrasts made and implied, for the topics for reflection are chosen from the chief evangelical criticisms of the church, but there is no offensive mounted and there is a pedagogically effective strategy of unfolding Roman Catholic self-understanding on issues of mutual concern. Bishop Leibrecht has adopted the standard procedure of dialogue, namely, spelling out one's own position without attacking the position of the dialogue partner. The bishop's doctrine a fundamentalist will in all likelihood reject but will, along with the Catholics to whom it is addressed, find herself better instructed. There is no anger or annoyance, no accusation, no attempt to explain fundamentalist belief away, and no invidious comparison. The entire focus of the letter is an explanation of Catholic faith, rather than a refutation of the faith of others.

Among the American bishops at the time, Archbishop John Whealon of Hartford showed the most concern with fundamentalism. He chaired the NCCB committee that wrote the 1987 letter and wrote two essays on the subject, appearing in *America* in 1985 and 1986.[6] The titles, "Fighting Fundamentalism" and "Challenging Fundamentalism," express well the alarm with which he viewed the situation: biblical fundamentalism poses "a "massive challenge" to the clergy and catechists.

In the first essay, little more than a summary of the analysis and characterization of fundamentalism found in the NCCB letter to be released two years later, Whealon urges that the means are at hand to meet the challenge in the form of the lectionary, a new translation of the scriptures, the second edition of the *Jerome Biblical Commentary* (released shortly thereafter), commentaries, books, tapes, and so on. The answer to the fundamentalist challenge is "to get this knowledge into the minds and hearts of all our Catholic teachers and students, and also to get it into our textbooks in a way that shows a knowledge and love of the Bible."[7]

The second essay describes at length an address of Archbishop Whealon's attended by a large crowd of Catholics and fundamentalists, the latter apparently including a good number of former Catholics. In the address, he summed up reasons to admire fundamentalist churches—"Their love of the Bible. . . . Their spirit of warmth and friendliness. Their care for other members of the congregation. Their dedication to Jesus Christ. Their moral standards. Their missionary outreach."[8] But he noted their deficiencies as well: no authoritative church, their defective ecclesiology, their truncated doctrinal sense, their lack of devotion to Mary and the saints, the absence of a sacramental life, their mistaken notion of inerrancy, and the absence of interest in ecumenism and social justice. He noted in the vigorous discussion period that followed that, while anti-Catholicism is present in some forms of fundamentalism, ". . . most Fundamentalists or Evangelical churches in the United States . . . are not anti-Catholic. They are interested only in living according to Jesus Christ and the Bible."

Archbishop Whealon admitted that statistics are hard to come by, but had no doubt that "hundreds of thousands of baptized Catholics have for one reason or another abandoned their Catholic faith for a 'Bible church'." What is the Catholic responsibility in this matter? An evangelical minister of a growing church in Waterbury told him that 80 percent of his congregation consisted of former Catholics and that the Catholic Church was doing a poor job of holding on to its own people. Whealon lists the reasons: catechetical efforts are failing to produce educated Catholics; Catholic sense of identity is weak; evangelization efforts must be increased in parishes; in spite of the resources available, Catholics are not "Bible-reading, Bible-loving, Bible-quoting, Bible-living . . ." people, a state of religious living of which he approves and desires for Catholics. In the end he quotes the pope on the need for prayer and immersion in scripture interpreted in the light of tradition so that one can "resist the temptation to place one's personal interpretation above or even in opposition to the authentic interpretation of God's word that belongs exclusively to the bishops of the church in union with the Pope."[9] The archbishop was in fact challenging Catholics leaders to resist the challenge posed to Catholicism by fundamentalists rather than challenging fundamentalists. In the usage adopted here, he wanted the Catholic Church to become a biblical Christianity while remaining a liturgical Christianity. In order to "challenge" and to "fight" fundamentalism, it is necessary that Catholics become a biblical people subject to the Magisterium. His challenge amounted to an effort at retention.

Several Vatican secretariats cooperated in collecting data from national episcopal conferences and other sources to produce a "Vatican Report on Sects, Cults and New Religious Movements."[10] The document was concerned with a more general and geographically widespread phenomenon than the impact of Christian fundamentalism on American Catholicism. But the concern surely included the American problem, and set it in the broader context of an international church struggling with its identity and defining its reactions to religious pluralism as well as to the ebb and flow of the religious interests and inclinations of a billion souls in hundreds of cultures. The document has its shortcomings, both in terms of the conceptuality drawn from the human sciences (e.g., a derogatory definition of sects and cults) and its theological rationale (there is no *theological* understanding of defection in evidence), but it both reflects current attitudes of Catholic leaders toward the challenges and will help shape the future reactions and strategies.[11] It is an official attempt to face what appears to be a huge difficulty in several parts of the Roman vineyard.[12]

What is the situation that the Vatican tries to explain? The concern is the phenomenon of massive loss of Catholics to these "sects and cults," precisely the same motive evident in the American bishops' response to fundamentalism. How does the Vatican explain the situation? In three ways. First, there are unmet needs and aspirations that the new religions meet. These are universal, and Catholicism itself seeks to meet them: the desire for community, for clear and decisive answers to questions of meaning, the desire for wholeness, for cultural identity, for personal recognition and importance, for a conviction of transcendence, for specific spiritual guidance, for hope, for participation and involvement. Not only do they offer to meet the needs and aspirations in word but also ". . . the sects seem to live by what they believe, with powerful (often magnetic) conviction, devotion, and commitment."[13] Momentarily, at least, the document has at hand an experiential point of contrast between the new religions and the old, namely, vital religions work and tired religions do not.

Second, the new religions use recruitment and conversion techniques that are underhanded and directed toward unworthy goals. They aim at achieving mind control by adopting abusive behavior modification techniques (1.5; 2.2). They may meet legitimate needs, but they do so inhumanely. They rob people of freedom.[14] In agreement with some of the American Catholic critics of fundamentalism, the Vatican psychologizes conversion to other religious bodies. But there are significant problems with this "explanation," not the least of which is the fact that it might explain Catholicism itself:

> Ironically, by framing the problem of religious pluralism partially,
> but not entirely, in the rhetoric of coercion, the Vatican report lends
> credibility to a perspective laden with secular and behavioral science
> assumptions. The brain-washing/mind-control metaphor implicitly
> medicalizes many realities of religious life and commitment, denies
> free will and conversion and legitimates a Freudian psychoanalytic
> bias in which virtually all religious experience is viewed as regres-
> sive. It is also a perspective that, when emphasized, obviates the
> need for critical examination and structural change within the
> church itself.[15]

The last point, the avoidance of self-criticism, is a rule of Catholic "corporate culture" to which I will return later. The medical metaphor we have already come across in both the periodical literature and monographs, and it is the rhetorical technique in the Catholic response to fundamentalism that is most open to methodological and theological objection. Its use also reveals how deeply the sects' gains among the nominally Catholic population has disturbed the otherwise urbane ecumenical rhetoric of theologians and bishops. When the sheep no longer recognize the voice of the shepherd, false shepherds are blamed.

The Vatican's solution to the problem called for a more holistic pastoral care by Catholic ministers, an increased inculturation of Catholic religious practice, especially prayer and worship ". . . with due respect for the nature of the liturgy and for the demands of universality"[16] and increased lay leadership and participation. The Vatican wanted the local churches to better meet the "needs and aspirations" it listed. It warned against naive irenicism, which overlooks the "ideological" and "economic forces" sometimes at work in the sects (perhaps an expression of worry that socially and politically conservative American groups are supporting evangelical missions in Latin America); it called on church leaders to exercise special care for the young; and it admitted that the Vatican II response to "other churches and religions" (dialogue) will fail in the case of the new religions. The Vatican was not at all interested in dialogue with them, whereas it cherishes dialogue with nonthreatening mainline Protestant churches.

Nonetheless, lest its concern be taken as a reversal of its positive and constructive attitude toward other religions, the Vatican did not want any diminishment of "true ecumenism." In fact, and in the end, the document was not satisfied with a negative response to the problem: "The challenge of the new religious movements is to stimulate our own renewal for a greater pastoral efficacy."[17] The document on the whole presented a balance of tensions evident in the other literature, voicing at the same time concern for a threat perceived to be huge and recommendations for "more of the same" solutions, with little or no sense that other possibilities of explanation and response exist. For example, the question is never raised whether Catholicism, under certain circumstances and perhaps even constitutionally, is unable to meet some "legitimate needs and aspirations," nor is the possibility faced that a radical change in Catholic practice may be called for, or that its understanding of the "demands of universality" may be seriously askew. The Catholic response remains Roman.

Finally, most suspect of all is the Vatican's explanatory appeal to cultural breakdown:

> A breakdown of traditional social structures, cultural patterns and
> traditional sets of values caused by industrialization, urbanization,
> migration, rapid development of communications systems, all-
> rational technological systems, etc. leave many individuals confused,
> uprooted, insecure and therefore vulnerable. In these situations
> there is naturally a search for a solution, and the simpler the better.

There is also the temptation to accept the solution as the only and final answer.[18]

But these are the very conditions under which religions, including Catholicism and Protestant Christianity, came into existence and spread, took root and prospered. Presumably they prospered because they spoke effectively and truthfully to the human situation, something that the prevalent religion did not. This is not to deny that breakdowns do occur, nor that they present grave difficulties, nor that religion is quite properly strongly linked to social and personal breakdowns. It is only to say that the appeal shows a startling lack of historical self-understanding, one that can be understood religiously as another example of the "mote and the beam."

The paragraphs on fundamentalism in a statement of the Pontifical Biblical Commission on biblical interpretation repeated most of the charges made against fundamentalism by theologians and by the preceding magisterial documents. The final paragraph was particularly unfortunate: it is stated or suggested that fundamentalism is "dangerous," deceptive, "illusory," an invitation to "intellectual suicide," and "injects into life a false certitude." The document displays a measured and balanced response to other "methods," including liberation theology and feminism, but explodes with revulsion toward fundamentalism. [19]

The episcopal and Vatican literature has its aims, the most evident of which is to warn Catholics. The bishops clearly think that the situation is no minor statistical variation, but poses a significant pastoral threat. The bishops know that Catholics are vulnerable to appeals from fundamentalists and other "sectarians." They must offer an explanation, and they do so in terms of the characteristics of the age and culture. They must propose a remedy, and so they do in specific terms of pastoral renewal and reform. But this, too, is not enough. They must not only explain the appeal of fundamentalism and the fact of widespread conversion of Catholics, but they must point out the doctrinal inadequacies and mistaken practices of fundamentalists. As fundamentalists turn to the Bible to "prove" that Catholicism is not Christian, so the bishops turn to Catholic doctrine and practice to indicate the inadequacies of the fundamentalist understanding and practice of Christianity. As fundamentalists might "explain" Catholicism as a diabolical distortion of the Christian faith, so the bishops' reach into widely accepted views of the peculiarities of the age and into popular psychological notions to explain the success and attraction of fundamentalism. One of the stark differences between the approaches of the two is that the aggressive evangelization of Catholics is not in the least matched by the Catholic literature, official and otherwise. The bishops do not target fundamentalists for evangelization; their writings are defensive, not evangelistic. Nor do they mention the small but significant defections of evangelicals from their churches to the Catholic Church. In this, they continue the centuries-long habit of American Catholics, that of minding their own religious business. For all their official talk of "evangelization," and for the one hundred thousand converts to the American church each year, Catholics are not convert hunters.

Although it may be out of place here, I cannot pass from the episcopal and Roman material without mentioning an essay in criticism of the National Conference of Catholic Bishops' statement by a former Catholic and now a conservative Protestant, Mark Christensen, a man who has himself done what has prompted this twenty year flurry of Catholic literature. He thinks ". . . the bishops' statement has addressed only a fraction of the problem"[20] when it traces the problem to a quest for certainty and acceptance of simple answers to complex questions. The problem is that Catholicism is a culture as well as a religion, and obscures Christ:

> . . . the difficulty we had with Catholicism was that this same power-
> ful force that had done such great things in history also over-
> shadows and obscures Christ! The effect of the obscurity for me was
> that, while I certainly grew up knowing about Jesus, I never realized
> who He is or why He came to earth in the first place. I knew Ca-
> tholicism. Like Theresa and my other ex-Catholic friends, I have
> been shaped by Catholicism as religious system and culture—but I
> never heard the gospel. . . . For reasons I don't nearly understand,
> millions of other former Catholics besides myself couldn't hear this
> Gospel within the Catholic Church. I urge Catholic leaders in this
> country to ask themselves why their most potentially ardent mem-
> bers must go elsewhere to find their spiritual food.[21]

In the literature as a whole the authors, whether popularizers or professional theologians or bishops, show little sign of any serious interest in fundamentalist or evangelical theology.[22] That is, they do not convey the impression that there is any respectable intellectual life in biblical Christianity. One finds no more than a cursory knowledge of its intellectual history or its important texts. Nor do the distinctions between the subgroupings of biblical Christians appear that are so important to understanding the movement and responding to it. Moreover, very little of the literature presents a program for dialogue, common reflection, or common action. In this respect, ECT is a thorough departure from tradition for Catholics as well as evangelicals.

One is forced to the conclusion that, were biblical Christians to give up evangelism and stop enticing Catholics into their communities, the Catholic literature would cease. Biblical Christianity apparently raises no theologically or religiously significant questions for Catholics. The case is quite different with Catholic reactions to liberal and neo-orthodox Protestant theology in the wake of Vatican II. The work of Tillich, Bultmann, Barth, Pannenberg, and others has been crucial for many Catholic theologians. Protestantism was taken as both an intellectual and spiritual opportunity for Catholics, but none of this appears in the literature on fundamentalism. Even the material on its best behavior displays little or no intellectual (as distinct from practical) curiosity; in fact, the various strata of the evangelical movement up to the *ECT* have been chiefly an object of defense, alarm, and scorn.

Moreover, there is a sobering irony to bishops' warning Catholics about biblical Christianity. The leaders of that Western religious community which most vociferously and dogmatically opposed the Enlightenment, and who created a vast counterculture in opposition to it, and which was opposed bitterly by it, must now warn their flock about simplistic and dogmatic Christian answers to the complex problems and stresses of the modern world! There is a further irony in the leaders of a church that, for most of a century, asserted without fear of contradiction both doctrines and theological opinions that their successors now with furrowed brow denounce in fundamentalists. What is absent from episcopal and Vatican letters is an even rudimentary interest in fundamentalism itself, no fellow-feeling for it, and no grasp of the possibility that it represents a serious alternative understanding of Christianity. The bishops and the Vatican are defending souls and tribal turf. They are capable of dealing reasonably with the possibility of nuclear war and with a systematically unjust economy, and of bringing spiritual and intellectual light to those topics, but they can only deal with a competitor Christianity as a threat. Still, and thankfully, there remains that slice of the literature embodying calm analysis and constructive interpretation of biblical Christianity by men such as Francis X. Cleary, S.J., and Bishop John Leibrecht, on which advances in the relationship between the two communities such as *ECT* could count.

# 14

# Conclusion: The Lion and the Lamb

Confession

Frederick Woodbridge, an influential Columbia University naturalist philosopher, wrote that individuality is a metaphysical fact.[1] His comment provides a starting point for an admission to the limits placed on my work by "perspective," part of the metaphysical fact of my individuality. History lived (my past and yours) and history written (our past caught in a perspective) have to be understood in the light of this. I would not have bothered to read and write had these two religious communities not caught my spirit, nor would I have written had I not thought it might prove worthwhile for them. Although I am only in a marginal way engaged in the discussion between them, I have an intellectual and spiritual commitment to both and to their well-being. That is part of my individuality and my perspective. Although I have tried throughout to be disinterested, I could not for a moment claim to be detached. I have rarely been the latter, and only with great effort have I ever been the former.

Catholic theology as a practice has had little appeal for me since my seminary days (1953–61), and less and less as time has gone by, for Catholic theology is not only ecclesial (which it must be to be Catholic) but also ecclesiastical (for me a sad fact). The first means that its foundation is the lived experience and intellectual tradition of Catholicism, and the second means that it falls under the hierarchical authorities of the Catholic Church. While I like being Catholic, I confess a personal antipathy for the controls and the attitudes of the caste that runs the Catholic religion, although I confess as readily that I am glad they do what they do. Someone has to, and they often do a decent job.

I know that the Catholicism I love, the *res catholica*, the community of people and the complex of practice, symbols, beliefs, aesthetic perception and artistic product, and theological achievement would not be what it is without the higher and lower clergy and all their pomps and works. As it is, I would describe myself as a communitarian liberal in politics, a catholic who is Catholic in his confession and in his culture, a man who hopes that "Christianity" is other than what evangelicals stereotypically take it to be in practice, belief, and theology, and a person who finds argument over religion and theological apologetics and dogmatics as it has been practiced by theologians distasteful, albeit fascinating as a subject of study. My antipathy is explained by the fact that I am not much of a team player. The Roman Catholic hierarchy is a great idea in theory but I would not want a daughter of mine to marry one of them— or, for that matter, marry a university or corporation president. Part of that dispositional immediacy of my psyche is a lack of ease with people who possess power and wield it. I find the wielding especially objectionable in religious matters. I do not object to authority, but I do object to power and the uses of it. This fact goes a long way toward explaining my sympathy for the Protestant critique of my church.

A lot has gone into this book, not least years of reading and teaching, and much more into its "attitude" and the curve with which the book is pitched. My father, who arrived in New York from Cobh in 1927, told me in my grammar school years that while I should respect the priests of the church, I should always remember that they do not know very much about life—about the things that went on between people outside the rectory, the things that escaped their notice and interest, or failed to win their approval. For example, he told me that I should never think that Jews were somehow less in the eyes of God than Christians. He knew that because he worked closely with Jews in his business and he found them more helpful to him and honest than he found his fellow Catholics, and made his friends among them. He didn't think the priests knew the truth about Jews. He also told me, and later wrote it in an autobiography, that "Negroes" deserved the same respect as whites. He worked with them, too, and once got into a fistfight with his job foreman who had insulted a black co-worker. He won the fight and lost the job. He and I both knew that some of our Irish American priests didn't care much for "Negroes." My father's side of the family were shanty Irish and my mother's lace-curtain Irish, but neither side cared for Jews and African Americans, as I recall. I have had a hard time being patient with bullies, anti-Semites, and bigots as a result of my father's doctrine, and felt that he held views odd in our east Bronx neighborhood, and, indeed, in his family and among his in-laws.

Protestants were another matter. Whereas Irish Catholics have no good historical reason to disdain Jews and African Americans, they have plenty of reason to disdain Protestants, especially the British varieties. My four Shea aunts and uncles from Ireland and my two Power aunts born in the Bronx were good Catholics and, like the priests, regarded Protestants as unfortunate people who were probably doomed because they did not belong to the true church and because they oppressed the Catholic Irish. My father regarded Protestants as peculiar ("they walk sideways, like a crab on the beach," he would say to make me laugh, "not straight forward like Catholics"). I was never to doubt where my loyalties lay and which people were my people. But he also told me soberly that the catechism and the priests were wrong to say that Protestants would not go to heaven because they didn't belong to the true church. He didn't know how they would get there (he wasn't a theologian!), but he was sure they would. Before my father was born—the sixth of nine children—his father and mother were disinherited and "put out on the road" by his grandfather's second wife. It was a Protestant family, the Powers, who gave them a cottage and a quarter of an acre of land to live on in Kilmoogue and who charged them no more than a shilling a year, and that only to save my grandfather's pride. The Powers would go to heaven, he knew, no matter what the priests said.

When I arrived at St. Joseph's Seminary in 1955, I soon discovered that a room in the new library had been set aside for Protestant anti-Catholic literature. Many an afternoon study period I spent there, skipping through the likes of Maria Monk and Rebecca Reed, anti-Jesuit novels, Josiah Strong and dogmatic tracts, no-popery literature and denunciations of Catholic compromise with paganism and Judaism, and highly excited pamphlets on the Blessed Virgin. I don't remember seeing any other seminarian in the room and can't recall at this moment a single conversation about the room and its contents. It seemed my secret room, a place to go when I was so monumentally bored by my scholastic theology textbooks that I couldn't stand another minute with them.[2] The room provided me with a slant on things other than that offered by my church history and theology textbooks. In class books, I was left no doubt about who was right and who was wrong and why. The Protestant literature shocked and amused me no end. Why, after a forty-year hiatus, I should return to such stuff is mysterious. It no longer shocks or amuses me, but to this day it interests me.

I knew about Lutherans, Presbyterians, and Methodists only in the broadest historical terms and through personal, if fleeting, ecumenical circumstances over the twenty years in which I exercised priestly ministry in New York and Washington. My deepest and best Protestant contact was with Protestant existentialist and neo-orthodox theologians such as Bultmann, Barth, Brunner, Tillich, the Niebuhrs, and, later, Schubert Ogden, whose work in fundamental theology and Christology fascinated me and whose tense, lucid, and utterly logical prose wore me out. They took the place of the scholastic philosophers and theologians who for six years I was required to read. Evangelicals in the American usage I did not come to know until I married in 1980 and was forced to resign an associate professorship at the Catholic University of America. This brought me to the religious studies department at the University of South Florida in Tampa. In the classrooms of that young and bustling university, I was met by large numbers of Southern Baptists, Southern Presbyterians of the Church of Christ and the Assemblies of God, Navigators, and Campus Crusaders. They didn't strike me as members of the same tribe as Bultmann, Barth, or Ogden. I got interested fast. What interested me most was the battle they waged (even against Catholic professors!) to uphold the Bible and the extraordinary price they were willing to pay for doctrinal purity. I had little idea at the outset that anti-Catholicism was so much a part of their heritage and so I made no connection between them and my secret room in the seminary library.

At the beginning of each new section of my courses in New Testament introduction and Jesus' Life and Teachings I would announce that I was a Roman Catholic, and a student or two would leave immediately. At the end of the first class in the second trimester, a young lady approached me and *sotto voce* asked: "Are you born again, Dr. Shea?" I said something to the effect that Catholics like me get born again regularly, a cute answer that I now regret. She knew I was not a member of the same tribe as she—she left and dropped the course. She had my number. How could a person still in the old Adam teach New Testament to a person in Christ? That was my personal introduction to American evangelicalism. I then had a connection to what I had heard on Sunday morning while running the AM band. I got a small grant the following summer and spent the two months in the library reading about revivals, the frontier, and fundamentalists.

When I resigned the priesthood in 1980, I experienced a surprising sense of release from two small weights of my life: first, I would not have to preside at the Eucharist and preach again, and, second, I would not in a classroom have to think of myself and behave as an ecclesiastical theologian. I conceived the great joy of being a lay Catholic and a teacher of religions including my own. Although I had and still have admiration for the work done by my theologian colleagues at Catholic University of America, I was and remain unable to place myself and my own work as part of a Christian mission or as in any way representative of the teaching *magisterium* of the Catholic Church.

While I am a sacramentalist in my feeling and thinking when it comes to detecting the grace of God in things and actions, in sacramental signs and marital love, and in the very existence of the Church, I long ago found the aura of sacrality surrounding Catholic clerical life to be objectionable and suffocating. It initially attracted me, but in the end repelled me. That sacrality draws many lines. Although affirming the religious values and the value of the beliefs of the Catholic Church, and much of its way of life and its discipline, I also think that the biggest mistake the church (the whole church and not just the clergy) has made historically is the way in which it has idealized and sanctified its hierarchic structure. What the church leaders think is a divinely established pecking order I conclude to be a solution to a set of problems facing the Christian churches between the second and the fourth centuries, one that I find to be often effective but just as often dispensable. Not that I would recommend that it be dispensed with, for I do not find any other established church polity significantly more attractive or promising, but still it is wearing on the human (and perhaps the divine) spirit that these men made so much of themselves and their work, and have shown themselves unable so often to listen to anyone but each other and their superiors. The disappointment of the past year (2002) in the bishops' handling of clerical sexual abuse has only served to confirm my decades-old dislike and distrust of them as a group. Instead of seeing ministerial structure as emergent service to life, they see it as designed in eternity, imposed on history, and isolated from ordinary life. This is a great burden slung on the church's shoulders: the sacredness of the priestly caste. Luther and Calvin saw this clearly, yet made a series of silly and damaging judgments about it. They put Satan at the design table. They tried to destroy something that was a good idea but needed reformation. It still needs reformation. The Protestant reform did not help in this regard; it served to turn up the Catholic sacral gas and, as a result, the clerical balloon ascended even higher.

But this is not a book about the papacy and the episcopacy, although they play a large role in the narrative—it is a book about evangelicals and Catholics. Now that I have had my say about some of the peculiarities of my perspective and acquitted my conscience on that score, I return to the topic.

## Hypotheses and Assumptions

I have asserted frequently as a broad historical context for my discussion an evangelical rethinking of the gospel and culture institutionalized in the National Association of Evangelicals and the Catholic version of that rethinking at Vatican II. That this context is debatable I gladly admit. I think it will withstand criticism, but whether it holds or not, the end of Christendom does not mean the churches' uneasiness with modernity has ended. To bury Christendom is not to marry modernity. If *ECT* proves anything, it is that conservative evangelical and Catholic leaders understand and accept this. They were anxious to make their way in the world but not on the world's terms. They sought to bring the gospel message back to the public square, not to take the square over (I hope!), nor to be taken over by it.

When Catholics face contemporary biblical Christianity, they see a reflection of their own church's reaction to important features of modern world.[3] Both Catholics and evangelicals have in common a quality of experience that the American diplomat George Kennan recently admitted about himself, that he remained a "guest of one's time and not a member of its household." As the beloved disciple wrote: "We know that we belong to God and the whole world is under the power of the evil one" (I John 5:19).[4] The Roman Catholic Church has passed through a vigorous struggle with modern culture, and its struggle peaked at the same time as the American Protestant battles over Modernism, when the twentieth-century fundamentalist form of evangelical Protestantism appeared. Because of its doctrinal and organizational differences from Protestantism, the Roman Catholic Church solved its difficulties with theological modernism differently and more effectively. In the nineteenth and the twentieth century, the popes denounced political democracy, freedom of religion, a free press, the separation of church and state—as well as economic exploitation of workers by capitalists and the weakening of the family. The popes and their men regarded Catholics who showed any interest in a constructive engagement with modern culture and politics with grave suspicion, and theologians who attempted to adopt and adapt modern methods of historical study were excommunicated or cowed into silence. Metaphorical blood was shed. The name for this Roman Catholic version of fundamentalism is *integralism;* it is the dominant form of the Roman Catholic reaction to modernity from the French Revolution to the second Vatican Council.[5] It remains a powerful weapon in the Roman Catholic tribal armament today.[6] Essentially, and at its most ambitious, integralism is the Catholic reaction to the totalizing tendency of modern naturalism, calling for the creation of a Catholic culture capable of excluding naturalism, a Catholic counterpart to the America fundamentalist cultural separatism and eschatology.

Nor has the Roman Catholic *aggiornamento* with its new affirmative engagement of modern culture and politics removed the Catholic suspicion of Western secularism and its systematized appetites for wealth and markets. Surely this vigorous Catholic response to the modern secular organization of life delivers a platform for conversation and cooperation with biblical Christians. If negative characterizing of one another were to be replaced by exploration of common interest in mitigating the effects of Enlightenment instrumentalism and pseudoprogress, then surely Christians will learn and the world will change.

Still there is residual and justified concern about leaders of both communities and their sanctified appetites for control of culture and politics. Still some evangelicals hanker after a Christian America, still some Catholics want public morality bound to Catholic moral teaching, still there is the common appeal to a natural law unbreakable even by those who do not recognize it. George Mavrodes, an evangelical philosopher of note, recently warned of that deep Christian yearning for Christendom.[7] But it seems to me that the respective recognitions of the end of the Catholic dream of a restored Christendom, and of a Protestant nation and an evangelical empire, are decisive and final.[8]

To long for Christendom at this point would be akin to a Muslim dream of a revival of the Caliphate.[9]

Other circumstances and conditions impel evangelical and Catholic conversation: the brute, experiential facts of another century of war, the Holocaust, policies legalizing abortion and threatening to legalize mercy killing and suicide, and American cultural and religious pluralism. In common evangelicals and Catholics have found out how far tribal hatred and fear have taken the modern world, and both know what happens in a society that no longer believes in life. Even were the two sides not Christian, these circumstances would drive them into one another's arms. The same circumstances have forced a change in Catholic ways of speaking about Jews, and brought the pope to pray with an unusual assortment of religious leaders from round the world's religion.

## The Protestant Problem

I want to be careful at this point, for I do not want to get into the theological side of the debate, although to avoid it seems impossible. On the one hand, there are questions of my competence and, on the other, my interest. My interest, so far as it is theological at all, is in the theology of the church and its mediation of religious meaning in history. That, to my understanding, is the theological point at issue between Protestants and Catholics. The tumultuous battle over faith, grace, and freedom, once one realizes all three terms have limited and partial meaning in concrete experience and bear on the mystery of the soul, has become to me the outline of an unlighted ship passing in nearly complete darkness. I have to force myself to pay attention, whereas I am caught immediately by Arianism, Gnosticism, and the historical and social existence of the church. The study of evangelical and Catholic exchanges has lead me to the conclusion that the problem on both sides is primarily imagination, its limits and uses—as it is with Arianism, Gnosticism, and the structure of the church. Catholics and evangelicals have biases (some would say convictions, I suppose) so powerful that their imaginings of each other, both eschatological and historical, have at times become Manichean in their dimensions. I ask: Are these people living in the same world, and are they living in the same world I am? First, the evangelical side.

The charges historically made against the Catholic Church, except the ones that can be made just as well against Protestants (for example, murder of the saints in the wars of religion and persecution), do not add up. In my sixty-seven years of Catholic practice and twenty-seven years as a Catholic clergyman, with a concurrent fifty years of reading and paying attention to the life around me, I do not see what the Protestant critics tell me is there. Doctrines of the Reform and Counter Reform, that minefield of abstractions and battery of negative energies, are not the primary question here, and I happily leave them to the historical and systematic theologians to make what sense they can of them. The charge is that Satan rules the Catholic Church; that Catholicism is idolatrous; that the sacrament of penance is blasphemous; that Catholics are not Christians; that belief in the Real Presence violates common sense and scripture; that the priests and bishops of the Church are money-grubbing imposters, burdens on the poor, charlatans, and extortionists; that Mary the mother of Jesus has become a goddess for the Catholic Church; that praying before statues, using the rosary, lighting candles in church and praying for the dead are all superstitious and anti-Christian; that Pope Pius, Pope John, Pope Paul, and Pope John Paul (to mention only my popes) are the Antichrist. What is a simple Catholic to say to all this? Whatever existential discomfort Catholic belief and practice may cause evangelicals, the distortion of Catholic belief and practice in all this has to raise the question of what private, inner-ecclesiastical game these polemicists are playing, for their own amusement and that of their audience. What they have said has only the most superficial connection with what Catholics are and do. The problem, then, is the evangelical imagination. They have created a playground of images, loosed from careful discrimination.

What David Tracy called the "dialectical imagination" is operating without reasonable control.[10] Every imagining provokes a moment of denial and affirmation. The theological problems with the Protestant story are, I suspect, its understanding of faith, grace, and freedom (evangelicals struggle to talk about living and being saved as one "motion," but their instinct remains to see it in terms of dialectical oppositions of grace and sin); the blinders imposed by the slogan of three *sola*'s of the Reform; an inability to understand, in the salvation of the individual in relation to the church (solidarity and salvation), that the church has ontological status; a mistaken insistence on an insoluble tension between freedom and order. They are wrong, in my understanding, about faith and works, and they distort history and human nature in their myth. The anthropology is a mess: for example, what Van Til claims to be scriptural about the relations between the gospel and culture is a perfect example of the dialectic in operation, and the failure to identify in the basic Christian story the unity of the God of creation and God the redeemer. Van Til and others use the scriptures not as a starting point and a check for reflection, but as a set of prescriptions and proscriptions. For all their support of the gospel of freedom and grace, it seems to me that, like Catholics, they have often turned it into law.[11]

The myth of Satan's possession of the Catholic Church is perhaps the silliest part of the evangelical story and easiest to dismiss. I recommend as an antidote a reading of George Weigel's biography of John Paul II.[12] Even with a good bit of critical salt on the biography's filiopietistic tail, can anyone imagine this man as a tool of the Evil One? But solidarity and salvation is another matter. Are we to imagine that salvation is a gift to individuals who then go on to decide to form a church, or does God's grace constitute a community of lost souls (say, Twelve of them!) by membership in which the souls are no longer lost? This is the heart of the issue: is it an entire people or individual persons that God saves? Van Til, the biblical dialectician, would tell us that this is a conundrum smelling too much like the Greek problem of the one and the many, another Catholic philosophical presupposition to what should be a presuppositionless soteriology. The Thomist in me responds: the biblical doctrine itself leads one to a high (Catholic) ecclesiology, for no one is saved outside the will to save a people, a community, a church, the human race, a cosmos.

Evangelicals have churches and are a church, but they are historically suspicious of churches and of authority in them (they are made up of and led by morally crippled human beings, after all, and how could God act through such people?). In fact, they often behave as Catholics do but do not believe as Catholics do. The Catholic wants to take the argument over salvation in another direction, to watch the play of grace in the history of humanity, to watch its social web a-building, to inspect the always double-sided (individual and communal) presence of God's grace. Again and again there appears the image of the individual and his Bible. Campbell's way of seeing this contrast is stark: the Bible—freedom and hierarchy—religious and political oppression. But does the Bible need an official, communal interpreter? Of course not, Campbell would say, for the Bible is perfectly plain. And the result of Campbell's misplaced confidence: sectarianism, denominationalism and a million popes, fragmentation of the community and spiritual anarchy, says the Catholic. And if the Bible does get an interpreter, asks the Protestant? You get Roman Catholic religious tyranny and clericalism. Tough choice. Priority of the church over the Bible is England's, Purcell's, Hughes's, and Gibbons's answer to biblical Christianity: the revelation was entrusted to witnesses, and the witness continues in Protestant as well as Roman Catholic preaching and teaching. And tradition continues in evangelical as well as Catholic forms. And authorities arise even though they are not called bishops. The church is there, the primary outcome of God's love, a God who would not leave us alone, apart from him/her or *apart from one another.*

Now this seems to me an argument worth having, an argument in which historical and social investigation can offer a significant service to theology, and an argument from which each side can benefit even when agreement escapes them. The anti-*ECT* argument about grace and freedom in Romans is, the critics admit, another call to renew the Reformation battles that have never led anywhere except more separation. The sixteenth-century Reform we need to leave in the sixteenth century, and give Augustine and Pelagius a rest. We have enough to reform in the twenty-first century.

## The Catholic Problem

Mayhew and many of the evangelicals, rationalist and pietist, worry that Catholics are idolaters. There is something to it, but the charge is a few decisive steps beyond the facts. If Protestants did with statues what Catholics do, the Protestants would be idolaters, beyond question. What gets the evangelicals worked up is the Catholic exercise of analogical imagination and *sometimes* without an explicit enough dose of dialectical imagination. Again, the historical relations between Catholicism, on one hand, and paganism and Judaism, on the other, are both complex and affirmative to some degree. This fact does not bother Catholics, but it clearly bothers evangelicals. Within the Roman Catholic sacramental universe, where nature and grace seem to fuse indiscriminately, objectionable enough by itself for evangelicals, redemption becomes inextricably identified with clerical caste and hierarchy (apostolic succession). The Roman Catholic Church has deposited all its communal authority in a clerical autocracy (along with the occasional, unscheduled prophet such as Francis or Catherine of Sienna, who dwelt in that liminal world between the laity and the powerful clerics). There seems no solution to any problem without an exercise of inherited power and obedience to it. Whatever the adjustments, whatever tacking to the wind, that went on at Vatican II and in the decades since, it is clear that part of the "essence" of Catholicism is clerical/hierarchic control of property, language, and performance—and, therefore, divine grace. Apostolic succession is about power in the church, even if it works for the good as in the cases of repelling Arianism and Gnosticism.[13]

Reclericalization of Catholicism has been one of the aims of the present pontiff, John Paul II. He has recentered the church on the papacy and recentered the parish on the priest. For a few fleeting years after the council it seemed to many that the bishops had decided that lay Catholics should have some say and some role in the administration and ministry, and that the bishops might take on a significantly larger role in a collegiate governance of the church. The issue for this pope all along has not been modernization, *aggiornamento,* but specifically the power to rule in the face of it. Whereas "liberals" like myself might hope for a significant change, if there is any change it will have to happen by papal fiat. Given the unlikelihood of that, the Catholic higher clergy are what they are and they do what they do, and it is that which distinguishes the Roman Catholic Church and makes it successful in its own way. But it has made immense mistakes. The caste resisted modernity at every turn (except the spirit of centralization and bureaucracy) so indiscriminately and intensely that the papacy for a century and a half became an alternation of neurotic prophet and carping grandmother of the Christian movement. It went so far in the modern period as to puff its Western patriarchal synods (Trent and the Vatican Councils) into ecumenical councils, daring to speak as if they represented the whole Christian church, daring to make dogmas binding on the whole church. Ironically, then, the strong point of the Roman tradition, that is, placing the Bible in the liturgy, and its ordered sacramental universe over every irruption of spiritual power, is also its weakness. Without the biblical *kerygma*, it would soon and easily become another wisdom tradition, and without the irruption of prophetic spirit that causes it to tremble, it would be moribund, another "religion" in Barth's pejorative sense of another human effort to reach God.[14]

If, as is probably the case, neither side can change (it may be the positive divine will after all that there forever be evangelicals and Catholics!), it is heartening to think that evangelicalism and Catholicism may be complementary in addition to incompatible and permanent, that the dialectical and analogical imaginations are two moments in one Christian movement in history. To change the framework of discussion we may ask: Is each necessary to the other? In fact, the survival of Protestantism may be essential to the health of the Roman Catholic Church, and vice versa. We recall Paul Tillich's systematic distinction between the Protestant principle and the Catholic substance, and his insistence in 1963 that they are to be constructively as well as dialectically interrelated:

> Finally, Protestant systematic theology must take into consideration the present, more affirmative relation between Catholicism and Protestantism. Contemporary theology must consider the fact that the Reformation was not only a religious gain but also a religious loss. Although my system is very outspoken in its emphasis on the "Protestant principle," it has not ignored the demand that the "Catholic substance" be united with it, as the section on the church, one of the longest in the whole system, shows. There is a *kairos*, a moment full of potentialities, in Protestant-Catholic relations; and Protestant theology must become and remain conscious of it.[15]

We might, from Tillich's perspective on the complementarity of principle and substance, correct Archbishop Hughes's sharp and insightful judgment as to the fundamental instability of evangelical Protestantism. It is not the case that evangelical religion is inherently unstable; rather, it is a remarkably stable search for authentic authority rather than simply a negation of all authority; and the stability of Catholicism is always in need of prophetic critique lest its sacramental discovery of grace in things become idolatry and the work of its sacral authority turn demonic. Perhaps what we have seen as two pieces of an original unity, ripped apart in the sixteenth century, *sub specie aeternitatis* may in fact be two complementary sides of a single movement, each needing a little help from its recovered friend. This is what I hope for evangelicals and Catholics. For it to happen, evangelicals will have to bring a bit of control to their exercise of dialectical imagination that constantly rejects analogy, and Catholics will have to learn that dialectical imagination is important to their communal life. As an example of what an "evangelical Catholicism" or a "Catholic evangelicalism," a Catholic theology with a strong component of dialectic in it, I point to Hans Kung. We already know how he upset Rome, and so we recognize the strain such a theology places on what Rome likes to call full communion.[16]

## The Myths

The Reformation was more than a tragedy and a mistake, it was a sin for which repentance rather than celebration is demanded (no mere historian could make a comment like this!). It poisoned the Christian well, biblical, liturgical, and psychological. Trent and its aftermath were every bit as much the sin and distortion. While addressing the spiritual desuetude of Western Catholicism, it closed the door to millions by anathematizing the partial but genuine religious and theological insights of the Reformers and their legitimate demands. The Reformers, on their part, to protect themselves and safeguard their insights, left the Romans in charge of the largest Christian church in the world, with undesirable consequences for Catholics as well as Protestants. We will only get as far as ECT and no further unless we recognize in common the disaster in the sixteenth century. The Roman Church failed in some significant ways to reform itself at Trent and the two Vatican councils. The criticisms evangelicals and Catholics have been making of each other for five centuries are correct, but they have not in common taken responsibility for the causes of validity of those criticisms. Grounds in history to reshape the Evangelical and Catholic stories are available. Each side needs to do that painful reshaping in its own ecclesial situation.

But as things have been, Protestants tell the myth of the declension of the early faith in order to justify their rending of Christian communion, and Catholics must tell of the Protestant reform as a declension and the destruction of the church and Christendom in order to cover their own unwillingness to hear public criticism of authority and the uses of power in the church and of its compromises with folk religion, and in order to counter the Protestant myth. Both myths are absurd from the point of view of current historical knowledge, both are products of the biases of tribal contention, but the myths hold. What Hecker and Hughes argued in the nineteenth century, John Paul II assumes in the twentieth, adjusted though it is for new ecumenical circumstances. All three are restorationist, albeit in somewhat different ways. The church they see is the religion of the Father in which the church is the ever-innocent Mother injured by her ungrateful children. The Mary of doctrines and Catholic worship is not half so hard to take as apologists' image of Mater ecclesia.

The Catholic myth is of original and enduring order subduing chaos; the

Protestant myth is light triumphantly breaking out of the darkness of order and structure chaining Spirit and Christian freedom. In its own view, Protestantism is the religion of the Spirit, the true Christianity—which, ironically, turned out to be as patriarchal as Rome in its practice, with less room for the feminine, and no way of testing the spirits! The religion of order needs spirit, the religion of spirit needs order. The real issue is how these Christianities combine the two and give their gifts to one another without one destroying the other, as they have meant to do for five centuries. Even the present pope catches a bit of this problem in *Ut unum sint* (1995) when he asks for forgiveness for the sins of his predecessors:

> Among all the Churches [i.e., Roman and Orthodox] and Ecclesial Communities [i.e., Protestant], the Catholic Church is conscious that she has preserved the ministry of the Successor of the Apostle Peter, the Bishop of Rome, whom God established as her "perpetual and visible principle and foundation of unity" [Lumen Gentium No. 23] and whom the Spirit sustains in order that he may enable all others to share in this essential good. In the beautiful expression of Pope St. Gregory the Great, my ministry is that of *servus servorum Dei*. This designation is the best possible safeguard against the risk of separating power (and in particular the primacy) from ministry. Such a separation would contradict the very meaning of power according to the Gospel: "I am among you as one who serves" (Luke 22:27), says our Lord Jesus Christ, Head of the Church. On the other hand, as I acknowledged on the important occasion of a visit to the World Council of Churches in Geneva on June 12, 1984, the Catholic Church's conviction that in the ministry of the Bishop of Rome she has preserved, in fidelity to the apostolic Tradition and the faith of the Fathers, the visible sign and guarantor of unity, constitutes a difficulty for most other Christians, whose memory is marked by certain painful recollections. To the extent that we are responsible for these, I join my predecessor in asking forgiveness.[17]

John Paul goes on in the following paragraphs to tell once again the story of Peter's primacy among the apostles. The halting attempt to heal the wounds of the post-Reformation church is enfolded in the rhetoric of papal mission. Although he would be the last to accept any weakening resolution to the "difficulties" presented by the exercises of the Petrine office (so it seems to me), it is difficult to imagine a pope who could. The popes are trapped in a cage of their own construction, historically speaking. Within the Catholic communion, the bishops long ago accepted his authority over them all, and since have proved themselves unwilling or unable to redefine or circumscribe his jurisdiction "immediate and direct" over all the entire church, including in principle

Orthodox as well as Protestant churches.[18] It is as if the East-West schism and the Reformation have taught the popes nothing, although they and their claims of Petrine authority were key to both.

The Catholic Myth at this point appears to be indestructible: Peter and the apostles got ordained at the Last Supper, the Bishop of Rome and the bishops of the churches pass on that ordination, all by the will of Jesus himself. The primacy of the Bishop of Rome is a lynchpin of the Catholic myth, and canonical jurisdiction over the churches is its direct implication. If indeed the popes have come to serve the unity of the church, their failure must rank high in the historical list, and it must deeply trouble the present occupant of Peter's chair. By contrast, it should no more rankle him than the sins of other Christians rankle them.

If historians can correct the Protestant myth, one might say, there is no reason why it cannot correct the Catholic one. But one must face the fact that even in a thoughtful and sincere attempt to embrace the ecumenical discussion of authority and its exercise in his encyclical *Ut unum sint*, the present pope can find no way to do it and has to ask his fellow Christians, especially those not in communion with him, for help.[19] But is anyone hopeful that a correction here or there in Peter's part in the story is going to reshape the Catholic Church, or that any significant correction to the story would be accepted by any holder of Peter's chair? Suppose, for example, one were to suggest that Peter and the Twelve were not priests or bishops, that Peter never held even a metaphorical chair in Rome, that the episcopate was a creative invention of the second-century church to solve a critical problem and was never foreseen or commanded by Jesus, and that the Last Supper was not an ordination or consecration of a hierarchy (all of which have been more than suggested by scholars). Perhaps stranger things have happened than the successor to Peter taking correction to the story that justifies his position in the church, but I can not recall one. John Paul II, no more than any of his predecessors and his successors, is interested in any history except that which confirms their faith in God's presence to them and through their ministry to the church. But in continuity with the calm insistence of other Protestants, evangelicals are called to promote unity in truth by helping the pope to define a more fitting and acceptable ministry of unity to the church.[20]

Blanshard and Boettner, and others, were convinced that papal spiritual power over the temporal order and over Catholics is incompatible with democracy. It seems that history has delivered an answer that has been confirmed by the second Vatican Council: Christendom is not, Catholicism is, and this is precisely what the American bishops have taught from the beginning of their tradition on church and state with John Carroll of Baltimore. We saw it in our account of Bishops England and Purcell, it was clear in the pastoral letters of the bishops, it reverberated through Al Smith's response to Charles Murray in 1927, O'Neill's criticism of Blanshard in 1952, and through John Courtney

Murray's theoretic solution adopted in its principles by the second Vatican Council in 1965. Jack Chick and Dave Hunt keep the nativist/evangelical flame.

The unintended intellectual legacy of the Reformation is resident in the existence of two initially plausible accounts of Christian church and two ways of religious life accompanying them[21]. An intellectual grace that came with the birth of a second myth was the origins of "scientific history," along with its practice and use by church historians and theologians, and the ultimate collapse of both at the hands of responsible historical reconstruction. The two mythical accounts were so disparate and opposed, one so eagerly accepted by each side and utterly exclusive of the other, that attempts to find out "what really happened" were inevitable. The Catholic Myth (stability of divinely instituted structure) preceded, and then was tailored to answer to, the Protestant myth (creation of early Christianity, declension, and re-creation, following a supernaturalized Deuteronomic model). For Catholics Protestantism is the decline—or a radically incomplete version of the church; for Protestants, the Roman church, with its spiritual arrogance, its quest for universal power, and its various worldly lusts, is the source of corruption.[22]

Part of the Catholic burden after the Reformation was to retell the story in the light of it. Baronius and Bellarmine reclaimed the history of the Christian church from the Centuriators. Satan seizing the papacy in the Medieval and Renaissance church was taken to be a distortion of the dialectic of sin and grace in the church's history; the correction of the Protestant myth became an opportunity to grasp and tell the story of the foibles and moral horrors possible in any life, anywhere, at anytime, among Reformers as well as popes, and not a story of declension and Satanic possession. The gospel and grace and sin were in the history throughout, Alexander VI, Julius II, and Leo X were no one's ideal bishop, reform was going forward apace (as it always had!) with the light and shadow present in all we do, not the total darkness triumphantly dispelled by Luther, Calvin, Zwingli, and Cranmer. Hughes's response to Nicholas Murray's savage attacks on the priesthood was to tell the story of culture's declension under Protestants (Hughes was a perfect counterpuncher), part of the Catholic story up to Pius X, and Cardinal Ottaviani's draft agenda for Vatican II. It ended there, at least for now.

The Catholic story was in some ways as morally tendentious as the evangelical. For evangelicals, paganism and Judaism and Satan were brought into the Protestant story to explain a Catholic Church in declension from a pure apostolic church, to expose the intricacies and the details of the papal program of corruption, just as for Catholics Satan, various lusts, and hatred of lawful authority explain the fact as well as the excesses of the reformers. Campbell justifies murder by saying that the Reformers were once Catholics who were taught murder and persecution in that church. From the Catholic perspective, what the Protestants saw as a demonic millennium should be understood as a tale of grace complementing and challenging fallen nature in constantly new circumstances, a story of continuity and God's faithfulness and not radical discontinuity: Peter was there, in Rome, the first bishop of Rome, the first pope, and so on and so forth. Responsible historians have stopped arguing clashing myths and have given us an even-handed historical account of Christianity, leaving the compressed and contested doctrines to one side, except as parts of the account. As well as a historically reliable account, we have a careful distinction between historical inquiry and theological reflection not possible in the age of the Reformation and in the battles we have recounted in this book.[23]

## Biblical and Liturgical Christianity

J. Gordon Melton, in the *Encyclopedia of American Religions,* classifies Christian churches and American religions into "families," distinguishing between liturgical Christianity, which are the Roman and Old Catholic churches, on the one side and, on the other, the Anglican, Presbyterian, Methodist, Holiness, Pentecostal "Families." He thereby categorizes churches, chiefly by genealogy, in a quiet and objective way, promoting the sort of descriptive scholarship for which he is justly famous. Some might think that the distinctions are the result of observation of superficialities. I do not think so. The device is helpful not only in organizing a reference work but in challenging the reader to distinguish the lilies and the daffodils in the American Christian meadow. Earlier in this book, I proposed the term "biblical Christianity" to hold together the plethora of American denominations that made up the "Evangelical Alliance" of the nineteenth century, including groups as disparate as Presbyterians, Methodists, and the Restorationists, and the fundamentalist and evangelical movements of the twentieth century, and to couple it with Melton's "Liturgical Christianity." It seems to me evident that Roman and Eastern Orthodox churches, including Roman schismatic groups from Old Catholic to Lefebvrists,[24] belong among the liturgical churches, and I might throw in "the Anglican family" and even some Lutheran groups if it made them happy.[25]

A different question, one that Melton anticipated, is: can you have a Christianity that is only one of the two, biblical or liturgical? Surely, an objector might say, by drawing this distinction you distort the field from the outset. An anthropologist might answer that purity in this case is absurdity. Although there are religions without a book, there is no such thing as a religion, never mind a Christianity, which is nonliturgical or aliturgical, or at least nonritual. And what would a Christianity be like were it unrelated to the Bible? The biblical story and so the Bible are essential to Christianity in any form. No form of Christian church is without worship and so without liturgy however restrained—and so the Quakers observe a liturgy of prayerful communion.

Melton recommends a descriptive scale here and does not enter issues of normativity, but surely both Bible and liturgy are normative for Christianity.

In the description, however, there is no doubt at all that there are biblical and liturgical churches on a sliding scale. Every Sunday morning at 11 A.M. the people of God walk up the steps of Tower Grove Baptist Church in the Shaw neighborhood of St. Louis with Bible in hand and sit for the forty-minute sermon turning onion leaf pages to check on the minister—and do not tell me that is not liturgy. And, at 10 A.M., just a few blocks away, Fr. Brown at St. Margaret of Scotland Catholic Church "hyssops" people of God with holy water, and nary one drop falls on the open pages of a parishioner's Bible—but do not tell me that "hyspopping" isn't biblical.

At this point, I merely want to make it clear that the charge that the Catholic Church is not biblical and the countercharge that evangelicals are not liturgical and sacramental in fact mean that neither is "enough" of what it should be in the eyes of the other. But surely the Christian churches are both biblical and liturgical. At the same time, there really is some value to the distinction. The Catholic Church is liturgical in some sense that the Presbyterian church is not, and the Baptists are biblical in some sense that the Catholic church is not. None of those "senses" should prove difficult to specify.

There is another terminological distinction that plays into evangelical-Catholic relations, that is, between Catholicity and Christianity. For most of the five hundred years of the protest movement against the Catholic Church, evangelical Christians have been quite sure that the Catholic Church is not Christian. This, of course, is closely related in evangelical polemics to the charge that the Catholic Church is not biblical, and more is at issue here than whether you carry your Bible under your arm or in a procession, or have Bible study groups. A negative answer to the question, Is the Catholic Church Christian? is the only answer that justifies the schism of the sixteenth century and its contemporary remnant. In other words, there would be no biblical Christianity as a term of distinction had the Catholic Church been a Christian church to begin with. Brother Martin would have died peacefully in his monastery bed had the Catholic Church professed real—that is, biblical—Christianity. But it did not, in his view, and so we have evangelicals. The conviction that the Roman Catholic Church is not Christian (not biblical) would seem to be the very heartbeat of the Reformation, and it is no surprise that it continues to beat among evangelical Christians to this day.

By contrast, only on a positive answer to the question, Is the Catholic Church Christian? does the Tridentine Catholic Church possess legitimacy. Since the sixteenth century, the Catholic Church has been intent on reuniting Christians based on the conviction that the Catholic Church is indeed Christian in its faith and practice, and has been just as intent on proving that the churches of the Reformation are not legitimate Christian churches or are only partly Christian. Some Catholics still think this, not least Cardinal Ratzinger and His Holiness.[26] Yet the scene grows more complex for each side. Evangelicals recognize the biblical character of much of Catholic belief and practice, and find themselves hand in glove with Catholics in the struggle for a deepened Christian imprint on American culture, and Catholics recognize undeniable elements of the "true" church in evangelical communities. Is this is a case of Esau and Jacob at the Jabbok, brothers on the verge of making up an old quarrel (Gen. 32, 23ff.)? May they get over it, we may be tempted to say! But to a person such as myself, to whom the tension of the argument is much more a sign of life than is a facile surrender to brotherly love and reconciliation, the old Protestant argument needs revisiting.

The Reformers and their nineteenth-century progeny may be close to the truth in their answer to the question, Is the Catholic Church Christian? than Catholics would be inclined to admit. In fact, if one accepts—a big "IF" for most of us, I assume—the evangelical definition of Christian faith as Christocentric, bibliocentric, proclamatory (kerygmatic), missionary-conversionist, exclusivist, blood-sacrificial, and apocalyptic—I for one (Catholic) would not regard myself as Christian and would happily cede the term to evangelicals. By inheritance I stand with the Grand Inquisitor, as has the Roman church: order and communal piety over chaos and gospel freedom. But I am loath to cede the title "Christian" to evangelicals and remain convinced that the Catholic mode of use of the Bible is substantially correct, and I would want to revisit the Catholic claim to Christianity and review the evidence for it (but not here!). Even advancing on strictly evangelical criteria, with Charles Hodge, I recognize that the Pauline gospel—not to say the Johannine and Matthean, let us give thanks for them—is central to the Catholic version of Christianity, whatever shadows it has allowed to play on it.

So, the terms *evangelical* and *Catholic* do differ, they do at least mark quite different Christianities, a difference so stark that it raises the issue whether they are or can both be Christian—or is it possible that the Protestants, most of them then and many of them still, are correct when they argue that we have here two religions as different from one another as Christianity is from Judaism? I realize that in this age and for most of us this proposal appears facetious, or even manipulative, but I ask you to exercise some Christian patience. I am confessing at least an ambivalent state of mind on this very important question. I would prefer to restate the question: Is there a Christian tradition or are there and have there been from the beginning Christian *traditions,* one of which can be located in Rome. Perhaps I could put it this way: I am quite sure that I am a Catholic but I am far from sure that I am or want to be a Christian, and so when I turn to the Catholic Church I am inclined to downplay those elements of it which are putatively biblical (Pauline) and to emphasize those elements that might be construed as tangential to biblical Christianity as it is construed by evangelicals. When I turn to evangelicals I find their Christianity quite

narrowly biblical (i.e., Pauline), ahistorical, fanciful, and ecclesially irrespon-
sible (as any good Catholic would!).

What is biblical Christianity? Biblical Christianity, for its evangelical practitioners, is in the first instance the faith and practice described in the Bible.
Christianity is also the religion gathered around the Bible, the church that prays
and thinks and writes under the inspiration by the Bible and that is ruled in
its language and behavior by the Bible. Like our own American Constitution,
the Bible is at once a text and focal symbol, what John Randall, the naturalist
philosopher, would call a "conjunction" as well as a noun. The Bible is not a
book only, it is a way of life. One might say that in the sixteenth century, Divine
Providence devised a strategy for meeting the rising culture of modernity, a
portable Word of God addressed to each literate believer, like a personal letter,
making it possible for each person to find divine instruction for a way of life
without the need of a guiding community.[27]

But further: the Bible provides the only rule for Christian faith and practice. The church itself is not a rule, it is a community under rule. The primacy
of the Bible negates the primacy or separate status of any other canon including
the church fathers, councils, creeds, and ecclesial authorities, practices, and
doctrines. Any other authority, any other rule, is unauthentic unless it is
grounded in the Bible. As Alexander Campbell put it in his debate with Bishop
Purcell, "Divine authority cannot exist, but in the holy oracles; against any other
pretended infallible standard, all men should protest." A creed, then, is binding
not because a church has agreed on it and used it as a test or a formula in
baptism, or because the saints who have gone before us vouch for it, but only
insofar as it is biblical doctrine. A creed is not an addition, it is a reflection.

In the especially intense forms of evangelical Christianity the Bible is also
the limit to belief and practice. Immigrants from Ireland, Thomas Campbell
and his son Alexander aimed their Restoration Movement at shaping a Christian community life that was purely biblical and that cut across evangelical
denominationalism, and was not weighed down by any ecclesiastical tradition
whatsoever: "Where the Scriptures speak we speak," they intoned, and "where
the Scriptures are silent we are silent." Impossible to live by, of course, and
the endlessly talkative Campbells were the first to violate their own rule. In
fact, the Campbells took the meaning of biblical Christianity to its logical next
step and made of the Bible a blueprint for the Christian church, insisting that
no historical accretion or expansion of the structure of the church and its beliefs
beyond the description of it in the New Testament texts be credited. Should
the church have music? Not a biblical church! Should there be a creed? Never!
"No creed but Christ!" and "No book but the Bible!" Should there be a central
judicature deciding matters of belief? There is none in the Bible.[28]

Moreover, for biblical Christianity, the Bible provides a table of contents
for doctrine, and doctrine is little more than the restatement of biblical texts.
Theology, in its turn, does no more than excavate the doctrines and connect

the dots. The Bible, as nineteenth-century Americans repeated, has a "system" and it is the job of theology is to reproduce it. In addition to the contents of the church's belief, the Bible delivers the table of contents for the anti-Catholic tract, for the Catholic Church is constituted by nonbiblical and antibiblical teaching and practice, as can be easily determined by comparing its "system" to the "system of the Bible."[29]

The Bible is as well the storehouse of divinely inspired images of, even codes for, the distortions of the Roman church. You can find in it not merely correct doctrines but descriptions of the horrors that have been and the horrors yet to come, the chief satanic instrument of which is the Roman Catholic Church. The Bible teaches not only what Christianity is but what it isn't, and, when a church is not what it should be, it may turn out to be a mirror-reverse image of Christianity. As the Bible displays the light of God and darkness of Satan, as the anti-Christ is the reverse Christ, so the Bible displays the true and the false church.

But the Bible is first and foremost the book of God, the book in which God and Christ and salvation are found, and only secondarily a source book for anti-Catholic polemic. The Bible in its most important sense is the house of God in which the saints dwell, and the estranged are welcomed and instructed and sanctified and comforted.[30] Together the converted practice biblical Christianity. The Bible did instruct people on the Catholic Church, but the constructive uses remain—the Bible fed and feeds faith and hope among those who also happen, justifiably perhaps, to fear Catholicism.

The Bible, then, sets forth the church's faith and practice, and in doing so, defines what a Christian church is. Belief and practices not based on biblical teaching are illegitimate. They must be "there" in the text or at least not logically opposed to what is "there" in the text. An important factor in determining what really is in the text is the hermeneutical habit induced by Luther's favoring of Romans and Galatians. The habit of establishing a canon within the canon continues among American evangelicals, with Romans and Galatians used as a goad to the Catholic Church to this day. But each of the evangelical traditions has its additional cap-pistols within the canon, and over them they divide among themselves, Pentecostals, for example, dividing from Reformed, or the Campbellites dividing from Baptists, Methodists, and Presbyterians. And so "tradition" has an application to evangelicals, at least in the sense that, although the entire biblical text is "Spirit-breathed," some parts are breathed more heavily than others. But, still, even when "tradition" is reluctantly allowed a role, the Bible precedes the church and the interpreter. It is no construct; it is a datum.

In practice Catholics, too, establish more and less important texts, and are every bit as likely as evangelicals to use one text to balance and even to counter others in order to support whatever it is they do and believe. Catholics pounced on Matthew 16 and John 21 to find support for the papacy. But they had and have the advantage of a reified hermeneutical habit and call it the Magisterium, the power by which the church teaches and interprets the Scriptures correctly. For them, too, the whole Bible is the Word of God and is fit for use as the leaders of the church choose to use it. Their canon is not within the canon, but the Magisterium is used much to the same effect as the evangelicals' rule of salvation by faith and grace alone, and by that rule to mine the meaning of the scriptures and to divide true from false Christianity.

Let us take a case for contrast, namely, the Orthodox Presbyterian Church (OPC) and the Roman church on the ordination of women. As sad as it makes the small evangelical church, itself a breakaway from the Presbyterian Church U.S.A. in 1936, it must "terminate our existing Ecclesiastical Fellowship as of July 1, 1997" with the Christian Reformed Church (CRC), because the Christian Reformed Church decided to "certify certain women as 'candidates for ministry'."[31] What is at stake for the OPC is the rule of the Bible: the CRC Synod had "opened the special offices of 'elder, minister, and evangelist' to persons biblically prohibited from holding them. The inviolability of the passage is particularly incisive. God declares, 'I do not permit a woman to teach or to have authority over the man'" (I Tim. 2:12). The CRC cannot do what is clearly prohibited by St. Paul and God.

In the Catholic counterpart, *Ordinatio sacerdotalis,* the Apostolic (i.e., papal) Letter reiterating the Catholic church's prohibition of the ordination of women to the priesthood,[32] the Roman Congregation and the pope ignore the only biblical text that explicitly supports their position by forbidding women to hold authority over men and speaking in church assemblies (I Tim. 2:11–15). Even though they do cite the epistles to Timothy and the first to Corinth to other effect, they argue instead from the "unbroken teaching and practice" of the church east and west to the same position taken by the OPC, that is, that the Catholic church cannot ordain women without being unfaithful to its apostolic heritage. When the OPC decided to stick with Paul and God, and when the Roman Church decided to stick with its "unbroken tradition" and to pass over the biblical text without comment, we get to the heart of the matter of what biblical Christianity is. *Quod Deus scripsit, scripsit!* say the biblical Christians. *Quod ecclesia scripsit, scripsit!* say the liturgical Christians. For the latter, the *vox ecclesiae* is the *vox dei.* For evangelicals there is only one edition of the *vox dei,* while for Catholics a Talmud (*vox ecclesiae*) is being added to Torah.

Each position is an answer the question in the sixteenth century: Who is a true Christian and what is true Christianity, or How am I to be saved? You can only be saved by believing and living under the Bible. You can only be saved by joining the true church in its worship of the triune God under the pastors appointed to lead the worship. The answers delivered in the sixteenth century need reexamination.

The Reformers gave the priority to the Christ-event and to the book that proclaims and explains and provides access to it in faith. The Bible also provided surety needed when the church grew corrupt and Christendom weakened, when the hierarchy and the sacramental system with its common Eucharistic worship could no longer be taken as defining points. To the Bible the Reformers could appeal to cut through the luxuriant growth in Catholic belief and practice, and to get some control over the community overseers. Bibliocentrism is one Christian answer to the end of Christendom as the badge of membership in the true church and the loss of its ideal of the single empire and the single church, as the empire fails and gives rise to nation-states with their implicit demand for national churches and for the dismantling of the transnational church with an extranational center. To end the formalism of membership, to make membership *real*, the Reformers call for personal experience of transformation described in the Bible over against the criteria of acceptance of authoritative teaching and participation in sacramental worship credited as authentic by the teachers. Biblical Christianity occurred not in the "primitive church" as the Reformers thought, but at "the waning of the middle ages." With it, the invention of printing and the renaissance of classical learning and culture precipitated the rise of historical consciousness.

Biblical Christianity's strengths were the reformers' call for personal commitment over formal adherence, and the Bible's portability (the printed Bible be with you!). The latter proved to be a formidable means to preserve faith and witness. No matter the bishop, no matter the sovereign, universality and authenticity are assured by personal faith and the book. The weaknesses of the evangelical myth of biblical Christianity were its intense individualism, its concentration on the event over process, its easy potential for Gnostic interpretation, its profound suspicion of human authority and sacramental mediation in religion, and its centrifugal energies. It is a wonder, from the Roman Catholic perspective, that orthodoxy survived at all in Protestantism. Evangelicals would admit it did not survive unscathed, and, in the second place, preserving orthodoxy turned out to be not so impossible a task, since the continuity between the Bible and the creeds and the great councils is fairly evident. Language does have its contents and its rules, and the latter bind meaning and common sense together, even with wanderers on the scene such as Jacob Arminius, Channing, and Parker. Orthodox doctrine did survive and Protestantism kept the founding story straight. The revivals in American evangelicalism have not been about spiritual experience only but also about the "fundamentals" in the Christian story. All this helped to keep Unitarianism and universalism and the like at bay.

Catholicism (i.e., liturgical Christianity) had come to stress the priority of process and order over discrete events, of continuity and repetition over dialectical breaks, and of mediated experience over direct. The liturgy is a prime mediator of redemptive meaning, not only a source but also a control of that meaning's expression. The Catholic Church had already proved as suspicious of direct experience of the divine in mysticism as Protestantism would prove suspicious of authoritative mediation of religious meaning by a hierarchy. The Catholic reaction to the Reformers predictably came down on the side of institutional continuity and sacramental experience, and for what had been over a millennium Christian practice. Hierarchy provided stability by permanence in structure, by repetition of the sacramental mystery, and confidence in the presence of the Spirit (infallibility of the Magisterium and indefectibility of the Church) in a historical community through changes in cultures, and by the Catholic absolutes of doctrine and structure. To this day, the canonical responsibilities of a bishop are to teach, to provide for and insure orthodox doctrine, and to oversee authentic worship.[33] With lapses, of course, this is exactly what bishops have done since the second century. Liturgical Christianity reaches its full flower when the Western Catholic bishops agree that there is not just this or that assembly with its priest-president, not just the liturgical worship of this and that diocese with its bishop-president, but that every liturgy, local and diocesan, is joined to a universal liturgy presided over by the bishop of bishops, Peter's successor. "Communion" starts with and rests on this.

Insofar as one can use a word such as absolute in the contemporary cultural context without confusion and provocation, the Catholic absolute has been the structured community and its possession by the Spirit rather than the Bible, although the Bible is one of the twin focuses of the liturgy. Although Christendom as an ideal ended in fact with the Reformation and the Enlightenment, and in theory at Vatican II, the longing for the absolute has assuredly not ended.[34] Meeting it is one of the strengths of the contemporary as well as the historical Catholic Church.[35] Other related strengths such as hierarchy and sacraments are matched by the weakness of historic Catholicism: its submergence of the individual Christian in the hierarchic church and the worshiping assembly, its exaltation of formal authority, its inability to agree to the existence of a complete form of Christianity different from and outside of itself, and its often overbearing patriarchal condescension. Roman Catholicism is allergic to anarchy—which is what Rome as well as its evangelical enemies alike mistakenly saw as an allergy to political freedom.

But how shall Catholics answer the perennial and pressing question, what is true Christianity? There must be a story, a narrative. They had to reclaim the story in parts and as a whole and tell it so that there is permanence in change or, better, no change at all, and that the papacy had been the lynchpin all along. In the Roman Catholic story, the Bible belongs *in the liturgy* where it had been from the beginning, properly interpreted by the president of each liturgical assembly, linked to the liturgy of the local bishop and through that to the Roman bishop and his liturgy.

Both evangelical and Catholic myths stand on the Jewish and Christian witness to God's historical presence to a people. The myth of the biblical Christian has the burden of also explaining how God and God's people got separated for a millennium (500–1500), and how the once-dead letter came to life. The Catholic Myth must explain how parts of the body of Christ became separated from the one true church, and, although they are not the true church and not true churches, they are nonetheless truly Christian. In the overarching myth of creation and redemption, such painful and mysterious facts could only be explained by a combination of providential will and Satanic irruption. Thus, both forms of Christianity, in their similarity and opposition, have stood and spun their doctrinal and narrative webs.

In a post-Christian, ecumenical age, how should we handle sharp doctrinal differences that will not go away? The Reformation is long over, but the doctrines were critical to it. Both forms of Christianity badly need reformation now, including doctrinal. Separatism, cultural and ecclesiastical, has not worked for integralists or for fundamentalists in promoting communion among Christians. We cannot bury the doctrinal differences—authenticity on both sides is too precious a thing. Learn to live with them is a nice general rubric, and many on each side in the past and now perhaps most on each side have been trying to meet that rubric. In 1993, ECT proposed for Catholics and evangelical Protestants spheres of common action based on common faith, common problems, and common aims in society and culture. But ECT did not solve the doctrinal problem, because of the conviction of each community that it is the only fully adequate way of Christian faith and that the other is defective. The Protestants in the middle of the doctrinal spectrum long ago learned to get along in spite of differences and to commit the differences to a long-term process of ecumenical discussion that involves the willingness on all sides to change.

Some evangelical Protestants to the right on the doctrinal spectrum have decided to rejoin the community of churches without yielding on doctrines, and so have Catholics. This is what was so surprising about ECT: the two groups of nonseparatist conservative Christians most sensitive to the "acids of modernity" and resistant to ecumenical compromise showed a willingness to cooperate (a classic ecumenical stand) while listing differences *without confronting them*. ECT II did not clear up the situation, and dropped the ban on mutual proselytizing agreed to in ECT I. Some activists on each side got to the point of frustration with American political and moral culture that they were ready to steer around the difference for the sake of "contending with modernity." Evangelicals have always suspected Catholicism of religious imperialism, of totalitarian ambitions; Catholics have always disdained Protestant divisiveness, anticlericalism, and anarchic instincts, and a logic that leads to nihilism. Neither has been given to seeing truth or virtue in the other. Yet ECT stands, even under severe criticism. But what about those differences? The issues aren't going to go away. How should we handle them?

Solving the Doctrinal Standoff

The necessity of learning that the church learns—it does not repeat, and that it does not know everything already—is the first step to be taken by evangelicals and Catholics together. That "the church learns" is the answer to the Roman boast of "the impossibility of change in an infallible church" and to the Reformed evangelical obsession with doctrinal orthodoxy. *Semper idem*, always the same, was the episcopal motto of Alfredo Ottaviani, the Cardinal lion of Catholic immobilism. It also was the answer to the always threatening moribundity of a Christianity tied to the biblical or conciliar or papal literalism (the latter is what liberal Catholics call "Catholic fundamentalism").[36] The church adjusts to cultures, for example, to the American experience, by what is now called by Roman theologians "inculturation." The two Christianities need to explore the religious life and traditions of the other, and especially to analyze together the promise and perils of modernization and even of postmodernism. There is surely enough religious vigor in each community to insure its survival and health, and enough decency in each community to overcome the legacy of fear and hatred that has infected their historical relations and to support a respectful conversation. They have a lot to tell one another about their respective struggles with modernity, and a lot of struggle yet to come in that they need one another's support. Specifically, on the theological level, a mutually critical dialogue on matters of ecclesiology and biblical faith is needed (it is well begun, most recently at the Wheaton Conference of 2002) to sharpen up differences as well as to uncover commonalities. A broad discussion over the next two decades of the relation between faith, religious practice, politics, and culture might underscore the common complaints about the corrosive effects of modern intellectual and popular culture on religious and family life.

In the case of evangelicals and Catholics, it is particularly required that the discussions between theologians and other intellectuals be made and kept public, for here it is not churches negotiating, and every step will need direct and immediate publicity if the two communities are to be educated about one another. They might even in common make a decisive difference in the impact modernization is having on the southern hemisphere, and they might begin to discuss the opposition between them in Latin American nations. Although neither Catholics nor evangelicals easily enter on ecumenical explorations of this sort (and "hard" evangelicals and fundamentalists, and traditionalist/integralist Catholics never do), that they do so is imperative for the health of both communities and the health of the public arena in general. Not that I am optimistic about the chance for a quick end to mutual distrust and dislike, for tribalism is a permanent feature of human life, and its ambiguities will remain. I still find it almost impossible to pull down the voting lever on a Republican in spite of my agreement with many of them about abortion. Nor am I sanguine that any of the large doctrinal differences can be resolved, but pessimism is no reason to stand still.

Roman Catholic *aggiornamento* and its constructive engagement with modern culture and politics have not at all removed the Catholic suspicion of Western secularism and its systematized appetites for natural wealth and markets.[37] Surely this vigorous response to the modern secular organization of life delivers a platform for conversation and common action. So, too, with evangelicals interested in the formation and transformation of culture. If negative characterizing could be replaced by exploration of common interest in mitigating the effects of Enlightenment pseudoprogress and material and spiritual exploitation of the poor, then surely the church will learn and our world will change. If they will explain doctrines with one another, this time patiently and charitably, perhaps common discovery can replace mutual rejection.

The necessity of mutual recognition cannot be escaped. These two are distinct but valid forms of Christian witness. As much as I am uncomfortable with this question, I have had to accept it as a working hypothesis. I do so hypothetically because such a judgment ought to be an outcome of a theological discussion rather than an assumption. I do so for academic reasons: objectivity. And I do so because of the Christian belief in history and God's part in it, that is, I do not believe that these two communities have been abandoned Christ or that Christ has abandoned them.[38] I find aspects of both communities repulsive and reprehensible but still do not believe that Christ has abandoned or been abandoned by either.

If Catholics are right about Purgatory, there are many ministerial and hierarchic souls that will need painful cleansing before entering the vision of God. The venial sin that impedes the relationship between the two is that neither will recognize the other as fully Christian—even the signers of *ECT*—and the ground for that refusal is the tribal self-definition of each as the norm of Christianity. By each community's criteria of authenticity the other is not an authentic Christian community or not a church. The opponents of even so modest and circumscribed an effort as *ECT* are shouting "Remember Trent!" and "Remember Regensburg!" as if *ECT* were a theological equivalent of Pearl Harbor. There are real problems here—evangelicals (hard or soft) are not a church and so can not "recognize" anything. They think they *can* recognize a true Christian, and that is what the soft evangelicals are doing when they peer intently at the Catholics, trying mightily to pick out the true Christians among them. Even when they have discerned the saved, they cannot speak for their evangelical colleagues who have concluded, with much precedent, that participation in the Catholic "system" is *prima facie* evidence of defective conversion. They can only prod the holdouts by example and appeal, and on any important matter are sure to meet opposition—as did the NAE when it was founded.[39] The response to *ECT* carried an implied threat of separation. Rome was not officially represented at the *ECT* table (the oddness of Catholic representation has been noted) and Rome may not approve any document that comes from any even recognized and formally established dialogue. Moreover, Rome has been unable to bring itself to recognize Protestant churches as churches because of its peculiar theological problem with the term church and its attachment to apostolic succession. Quite logically, for Rome there is and can be only one church, one body of Christ, and to be a Christian is equivalent to being in it.

To comment on the Roman Catholic side of this impasse, I would say that, if there is such a thing as an empirically grounded ecclesiological judgment, it is this: Catholicism is not for all Christians. The church no longer proclaims as part of its public doctrine that it is the only religious community to which one may belong (granted, the "may" needs exegesis), but it is far from admitting that the Catholic Church does not and even cannot accommodate the spiritual needs and theological insights of every Christian. It ought no longer to pretend to do so. Everyone ought to be in the one true church. The Catholic Church is a home or the home for every Christian who can and will accept its peculiar sense of order and sacrament, but hundreds of millions of Christians do not and will not, short of another surprise on the Last Day.

To my knowledge, Rome has never publicly admitted that Protestant churches represent permanent and valid organizations of the Christian community; nor has it admitted that biblical Christianity represents an entirely valid and adequate witness to Jesus. It cannot do so, I believe, without changing its criteria of authenticity, the chief among which are communion of faith and worship with the bishops and the bishop of Rome. However that may be, biblical Christianity is another Christian tribe, there, real, living, active, preaching, teaching, baptizing, celebrating the Eucharist, filled with faith, hope and charity but with distinctive spirituality which is not compatible with the Roman Catholic but that is Christian nonetheless.

Although the ecclesial and ecclesiological virtues and vices of each are primarily a matter of internal evaluation on each side, they must be a subject of critical dialogue. But the differences should no longer propel the evangelical side to the judgment that Catholicism is another religion than Christian, or perhaps no religion at all. Just as there are "Judaisms" rather than Judaism, so there are Christianities rather than simply Christianity, or churches rather than the Church. The break of the Reformers from the Roman Church, no matter what we may think of it as a moral option (as I said earlier, I think it was not just a mistake but also a sin, inflicting an ontological and psychological wound on the Christian church from which it has not recovered) is no less worthy of simple historical acceptance as the break of the early Christians with the religion of Moses, even though it is not as sharp, or the irretrievable breakdown of a marriage. Evangelicalism never became a new religion, as Christianity did in the first century, any more than Catholic Christianity is a different religion from the "early" church. The doctrinal and symbolic spine remained, the worship form is continuous, pretty much the same Bible is read. True, no one would confuse the Yale Divinity School chapel with the Shrine of the Immaculate Conception, but both are homes of Christian worship. Wherever two or three are gathered, he is there and his Spirit with him, and so the church is constituted. The small intentional gathering of Christians is a Christian church, as the embryo or fetus is a human being. A local church is a real church.

If stopping Catholic leakage to evangelical churches remains a Catholic concern, then a strategy is needed other than polemic and denigration. I would start by taking it for granted that biblical Christianity is a viable form of Christian life, that is, I would treat it and them as churches rather than as bluebottle flies or conventicles of anarchists, with at least the respect a Catholic would give a Hindu and to Hinduism and, as a consequence, assume that Catholics turn to evangelical communities and to the Bible for good reason, just as many Catholics today would understand why a Catholic might become Lutheran or Orthodox. Hundreds of Catholic priests, married and with families, have left the Catholic Church and have had their orders accepted by the Episcopal and Anglican churches, and there has been only the most ecumenically sensitive response to that phenomenon on the Catholic side, and nearly one hundred Anglican priests have taken the road in the other direction, from Canterbury to Rome. The "loss" in these cases may even be received in each communion as a relief! The reasons why "hundreds of thousands" or even millions of Catholics have joined evangelical and fundamentalist churches may be at least as respectable and reasonable as those of the priests, and deserve respect and tenders of good wishes. I do not suggest this because it is the ecumenically correct thing to do but because in what Christian church a person finds the salvation promised by God is a matter of divine providence and personal freedom. Leakage is a theological and religious problem only when there is but one true church and the rest are false or incomplete.

Moreover, surely the fact of the largest defection of Christians from the Catholic Church since the sixteenth century demands an examination of the church's limitations as commentators and bishops have admitted. Because the Catholic Church did not perform such an examination in the sixteenth century, there is perhaps little hope that it will do so now, but one can always have a little hope. Is it capable of facing the possibility that "One" doesn't mean only, that "Holy" doesn't mean perfect (even as a corporate or an ideal person), that "Catholic" doesn't mean complete, that "Apostolic" may mean more or other than continuity of officers in offices, and that all four can be found elsewhere than in the Roman communion?

Roman ecumenical documents show the effort to offer ecclesiologically affirmative evaluations of modern forms of church polity that have historically proven themselves in their support of communal and individual fidelity to redemptive grace, but still they imply that these "communions" can at best be considered made up of "anonymous Catholics."[40] These forms of church order have been the instruments of salvation of millions in the face of wars and rumors of wars, the Enlightenment, and the rise of capitalism and socialism, every bit as well as the Roman Catholic Church has. The judgment of Catholic leaders and theologians over four hundred years has been that Protestants fall short without hands-on apostolic succession and communion with Rome when the fact is that the broken communion is also Rome's responsibility and sin. The position needs reconsideration.

The necessity of sticking by one's principles would hardly seem to be a lesson either Catholics or evangelicals need reiterated. The mutual criticism has been strong, pointed, and long a matter of record, although in our ecumenical age often transposed into the form of dialogue, and all of it is based on cherished and hoary principles. I suggest that Catholics pay very close attention to evangelical criticism of Catholic belief and practice, under the possibility that some if not most of it is worth attention. As most of our authors indicate, even if they would certainly not agree with my statement of the case, Catholics are not biblical or Bible people. They are not what Archbishop Whealon wanted, much less Nevins or Blanshard. Every one of our commentators would agree that they are a sacramental or liturgical people. Evangelical critique of Catholic sacramentalism is as much needed as Catholic critique of prophetism and biblicism. Moreover, the Catholic Church is controlled by a hierarchy and is in no way democratic or congregational for all the theological chatter about the local church and episcopal conferences and Roman synods. Is this theologically beyond criticism and question? Has the Catholic Church yet reached the point at which the laity will be taken into the administration and ministry of the church? Five centuries of alienation, four decades of talk have produced little or no change in the clerical stranglehold on power in the Catholic Church. God forbid that evangelicals should abandon the principle of equality of all Christians in the church as well as before God!

Furthermore, although their theologians and bishops constantly remind themselves and the Catholic laity of their "rich heritage in spirituality," perhaps Catholics are an impoverished people spiritually. Like the Bible, the Catholic literature of spirituality is there, but inactive and unused by most clergy as well as by the laity, in spite of heroic efforts such as the Jesuit planting of the Spiritual Exercises in a lay spirituality movement. Perhaps the laity are as spiritually undernourished as are the Catholic bishops who coddled priestly pedophiles and ephebophiles (then again, perhaps not).[41] Catholics are a people with many shepherds in whose voices it is all too often difficult to discern the voice of the True Shepherd and who are not in a position to mediate the "rich spiritual heritage." Many an ex-Catholic convert to a fundamentalist church would tell us that he or she never "heard the gospel" in a Catholic Church, and we can be sure that what he or she was hearing was not "the rich spiritual tradition." Perhaps they have not because they did not listen—or perhaps they did not because the teachers and preachers had not heard it themselves and spoken it. These are the common charges laid at the Catholic door, charges that sting and that need more than mere homiletic address by theologians in the closing paragraphs of their essays and by bishops in their occasional letters. The tradition is crippled insofar as it is ignored or mishandled by an unconverted and ill-educated ministry.

The way forward between Catholic and biblical Christianities is not silence anymore than it is polemics, but that way is mutually respectful theological and religious criticism based on each taking the other fully seriously as a Christian community. If biblical Christians cannot take liturgical Christianity as a valid form of Christian witness and life, if liturgical Christians cannot take biblical Christianity as a valid form of Christian witness and life, if they cannot recognize each other as churches of Christ, then the hope for Christian maturity is dim indeed.

The necessity of stanching hatred and polemic needs no political or even theological justification. It is simply a matter of decent Christian behavior. Apologetics should be an effort to explain one's own faith and the faith of one's community, not to apply a buzz saw to the position of others. Catholics and evangelicals need to drop the polemics, even though there are plenty of good reasons for them. As Gabriel Daly noted, ecumenical charity ought to rule even when it remains unilateral. Can evangelical hatred and fear of Catholicism come out of the depths of commitment to Christian witness? As a Catholic, I must ask: Is it possible that the love of Christ impels us to incivility and meanness? As for the Roman church, it not only lives and works for the gospel of Christ—alas, it makes a great deal of itself. Yet it elicits Christian loyalty and service. Yes, there is a species of truth to Mayhew's charge of idolatry, namely Catholic ecclesiocentrism. But Christian faith and hope do not deliver Protestant hatred and fear, nor Roman self-concern, complacency, and arrogance. The fountainhead or foundation of faith is the cross, the surrender of the "self." Hatred and complaisance are not signs of truth or trust, they are signs of broken faith or none at all. Kindness is a fruit of the Holy Spirit. Where it is not, the Spirit is not.

The stranger gets the attention of the tribe, which takes the stranger to be at once a threat and a promise, both fascinating and fearful. The potency of the stranger matches the potency of the tribe, for good or ill, and the tribe's response to the stranger is ambiguous. The Christian tribes have been for a thousand years especially torn, for they should never have self-protection and survival as the fundamental value. Their Lord did not. So it must take even the threat and its own fear as a moment to be transcended in acceptance and even love. The interactions between liturgical and biblical Christians, whichever is the lion or the lamb, must run along these lines, although they have not up to this point. Christian churches must find the grace of God at work in one another. In the dynamic of the tribe and the stranger, the stranger speaks, willy-nilly, with the voice of God. This was the gamble of *ECT*, and it ought to be the gamble of every Christian, biblical and liturgical.

# Notes

## I. TERMINOLOGY, MYTH, AND TRIBES

1. *Evangelicals and Catholics Together: Toward a Common Mission*, ed. Charles Colson and Richard John Neuhaus (Dallas: Word, 1995), xv–xxxv.

2. Basil Meeking and John Stott, eds., *The Evangelical–Roman Catholic Dialogue on Mission, 1977–1984* (Grand Rapids: Eerdmans, 1986); Roy Honeycutt, "Issues in Southern Baptist–Roman Catholic Dialogue," *Review and Expositor* 79/2 (Spring 1982): 199–395; "Presbyterian and Reformed–Roman Catholic Dialogues," in *Building Unity: Ecumenical Dialogues with Roman Catholic Participation in the United States*, ed. Joseph A. Burgess and Jeffrey Gros (New York: Paulist Press, 1989), 373–435; and reports of discussions between Catholics and Lutheran, Reformed, Pentecostal, and Evangelical representatives in *Deepening Communion: International Ecumenical Documents with Roman Catholic Participation*, ed. William G. Rusch and Jeffrey Gros (Washington, DC: United States Catholic Conference, 1998).

3. D. G. Hart, "An Old Protestant on American Christianity," *Regeneration Quarterly* (Winter 1995): 27–29. The participants were not entering a theological dialogue; rather, they attempted to address a cultural crisis from a religious perspective, a matter of practice based on some presumably common doctrines. That the participants should have so presumed is precisely what is at issue for "old Protestants."

4. A follow-up statement, "The Gift of Salvation," was published in January 1998. It was followed by a statement by evangelical theologians, many of whom had been critical of *ECT*, "The Gospel of Jesus Christ: An Evangelical Celebration." Both can be found in R. C. Sproul, *Getting the Gospel Right: The Tie That Binds Evangelicals Together* (Grand Rapids, MI: Baker Books, 1999), 185–95. The dialogue continues in *Your Word is Truth: A Project of Evangelicals and Catholics Together*, ed. Charles Colson and Richard John Neuhaus (Grand Rapids, MI: Eerdmans, 2002).

5. The relation of the churches to Islam is clearly a momentous one, perhaps the greater in world-historical terms. But the relation of the church and the synagogue has an element of conscience and heritage to it that is duplicated in no other. For a review of the basic differences to be addressed by Christians, see Jacob Neusner, *A Rabbi Talks with Jesus* (Montreal: McGill-Queens University Press, 2000), and *Children of the Flesh, Children of the Promise, A Rabbi Talks with Paul* (Cleveland: Pilgrim Press, 1995).

6. The ideologies are expressed in terms such as modernism, modernity, the Enlightenment, secularism, and now postmodernity. See Michael J. Lacey, ed., *Religion and Twentieth Century American Intellectual Life* (New York: Woodrow Wilson Center and Cambridge University Press, 1989) and W. Shea and P. Huff, eds., *Knowledge and Belief in America: Enlightenment Traditions and Modern Religious Thought* (New York: Woodrow Wilson Center and Cambridge University Press, 1995).

7. For an attempt to deal with the sometimes conflicting horizons of Christian theology and philosophical naturalism, see William M. Shea, *The Naturalists and the Supernatural* (Macon, GA: Mercer University Press, 1984).

8. Paul Blanshard, *American Freedom and Catholic Power* (Boston: Beacon Press, 1947). For a discussion of the cultural ethos of postwar American anti-Catholicism and Blanshard's reflection of it, see John T. McGreevy, "Thinking on One's Own: Catholicism in the American Intellectual Imagination, 1928–1960," *The Journal of American History* 84 (June 1997): 97–130.

9. See, for example, John Ankerberg and John Weldon, *Protestants and Catholics: Do They Now Agree?* (Eugene, OR: Harvest House, 1995).

10. Richard J. Neuhaus, *The Naked Public Square: Religion and Democracy in America* (Grand Rapids, MI: Eerdmans, 1984) and Pope John Paul II, *The Splendor of Truth* (Washington, DC: United States Catholic Conference, 1994).

11. G. C. Berkouwer, a Dutch Reformed theologian highly respected in American Reformed evangelical circles, and American conservative evangelicals such as the theologian David Wells in the wake of Vatican II penned constructive yet still highly critical appreciations of the Council. See G. C. Berkouwer, *The Conflict with Rome*, trans. H. de Jongste (Philadelphia: Presbyterian and Reformed Press, 1958). Compare his *The Second Vatican Council and the New Catholicism* (Grand Rapids, MI: Eerdmans, 1965); David F. Wells, *Revolution in Rome* (Downers Grove, IL: InterVarsity Press, 1972).

12. Jack Chick's pamphlets, tracts and several books are available from Chick Publications P.O. Box 3500, Ontario, CA 91761, and online at *postmaster@chick.com;* see Tony Alamo (aka Bernie Hoffman), "The Pope's Secrets" (Alma, AR: Holy Alamo Christian Church, n.d.), and J Gordon Melton, *Encyclopedic Handbook of Cults in America* (New York: Garland, 1992), 183–88.

13. John Warwick Montgomery, *Ecumenicity, Evangelicals, and Rome* (Grand Rapids, MI: Zondervan, 1969); and Bernard Lonergan, *Method in Theology* (New York: Herder, 1972), 235–38.

14. W. Shea, "The Future of Graduate Education in Theology," Patrick Carey and Earl Muller, S.J., eds., *Theological Education in the Catholic Tradition* (New York: Crossroads Press, 1997).

15. Martin E. Marty and R. Scott Appleby, eds., *Fundamentalism Observed* (Chicago: University of Chicago Press, 1991).

16. David W. Bebbington, "Evangelicalism in Its Settings: The British and American Movements since 1940," in Mark Noll, David W. Bebbington, and George A. Rawlyk, eds., *Evangelicalism: Comparative Studies of Popular Protestantism in North America, the British Isles, and Beyond, 1700–1990* (New York: Oxford University Press, 1994), 365ff.; and Mark Ellingsen, *The Evangelical Movement: Growth, Impact, Controversy, Dialogue* (Minneapolis: Augsburg Press, 1988). Others suggest that the "all-important symbolic markers" are "a personal relationship with Jesus Christ" and "obedience to the authority of the Bible." See Christian Smith, et al., *American Evangelicalism Embattled and Thriving* (Chicago: University of Chicago Press, 1998), 124. For a brief overview, see B. L. Shelley, "Evangelicalism" in Daniel G. Reid, ed., *Dictionary of Christianity in America* (Downers Grove, IL: InterVarsity Press, 1990), 413–16. The forms or subspecies of evangelicalism far surpass the subspecies that can now be distinguished within Catholicism, but adjectives grow increasingly important for both nouns. For a collection of essays on the stems and branches, see Donald W. Dayton and Robert K. Johnston, eds., *The Variety of American Evangelicalism* (Knoxville: University of Tennessee Press, 1991). The difficulties are discussed at length in Jon Stone, *On the Boundaries of American Evangelicalism: The Postwar Evangelical Coalition* (New York: St. Martin's Press, 1997).

17. See Randall Balmer, *Mine Eyes Have seen the Glory: A Journey into the Evangelical Subculture*, expanded edition (New York: Oxford University Press, 1993) and *Blessed Assurance: A History of Evangelicalism in America* (Boston: Beacon Press, 1999).

18. Joel Carpenter, *Revive Us Again: The Reawakening of American Fundamentalism* (New York: Oxford University Press, 1997).

19. Sydney E. Ahlstrom, "From Puritanism to Evangelicalism: A Critical Perspective," in David F. Wells and John Woodbridge, eds., *The Evangelicals: What They Believe, Who They Are, and Where They are Changing* (Nashville: Abingdon Press, 1975), 270. Anti-Catholicism is the first of six on Ahlstrom's list of characteristics of American evangelicalism.

20. George Marsden defines it as "militantly anti-modernist Protestant evangelicalism," in *Fundamentalism and American Culture: The Shaping of Twentieth-Century Evangelicalism, 1870–1925* (New York: Oxford University Press, 1980), 4. For the bishops' usage, see "A Pastoral Statement for Catholics on Biblical Fundamentalism," printed in W. Shea, ed., *The Struggle Over the Past: Fundamentalism in the Modern World* (Lanham, MD: University Press of America, 1993), 327–32.

21. Mary Jo Weaver and R. Scott Appleby, eds., *Being Right: Conservative Catholicism in America*, and Joseph Komonchak's essay in it, "Interpreting the Council: Catholic Attitudes toward Vatican II." The differences among Catholics are such that evangelical authors often remark on them; see John Armstrong, ed., *Roman Catholicism: Evangelical Protestants Analyze What Divides and Unites Us* (Chicago: Moody Press, 1994). David Wells had commented on this surprising and not entirely welcome development twenty years before, as had John Warwick Montgomery. It would seem that "all that is solid melts into the air," even in the case of Roman Catholicism.

22. Avery Dulles, *Models of the Church* (Garden City, NY: Image Books, 1974).

23. David O'Brien, *Public Catholicism* (New York: Macmillan, 1988); and Patrick W. Carey, ed., *American Catholic Religious Thought* (New York: Paulist Press, 1975), especially Carey's introduction.

24. The term, new to me, was used widely at the Wheaton College "Conference on Evangelicals and Catholics" (April 11–13, 2002). Although attending carefully to the use of the term, I was unable to decide exactly what it meant. It may simply mean a Catholic who has accepted Christ's work through faith, supposing that there are many Catholics who have not and are therefore "uncommitted Catholics." Because I cannot say that I am born again in what I think evangelicals mean by that term, I am committed to the practice of the Catholic religion and, oddly, still an "uncommitted Catholic."

25. Ray Allen Billington, *The Protestant Crusade, 1800–1860, A Study of the Origins of American Nativism* (New York: Macmillan, 1938); Jenny Franchot, *Roads to Rome: The Antebellum Protestant Encounter with Catholicism* (Berkeley: University of California Press, 1994). The best study of nativism as a national phenomenon is John Higham, *Strangers in the Land: Patterns of American Nativism* (New York: Atheneum, 1963). Other academic comments on anti-Catholicism can be found in: Andrew Greeley, *An Ugly Little Secret: Anti-Catholicism in North America* (Kansas City: Sheed, Andrews, and McMeel, 1977); Robert Hueston, *The Catholic Press and Nativism* (New York: Arno Press, 1976); John S. Kane, *Catholic-Protestant Conflicts in America* (Chicago: Regnery, 1955). Popular and revealing accounts were written by Mark Hurley, *The Unholy Ghost: Anti-Catholicism in the American Experience* (Huntington, IN: Our Sunday Visitor Press, 1992), and by Michael Schwartz, *The Persistent Prejudice: Anti-Catholicism in America* (Huntington, IN: Our Sunday Visitor Press, 1984).

26. Richard Hofstadter, *Anti-Intellectualism in American Life* (New York: Random House, 1962).

27. The recent literature includes John Wolffe, "Anti-Catholicism and Evangelical Identity in Britain and the United States, 1830–1860," in Noll, et al., *Evangelicalism: Comparative Studies,* 179–97; John Wolffe, *The Protestant Crusade in Great Britain, 1829–1860* (New York: Oxford University Press, 1991); Harmut Lehmann, "Anti-Catholic and Anti-Protestant Propaganda in Mid-nineteenth-century America and Europe," in *Pietismus und Neuzeit. Luther-Verlag Jahrblicher zor Geschichte des Pietismus* 17: 121–34; Gary W. McDonogh, "Constructing Christian Hatred: Anti-Catholicism, Diversity, and Identity in Southern Religious Life," in O. Kendell White, Jr. and Daryl White, eds., *Religion in the Contemporary South: Diversity, Community, and Identity* (Athens: University of Georgia Press, 1995), 67–78; a lecture by Lynn Dumenil, "The Tribal Twenties: The Catholic Response to Anti-Catholicism," Claremont McKenna College, Claremont, CA., 1988; Mark Noll, "The History of an Encounter: Roman Catholics and Protestant Evangelicals," in Charles Colson and Richard Neuhaus, *Evangelicals and Catholics Together: Toward A Common Mission* (Dallas: Word, 1995), 81–114; Noll, "The Eclipse of Old Hostilities between and the Potential for New Strife among Catholics and Protestants Since Vatican II," in Robert Bellah and Frederick Greenspahn, eds., *Uncivil Religion, Interreligious Hostility in America* (New York: Crossroad, 1987), 86–109; Noll, *American Evangelical Christianity, An Introduction* (Oxford: Blackwell, 2001), 111–47; Peter A. Huff, "New Apologists in America's Conservative Catholic Subculture," in *Horizons, The Journal of the College Theology Society* 23/2 (1996): 242–60; William M. Shea, "Fundamentalism: How Catholics Approach It," in Francis Nichols, ed., *Christianity and the Stranger: Historical Essays.* Studies in Religion and the Social Order (Atlanta, GA: Scholars Press, 1995), 221–86; and John T. Mc-

Greevy, "Thinking on One's Own: Catholicism in the American Intellectual Imagination, 1928–1960."

28. Jacob Neusner, "Defining a Religion: A Method Exemplified in Defining Judaism," in *The Twentieth Century Construction of "Judaism": Essays on the Religion of Torah in the History of Religion*. USF Studies in the History of Judaism, vol. 32 (Atlanta: Scholars Press, 1991), 331–50.

29. Smithsonian Institution, Woodrow Wilson Center tape, 1986–87.

30. The key essays on myth and the New Testament remain Rudolph Bultmann's "New Testament and Mythology," in H. W. Bartsch, ed., *Kerygma and Myth* (New York: Harper Bros., 1961), 1–44, and Rudolph Bultmann, *Jesus Christ and Mythology* (New York: Charles Scribner's Sons, 1958). It is Bultmann's understanding of myth that I adopt and apply to what I regard as mythological telling of the history of the church born or heightened in the polemics of the sixteenth century, mythological precisely in the sense that the history is told by both Protestants and Catholics as a struggle between God's grace and Satan's snares. For discussions of the concept of myth in the study of religion, see Mircea Eliade, *Cosmos and History: the Myth of the Eternal Return* (New York: Harper, 1959). Reviews of the present status of the study of myth can be found in S. Daniel Breslauer, "Mythology, Judaism and," in Jacob Neusner, Alan J. Avery-Peck, and William S. Green, eds., *The Encyclopedia of Judaism* (Boston: Brill, 2000) 2: 939–60; Robert Segal, "Myth," in the *International Encyclopedia of the Social and Behavioral Sciences* (New York: Elsevier, 2001), 15: 10273–78 and Victor Turner, "Myth and Symbol," in the *Encyclopedia of the Social Sciences* (New York: Macmillan, 1968), 10: 576–81. See also Alasdair MacIntyre, "Myth," *Encyclopedia of Philosophy* (New York: Collier-MacMillan, 1967) 5: 434–37; T. Gaster, "Myth," *Interpreter's Dictionary of the Bible* (New York: Abingdon, 1962) 4: 481–87; E. Dinkler, "Myth in the New Testament," *ibid.* 4: 487–89; Heinrich Fries, "Myth," *Sacramentum Mundi* (New York: Herder and Herder,1969), 4: 152–56. Historians might well disagree with my usage and prefer a term such as *perspective* to designate the differences in putatively historical accounts. I cling to "myth" because, unlike perspectival explanations of the differences, "myth" seems the proper way to designate a narrative that brings God into the otherwise bare historical account. Thus, the perspective at issue in this sort of account necessitates such notions as providence and grace, and the clash of sin and salvation. I believe it is as impossible to construct such a narrative out of the data of the history of the Christian church as it is to construct divine Sonship out of the data of the life and death of Jesus of Nazareth. See Mark Noll's *Turning Points: Decisive Moments in the History of Christianity*, 31–34, for a use of the term *perspective* in accounting for differences in Protestant, Catholic, and Orthodox accounts of Christian origins.

31. The Protestant retelling of the church's story began with Luther. "In asides and fragments Luther framed an entirely new and revolutionary way of viewing the past; in him the new system is essentially complete; to the Protestant historians— Sleiden, Illyricus, Foxe—remained only the task of formulating the Lutheran system as systematic and chronological history." Anthony Kemp, The *Estrangement of the Past: A Study in the Origins of Modern Historical Consciousness* (New York: Oxford University Press, 1991), 75ff. The fullest formulation of the Protestant myth in the time of the Reformation is by Matthias Flacius Illyricus (1520–75), *Centuriae Magdebourgensis*, 3rd

edition published in Nürnberg in 1757. The first edition was published between 1559 and 1574 under the title *Ecclesiastica historica*. The myth is assumed by the anti-Catholic authors of the nineteenth century, and is retold in many forms. See, for example, the Adventist prophetess Ellen White, *The Great Controversy: Unseen Powers Struggle for Supremacy* (1888; reprint Napa, ID: Pacific Press, 1990), still distributed door to door. Detailed version of the Roman digestion of pagan myths and practices, resting on comparative religions and history of religions data, can be found in Alexander Hislop, *The Two Babylons, or Papal Worship Proved to be the Worship of Nimrod and his Wife* (1916; reprint London: A & C Black, 1932), and recooked by Ralph Woodrow, *Babylonian Mystery Religion* (London: Evangelistic Association, n.d.). It is ignored by most Protestant academic historians. Cf. Justo Gonzalez, *A History of Thought*, three vols. (Nashville: Abingdon Press, 1975), and Mark Noll, *Turning Points: Decisive Moments in the History of Christianity* (Grand Rapids, MI: Baker Books, 1997). It dominates Loraine Boettner's list of Catholic adaptations of paganism and appears even in works by so astute a theologian as J. I. Packer, the most eminent of the signers of *ETC*. See the latter's conference paper, forthcoming, InterVarsity Press, or on audiotape at the Wheaton College media center.

32. The Catholic answer to the story told by the Centuriators was first formulated by Caesare Baronio in his twelve-volume *Annales ecclesiastici* (1607; reprint Bari-Duces, Italy: *Consociatio Sancti Pauli*, 1880). Catholic historians have for a long time told the history in the fashion of the modern academy. For example, see Thomas Bokenkotter, *A Concise History of the Catholic Church* (New York Doubleday, 1979). The Myth, however, appears in basic religious texts such as the *Catechism of the Catholic Church* (1992; reprint New York: Doubleday, 1995), and in its modern *locus classicus*, the third chapter of *Lumen Gentium*. Catholics have evolved a secular telling of the story by historians now laid out beside the ancient and mythological telling. The compressed expression for the latter is the doctrine of apostolic succession.

33. The tension of this process is undeniable. Consult especially the Constitution on the Church in the Modern World (1965), the Decree on Ecumenism (1964), and the Declarations on Religious Liberty and on the Relation of the Church to Non-Christian Religion (1965) in *Vatican Council II: The Basic Sixteen Documents*, ed. Austin Flannery, O.P. (Northport, NY: Costello, 1996). To a limited extent the Myth is reasserted "authoritatively" in *Dominus Iesus* (Washington, DC: United States Catholic Conference, 2001) and in other recent documents, including the Apostolic Letter, *Ordinatio Sacerdotalis* (Washington, DC: United States Catholic Conference, 2001), on the ordination of women.

34. The reassertion of *mythos* over *logos* is nicely argued by the naturalist philosopher John Herman Randall, Jr. *Hellenistic Ways of Deliverance and the Making of the Christian Synthesis* (New York: Columbia University Press, 1970).

35. The Enlightenment story is retold by or supposed in many of the great philosophical texts of the modern era, including Kant and Compte. See it in John Dewey's *Quest for Certainty* (1919; reprint New York: G. P. Putnam's Sons, 1960), and in the works of minor American naturalists such as Sidney Hook and Corliss Lamont. A neat recitation can be found in Duncan Howlett's *The Critical Way in Religion: Testing and Questing* (Buffalo: Prometheus Books, 1980). The basic problem in cognitional theory underlying this philosophical tradition is discussed in Shea, *The Naturalists and the Supernatural*.

36. On the surface, postmodernism looks like the end of the Enlightenment myth and of modernism. But is it? Enlightenment and modernist ideals admit of a level of abstraction and universality that postmoderns find immensely uncomfortable and profoundly objectionable. The myth of Reason no longer rings true to them, yet they have no other tool than disciplined reason to correct the disciplined reason of their parents-in-myth. Like Hume and Kant, they use reason to show the limits of reason, and to construct reasonable solutions to the problems caused by the failure of Reason in ethics and politics. Cf. "Introduction," William M. Shea and Peter A. Huff, eds., *Knowledge and Belief in America: Enlightenment Traditions and Modern Religious Thought* (New York: Cambridge University Press and the Woodrow Wilson Center Press, 1995), 1–16; in the same work, see essays on postmodernism by Schubert Ogden, David Tracy, and Richard Bernstein, 321–46.

37. The term *tribe* is regarded by some social scientists as obsolete. It is certainly contested. For different views of its use and usefulness, see A. Gingrich, "Tribe," in Neil J. Smelser, ed., *International Encyclopedia of the Social and Behavioral Sciences* (New York: Elsevier, 2001) 23: 15906–9.

38. I. M. Lewis, "Tribal Society," in *International Encyclopedia of the Social Sciences*, 16: 146–51.

39. See Robert Wuthnow, *The Struggle for America's Soul* (Grand Rapids, MI: Eerdmans, 1989); see also William Shea, "Divided Loyalties," *Commonweal* 119 (9 January 1992): 9–14.

40. Mark Mazower, *Dark Continent: Europe's Twentieth Century* (New York: Alfred A. Knopf, 1999).

41. Dewey's theory of education is perhaps the best example of this. See John Dewey, *Democracy and Education* (New York: Macmillan, 1966), and John Dewey, *A Common Faith* (New Haven, CT: Yale University Press, 1934). On classicism, see Bernard Lonergan, *Method in Theology* (New York: Herder, 1972).

42. See the discussion of community in Philip Selznick, *The Communitarian Persuasion* (Washington, DC: Woodrow Wilson Press, 2002), and in Bernard Lonergan, *Insight: A Study of Human Understanding*, chapters 6 and 7, and *Method in Theology* (New York: Herder and Herder, 1972), chapters 3 and 4. For a provocative use of the concept "sacred society," see Darrell Fasching, *The Coming of the Millennium: Good News for the Whole Human Race* (Valley Forge, PA: Trinity Press International,1996), 28–37.

43. Ernst Cassirer, *The Myth of the State* (New York: Doubleday, 1955); John Herman Randall, *The Meaning of Religion for Man* (New York: Harper, 1968); and Carl Raschke, *The Interruption of Eternity: Modern Gnosticism and the Origins of the New Religious Consciousness* (Chicago: Nelson-Hall, 1980).

44. *The Grand Inquisitor*, in Fyodor Dostoevsky, *The Brothers Karamazov* (Chicago: Encyclopedia Britannica, 1952).

45. Fasching, *The Coming of the Millennium*.

46. Bernhard Asen, "From Acceptance to Inclusion: The Stranger in Old Testament Tradition," F. Nichols, ed., *Christianity and the Stranger: Historical Essays*, 16–35.

47. Roman Catholicism seems more important in the Protestant myth than Protestantism is in the Roman Catholic myth. The most evident reason is that for Catholics the Reformation, like the schism with the churches of the East, is only an episode in a much larger narrative stretching from Pentecost to the Last Day, while Protes-

tantism, granted its claim to apostolic origin, has chosen to begin its tale in the six-teenth century. In addition, why there need to be many Christian churches may be more difficult to explain than why there should be one when the corruption of the one is the explanation for the existence of the many.

48. Trutz Rentorff, "The Modern Age as a Chapter in the History of Christianity, or, the Legacy of Historical Consciousness in Present Theology," *Journal of Religion* 65/4 (October 1985): 478–499.

## 2. THE PERILS OF MODERNITY

1. Tertullian, *Liber de praescriptionibus adversus haereticos*, VII, in *Patrologia Latina* 2: .0019A.

2. See, for example, Norman Cohen, *The Pursuit of the Millennium: Revolutionary Millenarians and Mystical Anarchists of the Middle Ages* (New York: Oxford University Press, 1970).

3. For a review of literature and a bibliography on Darwin and religious reac-tions, see James C. Livingston, "Darwin, Darwinism, and Theology: Recent Studies," in *Religious Studies Review* 8 (1982): 105–16. And John Haught, *God After Darwin: A Theology of Evolution* (Boulder, CO: Westview Press, 2000).

4. The words are those of John Herman Randall Jr., in "The Changing Influence of Darwin on Philosophy," in *Journal of the History of Ideas*, 22/7 (October–December 1961): 452. He wrote in 1960 for a Darwin centenary celebration. He refers to an essay of John Dewey written on the fiftieth anniversary of Darwin's book. See Dewey, *The Influence of Darwin on Philosophy and Other Essays in Contemporary Thought* (Bloom-ington: Indiana University Press, 1965.1910).

5. The procedures and results of the Jesus seminar are only the latest outrage! See Robert Funk, *The Five Gospels: The Search for the Authentic Words of Jesus* (New York: Macmillan, 1993), 1–38. For a critical historical reading of the discoveries of the last two centuries and their accompanying ideological squabbles, see Philip Jenkins, *The Hidden Gospels* (New York: Oxford University Press, 2002); a theological rejoinder to the Jesus Seminar can be had in Luke Timothy Johnson, *"The Real Jesus": The Mis-guided Quest for the Historical Jesus and the Truth of the Traditional Gospels* (San Fran-cisco: Harper Bros., 1996).

6. Brief overviews of the history of biblical criticism can be found in the stan-dard dictionaries and encyclopedias such as *The New Jerome Biblical Commentary* (En-glewood Cliffs, NJ: Prentice Hall, 1990), *Peake's Commentary* (New York: T. Nelson, 1962), and the *Interpreter's Dictionary of the Bible* (Nashville: Abingdon, 1976), as well as in introductions such as Fiene-Behm-Kummel's *Introduction to the New Testament* (London: SCM Press, 1975) and Raymond Brown's *Introduction to the New Testament* (New York: Doubleday Anchor, 1998). For more detailed studies, see Robert M. Grant, *A Short History of the Interpretation of the Bible* (New York: Macmillan, 1963) and Jerry W. Brown, *The Rise of Biblical Criticism in America, 1800–1870: the New England Schol-ars* (Middletown, CT: Wesleyan University Press, 1969); Gerald P. Fogarty, S.J., *Ameri-can Catholic Biblical Scholarship: A History from the Early Republic to Vatican II* (San Francisco: Harper and Row, 1989), and Mark Noll, *Between Faith and Criticism, Evangelicals, Scholarship and the Bible in America* (San Francisco: Harper and Row, 1986).

7. For a brief account and interpretation of the revivals, see William G. Mc-Loughlin, *Revivals, Awakenings, and Reform: An Essay on Religion and Social Change in America* (Chicago: University of Chicago Press, 1978). The first of these events has been termed "interpretive fiction" by Jon Butler in *Awash in a Sea of Faith: Christianizing the American People* (Cambridge, MA: Harvard University Press, 1990), 164–65.

8. T. T. Martin, quoted in Willard B. Gatewood, ed., *Controversy in the Twenties: Fundamentalism, Modernism, and Evolution* (Nashville: Vanderbilt University Press, 1969), 19.

9. For a discussion and historical presentation, see Mark A. Noll, "The Rise and Long Life of the Protestant Enlightenment in America" in W. Shea and P. Huff, ed., *Knowledge and Belief in America: Enlightenment Traditions and Modern Religious Thought* (New York: Cambridge University Press, 1995), 88–124.

10. R. A. Torrey, A. C. Dixon, et al., eds., *The Fundamentals: A Testimony to the Truth* (Grand Rapids, MI: Baker Book House, 1980.1917).

11. Dyson Hague, "The History of Higher Criticism," in *The Fundamentals*, I: 32.

12. "Evolution in the Pulpit by An Occupant of the Pew," *The Fundamentals*, IV: 92.

13. For discussions of the movements and the essays, see Ernest Sandeen, *The Roots of Fundamentalism: British and American Millenarianism, 1800–1930* (Grand Rapids, MI: Baker Book House, 1970); George Marsden, *Fundamentalism and American Culture: The Shaping of 20th Century Evangelicalism, 1870–1925* (New York: Oxford University Press, 1980); and George Dollar, *A History of Fundamentalism in America* (Greenville, SC: Bob Jones University Press, 1973).

14. Several other traditionalist organizations also were formed. See Marsden, 152ff.

15. Curtis Lee Laws, "Convention Side Lights," *Watchman-Examiner* 8 (July 1, 1920): 834.

16. For the fundamentalists and the historians of the period, the terms liberal and modernist are used interchangeably; so also fundamentalist, conservative, and evangelical. I prefer to use the term liberal to designate those who are for the most part doctrinally orthodox and theologically moderate, who had not adopted the radical methodological stand of modernists such as Shailer Mathews and Shirley Case Jackson at Chicago Divinity School and the Catholic Alfred Loisy, and who maintained a position in favor of freedom of conscience and expression for church members. I reserve the term modernist for those who give evidence of believing that contradictions between scientific/historical conclusions and traditional religious beliefs are to be adjudicated solely by the canons of scientific and historical method. For the latter the source of authority in matters of knowledge seems to me to have clearly shifted from the church to the academic disciplines. Whether or not *all* of these people, from left to right, can and should call one another Christians is a question that I cannot settle.

17. See Marsden, 171ff. The sermon was printed in three popular Protestant journals within the month after it was delivered; see Marsden, 277, n1.

18. Shailer Mathews, *The Faith of Modernism* (1924; reprint New York: AMS Press, 1969).

19. Cf. Machen, *Christianity and Liberalism*, 52. I will discuss Machen's preference in the age of modernist Protestantism in chapter 8, when I explain how evangelicals have estimated Catholicism as a form of Christianity. It should be noted as well

that Machen rejected dispensational premillennialism, a cornerstone eschatological doctrine for most fundamentalists, and lacked any desire to see the Christian church(es) dominate or direct American culture. Machen resists ideological pigeon-holing, as does the church he helped found, the Orthodox Presbyterian Church.

20. See Mark Massa, *Charles Augustus Briggs and the Crisis of Historical Criticism* (Minneapolis: Fortress, 1990).

21. Westminster held its first classes in Philadelphia in fall 1929. For the Princeton and Westminster story, see Bradley J. Longfield, *The Presbyterian Controversy: Fundamentalists, Modernist, and Moderates* (New York: Oxford University Press, 1991), 162–80. For an interpretation of Machen's role in the controversy and his significance overall in the cultural crisis reflected in the fundamentalist-modernist battles, see D. G. Hart, *Defending the Faith: J. Gresham Machen and the Crisis of Conservative Protestantism in Modern America* (Baltimore, MD: Johns Hopkins University Press, 1994). Machen's colleague and friend Ned B. Stonehouse wrote *J. Gresham Machen: A Biographical Memoir* (Grand Rapids, MI: Eerdmans, 1954).

22. See D. G. Hart and John Muether, *Fighting the Good Fight: A Brief History of the Orthodox Presbyterian Church* (Philadelphia: The Committee on Christian Education of the Orthodox Presbyterian Church, 1995). Named at first as the Presbyterian Church in America, it was renamed after a suit was brought by the Presbyterian Church, USA. Machen's untimely death occurred within a year of the founding of the church. See Ned B. Stonehouse, *J. Gresham Machen, a Biographical Memoir*, 506–08.

23. Sandeen, 257–65; and Marsden, 164–95.

24. On the trial and its aftermath, see Marsden, 184ff. The charges are to a large extent unfounded. The leaders were pastors of large city parishes and were considerable figures in their communities, although they came from rural and often Southern backgrounds. They were college educated and most of them had (conservative) seminary training. Their leading theologian, Machen, was easily an intellectual match for the modernist opposition. For the variety of interpretations of modernism, see Marsden, 199–230; and, for biographical data, C. Allyn Russell, *Voices of American Fundamentalism: Seven Biographical Studies* (Philadelphia: Westminster Press, 1976). See Longfield on Bryan's role in the Presbyterian church and on other Presbyterian leaders of the time. See also Edward Larson, *Summer for the Gods: The Scopes Trial and America's Continuing Debate over Science and Religion* (New York: Basic Books, 1997).

25. Marsden, 4.

26. Gatewood, 24.

27. See Ferenc Szasz, *The Divided Mind of Protestant America, 1880–1930* (Tuscaloosa: University of Alabama Press, 1982). Harold Lindsell in *The Battle for the Bible* (Grand Rapids, MI: Zondervan, 1976) presents the case for inerrancy and the commonsense meaning of the Bible. The case involves the Bible's affirmation of its own inerrancy: the texts used are II Timothy 3, 16 and II Peter I, 12–21. The logic of the argument would be familiar to Catholics who find that the infallibility of the bishops and pope was infallibly defined by the bishops at the insistence of the pope.

28. See Revelation and I Thessalonians texts. On millenarian anti-Catholicism, see Sandeen, 17.

29. The positions are echoed in recent fundamentalist works; see Lindsell and Dollar. J. I. Packer, a British evangelical rather than an American fundamentalist, for example, once maintained that "... the various sorts of 'Catholicism,' on the one

hand, and of liberal Protestantism, on the other, are found wanting. In the course of the development which produced them, they have to a greater or lesser degree become something other than Christianity. They are the eccentricities and novelties, while Evangelicalism alone stands in the true line of Christian development." See Packer, *"Fundamentalism" and the Word of God* (Grand Rapids, MI: Eerdmans, 1958), 39; see also 46–51. Packer later changed his mind and became a signer of ECT. See the comment by Mark Noll in Colson and Neuhaus, eds., *Evangelicals and Catholics Together,* 81.

30. Ed Dobson, Ed Hindson, and Jerry Falwell, *The Fundamentalist Phenomenon: The Resurgence of Conservative Christianity* (Grand Rapids, MI: Baker Books, 1986), 27 ff.

31. Both Donald Bloesch and Alister McGrath lay stress on the continuity of evangelical faith with the medieval church. See their essays in John Armstrong, ed., *Roman Catholicism: Evangelical Protestants Analyze What Divides and What Unites Us* (Chicago: Moody Press, 1994). For others in the same volume the older view of stark discontinuity still holds; see W. Robert Godfrey, for example, and others severely critical of ECT.

32. This disengagement from the culture (political, social, and intellectual) is what the later neo-evangelicals found unacceptable. There are continuities as well, and so contrasts must be made cautiously. Fundamentalists make a good case that they represent both the Reformation and American Puritan positions in several respects, more clearly and more emphatically than do mainline Protestant churches. See Dobson, *The Fundamentalist Phenomenon.* But the fact remains that the larger and older bodies have tended to share in the culture and to regard one another as manifestations of the one spiritual church while the fundamentalists tend to be highly critical of selected aspects of the culture and to regard anyone who does not adopt a checklist of doctrines, signaled by but not exhausted in the doctrine of inerrancy, as unworthy of fellowship. See Dollar's distinctions between fundamentalists on the basis of purity of doctrine and militancy, and his discussion of fellowship and separation. For a brief version see George Dollar, *History of Fundamentalism in America,* http://www.seageronline.org.

33. For a discussion of the Princeton theology of inerrancy, see Marsden, 109–18; and Sandeen, 114–30 and 168–69.

34. For Machen's Calvinist theological leanings, see his radio talks, *The Christian View of Man* (1937; reprint Edinburgh: Banner of Truth Trust, 1965).

35. See *A Treatise Concerning Religious Affections* in vol. 2 of John E. Smith, ed., *The Works of Jonathan Edwards* (New Haven, CT: Yale University Press, 1959), 95. Edwards used holy affection as the first sign of the presence of the Holy Spirit.

36. Edwards was suspicious of dogmatic stands that led to separation when these stands appeared in the Great Awakening, and called Whitefield and Tennent to task for their intemperate and censorious speech. Bushnell's theological method amounted to a rejection of commonsense and dogmatic theological reading of the scriptures, and of the "logical and scientifical" exegetical method of New England theologians. On Bushnell, see W. Shea, "Religious Language and Theological Method," in Matthew Lamb, ed., *Creativity and Method: Essays in Honor of Bernard Lonergan* (Milwaukee: Marquette University Press, 1981), 153–72. Charles Hodge, Bushnell's contemporary, was the foremost exponent of "scientific" method in theology. See

Mark Noll, *The Scandal of the Evangelical Mind* (Grand Rapids, MI: Eerdmans, 1994), 182–85.

37. Donald Dayton and Robert Johnston, eds., *The Variety of American Evangelicalism*. On the general social action tendencies, see the essays in Leonard I. Sweet, ed., *The Evangelical Tradition in America*, and in David Wells and John Woodbridge, eds., *The Evangelicals: What They Believe, Who they Are, and Where they are Changing*.

38. The "new evangelicals" attempt to extend evangelical ethical concern to social issues on biblical grounds; see Robert O. Linder, "The Resurgence of Evangelical Social Concern (1925–75)," in Wells and Woodbridge, eds., *The Evangelicals*, 209–30. See Joel Carpenter, *Revive Us Again*, and Jon Stone, *On the Boundaries of American Evangelicalism: The Post-war Evangelical Coalition*.

39. Harold Lindsell, *The Battle for the Bible* (Grand Rapids, MI: Zondervan Publishing House, 1976). For a parallel Catholic reaction to softening of the integralist borderlines by Catholic scholars, see George Kelly, *The Battle of the American Church* (New York: Doubleday, 1979), and *The Crisis of Authority: John Paul and the American Bishops* (Chicago: Regnery-Gateway, 1981).

40. On creationism, see Anne Clifford, "Creation Science: Religion and Science in North America," in W. Shea, ed., *The Struggle Over the Past: Religious Fundamentalism in the Modern World*, 103–23.

41. His case is published in Jimmy Swaggart, *Catholicism and Christianity* (Baton Rouge: Jimmy Swaggart Ministries, 1986). There is a fine biography: Ann Rowe Seamon, *Swaggart, The Unauthorized Biography of an American Evangelist* (New York: Continuum, 1999).

42. *Time* reports in its July 1, 2002, issue that over thirty-five million copies of evangelist Tim LaHaye's and Jerry B. Jenkins's ten volumes of the dispensationalist novel *Left Behind* (Wheaton, IL: Tyndale House, 1995–2002) have been sold. See *Time*, pp. 44, 50–53. In typical evangelical fashion, La Haye has said that the Catholic Church is a false religion.

43. For sketches of the history of Catholic modernism and modernists and the papal reaction, see John J. Heaney, *The Modernist Crisis* (Washington, DC: Corpus Books, 1968); John Ratte, *Three Modernists: Alfred Loisy, George Tyrrell, and William L. Sullivan* (New York: Sheed and Ward, 1967); Alec Vidler, *A Variety of Catholic Modernists* (New York: Cambridge University Press, 1970). For an eminently readable recent history see Marvin O'Connell, *Critics on Trial: An Introduction to the Catholic Modernist Crisis* (Washington, DC: Catholic University of America Press, 1994); for contextual analysis of the crisis, see Lester Kurtz, *The Politics of Heresy: The Modernist Crisis in Roman Catholicism* (Berkeley: University of California Press, 1986); and the philosophical and theological aspects are nicely drawn by Gabriel Daley, *Transcendence and Immanence A Study in Catholic Modernism and Integralism* (New York: Oxford University Press, 1980).

44. Gregory XVI, *Mirari vos* (1832) in Claudia Carlen, ed., *The Papal Encyclicals* (Raleigh, NC: McGrath, 1981) I: 235–41; Pius IX, *Quanta cura* (1864) in Carlen, I: 381–86.

45. John J. Wynne, S.J., ed., *The Great Encyclicals of Pope Leo XIII* (New York: Benziger Bros., 1903), 441–53.

46. R. Scott Appleby, *"Church and Age Unite!" The Modernist Impulse in American Catholicism* (Notre Dame, IN: University of Notre Dame Press, 1992), 81–89. On the

papal construction of antimodern Catholicism, see Joseph A. Komonchak, "Modernity and the Construction of Roman Catholicism," Woodrow Wilson International Center for Scholars, Smithsonian Institution, lecture, May 9, 1985.

47. On the *New York Review* see Appleby, 117–58; see also Thomas Shelley, *Dunwoodie: The History of St. Joseph's Seminary, Yonkers, New York* (Westminster, MD: Christian Classics, 1993).

48. Leo XIII, *Providentissimus Deus* in Carlen, II: 325–40. For comments on the letters *Providentissimus Deus* and *Divino Afflante Spiritu*, see Raymond Brown, *The Critical Meaning of the Bible* (New York: Paulist Press, 1981), 1–41. The Catholic Church's official statements on scripture are discussed by Brown and Thomas Collins in "Church Pronouncements," Raymond Brown, Joseph Fitzmyer, and Roland Murphy, eds., *The New Jerome Biblical Commentary* (Englewood Cliffs, NJ: Prentice Hall, 1990), 1166–74.

49. Alfred Loisy, *The Gospel and the Church*, ed. Bernard B. Scott (1902; reprint Philadelphia: Fortress Press, 1979).

50. Marvin O'Connell, *Critics on Trial*, 241ff.

51. *Pascendi* and *Lamentabili* can be found in *On the Doctrine of the Modernists* (Boston: Sisters of St. Paul, n.d.).

52. Paragraph 39.

53. Paragraph 40. The condemned men understood fully that the pope and his men saw the issue in moral or spiritual terms rather than intellectual or even doctrinal ones. Some years after the crisis reached its peak in 1907 and 1908, the chief modernist, Alfred Loisy, looked back at the events that led to his excommunication and recognized that the pope demanded humility and obedience rather than acceptance of this or that theological proposition or doctrine. Nor was Pius X willing to accept mere professions of submission. See Loisy's *My Duel With the Vatican* (1913; reprint New York: E. P. Dutton, 1924), 252–53, 264, and 266–68.

54. See Lawrence Barmann, *Baron Friedrich von Hugel and the Modernist Crisis in England* (New York: Cambridge University Press, 1972).

55. On shunning, see "The European Free-Church Family," in J. Gordon Melton, ed., *The Encyclopedia of American Religions* (Tarrytown, NY: Triumph Books, 1991) I: 49ff. On Loisy's excommunication, see Marvin R. O'Connell, *Critics on Trial: An Introduction to the Catholic Modernist Crisis* (Washington, DC: Catholic University Press, 1994), 369–70.

56. James G. Livingston, *Tradition and the Critical Spirit: Catholic Modernist Writings* (Minneapolis: Fortress Press, 1991), xv.

57. On the Pontifical Biblical Commission, see Gerald P. Fogarty, *American Catholic Biblical Scholarship: A History from the Early Republic to Vatican II* (San Francisco: Harper and Row, 1989).

58. *Pascendi*, paragraph 55.

59. Pius XII, *Divino Afflante Spiritu* in Carlen, IV: 65–80. The pope seems to have in mind the attitude of Catholic integralists, which echoed the words of Bossuet: "There is no difficulty about recognizing false doctrine. . . . It is recognized at once, whenever it appears, merely because it is new." J. B. Bossuet, *Oeuve Completes* (Paris: Meguignon, 1846), 30: 419–420. It should be recognized that Benedict XV had in 1920 disowned the committees of vigilance in *Spiritus Paraclitus*. See the *NJBC*, 1167 ff.

60. "Christ the Subject: A Reply," in F. E. Crowe, ed., *Collection: Papers by Bernard Lonergan* (New York: Herder and Herder, 1967), 164–97. The attack came from another Jesuit, A. Perego, in "Una Nuova opinione sull'unita psicologica di Christo," *Divinitas* 2 (1958), 409–424.

61. The essays in question are: Myles M. Bourke, "The Literary Genus of Matthew 1–2," *Catholic Biblical Quarterly* 22 (1960): 160–75; and Richard J. Dillon, "St. Luke's Infancy Account: A Study of the Interpretation of Literary Form and Theological Meaning," *Dunwoodie Review* 1 (1961): 5–37. Bourke was charged in print with being a "new modernist" by an Italian theologian, Antonino Romeo; Dillon was subjected to criticism by a New York bishop, James Griffiths, who attempted to stop his ordination. This action was continuous with those taken earlier in the century in New York. For example, the seminary rector was removed, a Catholic theological journal of international repute, the *New York Review,* was crushed, one seminary professor's textbook on Holy Scripture was burned by his students at the order of the new rector, and one seminary professor was fired—not to be heard of in Catholic circles again. At Catholic University, in Washington, between 1910 and 1940, professors of scripture and theology were spied on, informed on, delated to the Apostolic delegate, put under enormous pressure to teach the orthodox line, and removed from their positions as a last resort. This was the case across the Catholic world, wherever the Pian Sodalities sniffed the odor of modernism. As late as 1939 a formal inquiry into the orthodoxy of faculty was conducted by the Apostolic delegate at the New York Seminary. See Thomas Shelley, *Dunwoodie,* for details. On the problems of scholarship at Catholic University of America, see Fogarty, *American Catholic Biblical Scholarship,* 78–119, 281–331. Fogarty also discusses the New York Seminary and the case of Myles Bourke, 286, 292, 379n22.

62. The Catholic weekly *The Wanderer* is an example; and see George Kelly, *The Battle for the American Church* and *The Crisis of Authority: John Paul II and the American Bishops.* See also his autobiography, *In My Father's House* (Garden City, NY: Doubleday, 1989).

63. "Constitution on Divine Revelation," paragraphs 9, 11, and 12 in Austin Flannery, ed., *The Basic Sixteen Documents of Vatican II* (Northport, NY: Costello Publishing, 1996).

64. Thus, the Roman Catholic position on inerrancy is *not* fundamentalist. It should be noted as well that in 1964 the Pontifical Biblical Commission accepted form and redaction criticism as methods for studying and interpreting the four gospels, something also unacceptable to fundamentalists and many conservative evangelicals. See Brown, *The Critical Meaning of the Bible.*

65. "Constitution on Divine Revelation," paragraphs 9 and 10, in Flannery, ed., *The Basic Sixteen Documents of Vatican II.*

66. John Paul II, *Fides et ratio* (Washington, DC: National Conference of Catholic Bishops, 1998).

67. This attitude pervades the documents of Vatican II. See the constitutions on the church in the modern world, on missionary activity, on non-Christian religions, and on religious freedom in Flannery. For an expression in theology, see Lonergan's essays on theology and contemporary culture in *A Second Collection* (Philadelphia: Westminster Press, 1975). The attitude was a great source of worry to some, among them former Missouri Synod Lutheran Richard J. Neuhaus in his *The Catholic Mo-*

ment: *The Paradox of the Church in the Postmodern World* (New York: Harper and Row, 1987), and to Catholics such as Avery Dulles, George Weigel, and James Vacarelli, who were concerned that the Catholic Church in America was becoming unacceptably and even dangerously Americanized. The tension is generated by church's role in the transformation of culture. What happens when the church runs into systemic evil in the culture? Or when the members of the church (intellectuals, perhaps) begin a process of assimilation to the cultural status quo rather than holding to Christian norms? At what moment in the church's attempted transformation of culture does the church become a prophetic critic?

68. See the essays by Gary Lease in the volumes of the Working Group on Roman Catholic Modernism of the American Academy of Religion (Mobile, AL: Spring Hill College, 1985–87).

69. See the essays of the AAR group; and also Komonchak, "Modernity and the Construction of Roman Catholicism" and Kurtz, *The Politics of Heresy.* See also O'Connell. Ferenc Szasz interprets American fundamentalism as a populist rejection of rule by specialists and bureaucrats; see *The Divided Mind of Protestant America* (Tuscaloosa, AL: University of Alabama Press, 1982).

70. Loisy, *My Duel with the Vatican.*

71. As we shall see, John England and the other leading American bishops of the nineteenth century did in fact imagine alternatives.

72. Michael Gannon, "Before and After Modernism," in John Tracy Ellis, ed., *The Catholic Priest: Historical Investigations* (Collegeville, MN: St. John's University Press, 1971), 341.

73. James Hennesey, *American Catholics* (New York: Oxford University Press, 1981), 217.

74. For an account of the metaphor "communion" and its role in Catholic ecclesiological theology from Adam Moehler to Pope John Paul II, see Dennis Doyle, *Communion Ecclesiology: Visions and Versions* (Maryknoll, NY: Orbis Press, 2000).

75. That the inerrancy dogma in the form in which fundamentalists accept it was in fact the ancient and inviolate teaching of Christianity is argued at length. See Lindsell, 41–71.

76. The classic statement is by Charles Hodge, "On Method," in his *Systematic Theology* (1873; reprint Grand Rapids, MI: Eerdmans, 1995). The method is outlined clearly by Packer, *"Fundamentalism,"* 101–06. For the historical developments, see Jack Rogers and Donald McKim, *The Authority and Interpretation of the Bible* (San Francisco: Harper and Row, 1979), and Robert Gnuse, *The Authority of the Bible: Theories of Inspiration, Revelation and the Canon of Scripture* (New York: Paulist, 1985).

77. *Pascendi* throughout nails down the modernists' naturalistic interpretation of the Bible and the church's life. This is why it is a "synthesis of all heresies." On the sacraments and the church in particular, see paragraphs 21–26. The attached list of condemned propositions, *Lamentabili,* deals with the sacraments in paragraphs 39–51.

78. Walter Ong, *The Presence of the Word: Some Prolegomena for Cultural and Religious History* (New Haven, CT: Yale University Press, 1967), 17–110; and *Orality and Literacy: the Technologizing of the Word* (New York: Methueun, 1982).

79. Harold Bloom, *The American Religion: The Emergence of the Post-Christian Nation* (New York: Simon and Schuster, 1992). Machen might well agree!

## 3. NATIVISM AND POLITICS

1. Ray Allen Billington told the story and supplied the evidence for a period of intensified nativist activity in his *The Protestant Crusade, 1800–1860*. In his first chapter he neatly and briefly laid out "the roots anti-Catholic prejudice." See Billington, 2–3.

2. John Foxe, *Foxe's Book of Martyrs*, William Forbush, ed. (Grand Rapids, MI: Zondervan, 1978).

3. Antonia Frazier, *Faith and Treason*. Oliver Ormerod, *The Picture of a Papist* and *Pagano-Papismus, London, 1606* (Norwood, NJ: Theatrum Orbis Terrarum, 1975).

4. John Cotton: *The End of the World*, vol. 14 of *A Library of American Puritan Writings* (New York: AMS Press, 1982). It includes *The Churches Resurrection* (1642) and *An Exposition upon the Thirteenth Chapter of the Revelation* (1655).

5. Cf. Michael D. Peters, *Jonathan Edwards's Politicization of Millennialism* (PhD diss., Saint Louis University, 2000); and Jonathan Mayhew, *Popish Idolatry: A Discourse delivered in the Chapel of Harvard-College in Cambridge, New England at the Lecture Founded by the Honorable Paul Dudley, Esquire*. (Boston: R. & S. Draper, Edes & Gill, and T. & J. Fleet, 1765).

6. See Everett H. Emerson, *John Cotton* (New York: Twayne Publishers, 1965), 54–84.

7. American Protestant critics of Catholicism had little idea how much the ancient ideal of Christendom played on their view of church and state and on their own practice.

8. Perhaps the second KKK (or more recently, the Aryan Nation) is the best example of nativism. It was explicitly racist, as well as anti-Semitic and anti-Catholic. But it was an organization proclaiming itself Protestant for Protestants.

9. Billington, 38.

10. On Hogan, see the article by Joseph M. Lafferty in *The Encyclopedia of American Church History*, ed. Michael Glazier and Thomas Shelley (Collegville, MN: Liturgical Press, 1997), 651–52. Also see Francis E. Tourscher, *The Hogan Schism and the Trustee Troubles in St. Mary's Church, Philadelphia, 1820–1829* (Philadelphia: Peter Reilly, 1930). Patrick Carey defines trusteeism as "a lay movement to adapt European Catholicism to American republican values by asserting the rights of lay governance and exclusive lay control of ecclesiastical temporalities." See Patrick W. Carey, "Trusteeism," *EACH*, 1396–1398. Carey has written an historical monograph on the movement: *People, Priests and Prelates: Ecclesiastical Democracy and the Tensions of Trusteeism* (Notre Dame, IN: University of Notre Dame Press, 1987).

11. Billington, 39–40.

12. Billington, 45–46.

13. For the encyclical, see Carlen, I: 235–41. *Quanta cura* and *Syllabus errorum* of Pius IX (1864). The definition of papal infallibility by the first Vatican Council (1869), and Pius X's antimodernist letter *Pascendi dominici gregis* and the accompanying list of condemned propositions, *Lamentabili* (1907), added fuel to the fear of the papacy.

14. Eamon Duffy, *Saints and Sinners: A History of the Popes* (New Haven, CT: Yale University Press, 1997), 217–21; J. N. D. Kelly, ed., *The Oxford Dictionary of the Popes* (Oxford: Oxford University Press, 1986), 307–09; and the *New Catholic Encyclopedia* (New York: McGraw-Hill, 1967), IV: 783–87.

15. Others in this first wave will be discussed in the next chapter. See Billington 56ff., on the beginning of the no-popery campaign.

16. Paul Straiti, *Samuel F. B. Morse* (New York: Cambridge University Press, 1989).

17. New York: Leavitt and Lord, 1835; reprint, New York: Arno Press, 1977. He followed this with *Imminent Dangers to the Free Institutions of the United States through Foreign Immigration* (1835; reprint New York: Arno Press, 1969). Two other books will be discussed later, one by Lyman Beecher and the other by Josiah Strong. Another, and perhaps the bestseller of the lot, was Maria Monk, *Awful Disclosures Of the Hotel Dieu Nunnery* (New York: Howe and Bates, 1936). A historical discussion of the book can be found in Nancy Lusignon Schultz's introduction to a reprint of it, *Veil of Fear: Nineteenth-Century Convent Tales* (West Lafayette, IN: Purdue University Press, 1999). That Morse was enamored of Miss Monk and in fact proposed marriage is mentioned by Schultz on the basis of two letters of James Fenimore Cooper; see Schultz, xxxi, n12.

18. The notion of a conspiracy among autocrats to destroy the American republic may seem nutty in retrospect, but it was more plausible at the time, much as Soviet and Chinese communism seemed a dire threat to the American republic in the 1950s and 1960s. Senator Joseph McCarthy's book on the "conspiracy" behind the fall of China to the communists might well be an apt Catholic parallel to Morse's work on Catholicism. See "McCarthy, Joseph Raymond and American Catholics," *EACH*, 872–874; and Joseph McCarthy, *America's Long Retreat from Victory, The Story of George Catlett Marshall* (New York: Devon, 1951).

19. *Foreign Conspiracy*, 23, 33.

20. 21, 36, 41–42, 45.

21. *Foreign Conspiracy*, 47. One can read another side to the suppression story. See a contemporary account, Giulio Cesare Cordara, *On the Suppression of the Society of Jesus*, J. P. Murphy, trans. (Chicago: Jesuit Way, 1999). For the story of the suppression and restoration, see William V. Bangert, *A History of the Society of Jesus* (St. Louis: Institute of Jesuit Sources, 1986), 2nd ed. Morse calls John England, bishop of Charlestown, a Jesuit (among other things). See Morse, 141. Lyman Beecher picks up the habit. One can understand the confusion. John Carroll, the first bishop, had been a Jesuit until the suppression of the order in 1773 by Clement XIII (of unhappy memory). Perhaps because other bishops who joined or succeeded him (like England and Hughes in New York) were "wily," they may have been supposed to be Jesuits as well. England spoke to a joint session of Congress in 1826. For over two hours he argued the compatibility of the U.S. Constitution and the Catholic Church. In fact, England "was the first theorist of separation of Church and state and freedom of religion." In other words, he advocated the end of Christendom. England was a formidable man, even if he was not a Jesuit. His address to Congress escaped Morse's notice, although it is hard to understand how. See *EACH*: 490.

22. *Foreign Conspiracy*, 55–56.

23. 61–62, 63. Cf. 57.

24. *Foreign Conspiracy*, 66ff., 70–71.

25. 89–90. Cf 88. Emphasis here and elsewhere is found in the original.

26. 112–13. As we shall see, the issue of loyalties was taken up directly by Catholic leaders again and again, and to no avail. Had the people of Morse's persuasion

adverted to them, they would likely have regarded such professions as prevarications. Part of the "theory" is that no one speaks for the Catholic Church except the pope, and he lies as well as they do when need be.

27. *Foreign Conspiracy,* 118–20. It turned out that these views were in fact the ideological basis of the American Native party, and of the later American Protestant Association and the still later American Protective Association, and, finally, of the renewed Ku Klux Klan in the twentieth century.

28. 128, 131.

29. Billington, 131–32. Morse's take on the Charlestown Ursuline convent burning of 1834 is a parody of moral reasoning: the nuns excited the mob when it had a perfectly legitimate concern for the safety of children, a just and proper feeling, even if no one can justify the burning. And Catholics orchestrated an overreaction to this unfortunate incident. Even Protestants fell into the trap set by popery and are brought to sympathize with the nuns. So the nuns were responsible for the burning of their convent and deserved no compensation. *Foreign Conspiracy,* 186.

30. *DRB,* 38. Lyman Beecher, *A Plea for the West,* 2nd edition. (Cincinnati: Truman and Smith; New York: Leavitt, Lord & Co., 1835). As for the convent burning in Charlestown in 1834, Beecher echoes Morse's evasion: "The late violence done to Catholic property at Charlestown is regarded with regret and abhorrence by Protestants and patriots throughout the land, though the excitement which produced it had no relation whatever to religious opinions, and no connection with any religious denomination of Christians" (65). With this astonishing statement, Beecher refused any personal responsibility for producing the alarmist atmosphere in Boston where he had preached antipopery for years, and sloughed off any Protestant responsibility for the convent burning. As Vincent Harding, his biographer, writes: "There, on the very night that he presented his 'Plea for the West' (August 11), a mob attacked and burned the Ursuline convent in nearby Charlestown. Though Beecher had not helped to incite this particular mob, it is doubtless that the spirit he represented was influential in the genesis of such an act" (36). One could surmise from his words that the convent was burned by a group of unchurched wild men who were overreacting in their secular concern for the liberty of oppressed women rather than acting in a context set by Protestant anti-Catholicism, and with plenty of ministerial stoking. Vincent Harding, *A Certain Magnificence: Lyman Beecher and the Transformation of American Protestantism, 1775–1863* (New York: Carlson Publishing, 1991). On Beecher's role, see also Schultz, *Fire and Roses,* 116–17, 160.

31. *Plea,* 31–32. See 1–50 for the case on need for education.

32. *Plea,* 51–53, 59.

33. *Plea,* 64, 63, 78ff. One must be skeptical of his claim, as in the case of similar claims by Morse, Strong, and Blanshard. The Catholic Church was viewed as intrinsically political by all of them and they each said as much. In addition, Beecher declares the old "declamatory, virulent, contemptuous, sarcastic, taunting, denunciatory, style is as unchristian as it is in bad taste and indiscreet." "We" will put up with the old style in Catholics and will not use it ourselves—though they "are fast using up both the sympathy and patience of the community in their behalf" by their "use of invidious terms, and the manifestation of a virulent, discourteous and contemptuous spirit . . ." (66, 67). Beecher failed to transcend the vituperative language he claimed was still used by Catholics. A "dark-minded population" is rushing upon us, not the

"*northern* hive but the *whole* hive is swarming upon our cities. . . . Clouds like the locusts of Egypt are rising from the hills and plains of Europe, and on the wings of every wind, are coming over to settle down upon our fair fields . . . while millions are preparing for flight in an endless succession" (72). Perhaps a northern hive would have been acceptable. Throughout this section of the book, there is no evidence of his truce on "vindictive" address. As in the case of his protestations about the convent burning, one is forced to wonder about his awareness of what he is writing.

34. 70–73. Emphases in the original.

35. *Plea,* 78–80.

36. 141. One wonders what he might have said had he not been a man of tact and taste. Alexander Campbell also gives the number of murder victims at fifty to sixty-eight million. The figure is cited frequently. I don't know the source of the estimate, but suspect that it may be the Centuriators of Magdeburg or Foxe.

37. Plea, 138–39, 142.

38. 151. He used Friedrich Schlegel, a German convert to Catholicism, who lectured on the need for restoration in Vienna in 1828. So, too, did Morse. Schlegel advanced a view commending a union of Austrian "despotism"—Metternich, that is, and the emperor—and popery. Beecher quotes Morse's *Foreign Conspiracy* in *Plea,* 157–59. He also quotes *Mirari vos* of Gregory XIV, 173–74. Like Morse, Beecher tags the Jesuits with a predominant and evil influence in this matter: clerical domination, he maintained, is intensified by the "predominant influence of the society of Jesuits," dedicated as it is to the cause of the papacy——"trained as courtiers, confessors, teachers, diplomatists, saints, spies, and working men, to influence and control the destiny of nations, and guided also by a morality which permits the end to sanctify the means" (147ff.).

39. *Plea,* 180–81.

40. *Controversy between Rev. Messrs. Hughes and Breckenridge on the subject "Is the Protestant Religion the Religion of Christ?"* (Philadelphia: Isaac Bird, 1833).

41. Christine Bochen, *The Journey to Rome: Conversion Literature by Nineteenth Century American Catholics* (New York: Garland Publishers, 1988).

42. Cf. Vincent Harding, *A Certain Magnificence: Lyman Beecher and the Transformation of American Protestantism* (New York: Carlson, 1991). Harding writes: "It was hard to know how seriously Lyman Beecher took the possibility of a true conspiracy to win the West on behalf of foreign Roman Catholic powers. Though it was an increasingly popular strain in American Protestantism, some persons suggested that he used this only as a means for raising more funds, since it made the issue sound more dramatic and crisis-laden." However, a couple of points suggest he was serious. First, there is his long-standing opposition to enfranchisement of even native unpropertied classes. He might well have been frightened at the prospect of millions of unpropertied Roman Catholic immigrant voters. Second, the Roman Catholic side of his argument on the school issue took a second place to the immigrant problem in his view—the conspiracy theory played in more closely with the immigration problem than with the Catholic school question. If his primary aim was to raise money he would have tied the schools with the foreign plot, but in fact he was disturbed more by Catholic immigrants than with foreign money for Catholic schools. Finally, he may very well have been forced to more prudence in his published book after the burning than in his sermons on its eve. Harding, 401–02.

43. See Henry Warner Bowden, ed., *The Dictionary of American Religious Biography* (Westport, CT: Greenwood Press, 1977), 439–40, and Daniel Reid et al., eds., *The Dictionary of Christianity in America* (Downers Grove, IL: InterVarsity Press, 1990), 1140–41, 1847–916.

44. Josiah Strong, *Our Country* (1891; reprint Cambridge, MA: Belknap Press of Harvard University, 1963), 2nd edition. The second edition includes an expanded chapter on Romanism. See also his *Expansion under New World Conditions* (New York: Baker and Taylor, 1900). See Paul R. Meyer, "The Fear of Cultural Decline: Josiah Strong's Thought about Reform and Expansion," *Church History* 42 (1973): 396–405. Meyer maintains that Strong's optimism about American destiny turned a bit toward pessimism in his later publications. He doubted a bit more the cultural superiority of Anglo-Protestant America. He softened during the militarism of the Spanish War period, and even his racism flagged. He tended more strongly toward Social Gospel Christianity. At that point it was the social gospel that needed expansion rather than the nation.

45. *Country*, ix and xxv.

46. x.

47. xxvi.

48. *Country*, 13, 40. By "the West" he means the American west, everything beyond the Appalachian Mountains. To push the image just a bit, what is to happen when the West catches its own tail in the East? Is this an endless wave, or shall the wave break? Hegel had the same problem.

49. *Country*, 53, 55, 57.

50. Strong quotes an essay by Edmund Purcell in H. E. Manning, ed., *Essays on Religion and Literature* (London: 1867), to this effect. The referent is Boniface VIII's *Unam Sanctam* and the medieval documents that stressed the authority of the papacy. The worry is constant from the time of the Reformation, and was reinforced in England and the United States by the English-Roman conflict over the monarchy in the sixteenth century. The pope did, after all, release the English Catholics from their oath of patriotic support for Elizabeth I. Leo XIII and Pius IX are cited as well, and even the archbishop of Cleveland (61) and the Vicar General of New York (63–64). We shall see this again and again, from Campbell in 1837 to Blanshard in 1948. Strong and the others assume, with good reason, that medieval Christendom remains the model of church-state relations for Catholics.

51. *Country*, 65. All of this is perfectly in tune with the letter of Charles Marshall to Al Smith in 1927, as well as with Paul Blanshard in 1948 (see later). Marshall was unconcerned about Smith's own loyalty and had no doubt of it. He was concerned with the official doctrinal position of the Catholic Church in opposition in principle to the American "experiment in ordered liberty," as J. C. Murray put it. See Charles C. Marshall. "An Open Letter to Governor Smith," *The Atlantic Monthly* 139 (April, 1927): 540–49; and Alfred E. Smith, "Catholic and Patriot: Governor Smith Replies," *The Atlantic Monthly* 139 (May, 1927): 721–28.

52. *Country*, 67.

53. *Brownson's Quarterly Review* 6(1/1852): 26. See *Country*, 70.

54. *Country*, 71. John J. McQuaid, bishop of Rochester, New York, said in 1876 in a lecture in Boston that "The state has no right to educate, and when the state undertakes the work of education it is usurping the powers of the church" (72). Orestes

Brownson and other ultramontanist Catholics were not overstating the case for papal and church "rights," as they conceived them. In the 1940s and 1950s, I was educated in an atmosphere of nostalgia for Christendom, which remained the "thesis" of church-state relations for some Catholic thinkers. The American Catholic James J. Walsh called his influential book *The Thirteenth, Greatest of Centuries* (New York: Catholic Summer School Press, 1913). He, and we, meant exactly that.

55. A cartoon dragon composed of Gilbert Keith Chesterton and Hilaire Belloc, two leading English Catholic apologists of the twentieth century. They, and other British Catholics, had considerable influence on the educational atmosphere mentioned in the previous note.

56. *Country*, 73–74.

57. 75–76; see also 77–78.

58. 79, 82, 83.

59. Quoted from Morse's *Confessions of a French Catholic Priest*(New York: 1837). Morse claimed to have the words from a conversation with and a letter from La-Fayette. Strong acknowledged that the authenticity of words has been challenged by Roman Catholics. See *Country*, 97n54. The words, and the attitude they reflect, are not found in Olivier Bernier, *LaFayette, Hero of Two Worlds* (New York: Dutton, 1983).

60. *Country*, 94, 90. But then why does he admit that an additional risk in allowing public support for Catholics schools is that Lutherans and Episcopalians might claim public money for schools of their own, hastening "the depletion and final destruction of the public school" (94–95)? What is the matter with these great schools that Episcopalians and Lutherans may prefer to set up their own? For Strong, as for many opponents of the private school system, the public schools are the training ground in American religious pluralism and in a unified culture (95ff.). There is a bit of hypocrisy on both sides of this issue. "Public schools are not sectarian," say the Protestants; "Catholic schools are necessary to avoid Protestantism and godlessness," say the Catholics. But the public schools were Protestant from the outset, as indeed they had to be, and only became secular and godless when the secular educationists got hold of them at the end of the nineteenth century; the Catholic schools were built and maintained to inculcate a loyalty and values that could never be obtained in any sort of public school system, Protestant or secular. See Stephen Macedo, *Diversity and Distrust: Civic Education in a Multicultural Democracy* (Cambridge, MA: Harvard University Press, 2000), for a full presentation of the argument over the schools. My disagreement with his position is registered in a review in *Theological Studies* 62/2 (9/01): 661–62.

61. *Country*, 216–17. The fourth peril, Mormonism, causes in him a horror matching that evoked by the Roman Church: "The civilized world wonders that such a hideous caricature of the Christian religion should have appeared in this most enlightened land. . . . Such an anachronism . . . this deep humiliation and outrageous wrong to women . . . the Mormon monster" (107); it is an "ecclesiastical despotism . . . [ruled by] . . . a pope who is not one whit less infallible than he who wears the tiara . . . [and] . . . out-popes the Roman" by getting new revelations in familiar conversation with the Almighty (108–09). The answer to it is Christian education by the denominations. The other perils include Intemperance, Socialism, Wealth, and the City.

62. 200–02.

63. *Country*, 213–14, 218.

64. There were plenty of respondents. See John McGreevy, "Thinking on One's Own," and James M. O'Neill, *Catholicism and American Freedom* (New York: Harper & Bros., 1952), 224–45. For a brief summary of Blanshard's career, see <http://www.harvardsquarelibrary.org/unitarians/blanshard.html>.

65. See Andrew Greeley, *American Catholics since the Council: An Unauthorized Report* (Chicago: Thomas Moore Press, 1985), and *The Catholic Myth: The Behavior and Beliefs of American Catholics* (New York: Macmillan, 1990). Greeley bases his summary views on four decades of sociological work, the results of which are available in dozens of volumes over the period.

66. 1930 twenty million, 1950 close to thirty million, and 1996 sixty million. Edwin Gaustad and Philip Barlow, eds., *New Historical Atlas of Religion in America* (New York: Oxford University Press, 2001), 157, figure 2.88.

67. Gregory D. Black, *Hollywood Censored: Morality Codes, Catholics, and the Movies* (New York: Cambridge University Press, 1994).

68. Paul Blanshard, *Personal and Controversial, An Autobiography* (Boston: Beacon Press, 1973), 28. Like Blanshard, H. G. Wells detested the Catholic Church. See Wells, *Crux Ansata: An Indictment of the Roman Catholic Church* (New York: Agora Publishing, 1946).

69. Blanshard, *Personal*, 40–41

70. 48.

71. 188.

72. 189. Henry Davis, S.J., *Moral and Pastoral Theology* (London: Sheed and Ward, 1935), 4 vols. The seventh edition was published in 1958. The book would have been used in English-language Catholic seminaries for the required courses in moral theology (Catholic ethics). Many of the seminaries used multivolume texts in Latin. Davis had earlier published *State Sterilization of the Unfit* (London: Burns, Oates and Washbourne, 1931).

73. *The Nation*(Nov. 1947–May 1948), vols. 165–66.

74. *Personal*, 201–02.

75. See John T, McGreevy, "Thinking on One's Own." McGreevy analyzes the plausibility of the liberal fears.

76. Loraine Boettner, *Roman Catholicism* and Dave Hunt, *The Woman Who Rides the Beast: The Roman Catholic Church and the Last Days*.

77. Paul Blanshard, *American Freedom and Catholic Power* (1949; reprint Boston: Beacon, 1958). Blanshard struck gold. He wrote several other books on the Catholic Church, and spent the winter of 1962 in Rome as an observer of the Vatican Council. See his reflections on that event and the documents in *Paul Blanshard on Vatican II* (Boston: Beacon Press, 1966). He followed *American Freedom* with *Communism, Democracy and Catholic Power* (Boston: Beacon Press, 1951); *The Irish and Catholic Power* (New York: Greenwood, 1972. 1953); *Freedom and Catholic Power in Spain and Portugal* (Boston: Beacon Press, 1962); and *Religion and the Schools: The Great Controversy* (Boston: Beacon Press, 1963).

78. *American Freedom*, 3, 4, 16, 20, 42, 50–51. See also 49–50, 22.

79. 22. On 28 ff., he recites the Protestant myth of early Christianity and the rise of the papacy in late antiquity and the early Middle Ages, citing Matthew 16 as the justification for it. Then he adds some some papal sinners, and the "declaration of war against modern political and social order" in the *Syllabus of Errors* and *Quanta*

*Cura* and infallibility, "the greatest intellectual blunder of Papal history—matched only by the social blunder of his namesake, Pius XI, in banning birth control . . ." (32). But in Blanshard's story sex plays a minor role, for he thinks that the American clergy and nuns keep their vows strictly. Here he differs from the anti-Catholic pornographic tradition (52). Blanshard's objection is not to the confessional as a sink of sin but to priests' use of the confessional for political purposes, for the "whole program," political as well as spiritual, ". . . to defeat British control in Malta, birth-control reform in Massachusetts, and democratic government in Spain." However, he does seem as sure that politics is conducted in the confessional as the older generation of evangelical pornographers were about "the sink of sin" (53).

80. 59–61.

81. *American Freedom*, 64.

82. 66. He never hinted in the book that there might be something to the Catholic case, nor did he make any suggestions about the "burden" Catholics (willingly) bear in double taxation. In the years my sons were in Catholic grammar and high school the "burden" grew from $3,000 to $10,000 a year, no feather considering a professor's salary. At the same time, our family paid taxes to support a stumbling pubic school system in the city of St. Louis. Willingly and without complaint I paid my taxes, and rarely thought about it, although I will say that public education is worth every cent and sacrifice. I would like to have had the money in my pocket, but not at the cost of my children's education in a Catholic setting.

83. He quotes a Catholic University Canon Law document of 1953 "Since there is no superior with whom appeal can be lodged when the Church and State have become involved in controversy as to their relative competence, the decision is to be made by the Church"; and then from the *Catholic Almanac* of 1948: "Under no circumstances may the Church be subjugated by the State. Whatever their form may be, states are not conceded the right to force the observance of immoral or irreligious laws upon a people" (63). But the government in the United States does express the will of the people as a whole, the people of all religions (64). How can it have a religion within it which denies that democratic rule of law?, he asks.

84. 73. He quotes Belloc from *The Contrast* (New York: Robert M. McBride, 1924). Belloc is not only correct in the distinction, but comes down on the right side of it. Blanshard comes down on wrong side. Why is he wrong? What sort of argument is needed to support his position? Protestant conviction is not significantly different in practice than the Catholic position on unjust laws. The two stood together in disobedience in the Civil Rights movement. Blanshard himself would have been with them. His annoyance at the transnational and, with respect to law, transcendent aspect of Catholicism is both pervasive and surprising. It seems obvious that no religion that claims a revelation can write a bank check to the state, the society, or the culture— or, or that matter, the church itself. Nor could any reasonable person, religious or secular. Blanshard, a man of liberal conviction, could not have done so himself had he given the matter more than a moment's thought.

85. *American Freedom*, 79–80; 323–24. Those who were being educated in Catholic schools at this time would, I think, be quite surprised at this all this. Blanshard himself would perhaps be surprised at the reported success of Catholic education, in this period and since. See Andrew Greeley, "My Research on Catholic Schools," in *The Sociology of Andrew M. Greeley* (Atlanta: Scholars Press, 1994), 508–26, and "The

Impact of the Roman Catholic Denominational School," 100–17. Blanshard reveals a startling uneasiness about nuns in this discussion. The life is unworthy of "American womanhood." He thinks it masochistic and medieval, submissive and self-abasing, isolated and obscure, unhygienic and alien. I very much doubt that he knew any nuns, something I regard as a significant loss in a civilized life. See 88.

86. *American Freedom*, 323–24. See also 80, 87, 88, 97.

87. 97, 85.

88. 134. Dewey, AS.2499: Its Anti-Democratic Implications," *The Nation's Schools* 39 (March, 1947): 21–22.

89. 279.

90. *American Freedom*, 281–92.

91. xi, 1, 2, 64.

92. *Religion and Education under the Constitution* (New York: Harper, 1949). Nothing in the *EACH* or in the *NCE*, but then there are not articles on Blanshard either. O'Neill is mentioned in an article, "Everson v. School Board," in the *NCE*, 5: 659.

93. James M. O'Neill, *Catholicism and American Freedom* (New York: Harper, 1952), xi–xii.

94. *Catholicism*, x–xi.

95. Many Protestant leaders expressed their concern about the implications of the McCollum decision. See "Statement on Church and State," *Christianity and Crisis* (July 5, 1948): 89–90, and the editorial comment in *The Christian Century* (June 30, 1948). See O"Neill, 55–58.

96. Everson 330 U.S. 1 (1947); McCollum 333 U.S. 203 (1948). See O'Neill, 41–43.

97. *Catholicism*, 68.

98. *Catholicism*, 65–68.

99. M. Searle Bates, *Religious Liberty: An Inquiry* (New York: Harper, 1945). Bates taught Missiology at Union Theological Seminary in New York. The study was done under the auspices of the Foreign Missions Conference of North America and the Federal Council of Churches. See O'Neill, 75 n1.

100. *Catholicism*, 77.

101. *Catholicism*, 80–82.

102. See William E. Gladstone, *The Vatican Decrees and their Bearing on Civil Allegiance* (New York: D. Appleton & Co., 1875) and *Vaticanism: An Answer to Reproofs and Replies* (New York: Harper & Bros., 1875); Friedrich Nippold, *The Papacy in the Nineteenth Century* (New York: G. P. Putnam's Sons, 1900); H. G. Wells, *Crux Ansata;* James Hastings Nichols, *Democracy and the Churches* (Philadelphia: The Westminster Press, 1951); Avro Manhattan, *Vatican Imperialism in the Twentieth Century* (Grand Rapids, MI: Zondervan Publishing House, 1965).

103. Quoted in Jay P. Corrin, *Catholic Intellectuals and the Challenge of Democracy* (Notre Dame, IN: University of Notre Dame Press, 2002), 380.

## 4. ROOTS

1. Mark U. Edwards Jr. *Luther's Last Battles: Politics and Polemics, 1531–46* (Ithaca, NY: Cornell University Press, 1983); see the Epilogue, and 190ff. On the historical

background of the Antichrist legend, see Bernard McGinn, *Anti-Christ: Two Thousand Years of the Human Fascination with Evil* (New York: Columbia University Press, 2000). On Luther's contribution to the myth of the Antichrist, see Anthony Kemp, *The Estrangement of the Past: A Study in the Origins of Modern Historical Consciousness* (New York: Oxford University Press, 1991), 66ff.

2. On the Pseudo-Isidorian Decretals, see Herbert Thurston, S.J., *No-Popery* (New York: Longmans, Green, 1930). On the Donation, *NCE* IV: 1000–01. The decretals were an eighth-century recension of an older document, the *legenda S. Silvestri.*

3. See *Exsurge, Domine,* the papal bull condemning forty-one of Luther's theological propositions, June 15, 1520. He burned it in public. The second, *Decet romanum pontificem,* excommunicated Luther on January 3, 1521. Both were issued by Leo X, the last of the Renaissance popes. For the story of the bull, see Ludwig Pastor, *The History of the Popes from the Close of the Middle Ages* (1923; reprint St. Louis: B. Herder, 1950), VII: 394–416.

4. See *Against the Papacy at Rome, Founded by the Devil,* in Eric W. Gritsch, ed., *Luther's Works* (Philadelphia: Fortress Press, 1966), 41: 295–301.

5. Edwards, 183.

6. On Gog, see Rev. 20, 8 and Ez 38, 2. On the "little horn," see Daniel 7:78.

7. Edwards, 110, quoting from Luther's *Refutation of the Koran* in which he maintains that Mohammad is not the Antichrist and that the pope is, and is far worse than the Muslim scourge of Europe and Christianity.

8. *Institutes of the Christian Religion by John Calvin,* John Allen, trans., intro by Benjamin B. Warfield, 2 vols. (Philadelphia: Presbyterian Board of Christian Education, 1936). Calvin's ecclesiology is found particularly in the fourth book. Chapter 2, "The True and the False Church Compared," contains his sharpest judgment of Rome. The quotation contains and, indeed, is framed by the curious and ambiguous proposition that true Christian churches may remain in the web of the false Roman church, a proposition that will become crucial to the later American Presbyterian arguments over the status of Rome as a Christian church. On the extent of Calvin's reliance on and agreement with Luther's ecclesiology and with his judgment of the Roman church, see Francois Wendel, *Calvin: The Origins and Development of his Religious Thought* (London: William Collins' Sons, 1965), especially chapter 5, "The External Means."

9. *Institutes,* IV, ii, 12. [Allen trans., 313–14].

10. *Institutes,* IV, vii, 14 [Allen trans., 411]. Same points are asserted in "The Necessity of Reforming the Church" in *Tracts and Treatises in the Reformation of the Church by John Calvin,* Henry Beveridge, trans., intro by Thomas F Torrance. Vol. I (Grand Rapids, MI: Eerdmans, 1958), 121–234, 219–20, and 276. For example: "You, the viceregent of Christ! Whose every thought, and wish, and action, are directed to the extinction of Christ, provided only the empty name remain, with which, as with a meretricious glare, you may deceive us! You, the viceregent of Christ, whom now the very children know to be very Antichrist! What kind of Christ will you fabricate for us, if you wish his image to be represented in your tyranny? We see a high priest of all impiety, a standard-bearer of Satan, a fierce tyrant, a cruel murderer of souls, in short, the son of perdition, whom the Apostle describes; and must we regard him as the viceregent of Christ? We see, I say, the wolf by which the sheep of Christ are devoured, we see the thief by whom they are carried off, we see the prowler

by whom they are slain, and still must we esteem him the viceregent of Christ?" (276).

11. The doctrinal/theological source for most of this heavy rhetoric may well be the different ecclesiologies. Against Trent, as well as among twentieth-century Catholic theologians who still regard the church itself as a sacrament of Christ and God, "The Church is not for Calvin a saving institution, seriously though he takes it. It is a visible fellowship of believers." K. Barth, in *The Theology of John Calvin*, Geoffrey W. Bromiley, trans. (Grand Rapids, MI: William Eerdmans and Sons, 1995), 269. See the pre–Vatican II ecclesiologies of K. Rahner, *The Church and the Sacraments* (New York: Herder and Herder, 1963) and E. Schillebeeckx, *Christ, the Sacrament of Encounter with God* (New York: Sheed and Ward, 1963), as well as the documents of Vatican II (Austin Flannery, ed.). See Dennis Doyle, *Communion Ecclesiology: Visions and Versions* (Maryknoll, NY: Orbis Books, 2000).

12. Oliver Ormerod, *The Picture of a Papist: Pagano-Papismus* [Facsimile of the 1606 printing by Nathaniel Fosbrooke] (Norwood, NJ: Walter J. Johnson, 1975). There is a notable pagination problem: there are gaps in page numbers (e.g., 203–64) but no gap in text. The dialogues have been misnumbered as well—there are two second dialogues and no third. S. J. Barrett identifies the author as a Cambridge scholar. See *Idol Temple Crafty Priests* (London: Macmillan, 1999), 32, 108–09. Ormerod does make a plea to Cecil on behalf of wandering scholars forced to drum up a few silver coins by teaching on the road, perhaps referring to himself. On the Gunpowder Plot, see Antonia Frazer, *Faith and Treason: The Story of the Gunpowder Plot* (New York: Doubleday, 1996).

13. Barnett says that Ormerod is "one archetype of the paganism charge," centering on idolatry, "systematically comparing ancient pagan religious beliefs and practices with those of Catholicism. Even nuns did not escape his glare. For nuns were only "remodelled [*sic*] vestal virgins . . ." Ibid., 108–09. Henry Ainsworth published *An Arrow Against Idolatry Taken out of the Quiver of the Lord of Hosts* in 1611, again on idolatry, showing Roman Christianity to be a counterfeit religion.

14. The controversies among historians over the plot and the trials are sketched by P. Coolsen, "Gunpowder Plot," in *The New Catholic Encyclopedia*, VI: 862–64, and in Antonia Frazer, *Faith and Treason*. The current *Encyclopedia Britannica* simply recounts the official (royal) version.

15. From *Picture*, 14–15, 21–22. Catholics took up the idolatrous customs of the "old ethnikes" (2ff). For example, Catholics have many gods (saints), one for every time and season, every country and town, for homes, for arts and sciences for sickness, danger, war, sea and land travel, sleep, doors and even hinges, mountains, apples, bees, woods, health, infants, childbirth. He wouldn't be surprised if we had one even for excrement—*propter excrementorum incrementum*! (8).

16. There are some mistakes or misprints in the original. The third is actually the second dialogue, and dialogue is regularly spelled diologue. In addition, the pagination suffers lapses.

17. *Picture*, 31, 34.

18. *Pagano Papismus*, 65–78.

19. Cardinal Bellarmine (1542–1621) stands out among the many authors cited. Cf. *Picture*, 102 ff. MT 16:18f is the contested text (along with others), and ecclesiology is a particularly important field of the criticism (*Picture*, 78–100). He takes up the

worship of angels, Marian doctrine, and the seven sacraments on 101–08 in a discussion aimed at showing how Catholics torture the scriptures to support their unscriptural doctrines, "rabinnically."

20. *Picture*, 114.

21. The letter to Lord Montegle [*sic*], which he himself turned over to Cecil thus exposing the plot, is quoted fully and attributed to Master Francis Tresham. It was the major piece of evidence against the plotters. Antonia Frazier thinks that Cecil had it written. Ormerod's minister says that "Lord Montegle" [ironically himself a Catholic] is a "most dutiful and loyall Subiect" (126). The king figured out the obscure meaning of the letter, namely that "fire" meant "explosives" hidden in the cellar chamber of the House of Parliament. Frazier, 124–26.

22. *Picture*, 131.

23. 112–13, 268.

24. 133–34, 135, 168.

25. 169, 182. "Iesuiticall plot" appears for the first time on 178. The issue of regicide looms large in British anti-Catholic literature. And yet a few decades (1649) later Cromwell had the head of Charles I lopped off.

26. *Picture*, 180–81.

27. 182–201.

28. 266.

29. John Cotton, *The Churches Resurrection, or the Opening of the fifed [sic] and sixt verses of the 20th chapter of the Revelation* and *An Exposition upon the Thirteenth Chapter of the Revelation*, published as vol. 14 in A Library of American Puritan Writings: The Seventeenth Century, under the title *John Cotton: The End of the World* (New York: AMS, n.d.). Originally published London: H. Overton, 1642.

30. Relation of saving grace continues in Bible churches of congregational polity and born again experience, and in Pentecostal and charismatic communities where witness to grace is crucial to ecclesial standing.

31. *Exposition*, 40.

32. *The Churches Resurrection*, 17. On the Renaissance origins of the myth, see Anthony Kemp, *The Estrangement of the Past*.

33. *The Churches Resurrection*, 19.

34. *Exposition*, 228.

35. *Churches Resurrection*,7, 34

36. Historians now date Boniface's brief reign from February to November 607 c.e.. See the *New Catholic Encyclopedia* II: 670; Kelly, *The Oxford Dictionary of the Popes*, 68.

37. *Churches Resurrection*, 7, 35–36, 225, 228.

38. *Churches Resurrection*, 7, 14, 13.

39. 230ff.

40. 16, 20.

41. *Churches Resurrection*, 22–24. In Cotton's work, the Jesuit Cardinal Robert Bellarmine remains prominent as the chief ideologue of the Tridentine papacy; see 28, 36, 55, 57, 113.

42. 54–56.

43. *Churches Resurrection*, 117–19, 128. See 80–97 for an opaque discussion of the meaning of the predicted forty-two months of the power of the Beast in Revela-

tion 13:5–6. *Churches Resurrection,* 80–97 indicates that Puritans were not immune from this Christian numerological play. Cotton assumes that he lives in the period of the forty-two months as he does that the name of the beast is hidden in the number 666. He is quite sure, on other than numerological grounds, that the mysterious period began in the short reign of Boniface III and that the church and papacy are the beasts. While participating in the play, he refuses to get caught in the trickier project of supplying definite chronological referents.

44. *Churches Resurrection,* 212.

45. Cotton's composition at this point may lead us to confuse Boniface III (d. 607) and Boniface VIII (d. 1303). The former was named "universal bishop" in 607 by the emperor Phocas, whereas the latter Boniface, an outstanding canon lawyer, added a *Liber Sextus* to the five-volume medieval *Corpus Juris Canonici* in 1298. The sin they have in common, in Cotton's view, is universalizing the rule of the papacy over the churches. Perhaps this explains his failure to distinguish them. At any rate, what occupies him in his commentary at this point is the number six. On the Bonifaces, see *NCE* II: 670–73.

46. *Churches Resurrection,* 253–54, 260–61. Fascination with the numerology of the Name is a constant in apocalyptic literature in general, and particularly in the evangelical anti-Catholic version. See, for example, the short book by Robert Fleming, a dissenting pastor in the Church of Scotland, who made his study of history interpreted through biblical numbers the subject of an address in 1701, on the first day of the new century. The book, *An Epistolary Discourse on the Rise and Fall of Papacy,* was reprinted, with appendices, in Boston in 1794 by Adams and Larkin, and kept up to date in later printings. The interesting thing about Fleming's original work is that, whereas the careful if conventional calculations of the time of the Beast take up half of it, the other half is a sermon on the meaning and proper use of time. Fleming, like Cotton and Edwards, took a lot more from apocalyptic than anti-Roman propaganda. See Bernard McGinn, *Antichrist.*

47. Martin E. Marty, *Pilgrims in their Own Land: 500 years of Religion in America* (New York: Penguin Books, 1985), 132ff. See also *The Dictionary of Christianity in America* (Downers Grove, IL: InterVarsity Press, 1990), 720.

48. Mayhew mentioned at the outset that papal infallibility and supremacy had been handled by two of his predecessors. See Edward Wigglesworth (d. 1765), *Some Thoughts Upon the Spirit of Infallibility Claimed by the Church of Rome,* (Duldeian lecture, 1757), and Thomas Foxcroft (d. 1769), *The Pope's Supremacy, an Usurpation, a Lecture Delivered at Harvard College, May 13, 1761.*

49. Jonathan Mayhew, *Popish Idolatry: a Discourse delivered in the Chapel of Harvard College May 8, 1765 at the Lecture Founded by the Honorable Paul Dudley, Esquire* (Boston: R. & S. Draper, 1765), 6.

50. a. *Idolatry,* 10–11. Mayhew was an admirer of Locke and an advocate of Locke's staunch British common sense empiricism. With regard to saints receiving the prayers of devotees, he remarks; "It is a kind of worship, which supposes them to be omnipotent, omniscient, and omnipresent; since He alone who is possessed of those perfections, can be supposed to hear prayers at all times, from all parts of the earth at the same time; and able to grant such blessings" (33). Like the real presence of Christ in hosts, this is an outrageous violation of common sense: it is perfectly obvious that saints (who, of course, are finite and have ears) cannot hear all every-

where at the same time while God (who is infinite and does not have ears) can. The same commonsensical objection can be found throughout this literature. See, for example, John H. Gerstner, *A Primer on Roman Catholicism* (1948; reprint Morgan, PA: Soli Deo Gloria Publications, 1995).

51. *Idolatry*, 12 See Barrett on priestcraft.

52. *Idolatry*, 17.

53. 22–23.

54. 45ff. Hislop, *The Two Babylons*.

55. *Idolatry*, 48–49.

56. *Idolatry*, 50. Alas, says Mayhew in an endnote, "after repeated inquiry, the author could never obtain a sight of the whole *Rosarie* of the Virgin Mary, or of the whole *Mary-Psalter*." He had to rely on the reports of Henry Moore and others. John Adams claimed that in New England a Catholic was a rare as a comet or an earthquake. His brother Samuel, although he was very worried indeed about popery, couldn't find one Catholic in Charlestown. Within in half a century things would change in Boston. Marty, 141.

## 5. THE NATIONAL PROTEST

1. *Thoughts on Popery (New York:* American Tract Society, 1836) and *Practical Thoughts on Popery*. William Plumer [*sic*] published "selected Remains" and a memoir in 1836. This, along with the memoir of Nicholas Murray (see below), afford a (filiopietistic) look at what the Presbyterian pastorate was like in antebellum America. Nevins's collected sermons were published in 1837. Apppleton's *Cyclopedia of American Biography*, 1888, contains brief biographies of nineteenth-century notables some of whom did not make it into the *Dictionary of American Biography*.

2. See *Thoughts*, 75. The prescript says that he is concerned with Romanism as essentially a political rather than a religious institution——as Morse said. But that is not the case, and it is hard to understand how anyone who read the book would think so. The remark is accurate to a degree of Morse and Beecher but Nevins' is a different sort of book entirely. He may have intended to appeal to an American public for whom religion as such should not be attacked.

3. Mary and the saints pose the same problem to Nevins as to Ormerod in 1605 and John Gerstner in 1996: how shall they hear us since they are in heaven and we are on earth. Are they omnipresent? We do not ask persons to pray for us who are beyond hearing–(78–79), and how can they hear all of those who pray to them at once? "[Mary] . . . cannot hear, even if she could help. Do you suppose that her calm repose in heaven is suffered to be disturbed by the ten thousand confused voices that cry to her without ceasing from earth? Never" (79). The refrain is constant and no Catholic protest or explanation has been able to quiet it. See Andrew Greeley, "Mary and the Womanliness of God," in *The Catholic Myth* (New York: Macmillan, 1990), 243–54.

4. "You shall not carve idols for yourselves in the shape of anything in the sky above or on the earth below or in the waters beneath the earth, nor shall you bow down before them or worship them" (Ex. 20, 4; Deut. 5, 8–9). These verses Catholics have traditionally taken to be part of the first commandment, while Protestants take it to be the second. The latter have charged the former with cutting out the second in

order to promote worship of statues and saints and to protect church practice from a critical attack based on these verses.

5. Nevins took John Hughes to be the author of *The Christian's Guide to Heaven*, a widely used book of prayers and religious information (*Thoughts*, 80). In fact, the author was William Graham. The book went through more than a dozen editions in the nineteenth century. It was originally published in 1794 in London by P. Keeting. It was printed in Philadelphia in 1810 and in Baltimore in 1829, and it may have been this edition that found itself on Nevins's writing table. Hughes may have given the book its imprimatur or nihil obstat, and thus may have been taken by Nevins to be the author. From the volume Nevins takes the *Memorare* and the *Salve Regina* to continue his criticism of Catholic idolatry (65). In contemporary systematic terms Nevins is upset at what David Tracy call the analogical imagination. See David Tracy, *The Analogical Imagination: Christian Theology and the Culture of Pluralism* (New York: Crossroad, 1981).

6. *Thoughts*, 6, 18, 19, 20, 21, 22, 23, 24, 25.

7. 65.

8. 66. Nevins quotes here from the "Laity's Directory" of 1833. See "American Catholic Directories, 1817–1879" (New York: Eastman Kodak, 1952), microfilm.

9. 67–68. He apparently does not advert to a frequent claim that Catholics address the pope as "Lord God."

10. *Thoughts*, 72–75. Again, the "Rhemish New Testament" is cited. Alexander Campbell seems to have meant the Douay-Rheims translation of the Latin Vulgate, with notes. It was a bone of contention in the Campbell-Purcell debate, where Purcell denied its authenticity. See *Debate*, 422, 438–39. See "Excursus" at the end of this chapter.

11. *Thoughts*, 77–79.

12. 80.

13. *Thoughts*, 81–88.

14. 88–89.

15. It was Augustine who settled on the ten the way Catholics use them. S. M. Polan remarks: ". . . the acceptance of the enumeration of commandments as found in Deuteronomy by St. Augustine and many of the Fathers of the West has led the Latin Church, as well as the Lutherans, to use this enumeration. Confusion arises from the fact that the enumeration as presented by the text of Exodus, which appears also in the Jewish rabbinic tradition, was adopted by St. Jerome and the Greek Fathers and so has resulted in a usage by the Greek Church differing from that of the Latin Church. Protestants other than Lutherans and the Jews also use the enumeration of Exodus" (*NCE* 4:5). St. Augustine was probably not hoping to justify idolatry.

16. 93.

17. *Thoughts*, 93, 96. More on relics, 130–31.

18. 150.

19. 195.

20. *Thoughts*, 177–78.

21. Sometimes, perhaps more often than not, the debates took place in newspapers. For example, John Hughes and John Breckinridge, *Controversy between Rev. Messrs. Hughes and Breckinridge on the Subject "Is the Protestant Religion the Religion of Christ?"* (Philadelphia: Isaac Bird, 1833), Nicholas Murray and John Hughes, and in

the twentieth century, Charles Marshall and Alfred E. Smith. Others include J. P. Bland and John O'Brien, *The Catholic Church and its Relation to Civil and Religious Liberty* (Boston: Duffy, Cashman, 1880); J. F. Berg and N. Steinbacher, *Discussion Held in Lebanon, PA.* (Philadelphia: no publisher, 1849); *The "Catholic" Church and the Roman Catholic Church; in a Friendly Correspondence Between a Catholic Priest and an Episcopal Minister* (Baltimore, MD: John Murphy and Co., 1866); Elijah Lucas and Patrick Byrne, *The Great Controversy upon Catholicism and Protestantism* (Trenton, NJ: L. Field Whitbeck, 1875); *The Priest's Secret Oath: a Discussion between Rev. A. B. Ingram, Baptist Minister, and Rev. J. M. Kelly, Catholic Priest, at Corsicana, Texas* (no publisher, 1899); *The Roman Catholic Church and Free Thought: A Controversy between Archbishop Purcell of Cincinnati and Thomas Vickers Minister of the First Congregational Church of the Same City* (Cincinnati: First Congregational Church, 1898).

22. *A Debate on the Roman Catholic Religion between Alexander Campbell, Bethany, Va. And the Right Reverend John B. Purcell, Bishop of Cincinnati Held in the Sycamore Street Meetinghouse, Cincinnati, from the 13th to the 21st of January, 1837. Taken down by reporters, and revised by the parties* (Nashville, TN: MCAT Printing Company, 1914). The meeting house was a Baptist church—see page 426.

23. The honor belongs to Methodism if you ignore the fact that the Disciples movement began in the nineteenth century. Cf. Gaustad and Barlow's *New Historical Atlas of Religion in America*, figures 2.102 and 2.144.

24. *Debate*, vii.

25. *Debate*, 12–13.

26. *Debate*, 19, 37. Participants in the theological arguments over dating the establishment of the papacy cite the year 606, while contemporary historians date the reign of Boniface III from February to November 607. See Eamon Duffy, *Saints and Sinners, A History of the Popes* (New Haven, CT: Yale University Press, 1997), 57, and *ODP*, 68.

27. 37.

28. 49.

29. Purcell argued, with a good deal of historical and biblical sophistication and some powerful rhetoric but to absolutely no avail, that Campbell was misreading history, indeed creating his own history at each step in his narrative, from the Bible to the Great Schism. Purcell's view of the progress and decline of the Christian church will occupy us when we tackle the Catholic side of things.

30. 125.

31. Cornelius favored receiving the Christians who had lapsed during the persecution by the emperor Decius (249–51CE) back into communion once they had done suitable penance, while Novatian opposed it. *ODP*, 17–18.

32. *Debate*, 95.

33. 95–96.

34. The *Ecclesiastica historia* was completed in 1574. Cardinal Baronius's *Annales ecclesiastici* (1588–1607; Barri-Ducis, Italy: L. Guerin, 1864–1883) was the effective Catholic refutation.

35. *Debate*, 101.

36. *Debate*, 125–28.

37. 143ff. Purcell argued that Eusebius of Caesarea (d. 340 C.E.), the first great church historian, established the importance of the bishop of Rome, and that all

comes to him from John the Apostle through Polycarp and then Irenaeus. In an interesting aside on historical knowledge, he claimed Eusebius was the very basis of all the knowledge we possess of the history of the early church, and Eusebius himself rests on tradition. "Tradition," Purcell says, "is but another name for history." Cf. 152. What was needed in the long story of these polemics is a serious discussion of history and tradition, but its time had not yet come. Campbell wanted eyewitnesses to the prominence of the Roman bishops and Purcell could only offer him the charged term "tradition." It is impossible to make out what either of them held on the subject. One seems to say that knowing is seeing and the other that history is believing.

38. Campbell read from Catholic Louis Du Pin (d. 1719) (*Debate*, 158–61), Purcell from Protestants George Waddington (d. 1869) (184–87), Robert Southey (d. 1843) (319–20), John Fletcher (d. 1848?) (109–14), and John Lingard (d. 1841) (307–10). They use Edward Gibbon (d. 1794), Caesare Baronius (d. 1607), Jacques Bossuet (d. 1704), and William Chillingworth (d. 1644) in shorter bursts, and quote often from the church fathers East as well as West.

39. 167, n.

40. 1261–1379.

41. 173–74.

42. Campbell's assessment of "the immoral tendency of the Roman rule of faith" (Romanists leave sinners uncorrected and the authenticity of their repentance untested) can be found on 242–67. The theme of the softness of Rome on sin is pervasive in American anti-Catholic literature. He, like his contemporaries, finds the picture of a young woman kneeling and confessing her "secret thoughts" to be very disturbing. The notion of celibacy is repellent to him.

43. *Debate*, 354.

44. 356–59.

45. There is nothing new or unusual in Campbell's discussion of his fourth thesis, that *She* [the Catholic church] *is the Babylon of John, the Man of Sin of Paul, and the Empire of the Youngest Horn of Daniel's Sea Monster* (281). He aped John Cotton's commentary on Revelation 13, with none of Cotton's modesty about Revelation 13:18. Only Rome among the kingdoms on earth has the name equivalent to 666 (288). In Campbell's reading of Paul in II Thessalonians 2:3ff., the Man of Sin turns out to be the pope who stealthily took on the leadership of the papal empire, using blasphemous titles, invading the church to become its center, claiming divine homage, lawless, deceiving by miracles (290). Like a dog worrying an old bone, chewed on by generations, Campbell concluded that the end of the Whore and the angels' song of the fall of Rome may come soon. The only thing he added to the old story is the opposition of the pope to the spirit and freedoms of the age, perhaps a reference to the recent *Mirari vos* by Gregory XVI (1832) who knew he might be the last pope (281–94). Purcell mocked Campbell's interpretation. That a pope or especially this pope (Gregory XVI) is the Antichrist is an absurdity—this pope's chief weakness is snuff (306)! Purcell remarks that Campbell "dashes headlong upon this rock of commentators" on which so many have been wrecked. Purcell had "so many wise men on my side, while all the monomaniacs are on his!" (299). Even "Alexander Campbell" could be made out to be 666!

46. 322–23.

47. He means the present Roman "system."

48. 325–30.

49. *Debate*, 335–36.

50. 337.

51. 341–42.

52. So Mark Noll in *American Evangelical Christianity*, (Oxford: Blackwell, 2001), 111–47.

53. *Debate*, 383; see 371; also 203 and 212 to the same effect.

54. Debate, 407; see also 411.

55. 415–16.

56. 314, 441.

57. 408–09.

58. *Debate*, 441.

59. 434. So John England in *Discourse Before Congress* at greater length. See chapter 9.

60. 435. Campbell will not accept Purcell's countercharge that Catholics have suffered Protestant persecution. Protestant "persecutions have not been as a drop in the ocean, in comparison to papal persecutions. . . . But we have an excuse for them. The first Protestants after the Lutheran Reformation, came out from a bloody and cruel mother, who has accustomed them to blood and slaughter, and taught them that the blood of heretics was a sacrifice, most acceptable to God" (410). The Catholic Church is thereby responsible for Protestant persecution of Catholics.

61. *Debate*, 440; see 446, 427.

62. *Debate*, 359. *Secreta Monita* can be found in *Pamphlets in American History*, CA 50. See the comments of Owen Chadwick, *The Popes and the European Revolution* (Oxford: Clarendon Press, 1981), 346.

63. *Debate*, 318, 338, 363. The text in question is Samuel Smith, *A Synopsis of the Moral Theology of the Church of Rome taken from the Works of St. Liqouri and translated from the Latin into English by Samuel B. Smith, Late a Popish Priest, Embellished with Four Engravings* (New York: Office of the Downfall of Babylon, Pittsburgh: Patterson, Ingram, 1836).

64. *Debate*, 422, 438–39.

65. *Debate*, 417–18.

66. The words quoted by Campbell appear in the first edition of the Roman Pontifical after Trent and still appear in 1962 Pontifical. Cf. Manlio Sodi and Achille Triacca, eds., *Pontificale Romanum. Editio Princeps (1595–1596)* (Vatican City: Libreria Editrice Vaticana, 1997), 87; compare Anthony Ward and Cuthbert Johnson, eds., *Pontificale Romanum, reimpressio editionis iuxta typicam anno 1962* (Vatican City: Edizioni Liturgiche, 1999), 52.

## 6. THREE PRESBYTERIANS AND THREE CONGREGATIONALISTS

1. See Richard Shaw, *Dagger John: The Unquiet Life and Times of Archbishop John Hughes of New York* (New York: Paulist Press, 1977) and Shaw's essay on Hughes in *EACH*, 661–64. The address can be found in *The Complete Works of the Most Rev. John Hughes, D. D., Archbishop of New York* (New York: Lawrence Kehoe, 1865), vol. II, 87–121.

2. Walter Blake Kirwan was an eighteenth-century Catholic priest and convert to

the Church of Ireland from the Catholic Church. See Prime, 267–68. See "Kirwan" (Nicholas Murray), *Letters to the Rt. Rev. John Hughes, Roman Catholic Archbishop of New York* (Philadelphia: Presbyterian Board of Publication, 1851. He also published under the same alias with the same publisher a *Second Series* of letters to Hughes and then a *Third Series*. In the same decade *The Difference Between Popery and Protestantism in a Letter to an Enquiring Friend* appeared under the same publisher, no date. After the first series had appeared on the pages of the New York *Observer* Murray was publicly known to be the author. Hughes's reply was titled *Kirwan Unmasked in Six Letters Addressed to Rev. Nicholas Murray of Elizabethtown, N. J. by the Right Rev. John Hughes, D. D.* (New York: Dunigan & Brothers, 1851).

3. Billington, 252–54. On the function of the Moderator, see "Church Officers" in the *Evangelical Dictionary of Theology*, ed. Walter A. Elwell (Grand Rapids, MI: Baker Books, 1984), 244.

4. Shaw, 256. The fact that Hughes was in Rome is implied by Murray's reference to "those whose chief aim and grand ambition is to wear a fillet made from the wool of holy sheep." See Nicholas Murray, *The Decline of Popery and its Causes. An Address delivered in the Broadway Tabernacle on Wednesday Evening, January 15th, 1851* (no publication data available). Murray's memorialist, Samuel Prime, commented on Hughes's lecture as one would expect: "Its artful perversions of history, its subtle philosophy, and plausible eloquence were well fitted to mislead the hearer." Samuel Irenaeus Prime, *Memoirs of the Rev. Nicholas Murray. D. D.* (New York: Harper and Brothers Publishers, 1862), 308.

5. Muray, *Decline*, 337.

6. 338.

7. Billington, 94, 169, 173–76. Murray preached before the General Assembly in May 1842 at the request of the General Assembly of 1841, part of the series on the Catholic Church begun in the 1830s. The series was suspended at the Old-New Light split, and restored in 1842 until the 1850s when the series ended as part of a "new attitude toward Catholics," which amounted to a prudential rule to exclude denunciation of people they wanted to convert. Breckinridge's 1842 sermon is printed as *The Rule of Faith: Discourse to Vindicate the Incarnate Word* (Philadelphia: Presbyterian Board of Publication, 1942). This is the work referred to in this section. His brother John, a Philadelphia pastor, had already had a public exchange with Hughes when Hughes was a parish priest there himself. See *Controversy between Rev. Messrs. Hughes and Breckinridge on the Subject "Is the Protestant Religion the Religion of Christ?"* (Philadelphia: Isaac Bird, 1833).

8. Breckinridge cites Bellarmine's *De summo pontifice* and *De ecclesia militante*, exhibiting once again the prominence of this Jesuit Cardinal in the minds of the theologians of no-popery. See Robert Bellarmine, *Opera Omnia*, ed. X. Sforza (Naples: Joseph Giuliani, 1856), vol. I, book 3; vol. II, book 3.

9. These points are made on pp. 1–7 of the sermon.

10. *Rule*, 13–14, 8.

11. 20. There is a direct reference to Gregory XVI's *Mirari vos* (1832).

12. Note the formalism of the apocalyptic reference.

13. *Rule*, 25–26. He mentions the number fifty, and lists nine in 150 years.

14. 27, 32.

15. Billington, 173.

16. Charles Hodge, "Romish Baptism," *Princeton Review* XVII (July 1845): 444–70, and "Is the Church of Rome Part of the Visible Church," *Ibid.* XVIII (April 1846): 320–44. The Council of Trent anathematized the Protestant sacramental doctrines without pronouncing the sacrament of baptism administered by a Protestant minister invalid, as long as the matter, form, and intention of the minister are valid. For Hodge's critique of the Catholic Church, see his *Systematic Theology, passim.* The Catholic understanding of the conditions of validity Hodge seems to support. James Henley Thornwell responded to the articles by Hodge in "The Validity of Popish Baptism" in *Southern Presbyterian Review* 1 (July 1851): 12–52; 2 (October 1851): 177–207.

17. The Catholic view of the issue of the intention of the minister is quite different. See Kevin Irwin, "Sacrament," in Joseph Komonchak, Mary Collins and Dermot Lane, eds., *The New Dictionary of Theology* (Wilmington, DE: Michael Glazier, 1988), 910–22. For Catholics, it is the intention of the church that counts, not the personal beliefs of the minister. If the minister, whether lay or cleric, orthodox or heretic, Christian or atheist, intends to do what the church intends, the sacrament is valid. I doubt that Thornwell thought the church is an entity capable of an intention.

18. *Validity*, part 1: 16, 20, 30, 38, 39.

19. He quotes Bellarmine's refutation of the *mendacia* of the Reformers at length from the *De sacramentis,* and from the Roman Catechism's parallel of sacraments and moments in life, from birth to death. Bellarmine, *Opera Omnia,* III, 1 and 2. and *The Catechism of the Council of Trent* (Baltimore, MD: Lucas Brothers, 1850).

20. *Validity*, part 1: 41–42.

21. 47.

22. *Validity*, part 1: 47–52.

23. *Validity*, part 2: 178, 180, 185–86. The reformers did not believe that the Catholic sacrament is invalid and they did not have themselves or anyone else rebaptized—neither Lutherans nor Calvinists were Anabaptists. Thornwell nowhere considers this fact. Thornwell's position implies, first, that Luther and Calvin and the first generation of their followers may be in Hell, and, second, that all Catholics who join evangelical churches must be rebaptized, very odd positions for so learned a theologian. The crucial question on this point is whether Thornwell believed that water baptism is necessary for salvation.

24. *Validity*, part 2: 187.

25. *Validity*, part 2: 189, 191, 194.

26. Loraine Boettner, *Roman Catholicism* (Philadelphia: Presbyterian and Reformed Press, 1962); John Armstrong, et al., *Roman Catholicism: Evangelical Protestants Analyze what Divides and Unites Us* (Chicago: Moody Press, 1994); and R. C. Sproul, *Faith Alone: The Evangelical Doctrine of Justification* (Grand Rapids, MI: Baker Books, 1995).

27. It was published three years before his death in a journal produced by Charles Partridge, the great-great-(maternal)-grandfather of Professor Joseph Komonchak of Catholic University, and therein lies a tale. Charles Partridge, like the father of William James of whom he was a contemporary, was a spiritualist, a dedicated esotericist, and an all-round eccentric. He published this brief statement on Catholicism by Parker whose beliefs in this respect Partridge shared so far as to disinherit his daughter, who married an Irish Catholic named O'Brien. Without this union we would not have with us, four generations later, America's foremost Slavic Catholic

theologian. *The Spiritual Telegraph* expressed his interests. The piece also can be found printed in Theodore Parker, *The Rights of Man in America,* Centenary edition by F. B. Sanborn (Boston: American Unitarian Association, 1911), 354–58.

28. Ahlstrom, 293–316; for Bushnell's *Dissertation,* 317–427; and Charles Hodge on language and method, 251–93. On Bushnell, see Howard Barnes, *Horace Bushnell and the Virtuous Republic* (Philadelphia: American Theological Library Association and Scarecrow Press, 1991) and Mary Chaney, *Horace Bushnell: His Life and Letters* (1880; reprint New York: Arno Press, 1969).

29. Cf. Sydney E. Ahlstrom, ed., *Theology in America: The Major Protestant Voices from Puritanism to Neo-Orthodoxy.* The American Heritage Series (Indianapolis: Bobbs-Merrill Company, 1967), 62, 318.

30. (Hartford: Daniel Burgess, 1835), 5.

31. Infidelity may be exemplified by Shakerism. See *Crisis,* 20–22.

32. *Crisis,* 23. Perhaps he refers to Karl Wilhelm Friedrich von Schlegel's 1828 lecture, *Philosophie der Geschichte,* English translation (1828; reprint New York: Bell and Sons, 1893).

33. *Crisis,* 24.

34. 25.

35. (New York: William Osborn [*sic*], 1847), a public lecture given in May and June 1947 in "New York, Boston, and other places" and now published for the American Home Missionary Society.

36. *Barbarism,* 5–6.

37. 24.

38. 25.

39. In *Building Eras in Religion* (New York: Scribner's Sons, 1881), published in 1846 on his return from Italy, translated and widely distributed, and put on the Roman *Index* according to an editor's note. No sane person could imagine that a letter of this sort would cause anything except a momentary exasperation in the Pope, if he indeed saw it at all. Every bit as much as any letter to the editor, this one was meant for the public.

40. William M. Shea, "Religious Language and Theological Method," in Matthew L. Lamb, ed., *Creativity and Method: Essays in Honor of Bernard Lonergan* (Milwaukee: Marquette University Press, 1981), 153–72.

41. Marsden, *The Soul of the American University* and *The Secularization of the Academy,* edited with Bradley Longfield.

42. In epistemology Porter switched from Scottish Common Sense Realism to rationalist idealism in *The Human Intellect* (1868), an important book that should be read with John Dewey's *Logic, the Theory of Inquiry* (New York: Holy, Rinehart and Winston, 1938) and Bernard Lonergan's *Insight, a Study of Human Understanding* (New York: Philosophical Library, 1957).

43. (New York: M. W. Dodd, 1851). In this essay he relies for his "principle authority" on Jacques Cretineau-Joly's *Histoire Religieuse, Politique et Litteraire de la Compagnie de Jesus.* 5vols. (Paris: Paul Mellier, 1844–46). Cf. p. 5, note. He consulted as well one of the widely read exposes of the era, Andrew Steinmetz, *Novitiate, or a year among the English Jesuits* (New York: Harper & Bros., 1846). Porter makes a curious comment on the latter: "If any man desires to understand what kind of being a Jesuit

is made to be, especially in his internal self, and by what horribly unnatural process he is trained, let him read this volume. . . . If it should be suggested, that this is a romance and not a history, we have only to say that if it is not true, it deserves to be, and the Jesuits will certainly make it true, by adopting the system which it describes." Porter, *Educational,* 10, note.

44. There was a good deal more than the Jesuits ripping up the tracks! The Catholic reformation sponsored by the Council of Trent and the papacy worked, and the political and military support of the Reformers ran out, among other things. For an overall assessment, see Robert Birely, *The Refashioning of Catholicism, 1450–1700, A Reassessment of the Counter Reformation* (Washington, DC: Catholic University of America Press, 1999). On the problems presented to Catholic historians by the terminology, see John W. O'Malley, *Trent and All That: Renaming Catholicism in the Early Modern Era.* (Cambridge, MA: Harvard University Press, 2000). The classic twentieth-century Catholic study is Herbert Jedin's *A History of the Council of Trent* (London: Thomas Nelson and Sons, 1957–61), trans. Ernest Graf.

45. *Educational,* 21. It doesn't seem that Porter has seen the *Ratio Studiorum,* a new edition of which was published in 1832. He gets his knowledge of Jesuit education through Cretineau. See 23.

46. 16–18.

47. *Educational,* 44.

48. 46, 49.

49. 50–51.

50. *Educational,* 64. Porter regularly mixes moods. What must be, is; what should be, will be. He is walking in *terra incognita.*

51. 63–64.

52. 65n.

53. 68–69.

54. *Educational,* 70.

55. 73.

56. A Protestant student, near the end of doctoral studies in theology at Saint Louis University, told me conversion of Protestants to the Catholic Church was a great mystery to her since Catholics worship Mary as a goddess and are not permitted to think freely. The more things change . . .

## 7. HARD EVANGELICALS AND THE APOSTATE CHURCH

1. On Machen, see D. G. Hart, *Defending the Faith: J. Gresham Machen and the Crisis of Conservative Protestantism in Modern America* (Baltimore, MD: Johns Hopkins University Press, 1994).

2. The original name was Presbyterian Church of America. See R. Balmer, *Encyclopedia of Evangelicalism* (Louisville: John Knox Press, 2002), 430. For the story of the founding, see D. G. Hart and John Muether, *Fighting the Good Fight: A Brief History of the Orthodox Presbyterian Church* (Philadelphia: Committee for the Historian of the Orthodox Presbyterian Church, 1995), 27–40.

3. Loraine Boettner, *Roman Catholicism,* 1962 (Phillipsburg, NJ: Presbyterian & Reformed Publishing, 1989). He wrote several other works of systematic theology,

among them works on the millennium, immortality, and predestination. Chapters from his books, including *Roman Catholicism,* are published online at <http://www .soft.net.uk/arden>.

4. They both find support from three former priests, Emmett McLoughlin (Blanshard spells it McLaughlin), Leo Lehmann, and Walter Montano. The three were active public critics of the Catholic Church. Boettner, because his interests are religious, uses several more ex-priests, among them Charles Chiniquy, Lucien Vinet, and Joseph Zachello. See Lucien Vinet, *I Was a Priest* (Toronto: Canadian Protestant League, 1949); Charles Chiniquy, *The Priest the Woman and the Confessional* (New York: Fleming H. Revell, 1880); and *Fifty Years in the Church of Rome* (New York: Fleming H. Ravell, 1886). Statements on their conversion to evangelicalism by Lehmann, Chiniquy, and Zachello can be found in *Far from Rome, Near to God: The Testimony of 50 Converted Catholic Priests,* compiled by Richard Bennett and Martin Buckingham (Portland, OR: Berean Beacon Press, 1994).

5. *Catholicism,* preface to the 5th edition (n.d.), in which he claims that Vatican II has not changed the basic doctrines to which Protestants object, except to add one: Mary, Mother of the Church. Boettner was among the "leopards-don't-change-their-spots" people. Although the council recognized elements of truth in other churches and religious freedom, time will tell. Still "She" proclaims herself the true church and reaffirms papal jurisdiction and infallibility. The pope remains absolute ruler, x–xi. "On previous occasions Rome has changed her tactics when old methods become ineffective. But she has never changed her nature." The anathemas of Trent have not been lifted. The danger from Rome has not decreased, and has probably increased—— she remains irreformable at the very points where she needs reformation.

6. *Catholicism,* 1–18; 470.

7. *Catholicism,* 1–2.

8. 12.

9. *Catholicism,* 102–103.

10. 102–103. See the calendar on 7–8, and summary on 90. On Mary as the feminine "face of God," see Andrew Greeley, *The Catholic Myth,* 243–254. Although I find Greeley's analysis illuminating, Boettner would not be helped by it. The accuracy, not to say objectivity, of Boettner's presentation on this and several other matters was challenged by Edwin H. Palmer in the *Westminster Theological Journal* 26 (November 1963): 114–119.

11. Catholicism, 9–10.

12. *Catholicism,* 13, 16.

13. 43–74.

14. 46. See the Letter to the Hebrews, 9 and I Timothy 2:5.

15. *Catholicism,* 49.

16. 55, 57.

17. 89–90, 93, 96. Boettner suggests that Catholics, like Jews in the same formative period in each, developed an oral Torah in addition to the inspired written Torah. Jacob Neusner calls this the Judaism of the dual Torah to distinguish it from its predecessor Judaism. See J. Neusner, "Torah in Judaism," and Alan Avery-Peck, "Tradition in Judaism," in *The Encyclopedia of Judaism* 3: 1447–65. Boettner is quite right, but he regards this as a deviation from a "true Christianity" that preceded it.

18. *Catholicism,* 99.

19. 113, 126.

20. 132–67.

21. 134, 135. Boettner quotes a pamphlet by Marcus Meyer: "God has no mother." The pamphlet is titled *No Mother*, but no bibliographic information is given. Boettner himself did not address the question, "Did God die on the cross?" If God the Son wasn't "conceived of the Holy Spirit and born of the Virgin Mary," then he didn't "suffer under Pontius Pilate." Boettner is in a serious difficulty for an orthodox Christian if he cannot say that the *person* of the *Logos* was born and died. Who was born and who died then? See Bernard Lonergan, "Christ the Subject," in *Collection: Papers by Bernard Lonergan*, S.J. (New York: Herder and Herder, 1967).

22. *Catholicism*, 136. A recent example can be found in the Mexican devotion to Our Lady of Guadalupe, another "curious mixture of Romanism and Paganism."

23. See index entries under "Body," "Confessional," and "Seduction" in Franchot, *Roads to Rome*.

24. *Catholicism*, 201–02.

25. 210–11. See note 4, earlier.

26. 212–13, 217. Boettner must know all this from ex-priests. Did the ex-priests find a prurient interest and speak to it? At any rate, having spent twenty years in the confessional on Saturday evenings, and having confessed my sins to a priest for over sixty years I find a hyperactive sexual imagination at work in such claims.

27. Franchot, 125–127. See Jules Michelet, *Priests, Women and Families* (London: C. Cocks, 1845). Even more than a threat to American Protestant virtue, the confessional, according to Boettner, has been an international social and economic curse: Ireland, Spain, and France experienced "downfall" and "degradation" because of the confessional. The sacrament explains why they are inferior to their neighbor nations where Protestantism is professed. See Boettner, 215–16.

28. *Catholicism*, 273–74, 270, 281.

29. Crosses, crucifixes, scapulars, relics, and so on amount to "fetishism and sorcery" (284ff., 288ff.). Catholics even in an "enlightened country such as the United States" accept this or fail to denounce it (292). Pilgrimages, originating in the middle ages brought money to the church and still do at places like Lourdes, Fatima, and Guadalupe—the latter the shrine of a Mexican goddess absorbed into Mary by devotees.

30. *Catholicism*, 457–59.

31. 460.

32. *Catholicism*, 460.

33. For biographical data, see John M. Frame, his intellectual biographer, in *Cornelius Van Til: An Analysis of His Thought* (Philadelphia: Presbyterian and Reformed Publishing, 1995), and a shorter essay in Walter A. Elwell, ed., *Handbook of Evangelical Theologians* (Grand Rapids, MI: Baker Books, 1993), 156–67. See also a warmly appreciative biography by William White Jr., *Van Til: Defender of the Faith* (New York: Thomas Nelson Publishers, 1979). The brief article on him in the *Dictionary of Christianity in America* (p. 1211) has him retiring from Westminster in 1975, while the other sources put it in 1972.

34. *The Works of Cornelius Van Til, 1895–1987*. Logos Library System CD-ROM, available at Westminster Theological Seminary bookstore.

35. For example, in 1942 he was present at the meeting in St. Louis at which

plans for the formation of a new association of evangelicals were proposed, but neither he nor any representative of his Orthodox Presbyterian Church showed up for
the founding meeting in Chicago in 1943. My hunch is that he discerned that it
would take Christian orthodoxy in directions that neither he nor his church support.

36. "St. Thomas and Calvin, an Address Given by Dr. Cornelius Van Til, Calvin
College, 1949," and "Bernard J. F. Lonergan, S.J." Typescript dated 11/22/74. Both are
from the Westminister Theological Seminary Library, and the pagination in references follows the WTS typescripts. The piece on Lonergan is available in *The Works*
(Logos 2), cited earlier. The same critique appears when he treats other Catholic
thinkers: Maritain, Gilson, Teilhard de Chardin, and Hans Kung. See *The Works . . .*
There are valuable comments by Van Til on "Romanism" in his introduction to *The
Inspiration and Authority of the Bible: Benjamin B. Warfield*, ed. by S. G. Craig (Phillipsburg, NJ: Presbyterian and Reformed Publishing Co., 1948), 17–29.

37. "St. Thomas and Calvin," 6. He adds: "This principle does not come to full
expression in this life." He may mean that a gray area in this matter makes it impossible for any human being to judge another's life in faith.

38. "St. Thomas and Calvin," 8–18.

39. 20.

40. 22–23.

41. Van Til reviews Lonergan's important contributions to Catholic thought, *Insight, A Study of Human Understanding* (New York: Philosophical Library, 1957) and
*Method in Theology* (New York: Herder and Herder, 1972).

42. "Lonergan," 34, 38–39.

43. "Lonergan," 41–42.

44. If at all—he does not make a clear statement on the issue. Frame criticized
him on the point, implying that Van Til confused a person's theological and philosophical position with that person's Christian faith or lack of it. Frame, 350–52.

45. See David Tracy, *The Analogical Imagination;* and Hans Kung and David
Tracy, eds., *Paradigm Change in Theology: A Symposium for the Future* (New York:
Crossroad, 1991). The latter is a collection of essays by leading Catholic and Protes-
tant mediating theologians.

46. Chicago: Moody Press, 1994.

47. *Roman Catholicism,* 65–74. The title of Godfrey's essay is "What Really
Caused the Great Divide?" The documents by Calvin are "The Reply to Sadoleto"
(1539); "The Necessity of Reforming the Church" (1544); and "The True Method of
Reforming the Church and Healing her Divisions" (1549).

48. *Roman,* 79. Not that Protestant churches are much more faithful to the
scriptures, Godfrey remarks!

49. "Roman Catholic Theology Today," in *Roman,* 85–118. Karl Rahner is the
best example in his view, but far from the only one. He discusses Gregory Moran on
revelation, Raymond Brown on scripture, Josef Geiselmann on scripture and tradition, David Tracy, and Avery Dulles.

50. *Roman,* 89. As for conservative Catholicism, he mentions the Fellowship of
Catholic Scholars, Karl Keating, and Scott Hahn of the Franciscan University of Steu-
benville, Pennsylvania.

51. *Roman,* 90.

52. *Roman,* 101.

53. 113. See R. C. Sproul, *Faith Alone: The Evangelical Doctrine of Justification* (Grand Rapids, MI: Baker Books, 1995), and *Getting the Gospel Right: The Tie That Binds Evangelicals Together* (Grand Rapids, MI: Baker Books, 1999), for clear statements of the evangelical objection to *ECT*. Strimple addresses theologians while Sproul et al. insist on addressing the official documents because the theologians are too slippery and Romans live by official teaching. See "Resolutions for Roman Catholic and Evangelical Dialogue," in *Modern Reformation* (July/August 1994): 28–29. Among others, it is signed by Armstrong, Godfrey, Sproul, Strimple, and Michael Horton.

54. (Eugene, OR: Harvest House, 1995). Ankerberg also moderated and produced a video of discussions between R. C. Sproul, James Kennedy, and John MacArthur under the same title. It is available from the Ankerberg Theological Research Institute, Chattanooga, Tennessee 37414.

55. *Protestants and Catholics,* Appendix B: "How the Roman Catholic Church, the Papacy, and Catholic Tradition Arose." In this version the Catholic "system" was justified on the Old Testament priestly model (sacerdotalism appears in the early Fathers, c. 200 C.E.) and Pope Gregory I (540–604 C.E.) was the first pope—bishop, metropolitan of Italy, and patriarch of the West. Short-lived Boniface III disappears from the story. "If the official Roman Catholic Church begins to emerge anywhere, it is here" (255). Dates follow, from 310 (prayers for the dead) to 1950 and the dogma of the Assumption of Mary. See Boettner, 258–60.

56. Ankerberg, 160–61, 185–86. Dave Hunt, in *A Woman Rides the Beast,* has shuffled the cards of the Outline, but it is clearly discernable in his work as well. The Myth is operative, too, but the apocalypticism is veneer. Justification for the structural and substantive repetition must be found in the need to pass it on, much as the catechism form has lasted since the Reformation and Counter Reformation. As long as Catholicism remains, so must the Protestant criticism.

57. Ankerberg, 135. Of course, *ECT* doesn't make the claim of "all on either side" are Christians. In fact, *ECT* avoids the claim.

58. 136–38.

59. 187.

60. 215. See also 212, 219, 221.

61. See *Vatican Council II: The Basic Sixteen Documents,* ed. Austin Flannery (Northport, NY: Costello Publishing, 1995), especially the Decree on Ecumenism, 499ff. The term is not new. The American Catholic bishops used the term often. See the collection of their letters, Peter Guilday, ed., *The National Pastorals of the American Hierarchy, 1792–1919* (Westminster, MD: The Newman Press, 1954).

## 8. SOFT EVANGELICALS AND THE HERETICAL CHURCH

1. *DCA*, 238–39; *EDT*, 204. *DARB*, 94–95.

2. "Dr. Channing's Letter on Catholicism, &c," reprinted from *The Western Messenger* (Louisville KY: Morton & Smith, 1836) and "The Church: A Discourse Delivered in the First Congregational Church of Philadelphia, Sunday, May 30, 1841," in *The Works of William Ellery Channing* (1848; New York: Franklin, 1870), 428–446.

3. Letter, 9.

4. Letter, 10.

5. 12. What cause for hope could he be referring to in 1836? French liberal Catholicism of F. de Lamennais and his journal *L'Avenir*, and indeed all .iberalism had been condemned implicitly by Pope Gregory XVI in *Mirari Vos* in 1832. Perhaps he referred to the so-called Republican Catholics who supported the American revolution and had a hand in the writing of the Constitution. See David O'Brien, *Public Catholicism*, and Patrick Carey, *Roman Catholic Religious Thought*.

6. Letter, 14.

7. "Letter," 15. In Channing's view there is something Protestants can learn from Catholic practice, and, strangely enough, from the most execrated practice of all: auricular confession! According to Channing, the Protestant minister relies solely on preaching when what is needed is the art of personal communication between congregant and minister which fosters spiritual understanding and liberty of conscience all at once. There should be a Protestant version which eschews the Catholic confessional's intent to dominate conscience and limit liberty (17–20).

8. 20.

9. "Church," 437–38.

10. "Church," 440.

11. Calhoun, *Princeton Seminary* in 2 vols (Carlisle PA: Banner of Truth Trust, 1994), and Mark Noll, *The Princeton Theology, 1812–1921* (Grand Rapids: Baker Book House, 1983), 11–51.

12. Charles Hodge, *Systematic Theology*, 3 vols. (1932–73; Grand Rapids: Eerdmans, 1995). On verbal plenary inspiration see 1:153–68.

13. Mark A. Reynolds, "Charles Hodge's Ecclesiastical Elenctics: his Response to Catholicizing Tendencies in the Churches, 1837–1860," Ph.D. dissertation, Saint Louis University, 2000, 73–130. Much of what I report here relies on Reynolds's research, but my application of it is my own and not his responsibility. The major point of the dissertation is to rescue Hodge's creative theology from unjustified obscurity and misrepresentation, an effort I was convinced needed to be made since I first read the *Systematic Theology* in the early 1980s.

14. There had been a buildup over the previous decade. Among other related resolutions on the subject, the 1835 Assembly wrote: "The Roman Catholic Church has essentially apostatized from the religion of Our Lord and Savior Jesus Christ, and therefore cannot be recognized as a Christian church." Reynolds, 91ff.

15. *Iam vos omnes*, September 13, 1868. See *Documents of Vatican Council I*, trans. by John F. Broderick (Collegeville MN: Liturgical Press, 1971), 23–27.

16. Manuscript from Charles Hodge to Pope Pius IX, 1869. Firestone Library, Princeton University, and in the Hodge manuscript collection, box 28, file 49 of the Princeton Seminary Archives, Luce Library.

17. Notice how close this appears to be to the position of the evangelical signers of *ETC*.

18. See *Systematic Theology*, 1: 104–49 for his judgment of Catholic doctrine. It is highly sophisticated dialectical placing of the Reformed theology between the extremes of Roman ritualism and mysticism on one side and rationalism and what would later come to be called modernism on the other. Hodge discussed Roman doctrine at many points in his three volumes. Of particular interest is his discussion of the papacy as Antichrist. See 3: 812–36. He advanced several theological and historical arguments for the Protestant custom initiated by Luther and Calvin, but he insists

that even the attribution of the epithet to the papacy does not preclude Catholics from membership in the true church. In fact he maintains that it is undeniable that many Catholics are true Christians. He appears to be making as much sense of a Protestant usage as he can, but he himself is not given to speaking that way.

19. Reynolds, 130.

20. 250–51.

21. The story of the founding of Westminster is told by Bradley J. Longfield in *The Presbyterian Controversy: Fundamentalists, Modernists and Moderates* (New York: Oxford University Press, 1991), 173–80. Craig's resignation from the Board and Machen's trial and suspension from the ministry of the Presbyterian Church and his death are reported on 211ff. On both Machen and Craig see Ned B. Stonehouse, *J. Gresham Machen: A Biographical Memoir* (Grand Rapids: Eerdmans, 1954). See also D. G. Hart's fascinating intellectual biography of Machen, *Defending the Faith,* and his essay on Machen in the *Handbook of Evangelical Theologians,* ed. Walter Elwell (Grand Rapids: Baker Books, 1993), 129–43. On Craig see the *Dictionary of the Presbyterian and Reformed Tradition in America,* ed. D. G. Hart and Mark Noll (Downers Grove IL: InterVarsity Press, 1999), 71–72. Craig's *Christianity Today* born in controversy over Presbyterian modernism appeared from 1930 to 1949, and is to be distinguished from the *Christianity Today* founded in 1956, which is broadly evangelical rather than Presbyterian. "Samuel Craig" in DPRT, 71–72, and Balmer's *Encyclopedia of Evangelicalism,* 138

22. J. Gresham Machen, *Christianity and Liberalism* (Grand Rapids: Eerdmans, 1923).

23. For a discussion of the chief figures on the liberal side of evangelicalism, see Kenneth Cauthen, *The Impact of American Religious Liberalism, Second Edition* (Washington, DC: University Press of America, 1983). For a brilliant critique of the development of European liberal theology, see Karl Barth, *From Rousseau to Ritschl* (London: SCM Press, 1952). Machen was a good theologian and Barth was a great theologian.

24. Pius X, *Pascendi Dominici Gregis* and *Lamentabili Sane* (Boston: Daughters of St. Paul, nd.). For the historical circumstances, see Lester R. Kurtz, *The Politics of Heresy: The Modernist Crisis in Roman Catholicism* (Berkeley: University of California Press, 1986), and Marvin R. O'Connell, *Critics on Trial: An Introduction to the Catholic Modernist Crisis* (Washington, DC: Catholic University of America Press, 1994).

25. *Christianity and Liberalism,* 52. Machen tempts me to wonder what Hodge would have made of the Presbyterian modernists.

26. *Christianity and Liberalism,* 160.

27. Machen, *The Virgin Birth of Christ* (1923; 1930; Grand Rapids: Baker Books, 1975), x. See also his comments on Catholic interpreters, 127, 134, 143f.

28. It was printed as a pamphlet. See Samuel G. Craig, "The Revival of Theology in the Roman Catholic Church" (Philadelphia: Board of Christian Education of the Presbyterian Church in the United States of America, 1938), 21pp.

29. 4–5.

30. 12. He quotes Abraham Kuyper, the influential Dutch Reformed theologian, to the same effect: "Now in this conflict Rome is not an antagonist, but stands at our side, inasmuch as she also recognizes and maintains the Trinity, the deity of Christ, the cross as an atoning sacrifice, the Scriptures as the Word of God, and the Ten Commandments as a divinely imposed rule of life." 13. On Kuyper see Walter Elwell,

ed., *The Evangelical Dictionary of Theology* (Grand Rapids: Baker Books, 1984), 616. Heiko Oberman long argued that the Reformers were heirs as well as critics of medieval Catholicism see *The Reformation: Roots and Ramifications* (Grand Rapids: Eerdmans, 1994). So, too Stephen Ozmont. See the latter's introduction to the collection edited by him, *The Reformation in Medieval Perspective* (Chicago: Quadrangle Books, 1971).

31. Craig, 21.

32. The story of the National Association of Evangelicals is told by Joel Carpenter, *Revive Us Again: The Reawakening of American Fundamentalism* (New York: Oxford University Press, 1997).

33. Carpenter, 142–143.

34. 141.

35. Basic information on these groups can be found in the *Dictionary of Christianity in America* (Downers Grove, IL: InterVarsity Press, 1990).

36. Harold E. Fey, "Can Catholicism Win America? Etc." *Christian Century* (September–April, 1944–45), 61: 1378–80, 1409–11, 1442–44, 1476–79, 1498–99; 62:13–15, 44–47, 74–76. For an earlier Protestant attempt to answer the question, see John F. Moore, *Will America Become Catholic?* (New York: Harper, 1931). Moore is less worried than Fey.

37. Harold J. Ockenga, "Unvoiced Multitudes" in *Evangelical Action! A Report of the Organization of the National Association of Evangelicals for United Action"* (Boston: United Action Press, 1942), 19–40.

38. Ockenga, "Christ in America" *in United We Stand.* (National Association of Evangelicals Constitutional Convention: Chicago: May 3–7, 1943), 12.

39. *United We Stand,* 40. For Bradbury's address, see 16–27.

40. G. C. Berkouwer, *The Conflict with Rome* (Philadelphia: Presbyterian and Reformed Publishing, 1957). Trans from the Dutch by David H. Freeman.

41. See the biographical and expository essay on Berkouwer by Gary L. Watts in *Handbook of Evangelical Theologians,* ed. Walter A. Elwell (Grand Rapids: Baker Books, 1993), 193–207. The line was given to "standing firm against . . ." whatever the danger of the moment, but Berkouwer apparently mellowed as he aged.

42. *The Second Vatican Council and the New Catholicism* (Grand Rapids: Eerdmans, 1965), 32.

43. *Handbook,* p 203.

44. *The Second Vatican Council,* 19.

45. *The Second Vatican Council,* 27–30.

46. See his review, 178ff.

47. He examined the history of the phrase *extra ecclesiam nulla salus* from Cyprian on down. That history, he admitted, is not entirely one-grained or entirely triumphalist; *Second Vatican,* 186ff. Pasquier Quesnel (d. 1719) and Leonard Feeney (d. 1979) were condemned by Rome for their unconditioned exclusiveness, and Catholic theologians have sought ways of explaining how non-Catholics might be saved—invincible ignorance, baptism of desire, etc.

48. *Second Vatican,* 197. The Council remained ambiguous on this issue. *Dominus Iesus* (2000) from the Roman Congregation for the Doctrine of the Faith continues the ambiguity. See *Dominus Jesus,* National Conference of Catholic Bishops/United States Catholic Conference, www.nccbuscc.org/pope/doctrineoffaith.htm.

Rome seems caught between an acceptance of religions not only in tolerance but in respect for the truth found in them (*Nostra Aetate* of the second Vatican Council) and its traditional claim to be the one true Christian church and the one true religion. The debate among evangelical exclusivists and inclusivists reflects a similar tension, but in their case the problem is focused on the interpretation of scriptural texts.

49. *Second Vatican*, 202, 203, 206.

50. Reviewed by Van Til in *Interpretation* 20/4 (October 1966): 493–94.

51. David F. Wells, *Revolution in Rome* (Downers Grove IL: InterVarsity Press, 1972), with a forward by John Stott.

52. *Revolution*, 36, 114.

53. Among them are Leslie Dewart, Gregory Baum, Daniel Callahan, Eduard Schillebeeckx, Karl Rahner, and Hans Kung. Wells seems to have understood them to some degree and is much clearer in his comments on them than he is on John Henry Newman. See 42–43.

54. Revolution, 62. He relies heavily upon James Hitchcock, *The Decline and Fall of Radical Catholicism* (New York: Herder and Herder, 1971)). Hitchcock, a historian at Saint Louis University, remains an important critic of the liberal interpretations of the conciliar decrees. See Hitchcock's essays in *Years of Crisis: Collected Essays, 1970–83* (San Francisco: Ignatius Press, 1985).

55. This fits rather nicely with the traditional Catholic sacramentalism, objected to so strongly by most evangelical authors, and in it the church, the "true church," is the place where or means by which the person encounters God and Christ. So the essential note of Catholic ecclesiology is maintained even in its profound switch from exclusivity to inclusivity. He continues with Van Til's point that Catholicism's characteristic flaw began with its compromise with Greek philosophy. That compromise might be its characteristic strength he does not consider.

56. *Revolution*, 96–97.

57. Quoting from reprint, with permission of the *Institute on Religion and Public Life*, New York. The text can also be found in *Evangelicals and Catholic Together: Toward a Common Mission*, ed. Charles Colson and Richard John Neuhaus (Dallas: Word Publishing, 1995), xv–xxxiii.

58. The second picked up six new priests and dropped some of the Catholic laity and the bishops. One can only guess that the loss of bishop signers had to do with the storm of evangelical protest to the first document and the technical theological intent of the second. The leaders of the group, Colson and Neuhaus, edited a volume of essays by participants, *Thy Word is Truth: A Project of Evangelicals and Catholic Together*.

59. The critics are many, among them John Ankerberg, John Armstrong, Michael Horton, Ian Murray, Davis Duggins, and Scott Clark. The most astute comment has been made by Daryl Hart, "An Old Protestant on Americanist Christianity," in *Regeneration Quarterly* 1/1 (Winter 1995), 27–29.

60. Neuhaus, *The Naked Public Square: Religion and Democracy in America*. On the various eddies of conservative religion that cross denominational boundaries, and on the culture wars, see Robert Wuthnow, *The Restructuring of American Religion* (Princeton: Princeton University Press, 1988) and *The Struggle for America's Soul: Evangelicals Liberals, and Secularism* (Grand Rapids: Eerdmans, 1989) and J. D. Hunter, *Culture Wars: The Struggle to Define America* (New York: Basic Books, 1991).

61. No mention of homosexual rights, no opposition to birth control, no support for unwed mothers, orphans, workers, or blacks, no support for reduction of third world debt, nothing on the prohibition of alcohol, nothing on the slave trade for prostitution, or the depredations of capitalism, or the pollution of the environment. The politics seem evident, even had one not taken the hint of the political interests of the group from the fact that the organizers were Charles Colson and Richard J. Neuhaus. The tares were pulled.

62. Peter Kreeft, *Ecumenical Jihad* (San Francisco: Ignatius Press, 1996).

63. Evangelicals and Catholics show "a pattern of convergence and cooperation" in these matters, but it is not thereby a "partisan religious agenda." In fact "this is a set of directions oriented to the common good and discussable on the basis of public reason." One may wonder then why it was not so discussed. The answer is, I think, that the religious relationship between evangelicals and Catholics is as crucial to the signers as is their social agenda.

64. The most important recent document with reference to shared faith is "The Lutheran-Catholic Dialogue Joint Declaration on the Doctrine of Justification," *Origins* 28 (July 19, 1988): 120–27 and the comments by Cardinal Edward Cassidy, "Consensus Achieved, Vatican Official Tells Lutherans," *Origins* 28 (October 8, 1998): 286–288. *Origins* is the Catholic News Service document publication.

65. See Philip Jenkins, *The Next Christendom: The Coming of Global Christianity* (New York: Oxford University Press, 2002).

66. Thirty-six are listed in Richard Bennett and Martin Buckingham, eds., *Far from Rome, Near to God: The Testimony of 50 Converted Catholic Priests* (Portland, OR: Berean Beacon Press, 1994), ix–xii. For more one need only surf the Web.

67. I follow here the evangelical response to the Catholic concern. The Catholic side is discussed in chapter 12.

68. One can find "The Gift of Salvation" as appendix to R. C. Sproul, *Getting the Gospel Right: The Tie that Binds Evangelicals Together* (Grand Rapids: Baker Books, 1999), 179–84. It is followed by "The Gospel of Jesus Christ: An Evangelical Celebration," 185–95, drafted by evangelicals only, including four of the signers of *ECT II*, and signed by 114 others, including another half-dozen of the signers of either or both *ECT I* and *II*. Seven of the eighteen "Affirmations and Denials" seem to express matters of concern raised by evangelical cooperation in *ECT I* and *II*.

## 9. THE NINETEENTH-CENTURY BISHOPS AND ANTI-CATHOLICISM

1. *The National Pastorals of the American Hierarchy* (1792–1919), ed. Peter Guilday (Westminster, MD: The Newman Press, 1954). A provincial council is a meeting of bishops within an ecclesiastical province called by the archbishop; the plenary council was a meeting of the bishops attended by archbishops and bishops of the several American provinces.

2. For the growth curve, see Gaustad and Barlow, *New Historical Atlas of Religion in America*, 157, figure 2:28.

3. Guilday, 235.

4. Guilday, 19.39. Beside the signatures of Baltimore and Charleston we find

those of the bishops of Bardstown, Cincinnati, St. Louis, and Boston, and the administrator of diocese of Philadelphia.

5. Guilday, 27–28.

6. 78.

7. See Nancy L. Schultz, *Fire and Roses,* and her introduction to a reprint of Rebecca Reed's "Six Months in a Convent" and Monk's "Awful Disclosures of the Hotel Dieu Nunnery" in Schultz, ed., *Veil of Fear,* vii–xxxiii.

8. Guilday, 90–91.

9. 93. Schultz, in her introduction to Reed and Monk, puts the number of copies at over half a million over the twenty-five years preceding the Civil War.

10. Guilday, 123. The larger portion of the letter is taken up with the proper reading of scripture and the difficulties of translation and editions.

11. 150.

12. Guilday, 168–69.

13. Peter Clarke, "John England," *EACH,* 490. See also R. C. Madden in the *NCE* 5, 352–54.

14. The complete text of the Constitution of the Diocese of Charleston is printed in Patrick Carey, *American Catholic Religious Thought: The Shaping of a Theological and Social Tradition* (Mahwah, NJ: Paulist Press, 1987), 76–92. The words quoted can be found on 79ff.

15. John England, "Discourse Before Congress," *The Works of the Right Rev. John England, Bishop of Charleston, S.C., with Memoir, Memorials, Notes and Full Index,* ed. Hugh P. McElrone (Baltimore, MD: Baltimore Publishing, 1884), 2 vols. England's successor, Right Rev. Ignatius Aloysius Reynolds, edited the works in five volumes (Baltimore, MD: John Murphy, 1849). In this more extensive collection of England's works, we find "Letters on the Calumnies of J. Banco White Against the Catholic Religion," vol. 1, pp. 106–347, an important example of Catholic apologetics in answer to a book written by White, an ex-priest from Spain. There is a later edition of the works by Sebastian G. Messmer in seven vols, in Cleveland, 1908. For biographical data on England, see Patrick Carey, *An Immigrant Bishop: John England's Adaptation of Irish Catholicism to American Republicanism* (Yonkers, NY: U.S. Catholic Historical Society, 1982) and Peter Clarke, *A Free Church in a Free Society: The Ecclesiology of John England, Bishop of Charleston, 1820–1842* (Greenwood SC: Center for John England Studies, 1982), 2nd ed.

16. There follows a lengthy (219–223) analogy between a court procedure and a judgment regarding the facticity of the resurrection established on the basis of testimony. Hume's conclusion that no amount of eye witness testimony can justify belief in a miracle and that any other explanation of a peculiar event is preferable to divine intervention was likely in England's mind as he composed these pages. See *David Hume on Religion* (New York: Meridian Books, 1964), 205–229. The section was originally published as part of Hume's *Philosophical Essays Concerning Human Understanding,* 1747.

17. Sydney Ahlstrom, *A Religious History of the American People* (New Haven, CT: Yale University Press, 1972), 330. See also Charles P. Hanson, *Necessary Virtue: the Pragmatic Origins of Religious Liberty in New England* (Lanham, MD: University Press of America, 1998).

18. England, *Discourse,* 236.

19. England, *Discourse,* 236–37.

20. England deals in the body of his address with the Lateran Council and with Pope Pius V's action in 1569 against Elizabeth I.

21. 241–42. He then had to address specific concerns about the Inquisition and about the canons of the fourth Lateran Council, and he did so on the basis of his announced principle of the distinction of jurisdiction of church and state, and the distinction between what the church does and what Roman Catholics do, and by calling upon the nascent historical consciousness of his hearers—that age is not this age, and we must, as historically conscious persons, make this distinction (243–48).

22. He is likely referring to Henry Hallam, *History of Europe During the Middle Ages* (New York: Colonial Press, 1899), revised edition. Hallam died in 1859.

23. *Discourse,* 247–49.

24. Francis Patrick Kenrick, in 1830 bishop of Philadelphia and in 1851 archbishop of Baltimore, perhaps the finest theological scholar among the American bishops, published *The Primacy of the Apostolic See Vindicated* (Philadelphia: M. Fithian, 1845), taking substantially the same position as England on fourth Lateran and on the deposition of Elizabeth I. Although he adds considerable nuance to England's schematic presentation, he backs the claim that the popes acted within a medieval confederational context and not by a dogma of divine right. Even Boniface VIII, Kenrick maintains, understood that he acted by a quasi-prophetic power for the protection of the rights of the oppressed. See Kenrick, "Deposing Power," in *The Primacy,* 270–305. For a view of the character and travails of Boniface, see Kelly's *Oxford Book of the Popes,* 208–10.

25. Charles Marshall, "An Open Letter to Governor Smith," *Atlantic Monthly* (April 1927): 139, 540–49; "Catholic and Patriot: Governor Smith Responds," *Atlantic Monthly* (May 1927): 139, 721–28. Marshall got the last word in *Governor Smith's American Catholics* (Mahweh, NJ: Quinn and Boden, 1928). John Kennedy, "Kennedy's Houston Speech," in Albert J. Menendez, *John Kennedy: Catholic and Humanist* (Buffalo, NY: Prometheus Press, 1978), 119–34.

26. James J. Walsh, influential neurologist and amateur historian of Catholicism, made the case against "so-called progress" and for the glories of Christendom when the charge that Catholicism is intrinsically anti-intellectual was riding high. His response was to declare, indeed to prove, the superiority of Christendom in *The Thirteenth, the Greatest of Centuries,* 5th edition (New York: Catholic Summer School Press, 1913). It was reprinted as late as 1970. An important part of his evidence is the freedom of debate in the medieval universities.

27. John Courtney Murray, *We Hold These Truths: Catholic Reflections on the American Proposition* (1960; reprint Kansas City, MO: Sheed and Ward, 1988).

28. *Discourse,* 225.

29. *Discourse,* 227–32.

30. He follows Papias's second-century narrative of the order of the writing of the four gospels, although he doesn't mention this fact. Papias of Hierapolis (d. 130) is quoted in Eusebius, *Ecclesiastical History* (New York: Fathers of the Church, 1953), III, 39, 15–16.

31. *Discourse,* 213. What is a "great majority" he doesn't say, nor does he say why that should be have such weight.

32. J. M. R Tillard, "Bishop," *The New Dictionary of Theology*, eds J. Komonchak, Dermot Lane, and Mary Collins (Wilmington, DE: Michael Glazier, 1988), 132-38. "The problem of the origin, mission and nature of the episcopacy is one of the most difficult issues of the so-called Catholic ecclesiology" (132). There is no significant difference in the history of "Bishop" between Tillard and P. Toon in the *Evangelical Dictionary of Theology*, ed. Walter A. Elwell (Grand Rapids, MI: Baker Books, 1984), 157-58.

33. *Inopportunist* is a term designating bishops who opposed the definition of infallibility because they regarded the definition to be inopportune but did not oppose the doctrine itself. The category allowed opposition that would not turn out to be heresy *post factum*. See Earl Boyea's entry on Purcell in *EACH*, 1186-87. There is no biography. The story of Purcell's reign in Cincinnati is told by Robert Trisco, *The Holy See and the Nascent Church in the Middle Western United States, 1826-1850* (Rome: Gregorian University Press, 1962). Purcell's last years were marred by an economic disaster: his brother managed a diocesan fund, which should have had twenty-five million in it and ended up with a $2.5 million debt. See M. E. Hussey, "The 1878 Financial Failure of Archbishop Purcell," *The Cincinnati Historical Society Bulletin* 36 (1978): 7-41.

34. Campbell-Purcell *Debate*, 383.

35. Campbell quoted accurately from the bishop's oath. See *Pontificale Romanum, editio princeps 1595* (Vatican City: Libreria Editrice Vaticana, 1997), 87. The oath in this respect remains the same in the 1962 version; see *Pontificale Romanum redimpressio editionis iuxta typicam anno 1962* (Rome: Edizioni Liturgiche, 1999), 52.

36. *Debate*, 384-85.

37. 437.

38. 411.

39. 421-22. See also 407 and 411.

40. Jean Baptiste Bouvier, *Institutiones theologicae* (Paris: Méguignon and Le-Roux, 1841). See "Bouvier, Jean Baptiste," in *NCE*: II: 740. Bouvier was a Gallican theologian with typical anti-ultramontanist leanings, which may explain his willingness to circumscribe papal sovereignty. He later became a bishop and received help from Roman theologians in further editions of his *Institutiones*.

41. *Debate*, 427. "Collier" (?), according to Purcell, declared this part of the text of Lateran Council to be spurious. He may mean Jeremy Collier (1650-1726).

42. 431-35.

43. *Debate*, 434.

44. *Debate*, 434-35.

45. *Debate*, 446-47. Emphases are in the original printing.

## 10. JOHN HUGHES AND KIRWAN IN NEW YORK

1. Richard Shaw, *Dagger John: The Unquiet Life and Times of Archbishop John Hughes of New York.* (New York: Paulist Press, 1977), 62-70.

2. Stephan Macedo, *Diversity and Distrust: Civic Education in a Multicultural Democracy* (Cambridge, MA: Harvard University Press, 2000). On Hughes's role, see 68-72, 83-87. In telling the story, Macedo takes the view that denominational education, Catholic in fact, is divisive. It is the standard liberal criticism from the time of

Hughes. Its most prominent exponent in the twentieth century was John Dewey, not simply because Dewey did not like Catholicism but because he, like Macedo, looked on the public school as the nursery of democratic society and culture. I do not agree with their view on divisiveness and I do not think there is anything like sufficient evidence to bear it out. For a description of the public controversy over the schools, see Billington, 193–238, and Robert Francis Hueston, *The Catholic Press and Nativism, 1840–1860* (1972; reprint New York: Arno Press, 1976). Also see Andrew Greeley, *American Catholics Since the Council: An Unauthorized Account* (Chicago: Thomas Moore Press, 1885), 129–49; and *The Catholic Myth: The Behavior and Beliefs of American Catholics,* 162–81.

3. Shaw, *Dagger John,* 195–97. Slapping a nun would not have been taken kindly by the armed Irishmen who were ready to defend the churches at Hughes's call.

4. See Samuel I. Prime, *Memoirs of the Rev. Nichols Murray, D. D.,* for biographical details, and chapter 6 of this book for a discussion of Murray.

5. Prime, 282. This may be something of an overstatement, given the large sales of the sensational books by Maria Monk and Samuel Morse. Prime might be correct if he meant to restrict the remark to works of theological criticism, which Monk and Morse were certainly not. Prime, as might be expected, tells us that Murray was a champion of truth, while Hughes used his considerable gifts to defend the indefensible. See Kirwan (276).

6. In the *Complete Works of the Most Rev. John Hughes, D. D., Archbishop of New York Comprising his Sermons, Letters, Lectures, Speeches, etc.* (New York: Lawrence Kehoe, 1865), I: 577–636. On the conflict with Murray, see Shaw, 253–56, and Prime, *Memoirs,* 263–313.

7. *Kirwan Unmasked: A Review in Six Letters Addressed to the Rev. Nicholas Murray, D. D., of Elizabethtown, New Jersey, by the Right Rev. John Hughes, D.D., Bishop of New York* (New York: Edward Dunigan, 1951).

8. *Controversy between Rev. Messrs. Hughes and Breckenridge on the Subject "Is the Protestant Religion the Religion of Christ?"* (Philadelphia: Isaac Bird, 1833).

9. *Letters . . . First Series,* 50–51. In the same vein on the Irish Catholic clergy, see also Charlotte Elizabeth (Tonna), "Personal Recollections," *The Works of Charlotte Elizabeth (Tonna) with an Introduction by H. B. Stowe* (New York: M. W. Dodd, 1847), I: 47–69.

10. S. J. Barnett, *Idol Temples and Crafty Priests, The Origins of Enlightenment Anti-Clericalism* (London: Macmillan, 1999).

11. *Letters . . . First Series,* 36–37.

12. *Kirwan Unmasked,* 7–8.

13. 12–14. The infidelity Hughes refers to is Kirwan's own term for the state of his mind between his lapse from Catholicism and his conversion to "true Christianity." See *Letters . . . First Series,* p. 30ff. See also *Kirwan Unmasked,* 82.

14. *Kirwan Unmasked,* 23. 26.

15. 28–29. Murray sees the cause of the miserable state of the Irish in the nineteenth century ("my Ireland," as he puts it) in the oppression of the gullible Irish by popery and priest-craft. Hughes sees it as a result of English depredations and a badly deformed social and economic system. See Hughes, *A Lecture on the Antecedent Causes of the Irish Famine in 1847* (New York: Edward Dunigan, 1847).

16. *Kirwan Unmasked,* 30.

17. *Kirwan Unmasked,* 59–63; see also 66. Hughes also detects in Murray's standard of judgment of truth and falsity an echo of unbelief, for Murray habitually uses "common sense" when he judges Catholic doctrines to be "nonsense." Whose "common sense," Hughes asks? It sounds to him like the common sense of Theodore Parker's Unitarianism, not to say Voltaire and Thomas Paine (47ff). It is a fact that Murray constantly reaches beyond the evangelical affirmation of the bible as the rule of faith to the "common sense" of his intellectual culture to ridicule Catholic doctrines such as Real Presence and the notion of a sacrament. Hughes may have put his finger on a problem that does not rear its head in the Presbyterian church until the turn of the century in the modernist controversy.

18. *Bishop Hughes Confuted: Reply to the Rt. Rev. John Hughes, Roman Catholic Archbishop of New York by "Kirwan," Third Series* (Philadelphia: Presbyterian Board of Publication, 1851), 94.

19. *Reply . . . Third Series,* 103, 105.

20. See note 6.

21. Jack Chick and Dave Hunt and a dozen others exemplify it today.

22. He laid the cornerstone for the new St. Patrick's Cathedral on 50th Street and 5th Avenue on August 15, 1858, the Feast of the Assumption of Mary into heaven, before sixty thousand onlookers, a crowd considered to be the largest in the history of the country to that point. It was not finished when he died on January 3, 1864. See Shaw, 329ff.

23. *The Decline of Protestantism, and its Cause: A Lecture delivered in St. Patrick's Cathedral on Sunday Evening, November 10, 1850, for the Benefit of the House of Protection, under the Charge of the Sisters of Mercy* (New York: Edward Dunigan & Brother, 1850), 5. See *Pamphlets,* IV: CA 115.

24. *Decline,* 6.

25. *Decline,* 9. It is easy to see why Hughes and other Catholic apologists have trouble calling Protestantism a church, or Protestant communities "churches." Even Hughes's definition omits the term, which is vitally important in his conception of "the Catholic Church."

26. 10.

27. 11.

28. 12–13.

29. *Decline,* 13, 14.

30. 15. Hughes would understand in the same way the anomaly at the heart of Hodge's protest against the Catholicizing tendencies in American Protestantism in the nineteenth century. See Reynolds. Instability is also the issue in fundamentalist and evangelical protests against modernist Protestantism. See Machen and Van Til.

31. 19, 21.

32. *Decline,* 22–23. One finds in New England "congresses . . . clamoring for 'woman's rights'; claiming to be Christians, but forgetting their true dignity, as belonging to a sex rendered for ever glorious by the Virgin Mother of the Incarnate God . . . under Protestantism they are contending for 'woman's rights,' measured by a base human standard. They will not obtain them."

33. 25. Hughes might have been consoled for the persistence of Protestantism in the United Sates by Kennedy's election to the presidency in that very week, although he would not have been so by Kennedy's peculiar brand of Catholicism.

11. JAMES GIBBONS OF BALTIMORE

1. *EACH*, 584–87. Thomas W. Spalding, author of the article, also wrote *The Premier See: A History of the Archdiocese of Baltimore, 1786–1989*. The most important biography is by J. T. Ellis, *The Life of James Cardinal Gibbons, Archbishop of Baltimore, 1834–1921* (Milwaukee: Bruce Publishing, 1952). See also Gerald Fogarty, *Patterns of Episcopal Leadership* (New York: Macmillan, 1989).

2. It was there that he wrote *The Faith of Our Fathers, Being a Plain Exposition and Vindication of the Church Founded by Our Lord Jesus Christ* (1876; reprint New York: P. J. Kennedy & Sons, 1917), 110th edition. The preface to the 47th edition (1895) recounts that 250,000 copies had been sold, with translations into French, German, Spanish, Italian, Norwegian, and Swedish. By the 83rd edition, 1,400,000 copies had been published. The frontispiece of the 110th edition announced that 2,000,000 copies had been distributed. How many copies were sold and how many distributed free of charge is uncertain.

3. See Gerald Fogarty, "American Catholics: 1865–1908," *EACH*, 73–78. See also Fogarty, *The Vatican and the American Hierarchy from 1970–1965* (Wilmington, DE: Michael Glazier, 1985), 115–42.

4. *EACH*, 586. In his sermon in Santa Maria in Trastevere in 1887, Gibbons, praising the free institutions of the United States and the fact that "in the genial air of liberty she [the church] blossoms like the rose!" also added to his thanks to every class of Catholic his thanks to "our separated brethren of America who, though not sharing our faith, have shown that they are not insensible to the honor conferred on our common country, and have again and again expressed their warm admiration of the enlightened statesmanship, the apostolic virtues, and the benevolent charities of the illustrious Pontiff who now sits in the Chair of Peter" (*EACH*, 588). See Ellis, *Documents of American Catholic History* (Chicago: Regnery, 1967), 2: 461–63.

5. (Phillipsburg, NJ: Presbyterian and Reformed Publishing, 1962). For comparable content listings, see John Ankerberg and John Weldon, *Protestants and Catholics, Do They Now Agree?* Jimmy Swaggart, *Catholicism and Christianity* (Baton Rouge, LA: Jimmy Swaggart Ministries, 1986); Dave Hunt, *A Woman Rides the Beast: The Catholic Church and the Last Days*. William Nevins's *Thoughts on Popery* in 1836 reflects the same intellectual organization. The works differ by emphasis responding to the immediate political and social conditions under which they are written, but the differences are not such as to leave the reader confused as to the literary form. They are as a whole a tortured form of Christian catechism.

6. Boettner, 1.

7. Boettner, chapters 3 and 5, 6, 11.

8. Contrast Boettner's chapters 2 and 4 with Gibbons's 2, 3, 4, 5, 6, 7 (the church and tradition); and Boettner's 3 and 14 with Gibbons's 29 and 30 (the priesthood); and Boettner's 5, 6, and 11 with Gibbons's 9, 10, 11, and 12 (the papacy).

9. In 1960, still Boettner was obliged to write an attack on the Catholic schools and on Catholic attempts to get public money to support them (chapter 16).

10. Boettner has no chapter on faith and works either. The Protestant position permeates his book as much as the Catholic assumption permeates Gibbons's book. These Catholic authors assume that the Protestant dichotomy is, to use Dewey's term,

an invidious dualism, an abstraction, an instance of the fallacy of misplaced concreteness.

11. Gibbons, 5.

12. 7.

13. He mentions Charles Borromeo, Ignatius of Loyola, Alphonsus Liguori, and Philip Neri, all canonized saints of the Tridentine reform.

14. 21–23. This is a typical Catholic reading of the reform and the Reformers between Trent and Vatican II. A more careful reading was generally available in the 1967 *New Catholic Encyclopedia;* see articles on Calvin, Knox, Luther, and Zwingli, and earlier in Philip Hughes's *A Popular History of the Reformation* (New York: Doubleday Image Books, 1957) and *A History of the Church* (New York: Sheed and Ward, 1947), three volumes. But I was raised on Grisar's biography of Luther, which told the traditional Catholic story; cf. Hartmann Grisar, S.J., *Luther*, ed. Luigi Cappadelta (St. Louis: B. Herder, 1917), six volumes. A one-volume summary version was made available during my seminary years: Grisar, *Martin Luther: His Life and Work*, adapted by Frank Eble and Arthur Preuss (Westminster, MD: Newman, 1954). For a nineteenth-century example of the Catholic view on Luther, see Isaac Hecker, "Luther and the Diet of Worms" (1883) *Pamphlets in American History* IV: CA 977, 15–31 (microfiche).

15. Gibbons, 24, from Joseph De Maistre, *Du Pape* (Lyon: Pelagaud, 1878). See Jack Lively, ed., *The Works of Joseph De Maistre* (New York: Macmillan, 1965).

16. Gibbons, 29.

17. Gibbons, 38–40. The historical case for the Roman primacy was most fully made in this context by Francis Patrick Kenrick, Gibbons's predecessor, in *The Primacy of the Apostolic See Vindicated*. See also Louisville's bishop Martin J. Spalding, *Lectures on the Evidences of Catholicity* (Louisville, KY: Welb & Levering, 1857). He as well was a predecessor of Gibbons in Baltimore.

18. Gibbons, 37. The tables of doctrines are found on pages 34–37. For the continuance of the Catholic teaching on apostolic succession, see Francis Cardinal George's lecture at a Wheaton College conference on evangelicalism and Catholicism, April 10, 2002, forthcoming, InterVarsity Press.

19. 39–40.

20. 40.

21. 41.

22. 42. He cites *Psal. Contra. Part. Donati*, v. 235: "Venite fratres, si vultis, ut inseramini in vite. Dolor est cum vos videmus praecisos ita iacere. Numerate sacerdotes vel ab ipsa Petri sede et in ordinae illo patrum quis cui successit videte: ipsa est petra quam non vincunt superbae inferorum portae." *Traites Anti-Donastistes*, I: 183–84 (Paris: Desclee de Brower, 1963). The evangelical argument was made by Campbell against Purcell in which true spiritual apostolicity is traced through various heretical and schismatic movements, including Novatian in Rome and the Donatists in North Africa. Purcell responded as did Gibbons: Do you really want to claim those people as your spiritual ancestors?

23. Gibbons, 43. Mt 16:18.

24. Gibbons, 47. He quotes De Maistre again, *Du Pape*, I, 2, chapter 5.

25.   Among the Americans present only the bishop of Little Rock, Edward Fitzgerald (1833–1907), voted against it and he was one of only two bishops in the entire

international church to do so. Several Americans, with Archbishops Purcell of Cincinnati and Kenrick of St. Louis, chose to leave Rome before the vote to avoid opposing the inevitable. Forty years before this, Purcell could deny to Campbell that the pope was held by Catholics to be infallible. In the up-and-down moral history of the papacy this is among its most manipulative moments, ironically by a man recently proposed for sainthood. See Brian Tierney, *The Origins of Papal Infallibility, 1150–1350: A Study in the Concepts of Infallibility, Sovereignty and Tradition in the Middle Ages* (Leiden: Brill, 1972); August Hasler, *How the Pope Became Infallible: Pius X and the Politics of Persuasion* (New York: Doubleday, 1981); and Owen Chadwick, *A History of the Popes, 1830–1914* (New York: Oxford University Press, 1998). One part of an infallible hierarchy infallibly committed itself to the infallibility of its beleaguered leader after hooting down the substantial number of bishops who objected and while a large number of its own were on the way out of town to avoid voting. What can that hierarchy expect but the mockery and outrage of its critics and the despair of some of its own intellectuals? See Roland Hill, *Lord Acton* (New Haven, CT: Yale University Press, 2000) on William Gladstone, John Acton, and Joseph Dollinger, and others. Its match in paranoia and manipulation was the papal reaction to the Catholic modernist theologians forty years later under Pope St. Pius X. These were desperate times. In my view these are the low points in the two-century papal misdirection of the church in the face of the changes in European culture and politics, understandable perhaps but misguided. The papacy survived its mistakes and prospered, adding to the long list of empirical proofs of its divine foundation!

26. Chapter 7 is on the infallible church, chapter 8 on the church and the Bible, and 9–12 on the papacy. It seems logical to set the infallible church in place, and expatiate on the priority of the church over the Bible, before coming to that thorniest of doctrines in the Catholic crown, the infallibility of the pope.

27. Gibbons, 56.

28. 58.

29. Gibbons, 61.

30. 60.

31. See, for example, Mark P. Shea, *By What Authority: An Evangelical Discovers Catholic Tradition* (Huntington, IN: Our Sunday Visitor Press, 1996); David B. Currie, *Born Fundamentalist, Born Again Catholic* (San Francisco: Ignatius Press, 1996); Scott Hahn and Kimberly Hahn, *Rome Sweet Home: Our Journey to Catholicism* (San Francisco: Ignatius Press, 1993); and the essays in Dan O'Neill, ed., *The New Catholics: Contemporary Catholics Tell their Stories* (New York: Crossroad, 1987); and Patrick Madrid, ed., *Surprised by Truth: Eleven Converts Give Biblical and Historical Reasons for Becoming Catholic* (San Diego: Basilica Press, 1994). For an academic studies of converts to Catholicism, see Patrick Allitt, *Catholic Converts: British and American Intellectuals Turn to Rome* (Ithaca, NY: Cornell University Press, 1997); and Christine Bochen, *The Journey to Rome: Conversion Literature by 19th Century American Catholics* (New York: Garland, 1988).

32. Gibbons, 63.

33. Gibbons, 65–67.

34. See 57, 63, 65.

35. 67.

36. 69.

37. 69–70.

38. 70–71.

39. 73. He offers, as examples of the third, the sanctification of Sunday and prayer to the Holy Ghost. Neither is taught in scripture, there is no dominical or apostolic command of either. For his argument to hold Gibbons must assume that both are "necessary for salvation," or at least that they are commonly accepted as such by Protestants. His argument that the Bible is not prior to the church is the common Catholic position. See, for example, Isaac Hecker's version of it in "Protestantism vs the Church" (1883), in *Pamphlets in American History* IV, CA 977 (microfiche). He writes: "No book must be interposed between the soul and Christ." The church is the primary mediator of the love of Christ.

40. Gibbons, 73ff. The charge has been softened considerably since the second Vatican Council but was ubiquitous in evangelical polemic before that event. Those critics who retain the anti-Tridentine polemical traditions on the issue of faith and works are most likely to retain this one as well. See in Armstrong, Ankerberg, et al.

41. 73. He details the "plain facts" of Church practice and teaching in preserving, collecting, canonizing, translating the text of the Bible, touching on the third Council of Carthage (397 A.D.), Pope Damasus's commissioning the first Latin translation by St. Jerome (c. 382 A.D.), the Venerable Bede's translation into English (c. 735 A.D.), and the existence of fifty-six editions of the Bible in German, Spanish, French, Italian, Flemish, and Bohemian before Luther began his own translation. Gibbons recalls a Protestant friend who was surprised, on entering a Catholic bookstore, to find "an imposing array of Bibles for sale." "Be assured." he concludes, "that if you become a Catholic you will never be forbidden to read the Bible. It is our earnest wish that every word of the Gospel may be imprinted on your memory and on your heart" (75–76).

42. Gibbons, 79–81.

43. 87–88. He doesn't make mention of the argument made by Campbell and Murray, that even if Peter had been in Rome (neither would admit as much), there is no evidence, and indeed no likelihood, that he ever functioned as the founder or as *episcopos* of the Christian community there, and that had he been in Rome or had he any significant connection with the church there, Paul's failure to mention him in his letter to Rome is utterly unintelligible.

44. Gibbons, 89.

45. 90.

46. 93–94.

47. 95–96.

48. Among the many surveys of the Protestant-Catholic differences that express a decidedly different perspective on the nature of the Christian church, see David S. Schaff, *Our Fathers Faith and Ours, A Comparison between Protestantism and Romanism* (New York: Knickerbocker Press, 1928). A seminary professor, Schaff offers an academically impressive update on Protestant criticisms of the arguments made by Gibbons and Catholic apologists generally. In fact, Schaff has framed his substantial book as a response to Gibbons, among other nineteenth-century Catholic apologists, whose work he studied and evaluated. His work, however valuable, remains completely in the Reformation apologetic tradition and literary characteristics.

49. Gibbons, 99–110; 111–23. It is curious that at the very time when American

Protestants were most worried about a papal invasion and corruption of the republic, Catholics were most worried about the weakening of papal independence and authority. Neither of these pictures now seem very likely. What historians can now see is the growing strength of American republicanism, including its appreciation by Catholic citizens who showed and still show absolutely no interest in expanding "papal dominion," and the growing prestige and decisiveness of the papacy both within and without the church at the very time when it seemed to have felt most threatened. Surely there is a lesson of some sort in this for both sides. *EACH*, 584–87. Thomas W. Spalding, author of the article, also wrote *The Premier See: A History of the Archdiocese of Baltimore, 1786–1989*. The most important biography is by J. T. Ellis, *The Life of James Cardinal Gibbons, Archbishop of Baltimore, 1834–1921* (Milwaukee: Bruce Publishing, 1952). See also Gerald Fogarty, *Patterns of Episcopal Leadership* (New York: Macmillan, 1989).

## 12. WHAT HAVE CATHOLIC THEOLOGIANS MADE OF BIBLICAL CHRISTIANITY?

1. This chapter and the following are based on research, the first and more extensive version of which is found in F. Nichols, ed., *Christianity and the Stranger: Historical Essays, Studies on Religion and the Social Order* (Atlanta: Scholars Press, 1995), 221–86. A second and shorter version is printed in *Theological Studies* 57 (1996): 264–85.

2. Martin Marty and Scott Appleby, *The Glory and the Power: The Fundamentalist Challenge to the Modern World* (Boston: Beacon Press, 1992), 34–35; and Martin Marty and Scott Appleby, "An Interim Report on a Hypothetical Family," in *Fundamentalisms Observed*, Martin Marty and Scott Appleby, eds. (Chicago: University of Chicago Press, 1991), 814–43.

3. I could also use the terms hierarchical and sacramental Christianity, but I think that the liturgy is at the genesis of the other two.

4. I try here to use the terms *biblical Christianity* and *evangelical Christianity* interchangeably, recognizing that the later term may for some raise special issues having to do with the second birth, vicarious sacrifice, blood atonement, and so on. I can, if forced to it, refer to evangelical Christianity as fundamentalist in the light of its historical origins in the "militantly anti-modernist Protestantism" of the early twentieth century, its continued skittishness at contact with "ecumenical Christianity," and its never-ending concern with scriptural inerrancy. I prefer to use the term *fundamentalist* of those who use the term of themselves. Many evangelicals do not and will not.

5. William M. Shea, *The Struggle over the Past: Fundamentalism in the Modern World* (Lanham, MD: University Press of America, 1993). I refer occasionally to essays in this volume, one of whose criteria of acceptability was the absence of antifundamentalist polemic.

6. For example, the indexes of *Theological Studies*, *The Thomist*, and *Horizons: The Journal of the College Theology Society* list none. Only one of the essays to be discussed appeared in *Theological Studies*, and that is a general piece on sects and cults and not chiefly on fundamentalism. See John A. Saliba, "The Christian Church and the New Religious Movements," *Theological Studies* 43 (September 1982): 468–85. The closest one comes to scholarly journals in our list are those that publish materials

by scholars for the nonspecialist but theologically interested audience of intellectuals, such as the *Biblical Theology Review, Communio,* and *The Bible Today.*

7. Exceptions are John McCarthy, "Inspiration and Trust: Toward Narrowing the Gap between Fundamentalist and Higher Biblical Scholarship," in Shea, *The Struggle Over the Past,* 121–36; and Zachary Hayes, "Fundamentalist Eschatology: Piety and Politics," *New Theology Review* 1 (May 1988): 21–35.

8. George Marsden, *Fundamentalism and American Culture: The Shaping of Twentieth Century Evangelicalism, 1870–1925* (New York: Oxford University Press, 1980); Mark A. Noll, *A History of Christianity in the United States and Canada* (Grand Rapids, MI: Eerdmans, 1992); Nathan Hatch and Mark Noll, eds., *The Bible in America: Essays in Cultural History* (New York: Oxford University Press, 1982); James Barr, *Beyond Fundamentalism* (Philadelphia: Westminster, 1984) and *Fundamentalism* (Philadelphia: Westminster, 1978); and Ernest Robert Sandeen, *The Roots of Fundamentalism: British and American Millenarianism, 1800–1930* (Chicago: University of Chicago Press, 1970).

9. Brigid Curtin Frein, "Fundamentalism and Narrative Approaches to the Gospels," *Biblical Theology Bulletin* 22 (Spring 1992): 12–18. Not discussed in this chapter is the volume on fundamentalism edited by Hans Kung. Although it does contain essays by Catholics and essays on Catholic fundamentalism, it is chiefly concerned with international and world religions fundamentalism rather than with either American or Protestant fundamentalism. The only one among its authors who is considered a Catholic theologian is Hans Kung, and his contribution is concerned with fundamentalism in Catholicism. See Hans Kung and Jurgen Moltmann, eds., "Fundamentalism as an Ecumenical Challenge," *Concilium* (June 1992). (London: SCM Press, 1992).

10. E. D. Radmacher and Robert D. Preus, eds., *Hermeneutics, Inerrancy and the Bible* (Grand Rapids, MI: Zondervan, 1984), and Donald McKim, ed., *A Guide to Contemporary Hermeneutics: Major Trends in Biblical Interpretation* (Grand Rapids, MI: Eerdmans, 1986).

11. Frein, 16.

12. Later, in a discussion of the contents of an issue of *The New Theology Review,* I will refer to the essay of Zachary Hayes, whose discussion of fundamentalist hermeneutics rivals Frein's essay for detachment. For another essay by a Catholic biblicist but in a journal aimed at a less sophisticated audience, see Leslie Hoppe, "The Bible Tells Me So," *The Bible Today* 29 (September, 1991): 279–84. His point is that dispensationalist interpretation contradicts itself in that it does not interpret the text literally at all but through a set of nonbiblical beliefs.

13. Clifford G. Kossel, "The Moral Majority and Christian Politics," *Communio: International Catholic Review* 9 (Winter 1982): 339–54.

14. Kossel, 346.

15. Kossel, 348.

16. Isaac Hecker, *The Church and the Age: An Exposition of the Catholic Church in View of the Needs and Aspirations of the Present Age* (New York: Paulist Press, n.d.); and Richard J. Neuhaus, *The Catholic Moment: The Paradox of Church in the Postmodern World* (San Francisco: Harper & Row, 1987).

17. Kossel, 354.

18. The author refers in footnotes to the "usual suspects," Marsden and Barr, and to a few essays on evangelicals and politics. The essay itself is a piece of contem-

porary relevance, more an editorial than a piece of scholarship. It is distinguished by its balanced and constructive approach rather than any expert knowledge of evangelicalism. The attitude displayed here in matters of political cooperation might be displayed again on religious and theological issues, with what success or avidity it is hard to say. Kossel is concerned with the broad group of conservative evangelicals and does not use the term fundamentalist to describe his subject.

19. Roy Barkley, "The Fundamentalist Threat," *Homiletic and Pastoral Review* 88 (February 1988): 45–53. See page 46 on "hardbitten."

20. Barkley, 45.

21. Barkley, 48.

22. Barkley, 53. See Karl Keating, *Catholicism and Fundamentalism: The Attack on "Romanism" by "Bible Christians"* (San Francisco: Ignatius, 1988), and Steve Clark, "Those Terrible Fundamentalists," *New Covenant* 18–19 (January 1989): 9–10, other expressions of "orthodox" Catholicism.

23. Mary Ann Walsh, R.S.M., "Fundamentalists Give the Bible a Bad Name," *U.S. Catholic* 45 (April 1980): 26–32.

24. "When was the last time you heard a good homily?" she asks. Well, in fact, I hear one nearly every week in my parish church, and sympathize with those Catholics who do not.

25. Richard Chilson, "A Call to Catholic Action," *America* 155 (September 27, 1986): 133–48. Fr. Chilson was inveigled into an interview during the preparation of an anti-Catholic video, *Catholicism: Crisis of Faith,* in which he is used as an example of the ignorance of Catholics of their own beliefs. It is available from Lumen Productions, Cupertino, CA.

26. See also Mary Frances Reis, "Fundamentalism on the College Campus," *Emmanuel* 94 (November 1988): 490–97. Reis, at the University of Wisconsin in Milwaukee, wants to inform the "unsuspecting" Catholics about the strategies that await them. Primarily a description of campus crusading and the stages of the conversion process (Induction, Indoctrination, Decision), and the tools for recruiting and retaining, the essay is informative and frightening enough to make a parent of a child about to take off for college more than a bit nervous.

27. In addition to the essays discussed in the text, the same characteristics of clarity in doctrinal contrast, charity in attitude, and self-criticism are to be found in the following: James R. Higgins, C.S.S.R., "Which Came First, the Bible or the Church?" *Liguorian* 67 (August 1979): 21–25, and "A Catholic Looks at Fundamentalism," *Liguorian* 69 (October 1981): 48–53; Robert J. Hatter, "Fundamentalism and the Parish," *Church* 4 (Winter 1988): 17–25; Leonard Foley, O.F.M., "Catholics and Fundamentalists: We Agree and Disagree," *St. Anthony Messenger* 91 (July 1983): 15–20; and Peter Kreeft, a series on "Fundamentalists," in each issue of *National Catholic Register* 64 (October 1988).

28. Thomas M. Coskren, "Fundamentalists on Campus," *New Catholic World* 228 (January/February 1985): 38–42.

29. Francis X. Cleary, S.J., "How is the Bible to be Interpreted?" *Universitas* 2/4 (Spring 1977): p. 13; "Biblical Inerrancy and the New Criticism," *Universitas* 3/1 (Summer 1977): np; "Literal Interpretation of the Bible," *Universitas* 3/2 (Autumn 1977): 6.

30. *Dei Verbum,* paragraphs 11–12, in *Vatican Council II: Constitutions, Decrees, Declarations,* ed. Austin Flannery (Northport, NY: Costello Publishing, 104–6).

31. Cleary, "Literal Interpretation of the Bible," 6.

32. Raymond Brown, S.S., "Catholic Faith and Fundamentalism," *Priests and People* 5 (April 1991): 134–36. The points made are nearly identical to the appendix to his book, *Responses to 101 Questions on the Bible* (Mahwah, NJ: Paulist, 1990). In addition, however, the book deals with fundamentalism in questions 29–33, pp. 40–49. I shall discuss both the essay and the sections of the book here.

33. Brown, *Responses*, 44.

34. Brown, 47. See questions 32 and 33.

35. In an appendix to the book, "Expressing Catholic Faith so that Biblical Fundamentalists will not Misunderstand It" (137–42), Brown lines up ten questions of particular relevance to a Catholic conversation with fundamentalists, all of them doctrinal, and in each he pushes the doctrinal issue back to its scriptural basis or at very least to texts that shed light on the Catholic doctrinal position. There is no defensiveness or polemic involved. The same ten points are reprinted under the title "Catholic Faith and Fundamentalism" in *Priests and People* 5 (April 1991): 134–36.

36. He relies heavily on the 1981 edition of Ed Dobson, Ed Hinson, and Jerry Falwell, *The Fundamentalist Phenomenon: The Resurgence of Conservative Christianity* (Grand Rapids: Baker Books, 1981).

37. John Garvey, "Made for Each Other: The Fundamentalists-Humanist Complex," *Commonweal* 108 (January 16, 1981): 6–8. See p. 7.

38. Garvey, 7.

39. John Garvey, "Truth Flashes: What's Right about Jimmy Swaggart," *Commonweal* 113 (December 26, 1986): 678. He wrote this before Swaggart's much-publicized fall from grace. Cf. Ann Rowe Seaman, *Swaggart: The Unauthorized Biography of an American Evangelist* (New York: Contimuum, 1999).

40. Eugene LaVerdiere uses the term of the Catholic right in his article "Fundamentalism: A Pastoral Concern," *The Bible Today* (January 1983): 5–11.

41. Gabriel Daly, "Catholicism and Modernity," *Journal of the American Academy of Religion* 53 (1985): 773–796. See p. 776. See also his book, *Transcendence and Immanence: A Study in Catholic Modernism and Integralism* (New York: Oxford University Press, 1980).

42. Daly, "Catholicism and Modernity," 795.

43. Daly, 796.

44. For example, in the otherwise careful attempt at understanding and explanation of R. Scott Appleby, "Unflinching Faith: What fires Up the World's Fundamentalists?" *U.S. Catholic* 54 (December 1989): 6–13, esp. p. 11; in the essays of Catholic biblicist Eugene LaVerdiere, especially "Fundamentalism: A Pastoral Concern," 7–9; and, in a particularly confused essay by Damien Kraus, "Catholic Fundamentalism: A Look at the Problem," *The Living Light* 19 (Spring 1982):8–16, esp. 15.

45. Patrick Arnold, S.J., "The Rise of Catholic Fundamentalism," *America* 156 (April 11, 1987): 297–302, esp. 298 and 302.

46. Ibid., 302.

47. See Jacques Weber, S.J., "The Problem of Catholic Fundamentalism," in *Christian Adulthood, 1984–85: A Catechetical Resource*, ed. Neil Parent (Washington, DC: United States Catholic Conference, 1984). The broad usage of the term is now common, given its acceptance in The Fundamentalist Project for use of almost all militant religious protest against modernity. The habit seems firmly entrenched

among Catholic theologians since John Coleman's essay, "Who are the Catholic Fundamentalists? A Look at their Past, their Politics, and their Power," in *Commonweal* 116 (January 27, 1989): 42–47. Coleman does an admirable job connecting the concerns of current Catholic conservatives to those of the integralists in the first half of the century. I agree with the connection. The term *fundamentalist* applied to Catholics the like of James Hitchcock, however, is misleading.

48. Weber, 81.

49. James Hitchcock, essay in *Fundamentalism Observed,* ed. R. S. Appleby and Martin Marty (Chicago University Press, 1991), 101–41. "Catholic fundamentalism" is an oxymoron, in my opinion. Hitchcock was quite right to refuse its use of "activist conservative Catholics."

50. Weber, 82.

51. See Lonergan, *Method in Theology,* 235–37.

52. John O'Donohue, "The Dogmatic Perversion of Religion," *African Ecclesial Review* 28 (October 1986): 312–22, and "Fundamentalism: A Psychological Problem," *African Ecclesial Review* 29 (December 1987): 344–50.

53. "A Catholic organization nurturing lay spirituality." *DCA,* 846. Founded in 1930 in Spain, it has become favored in the pontificate of John Paul II as a worthy instrument in his restorationist policies. It is estimated that there are seventy thousand members.

54. O'Donohue, "Fundamentalism: A Psychological Problem," 344.

55. O'Donohue, 348.

56. O'Donohue, 350.

57. Thomas E. Clarke, S.J., "Fundamentalism and Prejudice" *Way* 27 (January 1987): 34–41.

58. Clarke, 38–39.

59. George MacRae, "The Poor You Always Have With You," *Catholic Charismatic,* 3 (December/January 1978/79): 15; and John Haughey, "Fundamentalism—An Afterward," *Catholic Charismatic,* 3 (December/January 1978/79): 45–46.

60. Richard Rohr, "Mary and Fundamentalism," *Catholic Charismatic,* 3 (December/January): 16–19.

61. Bill O'Brien, "A National Overview: The Question of Fundamentalism," *Catholic Charismatic,* 3 (December/January 1978/79):24–25, and Barbara O'Reilly, "Fundamentalism: Leader's Response," *Catholic Charismatic,* 3 (December/January 1978/79): 40–44.

62. Juan Lorenzo Hinojosa, "What Is Fundamentalism?" *Catholic Charismatic,* 3 (December/January 1978/79): 34–36.

63. Lawrence Boadt, "The Issue: Fundamentalism," *New Catholic World* 228 (January/February 1985): 2.

64. Edward Dobson, "Fundamentalism—Its Roots," *New Catholic World* 228 (January/February 1985): 4–9.

65. Thomas F. Stransky, "A Catholic Looks at American Fundamentalists," *New Catholic World* 228 (January/February 1985): 10–14.

66. Peggy Shriver, an official in the National Council of Churches, gives voice to mainline/liberal Protestant distaste for fundamentalism, describing it as a "mind set of certainty, obedience, authority, and absolute truth"—a "fortress faith" and a refuge. To her the troubles of the 1980s are a repeat of the troubles of the 1920s.

67. Eugene LaVerdiere, "Must a Christian Be Born Again?" *New Catholic World* 228 (January/February 1985), 20–22.

68. Brien E. Curley, "Fundamentalism and Its Challenge to Catholic Religious Education," *New Catholic World* 228 (January/February 1985): 34–37.

69. See also Richard Chilson, *Full Christianity: A Response to Fundamental Questions* (Mahwah, NJ: Paulist, 1985), discussed later.

70. *America,* 155 (September 27, 1986): 2.

71. Martin E. Marty," Modern Fundamentalism," *America* 155 (September 27, 1986): 134–135. Marty was the director of the Fundamentalist Project at the University of Chicago.

72. Marty, 135.

73. The Christophers, founded in 1945, is a Catholic movement devoted to fostering personal responsibility in seeking solutions to social problems. See *EACH,* 328–29.

74. William D. Dinges, "The Vatican Report on Sects, Cults and New Religious Movements," *America,* 155 (September 27, 1986): 145–54.

75. Robert J. Schreiter, C.P.P.S., "Introduction: The Challenge of Fundamentalism," *New Theological Review* 1 (May 1988): 3–4.

76. Dominic Monti, O.F.M., "World Out of Time: The Origins of the Fundamentalist Movement," *New Theology Review* 1 (May 1988): 5–20.

77. Hayes, 21–35.

78. Hayes, 34. In the same issue of the *New Theology Review,* Dianne Bergant, C.S.A, relies entirely on the work of James Barr in her essay on fundamentalist hermeneutics, "Fundamentalists and the Bible" (1: 36–50), and James Wall, the editor of *Christian Century,* briefly explains "The Rise of the Religious Right in American Politics" (1: 51–57).

79. Gabriel Fackre, "Positive Values and Honorable Intentions: A Critique of Fundamentalism," *New Theology Review* 1 (May 1988): 58–73.

80. Fackre, 64.

81. Theodore C. Ross, S.J., "Catholicism and Fundamentalism," *New Theology Review* 1 (May 1988): 74–87.

82. The fifth is Stanley B. Marrow, S.J., *The Words of Jesus in our Gospels: A Catholic Response to Fundamentalism* (Ramsey, NJ: Paulist, 1979). A Jesuit scripture scholar, Marrow set out to inform Catholics of the present state of New Testament scholarship. The book used a sketchy presentation of fundamentalist doctrine on the Bible to frame and provide contrast for a discussion of the outcome of critical approaches to the gospels. Fundamentalism is given short shrift (after the introduction, only a few paragraphs). His basic criticism of fundamentalism is somewhat sophisticated for this literature: implicit in the claim for the infallibility of the text is a claim for the infallibility of the interpreter. Thus," . . . in addition to the lack of thoroughness in its arguments and the failure to carry them through to their necessary conclusions, the fundamentalist position invariably runs the risk of the tyranny of its presuppositions." It leaves no room for interpretation, yet it must interpret; it interprets, but must appear not to.

83. Anthony E. Gilles, *Fundamentalism: What Every Catholic Should Know* (Cincinnati: St. Anthony Messenger, 1984).

84. Gilles, 14–25.

85. Gilles, 71.

86. Gilles, 5–9.

87. See Keating, *Catholicism and Fundamentalism*. This book was published by a press widely regarded in Catholic moderate to liberal Catholic academic circles as an organ of conservative Catholicism, much as the Paulist Press would be regarded as middle of the road or liberal. Keating himself is occasionally given to speaking of "orthodox" Catholics, and to occasionally expressing suspicion of contemporary Catholic biblical scholarship. On "orthodox" Catholics, see pp. 9, 129, 324, 329; on the biblical scholars, see pp. 121n2, and 324–325. Keating's basic approach is fully directly stated, along with his criticism of other Catholic strategies, in "Answering the Fundamentalist Challenge," *Homiletic and Pastoral Review* 85 (July 1985): 32–57. For a sample of his direct apologetic address to young Catholics importuned by evangelists, see his pamphlet *Pillar of Fire, Pillar of Truth: The Catholic Church and God's Plan for You* (San Diego: Catholic Answers, 1997). Albert J. Nevins, *Answering a Fundamentalist* (Huntington, IN: Our Sunday Visitor Publishing, 1990), similar to Keating in theology, is a handbook of answers to the issues raised in standard anti-Catholic repertoire I have called The Outline. For post-*ECT* discussions aimed at Catholics on the subject of fundamentalism, see Ronald D. Witherup, *Biblical Fundamentalism: What Every Catholic Should Know* (Collegeville, MN: Liturgical Press, 2001), and Eugene LaVerdiere, *Fundamentalism, A Pastoral Concern* (Collegeville, MN: Liturgical Press, 2000.).

88. They are willing to argue mightily about the historicity of the Gospel text in selected cases. See John Meier's three-volumes *A Marginal Jew: Rethinking the Historical Jesus* (Garden City, NY: Doubleday, 1991, 1994, 2002). They won't argue that the gospels are historical texts and inerrant, as one would expect fundamentalists and most evangelicals to do.

89. Charles Hodge, *Systematic Theology* (1873; reprint Grand Rapids, MI: Eerdmans, 1995), vol. I.

90. See Nicholas F. Gier, *God, Reason, and the Evangelicals: The Case Against Evangelical Rationalism* (Lanham, MD: University Press of America, 1987), and Peter Huff, "New Apologists in America's Conservative Catholic Subculture," *Horizons, the Journal of the College Theology Society* 23/2 (Fall 1996): 242–60. For an example of contemporary evangelical apologetics, see Norman L. Geisler, *Baker Encyclopedia of Apologetics* (Grand Rapids, MI: Baker Books, 1999).

91. Keating, 24–26.

92. Thomas F. O'Meara, O.P., *Fundamentalism: A Catholic Perspective* (Mahwah, NJ: Paulist Press, 1990).

93. O'Meara, 96.

94. They are Richard McBrien, another theologian at Notre Dame whose views of fundamentalism seem to have had a determinative effect on O'Meara's understanding of it; Raymond Brown, a priest who taught Scripture at Union Theological Seminary in New York; the American bishops' letter on fundamentalism; and Flannery O'Connor, a Catholic author of short stories. The first three surely count as critics of fundamentalism; Flannery O'Connor's "criticism" of fundamentalism is hard to separate from her "criticism" of humanity, for which she had the most extraordinary compassion and with whom she was fascinated. None of the first three critics display any such attitude toward fundamentalists or fundamentalism.

95. See Richard P. McBrien, *Catholicism* (Minneapolis: Winston Press, 1981),

1167–83; and his article "Roman Catholicism" in *The Encyclopedia of Religion* (New York: Macmillan, 1987) 12: 429–45.

96. O'Meara, 18. Emphasis original.

97. O'Meara, 81–93.

98. O'Meara, 7, 49.

99. O'Meara, 10, 13, 14.

100. O'Meara, 7, 13–14, 19, 22, 27, 29, 33, 50ff.

101. See O'Meara's "Fundamentalism and the Christian Believer," *Priest* 44 (3/88): 39–41, for more of the same.

102. O'Meara, 38–42. For candidates for this group, see P. Huff, "New Apologists in America's Conservative Catholic Subculture."

103. For further comments on the book, see William Dinges's review in *Record of the American Catholic Historical Society of Philadelphia* 101 (Fall 1990). On the problems of psychologizing, see William D. Dinges, "The Vatican Report on Sects, Cults and New Religious Movements," *America* 155 (September 27, 1986): 145–54.

## 13. BISHOPS AGAIN AND THE VATICAN

1. "The Challenge of Peace: God's Promise and Our Response" (1983) and "A Pastoral Letter on Catholic Social Teaching and the Economy," (1986) National Conference of Catholic Bishops. They are available at <http://www.usccb.org/cchd>. Printed copies available from the United States Catholic Conference, Washington, DC.

2. *Origins* 17 (11/5/87): 376–377. The signatories are: Archbishops John F. Whealon (Hartford), Theodore E. McCarrick (Newark), and J. Francis Stafford (Denver); and auxiliary bishops Alvara Corrada del Rio (District of Columbia), Richard J. Sklba (Milwaukee), and Donald W. Trautman (Buffalo).

3. Oscar H. Lipscomb of Mobile, Joseph Howze of Biloxi, William Houck of Jackson, and Raymond Boland of Birmingham, " 'Toward Your Happiness,' Catholicism and Fundamentalism: A Contrast," in Shea, *The Struggle over the Past*, 333–41.

4. The four points are enumerated in section 5 and the fifth in section 8.

5. John J. Leibrecht, "Sharing God's Life Together: On Being Catholic in the Bible Belt," A Pastoral Letter to the Diocese of Springfield-Cape Girardeau (November 11, 1988).

6. John F. Whealon, "Fighting Fundamentalism," *America* 153 (10/12/85): 212; and "Challenging Fundamentalism," *America* 155 (9/27/86): 136–138.

7. Whealon, "Fighting Fundamentalism."

8. Whealon, "Challenging Fundamentalism," 136.

9. 137.

10. "Vatican Report on Sects, Cults and New Religious Movements," *Origins* 16 (5/22/86): 1–11.

11. For a Catholic theological discussion of the problem before the Vatican document was composed, see John A. Saliba, S.J., "The Christian Church and the New Religious Movements," *Theological Studies* 43 (9/82): 468–85. For a careful criticism of the document itself by a specialist in American religious movements, see William D. Dinges, "The Vatican Report on Sects, Cults and New Religious Movements."

12. In his comments on the document, William Dinges mentions the estimate that Brazil will have nearly thirty-four million Pentecostals by the end of the century, that perhaps 30 percent of Puerto Ricans have joined Pentecostal communities, and that Latin America's Mormon population has tripled to one million. See also Philip Jenkins, *The Next Christendom: The Coming of Global Christianity* (New York: Oxford University Press, 2002).

13. "Vatican Report," 2.1.9.

14. 1.5, 2.2. Dinges remarks, "Nevertheless, there is little substantive evidence that the vast majority of participants in new religious groups are recruited through brainwashing or coercive tactics, or that they are kept in these movements by Orwellian-like mind-control techniques."

15. Dinges, 147.

16. "Vatican Report," 3.5.

17. a. "Vatican Report," 4.

18. "Vatican Report," 3.

19. See "The Interpretation of the Bible in the Church," *Origins* (January 6, 1994): 23/29: 499–524. The comments on fundamentalism are in section F, 509–10.

20. Mark Christensen, "Coming to Grips with Losses: The Migration of Catholics into Conservative Protestantism," *America* 164 (January 26, 1992): 58–59. See especially page 58.

21. 59. Steve Clark, one of the national lay leaders of the Catholic charismatic movement, similarly criticizes the bishops' statement but broadens the basis of attack. See "Those Terrible Fundamentalists," *New Covenant* 18–19 (January 1989): 9–10.

22. John McCarthy, "Inspiration and Trust: Narrowing the Gap between Fundamentalist and Higher Biblical Scholarship," in Shea, ed., *The Struggle over the Past: Fundamentalism in the Modern World*, 123–36; see also Ann Clifford, "Creation Science: Religion and Science in North American Culture," in *The Struggle over the Past*, 103–22.

## 14. CONCLUSION

1. Frederick Woodbridge, "The Problem of Metaphysics" in *Nature and Mind: Selected Essays of Frederick J. E. Woodbridge* (New York: Russell & Russell, 1965), 37–55. See 46: ". . . [T]he problem of metaphysics is fundamentally the problem of individuality, the definition of reality is primarily the definition of the individuality. . . . No metaphysics must be allowed to vitiate the basal proposition about reality, namely, that it consists of that which can be defined and grasped solely from points of departure absolutely individual in character. If reality is a system it is a system of individuals. If it is not a system, individuality is one of its essential characters." Woodbridge was part of an American revival of Aristotle at the beginning of the century. The essay was first published in 1903. For a discussion of Woodbridge, see W. M. Shea, *The Naturalists and the Supernatural* (Macon, GA: Mercer University Press, 1984).

2. I came on softer chairs and the works of Aldous Huxley and D.H. Lawrence in the library Reading Room on the other end of the second floor, along with Ernest Hemingway and Graham Greene. They filled many more hours than Maria Monk.

3. It does also when it faces New Age as David Toolan made out in *Facing West from California's Shores: A Jesuit's Journey into New Age Consciousness* (New York:

Crossroad, 1987). Unlike New Agers, however, Catholics and biblical Christians realize that sin is a fixture of the human condition not solved in the least by nude dancing in the moonlight and shucking guilt by ritualized union with nature.

4. Exercise the ususal caution with John's terminology. The world as he uses the term does not mean the cosmos, it means the world of human meaning gripped by sin. Still, in spite of that sin, everything that is, is through him and without him there is nothing.

5. See Joseph A. Komonchak, "Modernity and the Construction of Roman Catholicism" and Gabriel Daly, *Transcendence and Immanence*. Integralism is still favored in its pure form by Archbishop Lefebvre's Traditionalist movement, whose nineteenth-century orthodoxy is now found to be heterodox—a fate frequently shared by Catholic conservatives who learn too slowly. See William D. Dinges, "Roman Catholic Traditionalism" in *Fundamentalisms Observed*, 66–101.

6. The nub of it is found in the conservative response to Catholics who don't like this or that, "If you don't like it, leave!"

7. One admits that, like Dracula, it might return! But one's hope is stronger, resting as it does on *Gaudium et spes* and *Nostra aetate* of Vatican II. Professor Mavrodes voiced his concern at the Wheaton Conference, April 2002. See Thomas J. Curry, *Farewell to Christendom: The Future of Church and State in America* (New York: Oxford University Press, 2001), 3–11.

8. See D. G. Hart, *Defending the Faith;* Joel Carpenter, *Revive us Again;* and Martin E. Marty, *The Righteous Empire: The Protestant Experience in America* (New York: Dial Press, 1070).

9. I do not use the term Christendom exactly as Philip Jenkins does in his book, *The New Christendom*. My usage is political, his is religious and social as well. I follow Jose Casanova's usage in *Public Religion in the Modern World*.

10. David Tracy, *The Analogical Imagination*, 405ff.

11. My comments on their criticisms, of course, are Aristotelian/Thomist and as such may not further the discussion, but I make them to keep things honest.

12. George Weigel, *Witness to Hope: the Biography of Pope John Paul II* (New York: Cliff Street Books, 1999).

13. Doctrinally, orthodox Christianity would not have survived had it not been for the bishops of the fourth and fifth centuries. By contrast, does evangelical Protestantism represent a slippery slope to Gnosticism? Harold Bloom and Carl Raschke may be correct: *the* American religion (Bloom) or *the* modern alternative religion (Raschke) is gnostic. Biblical Christianity is a form of Gnosticism, an individual spiritual experience that is inherently antinomian and mystical (the old Catholic charge against Luther), and that is unable to live with a communal authority. In American culture, a culture of individual quests for satisfaction, orthodox Christianity may be entering a far more problematic situation than the conflict between rival orthodox Christianities. The old Gnosticism was taken to be a strike to the heart of Catholicism and not merely a problem of competition and "leakage." The fact that the old Gnosticism called forth the ever tighter ecclesiastical controls of post-Apostolic Christianity (what turned out to be early Catholicism) is a clue. There are signs that evangelicals recognize the problem (e.g., Northfield Institute and criticism of the self-help and pop evangelicalism). Christianity, Catholic and evangelical, may once again find itself a stranger in a strange land, not strange only because it is secular, but because it is

gnostic. On the interpretation of modern religion as gnosticism, see Harold Bloom, *The American Religion: The Emergence of the Post-Christian Nation* (New York: Simon and Schuster, 1991) and Carl A. Raschke, *The Interruption of Eternity: Modern Gnosticism and the Origins of the New Religious Consciousness* (Chicago: Nelson-Hall, 1980). Robert S. Ellwood Jr. has been a leader in the exploration of America's "alternative tradition." See his *Alternative Altars: Unconventional and Eastern Spirituality in America* (Chicago: University of Chicago Press, 1979); and also Ellwood and Harry B. Partin, *Religious and Spiritual Groups in Modern America,* 2nd ed. (Englewood Cliffs, NJ: Prentice Hall, 1988).

14. Karl Barth, "The Revelation of God as the Abolition of Religion," *Church Dogmatics* (Edinburgh: T. & T. Clark, 1956) I/2: 280–361.

15. Paul Tillich, *Systematic Theology* (Chicago: University of Chicago Press, 1963): III: 6.

16. Hans Kung, a theologian who earned his initial churchwide reputation at the second Vatican Council, was later pronounced not sufficiently Catholic to be considered a Catholic theologian. He does not regard the present Roman leadership to be Catholic enough themselves. For a brief sampling of Kung's theology, see *Signposts for the Future: Contemporary Issues Facing the Church* (Garden City, NY: Doubleday Co., 1978). For documents and an account of the dispute, see *The Kung Dialogue: Facts and Documents* (Washington, DC: United States Catholic Conference, 1980). In some respects, Kung is a model of evangelical Catholicism, but perhaps not what current evangelicals term a "committed Catholic."

17. *Ut unum sint,* paragraph 88. The Holy Father did not fulfill one of the conditions for absolution, enumeration of mortal sins. "Painful recollections" of others doesn't qualify for absolution, but perhaps the request for forgiveness is not the same as a request for absolution.

18. On papal jurisdiction, see *Pastor aeternus* of Vatican I (D.S. 360–3074). Also Patrick Granfield, "Pope" in Joseph Komonchak et al., eds. *The New Dictionary of Theology,* 779–84; and Granfield, *The Limits of the Papacy: Authority and Autonomy in the Church* (New York: Crossroad, 1987).

19. *Ut unum sint,* paragraph 96.

20. Anglican-Roman Catholic International Commission, *Final Report* (Washington, DC: United States Catholic Conference, 1982); P. C. Empie and T. A. Murphy, eds., *Papal Primacy and the Universal Church: Lutherans and Catholics in Dialogue* (Minneapolis: Augsburg, 1974).

21. See Anthony Kemp, *The Estrangement of the Past.*

22. Eastern Orthodoxy has its own myth, and in it the Romans and the Protestants are correct about each other and both have departed the faith of the ancient Christian church.

23. Francis Sullivan's *From Apostles to Bishops: The Development of the Episcopacy in the Early Church* (New York: Newman Press, 2001) is a good example of the distinction in practice. Mark Noll provides a model of evangelical historical discussion of the founding of the Jesuits and the Council of Trent in *Turning Points: Decisive Moment in the History of Christianity.* The distinctions are made theoretically in Bernard Lonergan, *Method in Theology.*

24. A. F. Allison, "Old Catholics," *The New Catholic Encyclopedia* (New York:

McGraw-Hill, 1967) X: 672–73. See also William D. Dinges, "Catholic Fundamentalism" in W. Shea, ed., *The Struggle Over the Past,* 255–280.

25. It is difficult to locate mystical Christian groups such as Quakers (what happens to Christianity when you do not need a Bible?) and hybrid originalities such as Mormons (what happens to Christianity when you have two Bibles?). As desserts to the main course, to his families Melton adds categories to cover the lot, among them metaphysical, mystical, magickal [*sic*], and gnostic families, where he is able to place New Thought groups, homosexual groups, and so forth. See J. Gordon Melton, ed., *The Encyclopedia of American Religions,* vol. I (Tarrytown, NY: Triumph Books, 1991).

26. *Dominus Jesus,* Congregation for the Doctrine of the Faith, with the approval of Pope John Paul II, August 6, 2000, published by the United States Catholic Conference, September 6, 2000. One does not have to torture the text to find it saying: "They may be Christian, but not enough, and they will not be until they become Roman Catholics" (<http://www.nccbuscc.org/pope/doctrineoffaith.htm>).

27. Of course, persons coalesced and communities of faith and worship were born.

28. Rarely has the mirage of a traditionless biblical church been so well articulated and so avidly pursued. See Richard Hughes, ed., *The American Quest for the Primitive Church* (Urbana: University of Illinois Press, 1988).

29. Hodge explained the project and exemplifies the way the "facts" of the Bible become a system. See his *Systematic Theology.*

30. Samuel S. Hill, "The Spirit of American Fundamentalism," and Bernard Ramm, "The Ethos of the Fundamentalist Movement," in William M. Shea, ed., *The Struggle Over the Past,* 209–22.

31. Letter from Donald D. Duff, Stated Clerk of the Orthodox Presbyterian Church General Assembly, Willow Grove, PA, to Dr. David H. Engelhard, General Secretary of the Synod of the Christian Reformed Church in North America, June 10, 1997.

32. John Paul II, *Ordinatio sacerdotalis,* issued May 30, 1994, in *Origins* 24/4 (June 9, 1994): 49, 51–52.

33. "By divine institution, Bishops succeed the Apostles through the Holy Spirit who is given to them. They are constituted Pastors in the Church, to be teachers of doctrine, priests of sacred worship and ministers of governance." Can. 375.1 in *The Code of Canon Law in English Translation* (Grand Rapids, MI: William B. Eerdmans, 1983). See Canons 330–41 for the responsibilities and powers of "The Roman Pontiff."

34. It floods the mind and soul of Pope John Paul (and strange to say, parallels the longing in the "evangelical mind"). See *"Veritatis splendor,"* in J. Michael Miller, C.S.B., *The Encyclicals of John Paul II* (Huntington, IN: Our Sunday Visitor Publishing Division, 1996), 674–771. On the importance of absolutes, see as well *"Evangelium vitae"* in the same volume, 792–894. For the contradictory position of modern thought, see John Dewey's *The Quest for Certainty: A Study of the Relation of Knowledge and Action* (New York: G. P. Putnam's Sons, 1929). The connection between faith and certainty is not as clear as the Catholic scholastic tradition has made it out to be, and the differences between Catholic thought on absolutes and the modern "method of intelligence" may not be irreconcilable.

35. For the search for certainty of contemporary converts to Catholicism, see Dan O'Neill, ed., *The New Catholics: Contemporary Catholic Converts Tell Their Stories* (New York: Crossroad, 1987).

36. John Henry Newman is the person most readily associated with the Catholic growth in historical consciousness (*The Development of Doctrine*), but the education of the Catholic public to it came with the changes promoted by Vatican II and the reflection that followed upon it.

37. Jose Casanova, *Public Religions in the Modern World,* and John Paul II, "Sollicitudo rei socialis" and "Centesimus annus" in Miller, ed., *The Encyclicals of John Paul II,* 426–77 and 588–650.

38. In addition, there are intellectual complications: How does one judge that a new, distinct religion has come into being? For example, Judaism to Christianity, Hinduism to Buddhism, Catholicism to Protestantism.

39. Joel Carpenter, *Revive Us Again.*

40. For the original of this adaptation, see Karl Rahner, "Observations on the Problem of the 'Anonymous Christian,'" *Theological Investigations* (New York: Seabury Press, 1976), 14: 280–94.

41. The Investigative Staff of the Boston Globe, *Betrayal: the Crisis in the Catholic Church* (Boston: Little, Brown and Company, 2002); and Philip Jenkins, *Pedophiles and Priests: Anatomy of a Contemporary Crisis* (New York: Oxford, 1996).

# Index